the american indian
in urban society

the american indian
in urban society

edited by

JACK O. WADDELL
O. MICHAEL WATSON

Purdue University

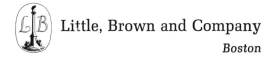 Little, Brown and Company
Boston

LIBRARY OF CONGRESS CATALOG CARD NO. 78-155318

SECOND PRINTING

Published simultaneously in Canada
by Little, Brown & Company (Canada) Limited

PRINTED IN THE UNITED STATES OF AMERICA

To Carol and Mary Jo

preface

Courses on the American Indian have been a part of the anthropology curriculum for many years. But despite the overwhelming body of literature, both ethnological and historical, the amount written for classroom use that focuses on contemporary Indians is negligible. The number of courses on modern Indians is growing, but students face a dearth of readily accessible resource material.

Journalists, educators, politicians, ministers, and social scientists other than anthropologists have been the ones to point out the dilemmas of present-day Indians. Recently, however, anthropologists whose field of study is the American Indian have conducted research among Indians who live on reservations, in colonies, and in cities, but much of the resultant data lies in unpublished graduate theses or manuscripts. Texts on urban studies or on ethnic minorities contain few pages devoted to Indians —

seldom a whole chapter. Despite their significance in United States' history and their value as a source from which theories and generalizations about man and culture may be drawn, enough information has not been available about these native Americans so their situation may be understood. As Indians strive to gain a social and economic foothold in a national political economy that historically has been devastatingly unkind to them, they encounter problems that are, in many ways, unique among minority groups.

Anthropologists have claimed that their discipline is empirical, that anthropology thrives on direct contact with native peoples, that as social scientists they go beyond statistics and surveys to become ethnographic reporters of the life-styles of people. Therefore, as anthropologists organizing a book on urban Indians, we had certain objectives. First, we wanted syntheses of understandings derived from anthropologists working among contemporary Indians that incorporated knowledge of New World ethnology and social anthropology. Second, we wanted primarily ethnographic articles or ones containing particularistic case studies. At the same time, we acknowledged the impossibility of covering all dimensions of the problems and all studies conducted among a diversity of American Indian populations by scholars from many disciplines.

Nine anthropologists and one American Indian have been called upon to answer the three questions underlying this book. Part 1 deals with this problem: What is the character, historically and currently, of the urbanization trends in America, as they have affected Indians? James E. Officer, who is Director of International Programs at the University of Arizona and has served as an Associate Commissioner in the Bureau of Indian Affairs, discusses the roles that the past and present federal Indian policies have played in the dislocation of Indians, including their migration to cities. Joseph G. Jorgensen of the University of Michigan has been studying how Shoshone and Ute Indians in small Western towns and colonies adapt to the stresses produced when they are denied access to crucial political, social, and economic resources; he reveals how American Indians in rural sectors are pressed into states of underdevelopment by the multiple influences of metropolitan political economies. Shuichi

Nagata of the University of Toronto discusses modern changes in reservation communities and agency towns resulting from social transactions with more urban centers; he bases much of his study on his fieldwork among the Hopi of Moenkopi and Tuba City, Arizona.

Part 2 explores this question: What is the character of Indian participation in the social institutions found in the city? Merwyn S. Garbarino of the University of Illinois at Chicago Circle, who has donated much of her time to casework and clinical problems at the Chicago American Indian Center, discusses the quality of life of Indians in Chicago. Peter Z. Snyder of the University of California at Los Angeles focuses upon the many dimensions of urban social environment, using Denver's Navajo population in his descriptive analysis. Robert S. Weppner of the National Institute of Mental Health Clinical Research Center (Lexington, Ky.) uses the same Denver population to discuss more intensively the economic aspects of urban social adjustments. Theodore D. Graves of the University of California at Los Angeles, also focusing on Navajos in Denver, analyzes drunkenness and drinking behavior, both very much related to the marginal social and economic positions occupied by Indians in the city. The section ends with a case study in educational innovation by Frank C. Miller of the University of Minnesota, which shows the positive results of Indian involvement in the building of a meaningful program at an urban university.

Part 3 attempts to answer the question: Why do some Indians "succeed" in adapting to urban life and remain in the city, while many other Indians, even some who "succeed," decide to return to their largely rural home communities? William H. Hodge of the University of Wisconsin (Milwaukee), a specialist in urban Indian anthropology, analyzes a family case history to reveal intra-family differences in rural-urban Indian migration; he raises questions that may guide future studies of the problem with which this section deals.

John W. Olson, an Assiniboine Indian and non-anthropologist who serves as a social casework director at the Chicago American Indian Center, shares his insights from the Indian point of view, to give the book an appropriate epilogue.

Although the Navajo may have been emphasized in this text,

we are not as concerned with tribal representation as with the major problems in urban living for American Indians. We hope the selections in this book will generate new understandings of these problems and stimulate new questions and research.

contents

the american indian
in urban society

PART 1   the american indian in
an urbanizing america

INTRODUCTION

Educators, policy-makers, planners, and the general citizenry are concerned about the urban crisis. Many formerly rural or small town people are now concentrated as voluntary "exiles" in urban ghettos of large cities, and the focus on urban problems has sharpened in recent years. However, for many decades the life styles of many kinds of people who have not had adequate access to the economic, political, and social opportunities that other segments of American society enjoy, have been subject to the advantages as well as the stresses and strains of an expanding, urbanizing, and industrializing political economy. This book will consider some of the ways in which American Indians have been influenced by, and have made their adjustments to, these urbanizing processes.

3

The presence of Indians in urban areas or cities is not anything new. In fact, as James Officer's chapter indicates, some Indians have been completely oriented to either cities, towns, or other nonreservation areas for many years and have not had any direct contact with reservations or any direct involvement with federal policies regulating reservation Indians. When we contemplate the many possible types of informal strategies that were developing and which governed the social relations of many whites with resident Indians in the locales where whites established their communities, we become aware of the fact that there is much more to contemporary Indian problems than can be gleaned from Congressional records or commissioners' annual reports, which relate primarily to reservation populations. While Indians, then, have always had to adapt their living conditions to the intrusive whites' farms, forts, missions, towns, and cities, not to mention their guiding ideologies, over the last few years the rapid rate with which American Indians have been migrating to various urban centers of the United States, combined with the growing emphasis upon problems of urban America, demands that attention be given to the problems Indian peoples encounter there.

As the three chapters in this section emphasize, more is involved than a simple migration to an urban ghetto for economic reasons; the problems of urban Indians are intricately related to the political and economic philosophies which have been developing in this nation since its foundation, and even before. In other words, the task is much broader than simply tracing Indians' movements to various urban centers to see how they are living. It must also include a study of the multiple influences of modern contemporary urban America which permeate rural areas to affect Indians on reservations, in rural colonies, or small town enclaves and an analysis of how the metropolis, as Joseph Jorgensen labels it, plays a special role in creating pockets of underdevelopment, whether in the cities or in the rural communities.

A particular strategy directs the order of the chapters, not only in Part 1, but throughout the book. Part 1 shows how the presence of American Indians in cities is related to attitudes and policies toward Indians which have been developing during the past two centuries; or, for those Indians who preferred to stay on reservations or in the rural colonies, how the influences of the metropolis have impinged upon them.

Officer presents a straightforward historical-descriptive chapter documenting the various kinds of policy formations at the governmental level which have had direct bearing upon the problems concerning special reserve lands set aside for Indians. He seeks to demonstrate how these governmental actions have, in so many ways, been significant forces behind the eventual movement of Indians to urban centers, or to small-town colonies or enclaves nearer their reservations or centers of aboriginal distribution.

The reader should be particularly sensitive to the crucial legislations, acts of Congress, and other policies or decisions, and should look intensively into them in order to understand their effect upon the American Indians more thoroughly as well as to see how the actions of a century or more ago are related to present problems. Interested students who want to get involved in classroom discussions should look at various sides of early issues to see how specific legislative decisions or court actions can be traced to a current facet of American Indian problems. Although decisions made a century ago cannot be reversed, nor, perhaps, their consequences, it might prove exciting to propose alternative strategies to those that were popular and to speculate on how the outcome might have differed.

It seems important to understand, for instance, what special interests motivated the founding fathers, or those with political and economic power, when establishing formal guidelines for governing relations with various Indian groups. How were trade matters to be regulated? How would sovereignty over land and subjects be exercised if sovereignty could be justified in the first place? How were "hostile" as opposed to "friendly" Indians to be dealt with? How were developments within the colonial policies of the European powers to be used? What policies were to be kept? What policies were to be thrown out or modified? Also, as the new nation began to expand its western frontier, what was to be done with these large populations of Indians? The Indian Removal Act of 1830, right or wrong, was a crucial decision, out of which many future attitudes and policies relating to American Indians became realities in the federal program.

Joseph Jorgensen tries to penetrate even more deeply the consequences of certain political and economic strategies by the non-Indian population which have been instrumental in promoting the state of underdevelopment found in most Indian communities or areas of occupation. He challenges a rather venerable concept in American anthropology, that of acculturation, as the force behind the Indians' adaptation, and, instead, credits the operating political and economic philosophy of the powerful interest groups in metropolitan America as the source of the debilitating effects upon the political, economic, social, and religious life of the American Indians. He develops the idea that the Bureau of Indian Affairs has also, in a sense, been trapped into this guiding philosophy and therefore, in many ways, has been party to the attempt to fully integrate American Indians into the American system of domination, exploitation, underdevelopment, and political contradiction. In this respect Jorgensen takes a more critical view of the role of the Bureau of Indian Affairs than does Officer. Jorgensen presents a specific case to show how the Utes have been brought into a state of underdevelopment as a result of their integration into this system of contradictory political and economic objectives. This idea should stimulate a great deal of thought, research, and discussion.

Shuichi Nagata in his chapter on reservation and urban communities presents a Hopi case and demonstrates how the Hopi and Navajo land is actually urbanized, albeit incompletely, as a result of influences from the urban setting. It is an even more specific case reflecting the impact of the metropolis in creating underdeveloped satellite rural communities such as agency towns and adjacent reservation villages. Some of the insights developed in Jorgensen's chapter are well illustrated by Nagata's study of the Hopi in their relationships to Tuba City and Flagstaff.

The chapters in this section are presented to show the student that there are many aspects of the urban Indian question that do not in any direct way involve moving into and living in cities. As Officer points out, though federal policy has been more directly concerned with reservation Indians, many of these policies, and many problems developed on reservations because of them, have some direct influence in the migration of Indians to cities. These movements to cities by reservation Indians have, in turn, had a clear impact upon the reservation communities or rural colonies, as both Jorgensen's and Nagata's chapters make clear.

The urban centers are also influential upon reservation areas that fringe them. Reservations are frequently fringed by small towns that are further oriented to a larger urban center. So whether or not an Indian lives in a city, the impact of the urban area upon Indian cultural communities, reservation or colony, is worthy of serious investigation.

CHAPTER 1   the american indian
                             and federal policy

JAMES E. OFFICER

PRE-REVOLUTIONARY POLICY

Among the legacies which the young government of the United States inherited from the British was the problem of what to do about the native inhabitants of the thirteen original colonies. Although relatively few in number, the natives were far too conspicuous to be ignored, especially in the frontier areas. In developing a policy for dealing with the Indians, the colonists relied heavily upon the experience they had previously gained while subjects of the British Crown. Thus, American Indian policy was modeled on that of the British and many concepts underlying this policy have endured to the present day.

The British had early accepted two basic principles to guide their relations with Indians. The first was that, even though they lacked formal title documents, Indians had a compensable interest in the lands they occupied and used. The second was that, being unsophisticated in the ways of Europeans, the Indians required the protection of the colonial governments. In 1633, the General Court of Massachusetts outlawed direct purchase of Indian land by individuals except with the court's permission. Virginia adopted a similar policy in 1655, and, later, most of the other colonies followed suit.

By the middle of the eighteenth century, the British Crown itself had begun to take an interest in the relations between Indians and the American colonists. In 1756, shortly after the outbreak of the French and Indian Wars, King George III appointed two representatives (whom he called superintendents) to regulate trade with the Indian tribes and to negotiate with them for the purchase of lands. In 1761, he acted upon a recommendation of the British Lords of Trade and decreed that all further applications for the purchase of Indian land would be processed through the British Lords of Trade, rather than by the colonial governments, and forwarded to him personally for approval. Two years later, he forbade all private purchase of land from the Indians and established the policy of licensing Indian traders through the crown, rather than through the legislative bodies of the various colonies.

At least two factors were responsible for King George's decision to centralize the administration of Indian affairs. First, in spite of laws passed by the colonies to protect the Indians from exploitation, colonial administrators often looked the other way and permitted abuses which harmed and angered the Indians. Second, such loose administration played into the hands of the French who were more successful in winning Indian allies than were the British.

The King's decision was not received with favor in some of the colonies, and in 1768 he felt obliged to return the authority for licensing traders to the colonial administrators. However, the crown-appointed superintendents remained (Kinney 1937:6–26).

INDIAN POLICY AFTER INDEPENDENCE

Following independence, colonial leaders found themselves confronted with the same problems which the British had previously faced: regulating trade with Indian tribes, acquiring land from them, and determining which level of government should be responsible for administering Indian affairs. The Articles of Confederation squarely placed the last responsibility in the hands of the federal government. The Constitution which followed was less specific in this regard, although it did confer upon Congress the power "to regulate commerce with foreign nations, and among the several states, and with the Indian tribes." Later, powers deriving from other portions of the Constitution were used to develop legislation for the implementation of federal Indian policy. Among these were the powers to make expenditures for the general welfare, to control the property of the United States, and to make treaties. Also important were the powers of Congress to admit new states and to prescribe the terms of their admission, to make war, to establish post roads, to create tribunals inferior to the Supreme Court, and to promulgate "a uniform rule of naturalization" (USDI 1958:21–22).

In negotiating with the Indians, the British colonies and the crown itself acknowledged certain rights of tribal sovereignty and, during the latter years of English rule, entered into treaties with the tribes. The fledgling United States government continued this policy. The first Indian treaty following American independence was concluded with the Delawares in 1778, eleven years before the adoption of the Constitution. Other treaties with the New York tribes, the Wyandots, Chippewas, Ottawas, Shawnees, Cherokees, Choctaws, and Chickasaws also preceded the Constitution.

Some of the states negotiated their own treaties with Indian tribes at this time, despite the fact that the Articles of Confederation clearly stated that Congress alone had the power to control the Indian trade and "all affairs with the Indians" (a doctrine restated in the Ordinance of 1786). Georgia, for example, signed a treaty with the Creeks at Shoulderbone in 1786, attempting thereby to acquire large acreages of Creek land west of the Oconee River (Prucha 1962:27). This was the first in a long series of incidents involving relations between Indians and the state of Georgia which culminated in the passage of an Indian Removal Act in 1830, and the practice of isolating Indian tribes which prevailed for more than a quarter of a century thereafter.

Indian administration in the United States, in the period between the Articles of Confederation and the adoption of the Constitution, was in the hands of three commissioners, each of whom headed a *Department* of Indian Affairs (Northern, Southern, and Middle). That these offices were considered important is demonstrated by the fact that the first three persons chosen to fill them were Benjamin Franklin, Patrick Henry, and James Wilson (Prucha 1962:28). Their duties did not differ in any significant way from those of the two Indian superintendents who had served previously under British rule.

In 1786, the Congress of the Confederation eliminated the Middle Department and, returning to the English precedent, changed the title of each department head to superintendent. Three years later, in 1789, the newly formed Congress of the United States established the War Department and, in line with the actions of its predecessor body, placed the responsibility for Indian affairs with the head of that department. The following year, Congress passed the first of the so-called "Trade and Intercourse Acts" relating to the conduct of Indian affairs. The first appropriation for Indian affairs as such was made in 1791; the amount was slightly over $39,000. Over the subsequent forty years, many pieces of legislation were to be enacted under the same rubric.

INDIAN TRADE

The problem of Indian trade was a major one in the early years of American history. Not only was it economically important, but the kind of relations prevailing between Indians and traders often affected the Indians' relations with others. When Indians were badly treated or plied with intoxicants, they frequently took to the warpath against the white settlers in their territory. Also, when displeased with American traders, they turned to those of other nations, an experience with which the British had become familiar in an earlier period.

So long as the British in the north and the Spanish to the south were considered threats to the sovereignty of the United States, leaders of the young nation felt it necessary to maintain Indian allies, and this meant assuring friendly relations with them. Since many of the social contacts between Indians and whites related to trading, this activity assumed great importance. Between 1796 and 1822, the United States government maintained trading houses where the Indians were guaranteed fair prices for the goods they had to sell and those they wished to buy. The first federal official with basic responsibilities in Indian administration was the Superintendent of Indian Trade, whose office was established in 1806.

The significance of trade with the Indians declined markedly after the War of 1812. With the British and Spanish threats no longer a problem, the federal government relaxed its previous careful regulation of Indian trade. The last of the trading houses was closed in 1822, the same year in which the position of Superintendent of Indian Trade was abolished.

THE REMOVAL POLICY

Emerging as dominant policy themes in Indian affairs after the war of 1812 were the twin ones of territorial acquisition and Indian isolation. The roots of this combined policy can be found in some of the treaties negotiated before 1800, but its real foundation was laid in 1802 when Georgia ceded to the United States the area which later was included within the states of Alabama and Mississippi. In return for this cession, the federal government promised to "peaceably obtain, on reasonable terms" the Indian title to certain lands within this area and to *all* the land inside the state of Georgia itself. President Jefferson saw an opportunity to comply with this promise in 1803, when the Louisiana Territory was purchased from France. In July of that year, he proposed removing the Indians from Georgia and other areas to the newly acquired lands west of the Mississippi River. Some of the Lower Cherokees living in Georgia, who were much harassed by the whites there, seemed amenable to this idea, but it had widespread opposition from the other Indians in Georgia, Alabama, North Carolina, and Tennessee. Later in 1803, Congress considered a bill to carry out Jefferson's plan, but while it passed in the Senate, it failed in the House of Representatives. The following year, Congress did authorize the president to work out exchanges of eastern lands for those in the west, provided the Indians would continue allegiance to the United States.

By the terms of treaties concluded in 1805 and 1806, the Cherokees ceded certain lands in Kentucky, Tennessee, and Alabama, but did not agree to removal. Removal was discussed with the Chickasaws in 1805, and with the Choctaws and Cherokees in 1808. In 1809, President Jefferson authorized a delegation of Lower Cherokees to visit Louisiana Territory at government expense. Many of those who accepted this offer reported favorably on what they saw, but the Upper Cherokees remained unconvinced.

Indian opposition to removal had become substantial by the time President Madison assumed office in 1809. Certain small groups of Indians who had previously gone west (including some Shawnees and Delawares who had settled near Cape Girardeau, Missouri, in 1793, and Cherokees who had moved west in 1795) had not liked living in the new area. Knowledge of their dissatisfaction was widely circulated among the other tribes (Kinney 1937:27–38). As the approaching war with Great Britain began to concern federal officials, the question of Indian removal was put aside temporarily. However, it was hastily revived at the end of the War of 1812.

President Monroe, in 1817, named John C. Calhoun as his Secretary of War. Calhoun was dedicated to the idea of Indian removal and he shared this dedication with General Andrew Jackson and with Lewis Cass, governor of the Northwest Territory. Together, they urged the acquisition of all Indian lands east of the Mississippi River and the transfer of all Indians wishing to continue to live in tribal status to the western part of the country. While they did not manage at this time to persuade Congress to pass a general act for Indian removal, Calhoun and Cass were in a position to proceed on their own in accordance with the authority granted President Jefferson in 1804. Cass centered his attention on the territory over which he presided, and as a result, concluded a number of removal treaties between 1817 and 1825. Calhoun, with Jackson's enthusiastic support, made certain the policy was applied to tribes in the southeast.

The first treaty contemplating Cherokee removal was signed in 1817. Another followed two years later. In 1820, the Choctaws agreed to be moved west of the Mississippi, and the following year, the Creeks ceded much of their land and promised to submit to removal. Among the Creeks and the Cherokees, however, the question of abandoning their territory was bitterly debated, and by no means all of these Indians were seriously considering a move to the west, in spite of the treaties.

In January, 1825, just before leaving office, President Monroe delivered a message calling for removal as the only means of settling the Indian problem. Secretary Calhoun backed him with a report stating the dimensions of the removal problem. In this report, he advocated removing more than 90,000 Indians to western areas, and recommended an appropriation of $95,000 for this purpose (Kinney 1937:41–44).

Not all those who served under Calhoun shared his enthusiasm for removal. In 1825, John Crowell, Indian Agent to the Cherokees, protested the way in which the Creek and Cherokee removal treaties had been negotiated. He pointed out that Creek Chief William McIntosh, who had signed the Treaty of 1825, was in danger of being assassinated by fellow tribesmen and requested federal protection for McIntosh. The request was not granted and a short time thereafter, when McIntosh authorized Georgia officials to survey Creek lands, he was hanged by the opponents of removal.

The treaty which the ill-fated McIntosh had signed was one whereby the Creeks agreed to cede all their lands in Georgia in exchange for equal acreages west of the Mississippi River. Early in 1826, a Creek delegation went to Washington to plead with federal officials to have the McIntosh treaty declared null and void. Sobered by the experience of the execution and perhaps by the criticism of such persons as Agent Crowell, administrators in the War Department agreed to seek revocation of the act affirming the Treaty of 1825. However, they insisted upon another treaty of cession, which was signed on the spot. The terms of the latter provided for surrender of certain Creek lands in Georgia in exchange for a perpetual annual annuity of $20,000. The new treaty also provided that a delegation of Creeks would visit the west to examine lands which might be set aside for them. The following year, the Creeks signed another treaty ceding all their Georgia lands. Thus, the violence visited upon Chief McIntosh failed to defer Creek removal for more than a couple of years (Kinney 1937:44–45).

By the time the Creek negotiations of 1825–27 were underway, Indian matters within the War Department were in the hands of the newly created Bureau of Indian Affairs (BIA) which Secretary Calhoun established without Congressional blessing in 1824.

The first head of the bureau was Thomas L. McKenney, who had previously been the Superintendent of Indian Trade. The most difficult problems with which McKenney was obliged to deal involved the relations between the Indians and the state of Georgia. Unhappy with revocation of the Treaty of 1825, the governor declared the Treaty of 1826 unconstitutional and, in this action, was backed by the Georgia legislature. In 1828, President Adams submitted the matter to Congress for its consideration. Sentiment in the House of Representatives was predominantly favorable to the Indians, but the Senate threw its support to Georgia. The full Congress thereupon recommended that the president settle the matter by purchasing the remaining Creek lands in Georgia (Kinney 1937:53).

The Creeks were not the only Indians with whom Georgia was battling at this time. The Cherokees had stubbornly resisted complete removal from their lands in Georgia, Alabama, North Carolina, and Tennessee, although some as a result of treaties in 1817 and 1819 had gone to settle in Arkansas territory. Those still in the east had by 1827 achieved a high degree of unity and were effectively governing themselves under a constitution adopted in that year. Georgians and other southerners maintained that adoption of a Cherokee constitution represented an effort by the Indians to set up a separate nation independent of the state's authority. Late in 1827, the Georgia legislature proclaimed that the Cherokees had no real title to their lands and should be evicted.

In 1828, Congress appropriated $50,000 to discharge the agreement of 1802 with Georgia, providing for the extinguishment of all Indian title in that state. That same year, the Cherokees who had previously relocated to Arkansas Territory signed a treaty agreeing to move farther west. The Cherokees remaining in Georgia and other eastern states refused, however, to be parties to this action. Outraged at their obstinancy, the Georgia legislature began enacting measures extending the state's laws over Indian lands.

Andrew Jackson, ardent advocate of Indian removal, became president in 1829, and quickly let it be known that he would pursue such a policy during his administration. He defended it as the only means of saving the Indians from complete extinction. Jackson's supporters introduced measures in Congress providing for exchanges of lands with all Indians still residing east of the Mississippi River. On May 28, 1830, a comprehensive act for Indian removal was finally passed.

The Act of 1830, one of the most important pieces of Indian legislation, authorized the president to set up districts within the so-called "Indian territory" (primarily the states of Kansas and Oklahoma today) and to prepare these districts for the reception of the eastern tribes. The act also provided authority for making land exchanges, paying for improvements on the lands being surrendered, assisting the Indians to relocate, and protecting the relocatees in their new habitat. The sum of $500,000 was authorized to carry out the provisions of the act.

By the time the Act of 1830 was passed, Indian removal was well underway in the states or territories of Ohio, Michigan, Indiana, Illinois, Minnesota, and Wisconsin (Harmon 1941:270ff.). Governor Cass had encountered resistance among some tribes in this large area, but in general, this resistance had proved less effective than that of the Cherokees in the southeast. The latter were much better organized than any of the other Indian groups in the country at this time. Although in Illinois, Kennekuk, the Kickapoo prophet, was able between 1827 and 1832 to resist in behalf of his followers the persistent pressure for removal, he capitulated and signed a treaty in 1832 agreeing to resettle on lands in Kansas (Spicer 1969:56).

THE INDIANS AND GEORGIA

During the entire decade of the 1830's, Georgia and adjacent southeastern states continued to provide the locus for the strongest Indian resistance to removal. In two landmark cases reaching the Supreme Court, the Cherokees won what turned out to be hollow victories over the state of Georgia. The first of these, decided in 1831, grew out of a plea by John Ross, Chief of the Cherokee Nation, for relief from the application of certain Georgia laws to the Cherokees. The motion which he filed with the court reviewed the various guarantees contained in the treaties between the Cherokees and the United States and complained that the action of the Georgia legislature was in direct violation of these. While the Supreme Court refused to assume jurisdiction in the matter on the grounds that the Cherokee Nation was not a *foreign state* within the meaning of the Constitution, Chief

Justice Marshall, in his analysis of the facts, asserted that the "acts of our government plainly recognize the Cherokee Nation as a state, and the courts are bound by these acts." Marshall also declared that "the relation of the United States to the Indian tribes within its territorial limits resembles that of a ward to his guardian. . . . They look to our government for protection; rely upon its kindness and its power; appeal to it for relief to their wants, and address the president as their great father. . . ." [1]

Shortly after Marshall's declaration, two missionaries named Worcester and Butler were indicted in the superior court of Gwinnett County, Georgia, for residing among the Cherokees, in violation of an act forbidding the residence of whites there without an oath of allegiance to the state and a license to remain. Worcester pleaded that the United States had, by virtue of its treaties with the Cherokees, recognized the sovereignty of this Indian nation and that, therefore, the laws of the state did not apply within Cherokee territory. He was tried, convicted, and sentenced to four years in prison.

Worcester's case was carried to the Supreme Court on a writ of error. In this instance, the court did assume jurisdiction and in 1832 reversed the decision of the lower court. In his opinion, Chief Justice Marshall stated:

> . . . they (state laws) interfere forcibly with the regulations established between the United States and the Cherokee nation. . . . They are in direct hostility with treaties . . . which mark out the boundary that separates the Cherokee country from Georgia . . . and recognize the pre-existing power of the nation to govern itself. . . . [2]

A number of points which Marshall included in his opinions in these two important cases have guided American Indian policy to the present day. These include the notion of Indians as "wards of the federal government"; the idea that tribes enjoy a sovereignty akin to that of the separate states, but unlike that of foreign nations (and, therefore, subject to the greater sovereignty of the United States government); and the concept that within their own territory Indians are not subject to the jurisdiction of

[1] *Cherokee Nation* v. *Georgia,* 5 Pet. 1 (1831).
[2] *Worcester* v. *Georgia,* 6 Pet. 515 (1832).

the states. Both of Marshall's Cherokee opinions are frequently cited in judicial decisions today.

In spite of the pronouncements of the Supreme Court, President Jackson moved ahead with his efforts to remove the Cherokees. In September, 1831, he sent Benjamin F. Currey of Tennessee into Cherokee country to oversee the task of enrolling the Indians for removal. Still divided on the issue, the Cherokees did not respond to Currey's mission. By persistent efforts, however, the federal government was finally able to conclude a treaty in 1835 calling for cession of all Cherokee lands east of the Mississippi River and removal to the west (Harmon 1941:189–191).

While pressing ahead with the removal program, the president and Congress also undertook to put some order into the administration of Indian matters. In 1832, Congress created the position of Commissioner of Indian Affairs and two years later gave its blessing to the previous action of Secretary Calhoun by passing an act "to provide for the organization of a department of Indian Affairs." The latter is regarded as the organic law of the Bureau of Indian Affairs, although some references still cite 1824 as the year in which the bureau was established. In truth, the Act of 1834 did not in any way alter the power of the Secretary of War or the commissioner, nor did it change the status of the Bureau of Indian Affairs within the War Department.

At least as significant from the standpoint of Indian administration as either of the above acts was the passage of omnibus legislation known as the Trade and Intercourse Act of 1834. In this action, Congress attempted to bring up to date the long series of separate acts going back to 1790, relating to the conduct of trade and the regulation of relations between Indians and whites within "Indian country." This act helped to define the territory within which state laws did not apply; certainly such a definition was necessary in the light of the Supreme Court pronouncements in the two Cherokee cases previously cited.

In spite of the Treaty of 1835, Cherokee removal was not easily accomplished. Three years after the conclusion of the treaty, General Winfield Scott was sent to Georgia with a contingent of troops to forcibly effect the movement of these Indians to the west. The result was the incident in American history well known today as the "trail of tears" (Kinney 1937:71).

Indian removal, by 1840, was well on its way to being an accomplished fact. A report published by Congress two years earlier showed that more than 50 treaties had been concluded since January 1, 1830, by the terms of which almost 200,000,000 acres of land had been acquired by the United States, with a probable value of $137,000,000. The total cost of this acquisition, according to the report, was about $70,000,000. The net profit was more than $67,000,000! [3]

Final removal operations continued with some of the Great Lakes tribes during the 1840's, and by the end of that decade, there were few Indians remaining in tribal status east of the Mississippi River and few lands west of the river not already occupied by relocated Indians or still hostile indigenous tribes. The day of a new Indian policy was dawning and it emerged in the years immediately preceding the American Civil War.

"CIVILIZING" THE INDIANS

Although the principal emphasis in American Indian policy during the first half of the nineteenth century was on acquiring Indian lands and resettling Indians in areas removed from white settlement, other policy considerations also began to assume importance during this period. These included the need for "civilizing" Indians, the establishment of a distinction between Indians who remained in tribal status and those who did not, and the desirability of giving individual Indians title to their lands, as opposed to permitting them to continue holding such lands communally.

Probably the first public act of a United States official related to promoting the civilization of Indians was the recommendation by Secretary of War Knox in 1789 that missionaries be sent among the tribes and that the Indians be given domestic animals to raise. Three years later, Rufus Putnam, at Knox's direction, went to negotiate with the hostile Indians near Lake Erie. He advised the tribes that "the United States are highly desirous of imparting to all the Indian tribes the blessings of civilization as the only means of perpetuating them on the earth." He went on to point out that the government was willing to undertake the

[3] From the establishment of the federal government in 1789 to 1850, the United States negotiated and ratified 245 treaties with the Indians. In the process, it acquired over 450,000,000 acres of land for less than $90 million. See Harmon 1941:297, 319.

expense of "teaching them to read and write, to plough and to sow, in order to raise their own bread and meat, with certainty, as the white people do" (Harmon 1941:17–18, 157–158).

The first treaty providing for any form of education for Indians was that concluded in 1794 with the Oneidas, Tuscaroras, and Stockbridge — tribes which had fought with the Americans during the Revolution. The terms of this treaty called for the training of some of the young Indian men "in the arts of miller and sawyer." Attempts were made to include similar provisions in the Creek Treaty of 1796, but the Indians objected (Harmon 1941: 158).

In 1802, Congress appropriated the first funds for promoting civilization among the "friendly" Indians. The $15,000 dedicated to this purpose was to be used to furnish domestic animals, implements of husbandry, and goods or money; and to appoint temporary agents to instruct the Indians in the ways of the white man's civilization. Annual appropriations from "the civilization fund" were comingled with other War Department appropriations for Indians in such manner that when President Monroe twenty years later called for an accounting of how the money had been spent, the department could not provide specific answers. Secretary Calhoun answered lamely that the principal use had been among the Cherokee, Creek, Chickasaw, and Choctaw for "spinning wheels, implements of husbandry, looms, and domestic animals" (Harmon 1941:159–162).

Even after the passage of the Act of 1802 establishing the civilization fund, the government continued to include provisions for education in its treaties with Indian tribes. The Kaskaskia Treaty of 1803 called for an annual appropriation of $100 to pay a Roman Catholic priest to "instruct as many of their children as possible in the rudiments of literature." The following year, a treaty with the Delawares provided $300 annually for ten years to be used solely for the purpose of "ameliorating their conditions and promoting their civilization."

Missionary groups by the end of the War of 1812 had assumed a lively interest in working among the Indians, both to convert them to Christianity and to educate them. In 1818, the House Committee on Indian Affairs recommended the establishment of Indian schools with aid from the missionaries. A year later, the full Congress responded by authorizing and appropriating a sum of $10,000 for this purpose. By 1823, there were twenty-one schools run by missionaries which were receiving some federal support and two years later, the figure had risen to thirty-eight (Harmon 1941:162–164).

During the 1820's, many Congressmen expressed opposition to the civilization fund because they considered it basically a means of subsidizing missionary groups for their own ends, rather than for the ends sought by the federal government. The legislators were not able to translate this opposition into successful proposals for change, however, and federal payments to religious organizations continued and were even increased. Thirty-two years after the civilization fund was established, the number of Indian schools under missionary direction had risen to sixty. Six religious denominations were in charge of the Indian education program and about 2,000 children were enrolled (Harmon 1941: 354).

Many of these early schools gave instruction in the Indian language, an educational approach which continued for nearly fifty years. Thousands of pages were printed in tribal dialects. The principal subjects taught the students were agricultural arts for boys and domestic arts for the girls. In a few instances, the missionary groups attempted to prepare young Indians for such professional pursuits as medicine and law, but Commissioner Medill in 1846 recommended the abandonment of this approach in favor of manual labor schools (Harmon 1941:356). Responding to his recommendation, the Bureau of Indian Affairs, with further assistance from missionary groups, established sixteen such schools during the following two years.

Of all the Indian tribes, the Choctaws had been most favored with appropriations for education prior to 1850. Including treaty payments, more than $1,000,000 had gone into the education program of this tribe. Interest in education was great also among the Cherokees, Creeks, and Chickasaws. By 1841, the Cherokees and Choctaws had established their own common school system, preceding many states in this regard (Harmon 1941:357–358).

Far more in the way of treaty payments went into Indian education than was invested for the general program prior to 1850. Many of the removal treaties contained provisions for payments to finance Indian education, and these annuities, like the general appropriations, usually found their way into the hands of the missionary societies.

WARD INDIANS AND CITIZEN INDIANS

In the concern with contemporary urban Indians, it is notable that federal policy in this early period was focused upon those Indians who lived in a tribal condition, occupying lands coveted by whites and warring upon them. The Indian who chose to live apart from his fellows and to "adopt the habits of civilization" might be offered moral support, but he was not helped in other ways.

Implicit in the earliest dealings with the Indians was the belief that tribal status and citizenship were incompatible. An Indian might be either a citizen or a member of an Indian tribe, but he could not be both. If he asserted his tribal membership, he was dealt with as an Indian; if he chose not to assert it, he might under certain conditions become a citizen and be treated like any other citizen.

At the outset, citizenship was conferred upon Indians primarily through treaties with the tribes to which they belonged. In accordance with the either-or principle cited above, the treaties usually provided that the Indians who became citizens would be allotted land in severalty, or outside the communal tribal pattern, and expected to lead "civilized" lives. The first federal statute granting citizenship to a whole tribe of Indians (the Brothertons) in 1839, also dissolved the tribe (Kinney 1937:110). Later statutes imposed such conditions as adopting the habits of civilized life, becoming self-supporting, and learning to read and speak the English language. The Winnebago citizenship act of 1870 offered these Indians the option of becoming citizens, provided they could prove to the satisfaction of the federal district court that they were sufficiently intelligent and prudent to control their own affairs and interests, that they had adopted the habits of civilized life, and that for the preceding five years they had supported themselves and their families. If satisfied with the proof offered, the court would declare them citizens and give them certificates entitling them to fee patents for their land and to a share of tribal property (USDI 1958:518). This act, although later in time than the period under discussion, demonstrates clearly the philosophy which prevailed. It also makes clear the existence early in American history of a distinction between "ward" Indians and "citizen" Indians, the former being considered eligible for federal assistance and protection, the latter, not.

Federal administrators early fell into the habit of presuming that all Indians who resided permanently away from their tribes were competent to manage their affairs without federal assistance. State and local governments, on the other hand, often resisted assuming any responsibility for indigent Indians within their jurisdiction, asserting that, citizens or not, these Indians were wards of the federal government and entitled to its help. These disclaimers have continued to the present day, and in spite of many judicial decisions and statutes, the distinction between Indians eligible for, and entitled to, federal assistance, and those who are primarily a responsibility of the local governments in whose jurisdictions they live, remains confused in many important respects.

OWNING LAND IN SEVERALTY

Usually related in some way at this early period to the eligibility of an Indian for citizenship was the kind of title he held to the land which he occupied and used. In order for him to become a citizen, it was generally felt that he must own the land in severalty — that is, outside the communal pattern of the tribes. Such ownership was regarded as highly desirable by a majority of the European immigrants to North America and was equated by them with a civilized, as opposed to a tribal, existence. It may be presumed that the earliest advocates of allotting the communal lands of the Indian tribes did so from wholly altruistic motives, although their approach to the matter was both shortsighted and ethnocentric. An Indian, they reasoned, who owned his own land could become a yeoman farmer, a highly desirable and civilized status.[4] On the other hand, one who continued to occupy and use an assignment of communal land from the tribe could not hope to achieve such an exalted position.

---

[4] At about the same time in Mexico, President Benito Juárez, himself an Indian, began advocating a similar policy with respect to land reform. He visualized Mexico as "a community of landed yeomen, of free, private landholders selling their produce and buying their wants in an open market." See Vernon 1963:36.

The Choctaw Treaty of 1805, made provision for allotments of land to a few named individuals, as did the Creek Treaty of 1814. In the latter instance, the recipients were those chiefs who had remained loyal to the United States in the War of 1812. General allotting of Indian lands was first proposed by Secretary of War Crawford in President Madison's cabinet. Following this suggestion, his successor, Calhoun, promoted the inclusion of provisions for allotments in the Cherokee Treaty of 1817, and many of those treaties which followed. Often the allotment provided for in these documents related only to certain tribal members, usually chiefs and persons of mixed blood. The Indians themselves undoubtedly influenced policy in this regard, for some, at least, did want to have title to their lands under the same conditions as their white neighbors.

Calhoun's successor as Secretary of War, James Barbour, publicly recommended a distribution of Indian tribal property among individuals in a statement made in 1826. The Choctaw Treaty of 1830 set up several classes of private landholders and made special provision for granting fee title to the lands held by Indians who chose to remain in the eastern states following removal. (In the Choctaw case, the treaty was patterned after that concluded with the Cherokees in 1817.) Ninety of the principal Creek chiefs were provided individual landholdings by the Treaty of 1832, which was signed the same year in which the first Commissioner of Indian Affairs, James Herring, expressed his preference for a general allotment program. One of his successors, Hartley Crawford, in his report of 1838, made the strongest statement of that time concerned with the relationship between owning land in severalty and civilization. He said that "common property and civilization cannot coexist."

By the time that George W. Manypenny became Commissioner of Indian Affairs in 1853, the precedent for allotment through treaty had become firmly established. However, it remained for Manypenny, one of the most important and influential of Indian commissioners, to raise allotment to the level of a major policy tenet (Kinney 1937:81–162).

THE END OF THE REMOVAL POLICY

As indicated previously, during the decade of the 1840's the program of removing Indians from the eastern half of the continent was largely completed. It was at this time, also, that the United States acquired dominion over many new lands in the west. Questions immediately arose as to the kind of policy to pursue with respect to the Indians residing in these areas.

In 1849, four years before George Manypenny became Commissioner of Indian Affairs, Congress created the Department of the Interior and transferred responsibility for Indian affairs from the War Department to the Interior Secretary. The missionaries were among the strongest supporters of this change, for they felt that Indian matters belonged in civilian rather than military hands. During the next twenty-five years, there were to be many attempts to return Indian affairs to the War Department but these all failed, and the Interior Department to the present day has exercised primary responsibility for implementing federal Indian policy (Manypenny 1880:379–394).[5]

Even before entering his post, Manypenny was aware that he must develop a policy to deal with the tribes in the newly acquired regions of the west. He was convinced that the previous removal policy had accomplished little with respect to integrating the Indians into American society, and he was equally convinced that integration was the only means of survival for the Indians.

The most basic policy change which Manypenny introduced was that of abandoning further Indian removal and establishing reservations of land for the western tribes within the general areas they were then occupying. This meant a new round of treaties, by whose terms the Indians would cede certain of their lands to the United States with the understanding that the federal government would thereafter guarantee them permanent use and occupancy of the remaining areas. Manypenny recognized that although this policy shift would provide a land base for the Indians, it would not accomplish any more than had the removal policy insofar as Indian integration was concerned. With respect to the latter, he proposed that a policy of allotment in severalty be followed. Like many of his predecessors, he believed that only through owning their lands individually could the Indians acquire

[5] Manypenny has an excellent description of the attempt by military leaders in 1876 to secure the return of the responsibility for Indian affairs to the War Department.

the habits of civilization which they would need in order to be successfully integrated. The two principal features of Manypenny's policy thus became the establishment of reservations and the allotment of land in severalty to tribal members.

One of the first of numerous treaties concluded during Manypenny's administration implemented both aspects of his policy and established a pattern for United States Indian policy over the next two decades. This was the Omaha Treaty of 1854, by whose terms the tribe ceded a large area of land in northeast Nebraska and had reserved to it other lands in the vicinity of the city which today bears the tribal name. Article 6 of the treaty authorized the president to allot the lands within the Omaha Reservation to individual Indians. The standard unit was to be eighty acres, and any acreage remaining after all members had received allotments was to be sold and the money deposited in the United States Treasury to the credit of the tribe. Many of the forty-one treaties negotiated during the four years Manypenny was in office contained similar allotment provisions (Kinney 1937:114–116).

GRANT'S PEACE POLICY

Manypenny's successors in the following eight years, although advocating allotment as firmly as did he, concluded fewer treaties and, therefore, were not able to carry the program forward at the same rapid pace. The outbreak of the Civil War was, of course, an inhibiting factor.

Toward the end of the war, Congress became increasingly concerned about the way in which Indian affairs were being administered; as a result, in March of 1865 it ordered an investigation into the treatment of Indian tribes. A joint committee of the House and Senate, under the chairmanship of Congressman James Doolittle of Wisconsin, spent two years hearing witnesses and gathering information. The report, issued in 1867, pointed out that the Indians were decreasing rapidly everywhere but in the Indian Territory. The boundaries of the reservations were constantly being violated by whites, and railroads crossing the plains were threatening the destruction of the buffalo. Conditions on the reservations were deplorable, with disease and starvation rampant. In spite of the critical nature of the situation, however, the committee members did not produce any substantial recommendations for change (Fritz 1963:29–30).

Much of the pressure for the investigation had come from missionaries who had been working among the Indians since early in the century. Many persons, including such military men as General Alfred Sully, Commander of the Northwestern Indian Expedition against the Teton Sioux, felt that only a "Christian influence" could save the Indians from extinction. By the end of the Civil War, strong support had developed in many quarters for putting religious leaders in charge of Indian affairs. Episcopal Bishop Henry B. Whipple was an advocate of this approach and also one of the first to propose the establishment of a "commission of men of high character" to oversee the entire program of Indian administration.

In 1866, Congress authorized the creation of an Indian Peace Commission to carry forward the negotiation of treaties with the western tribes. The commissioners were appointed the following year. Before commencing their work in the field, they met at St. Louis and decided to concentrate the Sioux, Crows, and other northern plains tribes in an area north of Nebraska and west of the Missouri River, and to establish reservations for the southern plains tribes in western Oklahoma; they also proposed setting aside lands west of the Rockies for the tribes in that part of the country. To some degree, this plan represented a return to the removal policy, since one goal was to clear Kansas and Nebraska of all hostile Indians (Fritz 1963:63ff.).

The Peace Commissioners concluded ten treaties during 1867 and 1868, providing for the establishment of 18 reservations. These proved to be the last of the Indian treaties. Congress in 1871 legislated that Indian tribes would no longer be dealt with through this device.

In 1868, the Society of Friends, which had the preceding year formed an alliance with the Episcopalians, met in Baltimore and prepared a memorial for incoming President Grant. Based on recommendations made by the Peace Commission and some military leaders, this memorial proposed that religious groups have the role of selecting agency superintendents; it was presented to Grant in January, 1869. Although he did not accept the recommendations of the Quakers, Grant did agree to experiment with the idea of greater involvement for the missionary societies.

One group of Friends was given control of the northern superintendency, including the state of Nebraska; another, the central
superintendency, including tribes in Kansas and the Indian Territory (by now reduced to Oklahoma only). The Five Civilized
Tribes were omitted from Quaker jurisdiction.

A short time later, in 1869, the Quakers and Episcopalians developed a proposal that funds for carrying out the recent Sioux
Treaty be administered by a board of five citizens authorized to
act jointly with the Secretary of the Interior. Again, responding
to pressure from the religious groups, Congress appropriated
$2,000,000 for the Sioux Treaty and created a board of ten com-
missioners to assist the Interior Secretary in administering the
fund. (The Board of Indian Commissioners continued in existence
until 1933, when it was finally abolished.) It was no surprise that
President Grant turned to the missionary societies for persons to
serve in this new assignment. The principal initial role of the
board was to oversee the use and disbursement of funds and
annuities provided the tribes pursuant to treaties, and prior to
the Civil War the inept, often fraudulent handling of this matter had been one of the principal issues raised by critics of federal Indian policy.

Although some military men, such as General Sully, favored
the idea of turning local Indian affairs over to religious organizations, Grant himself did not believe strongly in this policy, and
his concessions to the Quakers were as much a sop to them as an
indication of his desire to adopt a new approach. However, in
1870, Congress declared that military personnel would thereafter
be forbidden to hold civilian office. This frustrated Grant's earlier
plan to appoint army officers as Indian agents. He yielded,
therefore, to entreaties from the newly appointed Indian commissioners and agreed to permit other religious denominations to assume local responsibility for Indian affairs as the Quakers had
done. Thirteen different sects thereupon took over agencies
which served nearly all the Indians. This time, even the Five
Civilized Tribes were affected. The Baptists were placed in
charge of the Cherokees and Creeks; the Presbyterians, in charge
of the Choctaws and Seminoles. There is little evidence that
Grant was overly concerned with the religious leanings of the
Indians themselves; the Christian Church, for example, was
given jurisdiction over the Pueblo Indians of New Mexico who

had been Catholics, at least in part, for more than 250 years (Fritz 1963:72–86)!

Each denomination appointed an executive committee on Indian affairs, and all nominations to the Indian service, from the agent on down, were subject to the approval of these committees. Committee representatives attended an annual meeting in Washington with the Board of Indian Commissioners.

Subjecting Indians on the reservation to the control of the missionaries and those off the reservation (and presumably still hostile) to the control of the military is the basis for the Indian policy which largely prevailed for the next decade and a half. It is known today as "Grant's Peace Policy." Pursuant to it, the army began a campaign to persuade or force the off-reservation Indian tribes to accept grants of land to which they would thereafter be confined and within which they would be protected from white trespass. Because of the devastating effect of this confinement on many groups, a system of rations was undertaken, with the Indians supplied food and clothing. Without question, the two decades following the Civil War represent the period of greatest Indian dependence on the federal government. The rations system, handled by agency personnel, subverted the power of the traditional Indian leaders. The general allotment policy, finally extended to all tribes in 1887, largely finished the job except among the Indians of the Southwest who were more isolated, more economically self-sufficient, and who were not affected by allotment as were the other tribes.

On March 3, 1871, Congress enacted a bill which stated that "hereafter no Indian nation or tribe within the territory of the United States shall be acknowledged or recognized as an independent nation, tribe or power with whom the United States may contract by treaty." [6] This action might appear to have done away with the sovereignty of Indian tribes and paved the way

[6] The end of treaty-making was legislated in an appropriations bill (16 Stat. L., 566) approved on March 3, 1871. Thus ended a struggle between the Senate and House of Representatives, the latter body having long opposed negotiation with tribes through treaties. House members, within whose jurisdiction appropriations bills originate, felt they should have some say over the terms of settlements with the tribes, and since treaties were subject only to approval by the Senate, they were denied this opportunity. In 1871, House leaders refused to appropriate funds for carrying out provisions of the post–Civil War treaties unless the Senate would agree to abandon the treaty approach in dealing with Indian tribes. See USDI 1958:210–212.

for all Indians to become citizens; but, in fact, it did not. There was no accompanying action either to abrogate all previous treaties, nor to make a general grant of citizenship to Indians (as was finally done fifty-three years later in 1924). In the absence of the latter, the situation remained largely as before, with the Indians on the reservations practicing limited self-government, being excluded from the exercise of state jurisdiction, and becoming citizens only through special acts of Congress, none of which encompassed all tribes. On the other hand, the new policy did have some effect. For example, since 1796, Congress had forbidden leasing of Indian tribal lands except by treaty. The Act of 1871 did not change its predecessor statute in this respect and, therefore, raised the issue of whether such lands could thereafter be leased. Furthermore, since there were many tribes, especially in the Southwest, which were still not living on reservations in 1871, abandonment of treaty-making called for the development of a new procedure for setting up areas of land specially reserved for Indians. This matter was attended to through a series of special Congressional acts and through establishing reservations by executive order. The latter had been practiced to a very limited degree as early as 1855, but without statutory authorization by Congress. Congress did not act immediately after 1871 to provide the president with the authority to create executive order reservations, but he continued to do so. When, in 1882, his authority for such behavior was questioned, the Solicitor of the Interior Department delivered an opinion in which he conceded that Congress had, in fact, never given the president such authority, but that neither had it objected to his exercising it from time to time over the preceding three decades (USDI 1958:613–615). Still, the question of Indian entitlement to lands thereby set aside remained.

One important outcome of the stir over Indian affairs in the post–Civil War era was the establishment of Indian defense organizations, often dominated by missionaries and eastern intellectuals, to serve as a national conscience on Indian matters. From the outset, one of the largest and most important of these was the Indian Rights Association, formed in 1882, which remains active today. These organizations played a major role in the decision made a few years later to adopt a general allotment policy.

REVIVAL OF THE ALLOTMENT POLICY

The period of the 1870's was largely devoted to conquering and placing on reservations the few remaining hostile tribes. It is often referred to as the period of the Indian Wars, for it was at this time that the last of the powerful plains tribes, such as the Sioux, were defeated. Although the Apaches continued to cause problems in the Southwest until the ultimate defeat of Geronimo in 1886, the Indian Wars were largely over by 1880.

By this time, the country had been exposed for more than a decade to the reservation system, characterized by the issuance of rations and extreme Indian dependency. The missionary groups, in spite of their own involvement in trying to educate and train those Indians on reservations, were profoundly disturbed with what the long-range effects of such a policy would be. The only real purpose it seemed to serve was that of keeping the Indians isolated and protected, and even the role of protection was not wholly successful. Influential members of Congress were concerned with the mounting costs of providing for the Indians.

In such an atmosphere, influential policy-makers began seeking a new approach. The one they settled on was the allotment program to which Commissioner Manypenny had been so passionately dedicated. This was the era of homesteading, of the philosophy of the yeoman farmer ("forty acres and a mule"). Why not, many reasoned, give individual Indians the title to small acreages of agricultural land, provide them farm implements and seed, and instruct them in agricultural pursuits? At the time, it seemed a most logical method of assuring Indian self-sufficiency and preparing Indians for the assumption of full citizenship responsibilities.

In line with the new sentiment for allotment in severalty, Congress in 1875 extended the provisions of the Homestead Act to Indians, making it possible for those who did not have access to reservation lands to obtain homesteads on the public domain. Carl Shurz, one of the most powerful of the early Secretaries of the Interior, called for an allotment program in 1877, and two years later stated that many Indians also favored it (Kinney 1937:187).

Extending the Homestead Act was one of the first public acknowledgments by Congress that some Indians at least would not permanently make their homes on reservations, and is of importance, therefore, to a book about Indians who are oriented toward off-reservation urban environment. Another development of the same period has similar relevance.

An act of 1876 contained a provision that the Ponca tribe would be removed with its consent from Dakota territory to Oklahoma; in spite of the consent provision, the Poncas were forcibly removed during the administration of President Hayes. After remaining in Oklahoma for nearly two years, a small band of Poncas, under the leadership of Chief Standing Bear, fled northward to join the Omahas who had readied themselves to receive them. The Poncas were arrested and plans were made for transporting them back to Oklahoma. Friendly citizens of Nebraska engaged an attorney for the Poncas, and the resulting lawsuit was carried to the United States Supreme Court. In a now famous decision (*Standing Bear* v. *Crook*, 25 Fed. 14891), the Court held that Indians could not be denied the right to separate themselves from their tribes and to sever tribal relations for the purpose of becoming self-sustaining and living without support from the government. No massive exodus of Indians from the reservations followed this decision, but it did settle the issue of whether Indians had to live on the reservations assigned to their tribes. It also, by implication, reinforced the previously held belief that Indians who separated themselves from their tribes were expected to subsist without government aid.

The first general allotment bill was proposed in 1878, and although not enacted, the bill attracted widespread support. Two years later another, known as the Coke Bill, went into the legislative hopper. This bill also failed, but was reintroduced, and in 1884 and 1885 received enough votes to carry it through the Senate. By this time, the Indian defense organizations were solidly behind the idea of Indian allotment, and finally an act authorizing it was passed by both houses of Congress in 1887, known popularly today either as the Dawes Severalty Act or as the General Allotment Act (25 Stat. L., 388). Although officially repudiated as federal policy in 1934, this legislation has profoundly affected reservations in most parts of the country and unquestionably contributed to the movement of many Indians to other areas, including large cities in such states as Minnesota,

North Dakota, South Dakota, Washington, and (by later extension) Oklahoma.

Basically, the Dawes Severalty Act called for allotment of agricultural and range lands in severalty among tribal members. Each head of a family was to receive a quarter section (160 acres); single persons over eighteen were to receive an eighth section (80 acres), as were orphan children under eighteen; and other youngsters who had not reached their eighteenth birthdays were to receive one-sixteenth of a section. Each person was to be given a "trust" patent to his allotment, which meant it could not be alienated for a period of twenty-five years, at which time a full "fee" patent could be issued giving the owner authority to do with the land as he pleased. The president was authorized to extend the trust period in circumstances where he considered it appropriate. When all allotments had been made, the president could negotiate with the tribes for the purchase of the remaining (surplus) lands of the reservation, such purchase, however, being subject to Congressional approval.

The Dawes Act took account of the citizenship problem, again in the context of the difference between ward and citizen Indians previously described. It provided that once an Indian had received a patent to his allotment, he was to be subject to the jurisdiction of the laws of the state in which he resided and to enjoy full citizenship rights, provided he had been born in the United States. It further provided that any Indian who had voluntarily taken up residence apart from his tribe and "adopted the habits of civilized life" was thereby declared a citizen of the United States.

Insofar as Indians with allotted land were concerned, Congress reversed itself by the terms of the Burke Act of 1906, in which it legislated that thereafter allottees would not be eligible for citizenship until fee, rather than trust, patents had been issued and that state, civil, and criminal jurisdiction over their lands could not be asserted until the fee patent was forthcoming. Thus, this early attempt to resolve the problems of Indian citizenship and state jurisdiction over reservations was aborted.

Some parts of Indian country were exempted from the Dawes Act as originally passed. These included the territory of the Five Civilized Tribes, the Osages, Miamis, Peorias, Sacs and Foxes of Oklahoma, the Senecas of New York, and a small part of the

Sioux reservation in Nebraska. Two years after its passage, the act was amended to include the Peorias (along with the Weas, Kaskaskias, and Piankishaws with whom they were associated), and the Miamis. In 1891, the act was further amended to limit allotments to 80 acres, except for grazing lands which could be allotted in parcels of 160 acres. The legislation of 1891 also provided for limited leasing of allotments, and over the next ten years, Congress passed a number of amendments related to such limited leasing.

Administrators of the Indian Bureau wasted no time in implementing the allotment policy, in spite of the opposition of some tribes. Within a year after passage of the Dawes Act, allotment activities had been undertaken on ten reservations (Kinney 1937: 215).

OFF-RESERVATION BOARDING SCHOOLS

Following the Civil War, when adherents of an allotment policy were lining up supporters, another significant development occurred which is still today aligned in the minds of many with the Allotment Act and with forced integration of Indians. This was the off-reservation boarding school system. Although some of the religious institutions which carried the principal burden of educating Indians had maintained such schools quite early, credit for application of the idea to Indians generally is usually given to Lieutenant (later General) R. H. Pratt, an army officer who had become much interested in Indians while serving in Indian Territory. A firm believer in the importance of preparing Indians for integration, Pratt founded a school at Carlisle Barracks, Pennsylvania, in 1879. By removing Indians from the reservation and affording them an opportunity to live among whites, he felt that Indian assimilation would be speeded up. At the outset, missionary societies were more disposed to accept this approach than were federal administrators and for the first few years of its existence, the Carlisle School received more support from the Quakers and the Pennsylvania Dutch of the surrounding area than it did from the Indian Bureau (Beatty 1958:60–64). That the Pennsylvanians in the vicinity should have been interested is quite understandable in view of the fact that a basic element of Pratt's policy was the "outing" system, which might today be considered the first individual Indian "relocation" program. Boys and girls from the school were assigned to families in the communities and rural areas nearby, where they worked at farming or housekeeping to provide them with experience in these activities and to acquaint them with the living patterns of the white people, with whom they had previously had little contact (Leupp 1910:121–122).

By the early 1880's, the off-reservation boarding school concept had gathered wide support among federal Indian administrators, and the Bureau of Indian Affairs began to establish schools of its own in such states as Oregon, Kansas, Arizona, Nebraska, and Oklahoma (then, still Indian Territory). It proved a natural twin of the allotment policy, both being designed to remove the Indian from tribal status and integrate him into white society. It is understandable, therefore, that following the passage of the Dawes Act, great emphasis was placed upon educating the Indians in the new schools, whether they wished to go or not. In the next thirty years, Indian children would at times be forcibly removed from their parents and taken hundreds of miles away. Many did not return.

Federal administrators by 1890 were becoming aware that increasing numbers of Indians lived away from the reservations, some temporarily, others permanently. Both to assure educational opportunities for the urban Indians and to hasten their integration, the BIA began negotiating contracts with local public school districts to encourage these districts to assume responsibility for educating Indian children. Although the program moved slowly during its first decade, the enrollment of Indian children in public schools accelerated rapidly after 1900.

One other development following the passage of the Dawes Act had important repercussions in the field of education among the Five Civilized Tribes of Oklahoma. As indicated previously, these groups, within a few years after removal, had begun to operate schools of their own, with financial support coming primarily from treaty annuities.

Initially, the Five Civilized Tribes were excluded from the provisions of the Dawes Act, but within a few years after its passage (in 1898) Congress enacted special legislation to provide for allotting the lands of the Five Civilized Tribes and dissolving their local governments. Known as "the Curtis Act," this legislation paved the way for a number of other laws that closed the rolls of the tribes and, in 1906, transferred their schools to Indian Bureau control.

AMENDING THE ALLOTMENT ACT

The two most important of the many amendments to the Dawes Act were the Burke Act of 1906 (34 Stat. 182) and the Omnibus Act of 1910 (36 Stat. 855). It has already been mentioned that the Burke Act amended prior legislation by specifying the time Indians would become eligible for citizenship and be subject to the criminal and civil jurisdictions of the states in which they resided. This act included two other amendments of at least equal importance. The first provided authority for the Secretary of the Interior to issue a fee patent to any allottee whom he judged competent to manage his own affairs, without regard to whether the twenty-five-year allotment trust period had expired; the second directed that fee patents be issued to the heirs of all deceased allottees.

Prior to passage of the Burke Act, it was necessary for an allottee seeking a fee patent either to wait until the expiration of the twenty-five-year trust period (which even for the first allottees under the Dawes Act would not have come until 1912) or obtain a special act of Congress. Some Indians did seek private bills. These became a nuisance for Congress and also opened the door to unscrupulous politicians and lawyers, who sometimes charged the Indians fees for helping them obtain the necessary legislation (Leupp 1910:37–38). Commissioner Francis Leupp was one of those who supported the idea of eliminating such red tape and making it possible for competent Indians to obtain fee patents upon request. Despite the amendments of the Burke Act, however, fee patenting of land did not proceed rapidly under Commissioners Leupp and Valentine (1904–1913), neither of whom developed a clear-cut policy for determining competency and both of whom granted fee patents only upon application.

The decision to include in the Burke bill a proposal to issue fee patents to inherited allotments was based upon Congressional concern about the problem arising from ownership fractionation after the death of an original allottee. Congress had first perceived and dealt with this problem in 1902, when it amended the general Allotment Act to permit the secretary, at the request of the heirs, to sell an allotment and divide the proceeds. However, the heirs did not always wish to sell, so this proved only a partial solution. Commissioner Leupp and others felt that through fee patenting inherited allotments, further ownership fractionation growing out of restrictions against alienation of the land could be avoided.

A definitive attempt to deal with the so-called "heirship" problem was included in the Omnibus Bill of 1910. Section I of that act conferred upon the Secretary of the Interior exclusive authority to determine the heirs of an allottee who died intestate. It also authorized the secretary to confer fee patents upon the competent heirs and to partition the property when he considered it advisable. Where some of the heirs were held to be incompetent, the secretary might sell the land and distribute the proceeds.

Although the Act of 1910 seemed to provide all the necessary tools to deal with the problem of fractionated heirship interests in trust allotments, such, in fact, did not prove to be so. Federal officials who administered the act in the years immediately following its passage did not find it easy to settle on criteria for determining competency, nor did they always feel it wise to sell an allotment where one or more of the heirs was obviously incompetent. With notable exceptions (as during the administration of Cato Sells), they limited their responsibility to ascertaining the heirs and transferring the ownership interests to them in common, thus perpetuating, rather than alleviating, the problem.

Heirship was only one matter with which the Omnibus Act of 1910 was concerned; other problems grew out of the general Allotment Act with which its authors attempted to deal. Among these was the important matter of leasing Indian allotments and selling the resources they contained. Between 1891 and 1900, Congress had passed four separate pieces of legislation in an attempt to bring this problem under control.

The Act of 1910 authorized the secretary to lease allotments for periods not to exceed five years. It also provided authority for him to arrange the sale of timber on both allotted and unallotted lands. Although often overlooked by historians, this act is a most important piece of federal legislation related to natural resource development on the reservations.

Cato Sells, who became Commissioner of Indian Affairs in 1913, was a firm believer in removing the restrictions from the titles of Indian allottees and giving them full control of their property. The Department of the Interior began experimenting in 1916 with a program of "forced" fee patents (Sells called them "policy patents"). Instead of waiting until an allottee petitioned for a fee patent, as his immediate predecessors had done, Sells encouraged the issuance of such documents to all Indians considered competent to manage their own affairs. Secretary Lane, in 1916, established competency commissions, and with the aid of Commissioner Sells promulgated guidelines for determining whether an Indian should receive a fee patent and a certificate of competency. A policy declaration of 1917 included six rules for the guidance of those struggling with the issue of competency. The first of these related to patents in fee and contained the following statement:

> To all able-bodied adult Indians of less than one-half Indian blood, there will be given, as far as may be under the law, full and complete control of all their property. Patents in fee shall be issued to all adult Indians of one-half or more Indian blood who may, after careful investigation, be found competent, provided that where deemed advisable patents in fee shall be withheld for not to exceed 40 acres as a home.
>
> Indian students, when they are 21 years of age, or over, who complete the full course of instruction in the Government schools, receive diplomas, and have demonstrated competence will be so declared (Kinney 1937:292; also, 286–296).

The result of Sells's patent policy is well demonstrated by the Commissioner's Annual Report of 1920, the last issued by Sells before leaving office. In it, he pointed out that the number of acres of land allotted during successive fiscal years had declined in an irregular manner after 1910, the peak allotment activity having occurred from 1906 to 1910 inclusive. On the other hand, the number of fee patents had risen sharply after the initiation of the competency program of 1916. Statistical tables accompanying the report showed that around 135,000 of slightly more than 175,000 Indian allotments had been fee patented in whole or part, since the commencement of the allotment program in 1887.

In April, 1921, Charles Burke of South Dakota, who had previously been Chairman of the Committee on Indian Affairs of the House of Representatives, succeeded Sells as Indian Commissioner. In his annual reports of 1921 and 1922, Burke stated that he had abandoned the previous policy of the forced fee patent and returned to the policy of issuing these documents only to Indians who applied for them and could demonstrate competency. As a result, there was a marked decline in the number of fee patents issued after 1920. Many of those lands previously patented were sold out of Indian ownership in the period following World War I. In fact, through fee patenting and the sale of surplus lands, acreages held in trust for Indians declined from more than 132 million acres in 1887 to about 32 million in 1929 (Senate 1953a).

AWAKENING NATIONAL INTEREST IN INDIAN AFFAIRS

Two developments of the early 1920's focused attention on the Indian problem and led ultimately to a national survey of Indian affairs during the administration of President Coolidge. One was the introduction of a bill in Congress to settle the question of Indian land titles in New Mexico. Following the Treaty of Guadalupe Hidalgo, by whose terms New Mexico territory became a part of the United States, many white settlers moved onto lands which had been granted the Pueblo Indians by the previous Spanish and Mexican governments.

In 1922, the so-called Bursum Lands Bill was presented to Congress for its consideration. The bill proposed to establish a procedure by which white settlers could perfect title to lands they had entered and improved, believing them to be a part of the public domain and open to homestead, or privately owned and subject to conveyance. The proposed legislation placed upon Indians the burden of proving ownership, thus reversing the established legal procedure which required a person in adverse possession to prove ownership. Some 3,000 white squatters, representing with their families around 12,000 persons, and many thousands of acres were involved.

In order to defeat the Bursum Bill, nineteen separate Pueblo Indian groups met in November, 1922, and formed the All-Pueblo Council. The struggles of these Indians attracted national attention and resulted in the formation of two other Indian defense groups: the New Mexico Association of Indian Affairs (later to become the Southwestern Association on Indian Affairs) which largely concentrated its attention on local problems; and the Eastern Association on Indian Affairs (later to become the National Association on Indian Affairs, and still later the Association on American Indian Affairs) which focused its efforts at the national level. Because of the actions of these groups, the Bursum Bill was defeated, and in 1924, Congress passed the Pueblo Lands Act, providing that all Spanish grant lands lost by the Indians would either be restored to them or provision would be made for reparation payments (McNickle 1961–62:210–211).

The other Indian situation which produced a national clamor at this time was that of the Maricopa and Pima Indians on the Gila River reservation in Arizona. Although the tribal lands had not been invaded by white settlers, as was the case in New Mexico, the water of the Gila River upon which they depended for their agriculture had been appropriated by non-Indian farmers upstream. Thus, farming had all but disappeared on the Gila River reservation by the early 1900's. Church groups, especially the Presbyterians, as well as the Indian Rights Association, prior to 1920 had focused some national attention on the problem; still, a united effort was not mounted until around 1921, when, due to the activities of Reverend Dirk Lay, the Presbyterian synods passed resolutions related to the water problem. In July, 1923, Reverend Lay addressed 13,000 delegates at a world convention of the Christian Endeavor Union in Des Moines, and urged the delegates to petition Congress to authorize construction of a dam at San Carlos, the water thus husbanded to be used to benefit Indian lands. During the remainder of 1923 and throughout most of 1924, Presbyterian congregations throughout the country wrote Congressmen in behalf of the Pima and Maricopa Indians. Through these efforts and the personal intervention of President Coolidge, legislation was enacted in 1924 authorizing the construction of the large dam named for Mr. Coolidge (Hackenberg 1955:63–66).

Increased national interest in Indians at this time produced other important results. One was the passage in 1924 of an act conferring full citizenship on all Indians who had not previously been citizens.[7] The other was the commissioning in 1926 of a

---

[7] Although Congress in 1924 made all native-born Indians full citizens, some states continued to deny them the right to vote because of confusion

national study of Indian affairs; this responsibility was assumed under contract by the Institute for Government Research which, in turn, assigned this task to Lewis Meriam and a group of his associates. Two years later, Meriam and his colleagues completed the study called *The Problem of Indian Administration* (IGR 1928), without question the most comprehensive and objective survey of the American Indian situation ever made, covering a whole range of subjects related to federal Indian policies and recommending significant changes.

Among the subjects explored was the problem of the so-called "migrated Indian," who had left the reservation to live in urban areas (IGR 1928:667–742). By the late 1920's, there were large numbers of these Indians. Some had left the reservations after selling or leasing their allotments; others who had studied in off-reservation boarding schools and participated in the outing program never went back. The Meriam report contained significant criticisms of the outing program which had been standard BIA policy since the 1880's. However, the study recognized that in the case of reservations with meager economic resources and opportunities, tribal members needed federal help to speed their movement into communities affording opportunities for "labor and development." Thus, the Meriam report provided the foundations upon which today's off-reservation employment assistance program of the Indian Bureau is based, but more than twenty years elapsed before this recommendation was implemented.

The authors of the report noted that many off-reservation communities were unprepared, both financially and philosophically, to assume responsibilities for the social and economic advancement of the Indians in their midst and, further, that they generally regarded such responsibilities to be the exclusive domain of the federal government. In spite of the urban Indians' difficulties in obtaining social services from nonfederal agencies, Meriam and his associates did not recommend the establishment of special federal programs; instead, they suggested that federal efforts be directed toward establishing cooperative relationships with existing municipal agencies and encouraging them to pro-

---

regarding the wardship status. Following court decisions in 1948, Arizona and New Mexico — the last holdouts — finally extended the franchise to their Indian residents. See Hagan 1961:159.

vide assistance to Indians on the same basis as to others. Although the modern Indian Bureau "relocation" program departs somewhat from the Meriam recommendation in this particular, federal policy in general is still based on the premise that Indians living away from a reservation are the responsibility of the communities in which they reside. Some county and city governments have preferred to abide by the contrary doctrine of exclusive federal responsibility, leaving the urban Indian without assistance from either national or local agencies.

THE INDIAN REORGANIZATION ACT

Many recommendations of the Meriam report were formalized into law with enactment of the Wheeler-Howard or Indian Reorganization Act (48 Stat. 984, 985) in 1934. This is the last major piece of *omnibus* Indian legislation passed by Congress and provides the basis for federal Indian administration to the present day. The Indian Reorganization Act provided, among other things, that further allotment of Indian lands would cease and reservation lands previously declared surplus would be restored to Indian ownership. It provided authorization for the appropriation of funds to purchase additional land for Indian use. It encouraged the formation of tribal organizations and corporations, and established a revolving loan fund for the development of business enterprises. The act also addressed itself to the matter of Indian national resources and granted the executive branch of the government authority to frame regulations for the conservation of Indian soil and timber. It set up a system of special preference for the hiring of Indian employees by the Bureau of Indian Affairs.

Shortly before the Indian Reorganization Act was passed, Congress also approved legislation making it possible for the BIA to contract with state, local, and private educational, health, and welfare agencies to provide services to Indians. Known today as the Johnson-O'Malley Act (48 Stat. 596), this legislation was in response to recommendations in the Meriam report which called for enrolling greater numbers of Indian youngsters in public schools and supplying services to the Indian population through the same facilities supplying other citizens, rather than through special federal programs.

John Collier became Commissioner of Indian Affairs in 1933,

and served in that post longer than any other commissioner in history. The Indian Reorganization Act supplied the basis for the Collier Indian policy which the commissioner himself summarized in the following terms:

> The new Indian policy must be built around the group-dynamic potentials of Indian life. This meant an ending of the epoch of forced atomization, cultural prescription, and administrative absolutism. . . . In place of an Indian Bureau monopoly of Indian affairs, there must be sought a cumulative involvement of all agencies of helpfulness, Federal, state, local and unofficial; but the method must not be that of simply dismembering the Indian Service, but rather of transforming it into a technical servicing agency and a coordinating, evaluating and within limitations, regulatory agency (Collier 1954:5).

Between 1934 and 1941, the Collier Administration introduced many changes into the pattern of federal-Indian relationships. Yet, with the limitations in funds resulting from the Depression, these changes were not fully implemented, and before some of the most important changes could achieve permanent effect, the outbreak of World War II interfered.

INDIAN CLAIMS

The most significant piece of legislation emerging after World War II was the Indian Claims Commission Act (60 Stat. 1049), which provided tribes an opportunity to sue the federal government before a special tribunal to recover financial damages for many different types of grievances accumulated through the years. Although the United States Court of Claims had been established in 1855 to permit suit to be brought against the federal government, tribal claims based on treaties were excluded from general jurisdiction of the court. Like foreign nations, each tribe was required to obtain a special act from Congress to present a case, an expensive and time-consuming procedure. In spite of that fact, numerous Indian tribes did obtain the necessary legislation, and more than one hundred lawsuits were heard by the Court of Claims between the Civil War and 1946 (Lurie 1957:56–70). By that year, many Congressmen had become annoyed with the large numbers of Indian claims bills presented each session and were amenable to the idea of a single act which would give all tribes an opportunity to have their claims heard.

While many supporters of the Claims Commission Act undoubtedly felt it was necessary to overcome a longstanding policy of discrimination and some wished simply to be rid of an annoyance, there were others who viewed it in a different light. Sentiment in Congress during the war had grown more hostile to the idea of continuing the special relationship between Indians and the federal government indefinitely. It was clear that so long as many tribes had apparently legitimate unsettled claims, this relationship could not be easily terminated. Thus, the bill attracted support from Congressmen who considered it a means to withdraw programs designed solely for Indian benefit (Hagan 1961:167). Many of them believed that the claims awards would help to make tribes self-sustaining, thereby reducing the justification for such programs.

On the heels of the passage of the Claims Commission Act, the Commissioner of Indian Affairs was summoned to testify before the Senate Committee on Civil Service concerning the issue of withdrawal of federal services to Indians. Because the commissioner was too ill to appear, the burden of testifying fell on William Zimmerman, Jr., the Acting Commissioner. Zimmerman presented the committee with a statement of his views, in which he listed ten tribes as ready for federal withdrawal, and twenty additional groups for whom withdrawal would be feasible within five to ten years. Approximately 53,000 Indians were included within the first category, and 75,000 within the second. For the remaining tribes, Zimmerman indicated that a period of ten to twenty-five years would be required before withdrawal, depending upon the progress made in establishing an economic base for these groups (Province 1953:179–188).

THE BIA "RELOCATION" PROGRAM

About the time these Congressional views on the subject of "termination" of the federal-Indian relationship became manifest, the Indian Bureau independently began a small program on the Navajo and Hopi reservations, which was later to become confused with termination not only in the minds of the Indians, but in the minds of many federal officials. This program consisted of off-reservation job placement designed to relieve the pressure on reservation resources by assisting Indians to resettle in communities outside. Through this effort and with the help of the state employment offices and the Railroad Retirement Board, the bureau was able to find both temporary and permanent jobs for Navajos at off-reservation locations. Placement officers were assigned to Los Angeles, Phoenix, Denver, and Salt Lake City; initially, their function was to find employers willing to hire Indians and to notify their counterparts on the reservations (USDI 1951:36–37).

A year after the beginning of the Navajo-Hopi program, the bureau sought and received from Congress a small appropriation to extend off-reservation placement services to Indians in other areas. The Interior Department Appropriations Act of October 12, 1949 (including funds for fiscal year 1950) provided $100,000, and with this money the BIA hired placement officers to serve the Indians of the Aberdeen, Billings, Minneapolis, and Portland areas (Senate 1951:324). The following year, the bureau asked for $130,000 and Congress responded by appropriating $260,000. Heartened by this generosity, Commissioner Dillon Myer in his 1952 budget request boldly asked for more than $1,600,000; both Houses promptly trimmed this request, and the bureau ultimately received $576,000 for program operations during 1952. A significant increase over the previous year, the funds permitted the launching of a nationwide program. Early in 1952, Myer opened a placement center in Chicago and established a new branch in the Indian Bureau dedicated to what were now being called "relocation" services (Senate 1953b:473).

In presenting his budget request for 1953, Myer made a plea for the inclusion of a large vocational training component within the relocation program, and sought more than $8,500,000 to fund the total activity (Senate 1953b:471ff.). Unconvinced of the value of the new effort, Congress appropriated only $567,000 for relocation services and nothing for vocational training. This budget figure, a reduction from the previous year, remained more or less constant until 1956, when it was increased to nearly a million dollars.

Considering the fact that Congress in 1953 went on record favoring federal withdrawal from the Indian field and that many Indians and others have associated the termination program with the relocation program, it is significant that appropriations for relocation voted by this and the succeeding Congress remained at low levels. From a careful examination of the record, the conclusion drawn is that except for a temporal relationship, these two major tenets of federal Indian policy during 1946–1958 were not, in fact, the offspring of the same parent. Rather, a strong case can be made for regarding the Indian relocation program as a progeny of the Meriam report and a brainchild of Commissioner John Collier's staff.

During the 1930's, the Bureau of Indian Affairs for the first time conducted extensive surveys of reservation resources. These surveys made clear the size of the populations inhabiting certain reservations and the incapacity of these reservations' resources to support them. Following World War II, this matter came to critical attention on the Navajo reservation and, far more than any other factor, led to the development of a program of off-reservation placement for that jurisdiction.

Significant also in connection with attempts to establish a close association between relocation and termination is the fact that Commissioner Myer, considered perhaps unfairly to have been an ardent terminationist (Hagan 1961:161), did not in his congressional testimony or annual reports refer to the two in the same context. Myer genuinely believed that a better life was not possible for many Indians unless employment could be found for them in areas outside the reservations.[8] He was strongly seconded in his belief by one of his principal aides, H. Rex Lee, who had previously served with Myer in the War Relocation Authority and who later became the Deputy Commissioner of Indian Affairs.

FEDERAL WITHDRAWAL

However Commissioner Myer may have felt about a relationship between termination and relocation, there undoubtedly were persons at high levels in Washington during the 1950's who did relate the two programs' thrusts. Furthermore, the comments of certain Congressmen and Bureau of the Budget officials, documented between 1961 and 1968, suggest that this feeling of relationship survives today.

The enthusiasm for withdrawal of special federal services to Indians reached its peak in Congress in 1953 with the passage of House Concurrent Resolution 108, in which a majority of the

[8] Personal statement made to the author in 1969.

members of both Houses stated it to be the policy of Congress

> . . . as rapidly as possible to make the Indians within the
> territorial limits of the United States subject to the same laws
> and entitled to the same privileges and responsibilities as are
> applicable to other citizens of the United States, to end their
> status as wards of the United States, and to grant them all the
> rights and prerogatives pertaining to American citizenship.

As a result of this resolution, a number of small tribes and two large ones — the Menominees of Wisconsin and the Klamaths of Oregon — underwent "termination." By 1958, however, the termination thrust had lost much of its force, and Secretary of the Interior Fred Seaton stated the policy of his administration would not be to seek the withdrawal of federal services from Indian tribes without their understanding and acceptance. Similar policies have been enunciated by top officials of subsequent administrations, including President Nixon's. Still, in the eyes of many Indians, termination remains a threat.

Much more closely related to the termination thrust than the relocation program were actions taken by the Congress in 1953 and 1954 that implemented the policy statement contained in House Concurrent Resolution 108. On August 15, 1953, Congress legislated (67 Stat. 588) the transference of civil and criminal jurisdiction over Indian reservations to the states of California, Minnesota, Nebraska, Oregon, and Wisconsin (with a few specific exceptions), and the authorization of other states upon their initiative to assume jurisdiction. The legislation made no mention of the need for securing Indian consent before states could take over. Popularly known as Public Law 280, this Congressional action was vigorously opposed by a majority of the nation's Indian tribes. Finally, in 1968, the tribes were successful in amending this law to provide for the consent of the Indians before states could assert civil and criminal jurisdiction on their reservations.

On the same date as the passage of Public Law 280, Congress amended previous laws (67 Stat. 586) to permit the Indians of each reservation to decide whether and under what conditions intoxicants could be sold in Indian country. Thus, the century-old policy of prohibiting the sale of alcoholic beverages to Indians was reversed.

The following year, Congress transferred the responsibility for

Indian health services from the BIA to the Public Health Service of the Department of Health, Education, and Welfare. While this measure had the support of those Congressmen who favored termination, it also was supported by federal legislators who felt that the quality of Indian health services was extremely low and that the Public Health Service could secure the appropriations and the personnel necessary to raise the level of the services.

Importantly related to the relocation program was an action taken by Congress in 1956. In that year, a program of adult vocational training for Indians was authorized (25 USC 309). A ceiling of $3,500,000 was placed on the program; in subsequent years, this ceiling was progressively raised to its present level of $25,000,000.

Commissioner Myer, as early as 1952, had recognized the need for vocational training to assure those Indians participating in the voluntary relocation program some measure of success in maintaining employment in their new surroundings. As indicated earlier, Myer was not successful in selling this program to Congress during his administration, but as the relocation program became an established part of Indian Bureau policy, it gained support from more Congressmen.

In addition to the commencement of the off-reservation placement program and the institution of a related effort in vocational training, an additional development of the post–World War II period importantly affected the movement of Indians into urban areas. This was the special BIA education program for youngsters over twelve years of age who had received little or no formal schooling. There were an estimated 10,000 such youngsters on the Navajo reservation alone in 1946, and in the fall of that year, the Bureau of Indian Affairs began an experimental five-year program of accelerated basic and vocational education at the Sherman Institute in Riverside, California. Pleased with the results, it subsequently established similar programs at other off-reservation boarding schools and began including teenagers from reservations other than the Navajo.

The program was greatly accelerated in January, 1950, when the BIA took over an abandoned military hospital at Brigham City, Utah, and converted it into the Intermountain Indian School. This institution ultimately achieved an enrollment of more than 2,000, making it the keystone of the special program.

The most important emphasis in this educational effort was to prepare young men and women for employment, primarily in the schools' areas. In some respects, it resembled the "outing" program previously described, and for at least the first few years of its existence placed young women usually in home service (often as domestics) and young men in agriculture. As time passed, new employment and training opportunities were provided. That the emphasis was on employment away from the reservations is demonstrated by passages in a book written by an employee of the Indian Bureau and published by that agency. The author proudly points out that in 1959, one of the peak years of the special program, 449 Indian young men and women — 77 percent of the graduating class — were placed in off-reservation employment (Coombs 1962:115).

By 1960, the various programs directed toward off-reservation employment had begun to have a measurable impact on the size of the urban Indian population. In California alone, the number of urban Indians had nearly quadrupled over the preceding decade (Price 1968:169), largely because of substantial gains in the Los Angeles and San Francisco areas. Later analysis revealed that most newcomers were from reservations outside California. Many in the Los Angeles area had participated in the special education program at Sherman Institute; more in both areas had been processed through the BIA employment assistance centers in Los Angeles and the San Francisco Bay region.

With the change of administration in 1961, Secretary of the Interior Udall appointed a task force to study the Indian situation. The members of the group traveled widely throughout Indian country interviewing tribal leaders; they discovered that termination was still the issue of greatest concern to Indians and that, in the minds of many, the relocation program was a major arm of the termination policy. In spite of the latter belief, few Indians proposed that the off-reservation placement program be discontinued. Rather, a majority recommended that the voluntary aspects of the program be emphasized, that it provide better training and orientation, that it focus on local employment wherever possible, that its services be extended to Indians who had gone to the urban areas without BIA assistance, and that it be broadened to include more persons from the areas surrounding the reservations (USDI 1961).

Because the word *relocation* had so many negative connotations for Indians, the task force recommended that the bureau cease employing this term and that a new name be found for the branch of the BIA concerned with off-reservation placement activity. Commissioner Philleo Nash, who had himself been a member of the task force, implemented these suggestions, and the program was renamed simply "employment assistance." However, it is still better known both within the bureau and outside as "the relocation program."

Perhaps the most important development in Indian administration during the 1960's was the diversification of federal effort on the reservations. As previously stated, in 1954 the responsibility for Indian health was transferred to the United States Public Health Service, which proved overwhelmingly more successful than the Indian Bureau in obtaining appropriations. The result was a spectacular improvement in Indian health as well as the establishment of training programs for Indians interested in careers in nursing and other medically related fields. Also in the latter 1950's, the Indian Health Service began a program to supply reservations with better, safer water supplies and sewage disposal systems.

In addition to the Indian Health Service, other federal agencies such as the Social Security Administration and the Department of Labor were supplying services through state and local auspices to reservation Indians in the period before 1960. Also, the Bureau of Indian Affairs had begun the transfer of agricultural extension services to the various states. Through local public school districts, the Office of Education was contributing funds for Indian education. However, in general, these agencies did not maintain direct relationships with either individual Indians or Indian tribes.

The Department of Commerce, in 1961, began to have its first sustained contacts with Indian groups as a result of the Area Redevelopment Act. Under the aegis of the Area Redevelopment Administration, tribes prepared "Overall Economic Development Plans" for their reservations, and through the ARA, the Indians received financial assistance of various kinds related to the creation of job opportunities. By 1968, the ARA (now known as the EDA — Economic Development Administration) had expanded its activities on Indian reservations to such an extent that it was obliged to establish a special Indian office to assure program coordination.

Also in 1961, the Public Housing Administration (now the Housing Assistance Administration) first recognized Indian tribes as eligible to participate in its programs. Within a few years, more than eighty different tribes established housing authorities and began the construction of new dwellings on the reservations. The Farmers' Home Administration also started directing substantial sums toward construction of Indian reservation housing. During the period 1963–1965, the Accelerated Public Works Program, an arm of the Area Redevelopment Administration, invested nearly $2,000,000 in constructing or improving community centers on Indian reservations and in developing parks and playgrounds. In addition to providing a means for improved Indian housing, the Department of Housing and Urban Development also assisted with the construction of community centers through Neighborhood Facilities Grants. More recently, Indian tribes have taken advantage of urban planning grants made available by this department, and one reservation has been approved for participation in the Model Cities Program.

Of all the federal agencies which have come onto Indian reservations since 1960, the one with the most profound impact has been the Office of Economic Opportunity. Established in 1964, this agency was responsible for the initiation of tribal community action programs through which a variety of projects have been initiated. Included within the scope of the community action programs have been activities related to preschool education for children, vocational training for adults, agricultural extension, and housing. The Office of Economic Opportunity also brought to the reservations the services of VISTA volunteers and Job Corps camps. More than any other federal agency, the OEO has been responsible for the creation of new bureaucracies on the reservations, which in some ways compete with the existing bureaucracies of the Indian Bureau, elected tribal governments, and the Indian Health Service. The programs of the OEO, however, have provided Indians with new opportunities for decision-making, and in this respect have influenced relationships between the Indians and other federal agencies operating in the reservation setting. Shortly after its establishment, the Office of Economic Opportunity created a special Indian desk in recognition of the importance of its Indian programs.

Another federal department which in recent years has set up an office to coordinate Indian programs is Health, Education, and Welfare. This department now has several programs which relate to reservation Indians, especially within the fields of elementary and secondary education and juvenile delinquency.

It has often been necessary to change administrative procedures, develop new program ideas, and even amend existing legislation in order to qualify reservation Indians for participation in the federal programs just described; but these programs, primarily, have been administered for Indians within the same broad framework and by the same agencies that administer them for the general public. Thus, Indians have had to adjust to dealing with new sets of bureaucrats, most of them unfamiliar with the unique aspects of reservation life, and some of them reluctant to tailor existing programs to fit special reservation needs. The adjustment has been difficult for both sides and has led to the creation of "Indian desks" within federal agencies which previously did not have them, and to the establishment of new roles within tribal governments.

For the most part, the new Indian offices are concerned with coordinating or administering programs which relate to that segment of the Indian population living on or near the reservations. While Indians in other areas may benefit from public housing, community action, and manpower training programs, they do so, not as Indians, but on the same basis as other Americans in similar circumstances.

During the 1960's, the BIA greatly expanded its off-reservation training and placement effort, raising the latter — at least in terms of appropriations — to the level of a major program. In 1950–1959, BIA appropriations for both the vocational training and employment aspects of the program totaled slightly under $20,000,000. This total, in the following decade, was increased more than six times, to around $121,000,000. The sum available in 1969 alone was more than was spent during 1950–1959. Not all these funds were used to provide off-reservation employment, some being devoted to providing job opportunities in or near traditional Indian communities, but the bulk of the appropriations unquestionably was directed toward placing Indians in jobs away from the reservations.

The amount of money expended by the Indian Bureau per Indian relocatee has increased appreciably since 1950. At that time, the funds were used principally to find jobs and Indians who could fill them. Later, additional services were added, including transportation for a relocatee and his family to the training or job site, shipment of household goods, subsistence payments until the family began receiving a regular pay check, clothing allowances, and a range of counseling and orientation services. In 1967, the BIA began offering grants to relocated families to enable them to make down-payments on the purchase of homes.

Several other expensive additions to the employment assistance program were made by the bureau during the 1960's. Among these were the establishment of residential training centers where families could live while their breadwinners were undergoing prevocational and vocational training, the creation of a special orientation center in Seattle to help prepare Alaskan natives for urban life in the "lower 48" states, and inclusion for the first time of large families as participants in the off-reservation placement effort.

Although the Indian Bureau has progressively expanded its relocation activities, it has continued to regard the clientele for these activities as that portion of the Indian population residing on or near the reservations. Indians who relocate without bureau assistance may qualify for counseling from employees of the placement centers, but they are not considered eligible for the other services provided persons who relocate with bureau help. The Indian Health Service assists such Indians when they first move from the reservation, but only so long as they remain ineligible (because of residence qualifications) for health services administered to other indigent members of their communities.

THE RESERVATION "SYSTEM" AND THE URBAN INDIAN

The historical sketch presented in the preceding pages provides background for consideration at this point of the unique character of the reservation system. The system, in turn, is important for an understanding of the attitude of many urban Indians today toward federal agencies and programs.

To begin with, Indians within a reservation setting enjoy a closer relationship with the federal government than do most other Americans. While federal taxes help to finance many programs of benefit to citizens generally, few of these are actually *administered by* federal agencies. Instead, federal funds in the form of grants or loans find their way into the hands of *local* administrators. On Indian reservations, however, federal officials actually build and run schools, operate vocational training programs, provide scholarships to Indian students, supply medical care and hospital services, help individuals to find jobs, appraise lands, arrange leases, administer sales of minerals and timber, collect rentals, distribute checks to landowners, and supply general welfare assistance directly to Indian clients.

Not only are programs for reservation Indians administered at a different level of government from those for other Americans, but the quality of the programs is often different. Outside the military departments, only the Indian Health Service supplies its clients with cradle-to-grave medical and hospitalization services; no other agency at any level of government provides a program for training individuals and helping them to find employment which is as comprehensive as the employment assistance effort of the Indian Bureau; few local welfare agencies administer programs of general welfare assistance with the same flexibility as the Indian Bureau; and no other agency of government has a program of higher education grants like that maintained by the BIA.

When an Indian leaves the reservation and settles in the city, he does not lose his eligibility for the services which grow out of the federal trusteeship over Indian reservation land. If he has an interest in an allotment, he may benefit from services related to appraising the value of his allotment and the resources it contains, negotiating leases and sales, collecting rentals, royalties and sale receipts, and distributing income — all of which the BIA supplies to holders of trust allotments wherever they may be living.

It is the so-called "community" services — rather than those related to federal trusteeship — which do not usually follow Indians to the cities. Even in the case of persons relocated under Indian Bureau auspices, eligibility for such services is terminated in a short time. Within the BIA, the rationalization for withholding community services from Indians living away from the reservation has been that such individuals pay taxes in their communities and, therefore, should be served by the local agencies, which these taxes support, rather than by the Indian Bureau. Reservation Indians, on the other hand, contribute few tax revenues to local agencies and are often not subject to their jurisdiction. Therefore, special federal services are required for them.

The explanation in the case of the Indian Health Service is somewhat different. In the basic legislation establishing the agency and in subsequent appropriations acts, Congress has indicated that it intends reservation Indians to be the principal clientele served. Only in one instance (a clinic in Rapid City, South Dakota, operated for the benefit of Indians residing there) has it departed from this position.

The Indian who has recently migrated to the city from a reservation home encounters three new elements in his quest for assistance from public agencies. First, there is no agency which serves only Indian clients; he must stand in the same line with others in applying for and receiving such services. Second, he is usually eligible for help only if he is indigent. And, third, the character of services provided by state welfare institutions and public hospitals is different from that provided by the U.S. Public Health Service and other federal agencies whose services are geared primarily to the local Indian clientele in the Indian setting.

In an earlier day, many off-reservation Indians were persons who had voluntarily surrendered tribal status in order to enjoy full citizenship rights and the greater economic security which they felt could be found outside the reservations. These persons seldom expected or asked for special consideration. Other off-reservation Indians had no tribal affiliations or belonged to landless tribes. Many of these persons had never benefitted from special federal attention and were not sufficiently familiar with the reservation situation to know what services federal agencies were providing there.

Following the allotment program and the establishment of off-reservation boarding schools, a new class of Indians began to settle in the cities. These were "tribal" Indians — persons from reservation communities — some of whom, while not always satisfied with the services provided "back home" by the Indian Bureau, expected that agency to support them and come to their rescue in time of trouble in their new surroundings. By the twenties, when the Meriam report was prepared, the cities contained a sufficient number of these persons to be concerned about their impact, especially upon the welfare agencies. These Indians were also important enough as a class by this time to merit a lengthy chapter in the report.

Meriam and his associates observed that the feeling among migrated Indians toward the Indian Bureau was much more bitter than among those on the reservations. They attributed this bitterness to the following factors: many of the migrants had left the reservations because of difficulties with federal officials and objection to federal policies; as a group they were probably more "resourceful, energetic, and better educated" than other Indians; they were not so fearful of what might result from outspoken criticism of the BIA; and, finally, they had had "more opportunity to contrast what the government does for the Indians with what the ordinary city does for its citizens" (IGR 1928:671).

As a former official of the Indian Bureau, I can contrast the last conclusion of the Meriam survey with the one which I derived from many conversations with urban Indians during the 1960's. These Indians were much more displeased with the BIA because of its failure to provide them the same range of services provided their reservation kinsmen than because of the fact that the "ordinary city" does more for its citizens than does "the government for the Indians," as is suggested by the authors of the Meriam report. It may well be that the federal government in the last forty years has come closer to meeting the needs of Indian citizens than local governments have to meeting the needs of their constituencies.

Urban Indians today are no less bitter toward the Bureau of Indian Affairs and the Indian Health Service than were their counterparts forty years ago. Much of the leadership for the more militant Indian movements today has come from Indians who reside away from the reservations. That some of their bitterness relates to the question of eligibility for special federal services is documented in the words of the executive director of a new national organization composed of urban Indians. Formed in 1968 and initially funded with a $90,000 grant from the Ford Foundation, the group is known as American Indians United. In 1969, its executive director was quoted as saying that the purpose of the organization is "to strengthen the urban Indian's identity" and "to obtain for him both from private and Federal sources, the same services that are now provided for the reservation Indians" (BIA 1969a:3).

URBAN INDIANS TODAY

The 1960 census reported 165,922 "urban" Indians in the United States, which was about 30 percent of the total Indian population. Since the procedures by which census-takers identified Indians were different in 1950 and 1960, it is difficult to estimate precisely how much, in percentage terms, the urban Indian population increased during the decade. However, the BIA in a 1966 publication estimated the increase at 197 percent, as compared with a 70 percent increase in the "rural, non-farm" Indian population and a decrease of 28 percent in the number of Indians residing on farms (BIA 1966:2). Since much of the reservation Indian population falls into the "rural, non-farm" category, Indians seem to be moving into the cities at a rate considerably in excess of that at which the reservation population is increasing.

The BIA offers the following additional comments on the urbanizing trend:

> In terms of regional change, the urban Indian population in the West showed an increase of 228 per cent, with a 40 per cent decline among the rural farm group and an increase of 71 per cent in the rural, non-farm population. The shift in population occurred within States and from State to State. California was the main center of immigration as evidenced by the fact that the enumerated Indian population there doubled in ten years.
>
> Out-migration is having the effect of stabilizing the reservation populations in some areas. States in the Northwest and North Central sections of our country are experiencing a leveling-off of their Indian growth. The Southwest States of Arizona and New Mexico are the source of most of the increase in reservation population (BIA 1966:2–3).

There can be little doubt that urbanization of Indians has continued during the 1960's and — at least in terms of actual numbers — has accelerated. The BIA employment assistance program has been the factor of greatest importance in stimulating increases in the urban Indian population. During the 1950's, the Indian Bureau assisted nearly 30,000 Indians to relocate to urban areas, and provided vocational training leading to off-reservation employment for about 1,600 family heads, who together with their dependents numbered around 3,500 persons. Between 1960 and 1968, these figures — especially the numbers of individuals enrolled in vocational training programs — were substantially increased. Nearly 38,000 persons were helped to settle in cities, and vocational training was provided about 20,000 family heads, who with their dependents totaled slightly over 32,500 individuals (BIA 1968). In its 1970 budget requests, the BIA outlined a five-year program which would enable 58,000 additional Indians to take advantage of employment opportunities in urban areas by the end of 1974 (USDI 1969:16).

To which cities are the Indians moving in greatest numbers? The communities in which the Indian Bureau maintains employment assistance centers are registering some of the heaviest gains in Indian population. Southern California and the San Francisco Bay Area are two of the metropolitan centers most affected. But Indians also continue to migrate to the large cities near the reservations, such communities as Phoenix, Oklahoma City, Minneapolis and St. Paul, Portland, Rapid City, and Albuquerque.

Late in 1969, the BIA published estimates of urban Indian population and distribution (BIA 1969b). The very fact that the BIA, which has traditionally considered its clientele to be only Indians residing on or near reservations, should undertake to learn more about the Indians living elsewhere is indicative of a new federal interest in the broader dimensions of the "Indian problem." According to the bureau's estimates, seven American urban areas now have 10,000 or more Indian residents. Heading the list is Los Angeles County, within whose environs nearly 50,000 Indians may be residing.

The impact of the BIA employment assistance program is demonstrated by the fact that three of these seven areas — including the two with greatest estimated Indian population — are communities in which the Indian Bureau has long maintained field employment assistance offices. The oldest is the one in Los Angeles, which opened its doors to Navajos in the late 1940's; the office in Chicago was established in 1952. Shortly thereafter, the bureau began setting up offices in central and northern California, starting with an office in Oakland in 1955, and adding others the following year in San Francisco and San Jose. By the end of 1968, the BIA had assisted more than 23,000 Indians to move to the Los Angeles area either for direct employment or for vocational training. Nearly 12,000 had been helped to settle in Chicago, and more than 15,000 had gone to the San Francisco Bay Area with assistance from personnel in the Oakland and San Francisco field offices (BIA 1968).

Table 1.1 shows the estimated population of Indians within the seven urban areas where their concentration was felt to be greatest in 1969.

TABLE 1.1

Urban Areas with 10,000 or More Indians —
BIA Estimates — September, 1969

Urban Area	Estimated Indian Population
Los Angeles County	47,000
San Francisco Bay Area	18,000
Tulsa	15,000
Minneapolis–St. Paul	13,000
Oklahoma City	12,000
Chicago	12,000
Phoenix	10,000

The BIA report revealed other substantial concentrations of Indians in cities near reservations. Among the urban areas listed were Seattle, Gallup, Albuquerque, Rapid City, Sioux City, Milwaukee, Tacoma, Spokane, Portland, Crescent City–Eureka (California), Sacramento, Fresno, San Diego, Duluth, Great Falls, and Buffalo. It also took note of several emerging urban areas on Indian reservations, the most notable of which appears to be the community of Shiprock, New Mexico, on the Navajo reservation, where a large industry has recently begun operations.

What is the significance of the movement of Indians into the cities? Enough has transpired to provide some basis for prediction. From the point of view of individual tribes, the strongest impacts may come at the reservation level, for example, increasing demands from urban Indians that they be better represented on tribal councils. It is already evident that the nonresident members of many tribes have no faith in the desire or ability of present tribal leaders to protect their interest in the tribal estate. Young, aggressive, citified Indians often regard such persons as "Uncle Tomahawks" who are unnecessarily submissive to BIA and other federal officials. Council members who advocate investing income from successful claims suits in long-range reservation development programs are often outvoted by factions led by absentee members who prefer per capita payments. On such reservations as the Spokane, Colville, Flathead, and Blackfeet, the 1960's saw many bitter quarrels between factions composed of resident and nonresident members. In the Colville case, the off-reservation faction even went so far as to advocate liquidation of the entire tribal estate and distribution of the income resulting therefrom.

Another consequence of the urban movement manifest at the reservation level is the so-called "brain drain" of younger, better educated members upon whom the tribes must depend for future leadership. The outmigration of the past twenty years has included primarily individuals under thirty-five years of age. The industrial development program of the Indian Bureau — faced with numerous obstacles, including underfinancing and the isolation of many reservations in terms of transportation and communication — has enjoyed quite limited success, and employment opportunities remain inadequate to attract younger members back to their home communities.

The reservations will also be affected by the fact that, while preserving their interest in receiving benefits from the tribal estate, urban Indians over time will find their tribal ties attenuating, although they may retain a sense of Indian identity and participate in such pan-Indian movements as American Indians United. The whole topic of pan-Indianism is of great importance in discussing the migration of Indians to the cities. In concluding his report based on research among the Indians of Los Angeles, Price noted that:

> An awakened pan-Indianism . . . often becomes an additional dimension to, and sometimes a substitute for . . . tribal affiliations. Although only one-fifth of our respondents are socially active in pan-Indian associations, the great majority of Indians in the city clearly are ideologically and emotionally affiliated with pan-Indianism. Pan-Indianism thus seems to emerge as a stabilizing element — and perhaps a permanent part — of the adaptation of the Indian migrant to the metropolitan areas, and a significant facet of the ethnic diversity of the American city (Price 1968:175).

The impact of increased Indian urbanization could well be felt by federal agencies, too, including those with special Indian programs. Whether or not American Indians United will succeed in its campaign to extend to urban Indians all the community services which the federal government now provides those who reside on the reservations, there are some indications that the Indian Bureau and the Indian Health Service are modifying their traditional positions to some degree. Examples include the establishment with Congressional blessing of an Indian Health Clinic in Rapid City, South Dakota, and a decision by the BIA in 1969 to experiment with the extension of its housing improvement program (HIP) to some of the urban Indian families.[9] Previously, the HIP program has benefitted only reservation families who could not obtain improved housing by any other means. For several years, the Indian Health Service has provided medical and hospital care for indigent Indians recently moved to the cities until they satisfy the residence requirements for assistance from local health agencies. Since the early 1960's, the Indian Bureau has also followed a policy (which it has never publicized) of providing certain services to Indians in the cities when the failure to receive such services would force them to return to

[9] Although the BIA in its "Program Memorandum" to the Bureau of the Budget for Fiscal Year 1970 (see USDI 1969) proposed the extension of its Home Improvement Program to urban areas, this proposal appears to have been subsequently abandoned. On December 15, 1969, the Acting Commissioner for Community Service of the Indian Bureau wrote me that "we have no plans for an urban home-repair program."

the reservations (where they would again become eligible). However, relatively few individuals – and primarily only those in cities near the reservations – have benefitted from this policy. (The bureau does not maintain separate records for Indians in this category.)

Should the Indian Bureau and the Indian Health Service undertake on a broad scale to provide services to urban Indians, problems would unquestionably arise regarding the overlapping jurisdiction of federal and local public agencies. Historically, local agencies, especially with respect to social welfare and medical care benefits, have often resisted assuming responsibility for local Indians, while the Indian Bureau has fought – sometimes through lawsuits – to establish clearly the principle that Indians away from the reservations are entitled to the same public services from the same agencies available to other Americans in similar circumstances. A reversal of federal policy now would introduce a large measure of confusion into this situation and doubtless prompt some communities to withhold assistance from Indians they now serve.

On the other hand, as long as reservation kinsmen of the urban Indians receive desired special services denied the latter, as long as significant differences remain between the services (such as housing, medical care, and employment assistance) provided reservation Indians by the federal government and those provided the urban citizens, and as long as some local government agencies continue to regard Indians as a peculiar federal responsibility and attempt to deny them services, the issue of whether the "Great White Father" shall follow the Indian to the city will continue to evoke lively controversy.

BIBLIOGRAPHY

Beatty, Willard W.
    1958   "Education of the Indians." In *Encyclopedia Americana*, 1958
                ed., vol. 15. New York: Americana Corporation.
BIA (Bureau of Indian Affairs)
    1966   "Indians and the Federal Government." Xerox copy.
    1968   "Annual Statistical Summary, Branch of Employment Assis-
                tance."

1969a   *Indian Record* (BIA monthly newsletter). October, 1969.
1969b   "Urban Indian Distribution and Population." A paper prepared
           by the Community Development Office. Washington, Septem-
           ber, 1969.

Collier, John
1954   "The Genesis and Philosophy of the Indian Reorganization
           Act." In *Indian Affairs and the Indian Reorganization Act —
           the Twenty-Year Record,* William H. Kelly (ed.). Tucson: Uni-
           versity of Arizona.

Coombs, Madison
1962   *Doorway toward the Light.* Washington, D.C.: United States
           Department of the Interior, BIA.

Fritz, Henry E.
1963   *The Movement for Indian Assimilation, 1860–1890.* Philadel-
           phia: University of Pennsylvania Press.

Hackenberg, Robert A.
1955   *Economic and Political Change among the Gila River Pimas.*
           A Report to the John Hay Whitney Foundation.

Hagan, William T.
1961   *American Indians.* Chicago: University of Chicago Press.

Harmon, George Dewey
1941   *Sixty Years of Indian Affairs.* Chapel Hill: University of North
           Carolina Press.

IGR (Institute for Government Research)
1928   *The Problem of Indian Administration.* Baltimore: The Johns
           Hopkins Press.

Kinney, Jay P.
1937   *A Continent Lost — a Civilization Won.* Baltimore: The Johns
           Hopkins Press.

Leupp, Francis E.
1910   *The Indian and His Problem.* New York: Charles Scribner's
           Sons.

Lurie, Nancy O.
1957   "The Indian Claims Commission Act." In *American Indians
           and American Life,* pp. 56–70. *The Annals of the American
           Academy of Political and Social Sciences,* vol. 311, George
           Simpson and Milton Yinger (eds.).

McNickle, D'Arcy
1961–62   "Private Intervention." *Human Organization* 20 (Winter 1961–
           62).

Manypenny, George W.
1880   *Our Indian Wards.* Cincinnati: Robert Clarke and Co.

Price, John
1968   "The Migration and Adaptation of American Indians to Los
           Angeles." *Human Organization* 27 (Summer 1968).

Province, John
1953   "The Withdrawal of Federal Supervision of the American In-
           dian." In *Report with Respect to the House Resolution Autho-
           rizing the Committee on Interior and Insular Affairs to Conduct
           an Investigation of the Bureau of Indian Affairs.* House Report
           2503. Washington, D.C.: U.S. Government Printing Office, pp.
           179–188.

Prucha, Francis Paul
1962   *American Indian Policy in the Formative Years.* Cambridge, Mass.: Harvard University Press.
Senate (United States Senate)
1951   *Interior Department Appropriations for 1951.* Report on the Hearings of the Senate Appropriations Committee, pt. I.
1953a   *Report with Respect to the House Resolution Authorizing the Committee on Interior and Insular Affairs to Conduct an Investigation of the Bureau of Indian Affairs.* House Report 2503. Washington, D.C.: U.S. Government Printing Office. (See Chart 8, The Development of Federal Indian Relations, facing p. 1584.)
1953b   *Interior Department Appropriations for 1953.* Report on the Hearings of the Senate Appropriations Committee, pt. I.
Spicer, Edward H.
1969   *A Short History of the Indians of the United States.* New York: Van Nostrand Reinhold Co.
USDI (United States Department of the Interior)
1951   *Annual Report of the Secretary of the Interior.* Washington, D.C.: U.S. Government Printing Office.
1958   *Federal Indian Law.* Washington, D.C.: U.S. Government Printing Office.
1961   *Report to the Secretary of the Interior by the Task Force on Indian Affairs.* Washington, D.C.: U.S. Government Printing Office.
1969   "Program Memorandum: Indians. Fiscal Year 1970." Washington, D.C.: U.S. Government Printing Office.
Vernon, Raymond
1963   *The Dilemma of Mexico's Development.* Cambridge, Mass.: Harvard University Press.

indians and the
metropolis

JOSEPH G. JORGENSEN

INTRODUCTION [1]

How modern American Indians are integrated into the American political economy has received some anthropological analysis during the past thirty years. Anthropologists who have concerned themselves with *contemporary* Indian life have usually disregarded the political economic causes of Indian conditions and have employed an "acculturation" schema to explain why living Indian societies differ from their precontact forbears and from the dominant, contemporary, white or "Anglo" society as well.

[1] *Metropolis,* as used in the chapter title is not synonymous with *urban area, location,* or *city.* The hypothesis advanced in the third part of this chapter reveals its special meaning in this context.

Stages, contexts, or levels of acculturation achieved by Indians are usually loosely defined and measured in relation to the hypothesized norms for white society. Though actual measurements of white society are seldom made and variation in white society is almost never accounted for, in general, the more similar an Indian society is said to be to white society, the more "acculturated" the Indian society is. In this view the dominated society accommodates itself to the dominant society in stages.

The underlying assumption in these studies is that the direction change takes is from a primitive, underdeveloped society — i.e., a society with low economic output and low standard of living — to a civilized, developed society that becomes fully integrated into the dominant white society. Integration is achieved when "acculturation" is complete. The actual steps involved vary from context to context. There is no single path.

The acculturation framework provides a rather euphoric way to think and talk about what has happened to American Indians since contact. It assumes that before white contact Indians were "underdeveloped" and avoids analysis of why Indians are as they are today. Because this framework assumes that Indians will eventually become fully integrated into the United States polity, economy, and society just like whites, it is also meaningless. No matter what the condition of Indian society is when analyzed by the anthropologist, it is always somewhere along the acculturation path, headed toward full acculturation. Because acculturation explains everything, it explains nothing.

Recently the clichés and erroneous concepts of acculturation research have been challenged by Vine Deloria, Jr. (1969), an Indian author. Although Deloria's criticisms are sound, he does not adequately explain why Indians are as they are. It is clear, however, that the political, economic, and social conditions of American Indians are not improving, and this is the nub of the issue.

Underdevelopment, in my view, has been caused by the *development* of the white-controlled national economy, and the political, economic, and social conditions of Indians are not improving because *the American Indian is, and has been for over one hundred years, fully integrated into the national political economy.* Underdevelopment, paradoxically then, has been caused by the development of the capitalist political economy of the United States. This postulate is in direct opposition to the postulate that seems to underlie acculturation, and also suggests a basic contradiction in the American political economy. Before exploring this postulate, let us survey Indian conditions in the past several decades since they have *become* underdeveloped, and in a very cursory way, let us develop some idea of what the basic features of modern Indian life have been for these "acculturating" or "developing" people.

THE PROBLEM: THE PERSISTENCE
OF INDIAN POVERTY

The History of Indian Deprivation. In 1926 Lewis Meriam was commissioned by Secretary of Interior Hubert Work to survey Indian administration and Indian life. His report demonstrated that federal legislation and the niggardly funds allocated for Indian programs had injured rather than helped American Indians (Meriam 1928). It also showed that the Bureau of Indian Affairs (BIA), the government agency responsible for implementing federal policies and managing Indian affairs, had a long tradition of dry rot — i.e., unimaginative and undereducated mismanagers caught up in red-tape procedures — that had made it incapable of helping Indians particularly with their economic, health, education, housing, and legal problems.

Since the passage of the General Allotment Act (Dawes Act) of 1887, which was intended to civilize Indians and "free" them from communal land ownership, Indian reservation land had been drastically reduced by allotting acreage to each Indian family head and, in some instances, to other living Indians. The unallotted land became part of the public domain. By 1926, much Indian land was tied up in complicated heirship status, much had been sold or leased by Indians to whites, and Indian economic conditions, in general, were deplorable. Employment was almost nonexistent; family farming and ranching were not meeting subsistence needs. Thus, between 1887 and 1926 the underdeveloped Indians became more underdeveloped.

Meriam and his associates further showed that Indian health was particularly poor with a high incidence of disease — especially diseases that are correlated with poverty, like tuberculosis and trachoma — and a high infant mortality rate. Indian housing was so substandard — dirt floors, no doors, wretched sanitation, no running water — and Indian diet so poor that the two coalesced greatly to exacerbate Indian health problems.

Federal education policy since the 1880's took preadolescent children away from their homes and the so-called restrictive, backward influences of tribal life, and educated them in all-Indian boarding schools. The intention of the policy was to force rapid acceptance of white ways, and the optimistic notion behind it was that if a man is given an education, he will, ipso facto, make his own way successfully as a wage earner or petty capitalist-farmer or shopkeeper in white society. The Meriam report was critical of this education policy as well as the General Allotment Act of 1887, which was intended to bring the education-economic program to fruition and in a short time, to achieve the desired effects.

The Meriam report criticized the current state of Indian affairs, especially land and education policies, and made suggestions to solve the problems: Indian health and housing were to be improved; preadolescents were to be educated on home reservations; loss of Indian land through sale or lease was to be stopped; and greater federal appropriations were to be made to increase salaries to entice better qualified people to join the BIA. Characteristically, the report did not cover such questions as the need for massive funds to develop industries — agricultural or otherwise — under the ownership and control of Indians. Rather, it directed itself to the symptoms of the Indians' problems and to cleaning up the bumbling, underfunded BIA, hoping that good advice administered through this special appendage of the federal welfare enterprise would improve the individual Indian's lot until he became self-sufficient.

During the Hoover administration, federal appropriations doubled from 1929 to 1932, but slackened by nearly 20 percent in 1933 during the depths of the Depression. Most of the money went for education expenses, salaries of better trained personnel, and health and medical expenses, including the salaries of doctors, nurses, nutrition experts, and others involved in Indian health programs. Thus, funds were provided for the education dream, for a larger and better trained welfare bureaucracy to administer Indian affairs, and for maintaining and hopefully improving Indian health. This welfare program served to expand the BIA, improve health slightly, and keep the Indian education system going.

In 1934 during Roosevelt's first administration, the Wheeler-Howard Act, known best as the Indian Reorganization Act (IRA), was passed. The IRA provided for sweeping changes in Indian policies. Following the recommendations of the Meriam report it allowed for consolidation of Indian land and purchase of more land; development of tribal governments with constitutions and charters; financial loans to the tribal governments for the development of tribal resources; and development of day schools for Indian children on home reservations. John Collier was appointed Commissioner of Indian Affairs to implement these policies which were considered "radical" at the time (see Haas 1957).

The IRA did *not* decrease the powers of the BIA over Indian lives, even though tribal governments with constitutions were created. In fact, the IRA actually *increased* the powers of the Secretary of Interior over Indians. Many Congressmen and many lobbyists became irritated at Collier's implementation of the IRA, but their irritations and fears were premature. Because the program allowed land to be purchased for Indians, thus removing the land from state tax rolls, and because it was thought that it would be more difficult for private corporations to exploit resources on those lands if they fell into Indian ownership, state governments as well as agribusiness and mineral lobbies were opposed to the IRA and to Collier. Actually, mineral, farm, and rangeland exploitation became cheaper on Indian-owned land than on company-owned or leased federal land because a special tax exemption was implemented for lessees of Indian lands.

Shortly after World War II, Commissioner Collier was replaced and the Indian Claims Commission Act was passed allowing Indian tribes to sue the United States for redress of grievances, particularly for the loss of lands and broken treaties. Many thought that legal redress for these things and for inhumanities perpetrated against the American Indians was only just.

The Indian Claims legislation also paved the way for a new federal policy whose goal was the dissolution of the BIA and the termination of all treaty obligations of the United States to

American Indians. It was argued that once the old scores over land thefts and other inhumanities had been settled and Indians were taught how to spend money wisely, they could make their own way as responsible citizens (see Lurie 1957).

Aiming toward this goal of termination, following the passage of the Indian Claims Commission Act, the House Committee on Interior and Insular Affairs (HCIIA 1953, 1954) conducted an investigation of the BIA and some research on all United States Indian groups. Although the results made it clear that Indians were in dire straits and that the overwhelming majority opposed termination of federal government control and involvement, between 1950 and 1960 some groups were terminated with, it is alleged, their consent, and others without their consent. Most American Indian groups were not terminated, but they felt the pressure of such proceedings and were frightened by them (HCIIA 1954).

In response to the termination policy, the Commission on the Rights, Liberties and Responsibilities of the American Indian was financed in 1957 by The Fund for the Republic to begin a private investigation of federal Indian policies and the general living conditions of Indians. The investigation was a sequel to the Meriam investigation three decades earlier. An extensive summary of all investigations made by this commission was not published until 1966 (Brophy and Aberle).

If the Meriam report's analysis of the "Indian problem" had been correct and if the solution to that problem attempted through the implementation of the IRA had worked, in 1957 there would have been no need for another investigation. The solution suggested by Meriam, in my view, missed the crux of the problem, but the IRA did work satisfactorily, given the analysis and solution suggested by Meriam and accepted by Collier. Neither man, nor their advisors, seemed to realize that the "Indian problem" was due to the growth of the political economy of the metropolis.

The results of the commission's investigation showed the economic position of the Indian about 1960 to be less favorable than that of any other American minority group. Indian income was scandalously low; employment was meager, unstable, and temporary; and the Indian land base was smaller than in the previous decade. Indian health was poor when contrasted with whites, as was Indian housing, education, and local government (see Brophy and Aberle 1966). Relatively nothing had changed for the American Indian since 1934, except that some land had been reacquired, schools had been developed near reservations — about *half* of all funds went to education — the BIA staff had grown, and Indian governments exercised a modicum of control over reservation societies which were poverty-ridden and often pervaded with factionalism.

Deprivation among Contemporary Indians in California. The conditions of American Indians in California during 1960–65 (SACIA 1966, CFEPC 1966) illustrate the lot of Indians throughout the country. California is particularly good to assess because of its relatively large Indian population (45,000 in the mid-1960's), of which about 18–20 percent have migrated to California since 1955, primarily in quest of on-the-job training and employment. Moreover, only 19 percent of all California Indians live on, or adjacent to, reservations, and more than 50 percent live in urban areas. The national rural–urban migration, Indian and non-Indian, since 1955 has been marked, and California's urban areas have received huge numbers of migrants from other states and from its own rural areas. Nevertheless, the proportion of California Indians living in rural areas is still greater than that of any other ethnic group there — even though the many out-of-state Indian migrants to the Los Angeles and San Francisco–Oakland areas are included in the California Indian total.

In all measures of economy, education, health, and housing, the Indians of California rank below the white population and significantly below all other ethnic groups. Because family household size is related to household economics, it is not surprising to learn that Indians exceed all other ethnic groups in size of family households, with more than 25 percent having seven persons or more. The Indian family household *average* is 5.4 persons. This contrasts with a 2.9 average household size for non-Indians. In California, the Indian population is the most youthful ethnic group, whereas senior citizens are predominantly Anglo. Non-Indians live longer because of better nutrition, better medical care, better housing and the preconditions of better educations, occupations, and incomes. Moreover, the comparatively affluent whites can afford to move there to retire.

A survey of these "preconditions" to longevity reveals that in California less than 2 percent of the Indian population, including immigrants, have college degrees, and 43 percent have not attended school beyond the eighth grade. On the other hand, over 10 percent of the total adult population have completed college, and only 28 percent have not gone beyond the eighth grade. These percentages do not reveal the quality of education received, of course, and there is good reason to suspect that the Indian generally gets a poorer education. It can also be inferred that if approximately half of all federal funds for Indians are being used for education, either too few funds are being allocated, or other factors are causing Indians to drop out of school, the latter alternative being the case in my opinion.

In 1962 the median annual income of California Indian families ($2,800) was less than all other ethnic groups and only about one-third that of whites ($7,600). In the same year, the unemployment rate for Indians, using a narrow definition of employability,[2] was over 25 percent, or four times the state unemployment rate of less than 6 percent which was not based on nearly as narrow a definition of employability. Using this broader definition of employability, the same definition used for the rest of the United States' population, the figures are more startling. In 1960 only 68 percent of California Indian men were employed or even seeking employment, with only 31 percent of Indian women in this category. All forms of Indian employment during the early 1960's in California probably included no more than 60 percent of the employable population.

What kinds of jobs are Indians employed in? Table 2.1 compares the percentages of California Indians employed, by occupation, with those of the total state population employed in 1960; this reveals significant differences in the distribution of occupations. Fifty-five percent of employed Indians are categorized as laborers, domestic servants, or "occupation not reported," whereas

---

[2] *Employability* here means all Indians of working age who are not physically or mentally disabled, not students, not retired, and not encumbered by family responsibilities.

TABLE 2.1

Comparison of Employed Indians and Total Employed Population, California, 1960, by Occupation [a]

	Percentage of Total Population Employed	Percentage of Indian Population Employed	Difference in Percentages
Professional, Technical, Proprietors, Managers, Officials	24	8	−16
Clerical, Sales	30	10	−20
Craftsmen, Operatives	24	27	+3
Domestics, Service	11	18	+7
Laborers, Farm Laborers	5.5	17	+11.5
Occupation not reported	5.5	20	+14.5

[a] Data adapted from CFEPC (1966).

only 22 percent of the population are in these classifications. When skills and education are requisites — for such occupations as craftsmen, operatives, and clerical workers — only 37 percent of the Indians are so employed, compared with 54 percent of the population. When education and access to capital are requisites — for such occupations as professionals, proprietors, farm owners, and managers — only 8 percent of Indians hold positions, while 24 percent of the work force are so classified.

California Indians are not only out of work, but the work they have is generally unskilled and temporary. They stand on the lowest rungs of the occupation ladder, filling jobs that require few skills and no capital. These figures are more interesting, however, in view of the fact that 20 percent of the California Indian population has migrated there since 1955 in search of work. This is evidence of their self-selection of skills or motivation to acquire skills; therefore, these Indians probably possess more skills and more "desire" to improve their circumstances through working than Indian populations in other western states.

Some indicators of economic well-being show Indians to be in the lower percentiles. Predictably, California Indian housing is below the standards of comfort, decency, and safety set by the

U.S. Department of Health, Education and Welfare. A 1964 survey (SACIA 1966) classifies 90 percent of the houses as needing improvement, 39 percent of which could be improved and 51 percent needing complete replacement because of unsafe and unsanitary conditions. Sewage disposal facilities are unsatisfactory in about 65 percent of the homes; contaminated water is used in approximately 45 percent.

The health problems experienced by California Indians are great in comparison with the total California population; these problems are clearly correlated with lack of employment, poor housing, poor sanitation, poor nourishment, inadequate medical care, and the apathy generated by these conditions. The leading causes of death among California Indians contrast markedly with those for non-Indians. Although 37 percent of non-Indians die from diseases of the heart, only 20 percent of Indian deaths are attributed to these problems. About 20 percent of all Indian deaths are attributable to accidents, while only 6 percent of non-Indians die from accidents. Influenza, pneumonia, and tuberculosis account for about 10 percent of Indian deaths (except newborn) and for only 4 percent of non-Indian deaths. Cirrhosis of the liver accounts for about 7 percent of all Indian deaths, but only 2 percent of non-Indian deaths. The majority (100 percent in one California county) of diseases attacking Indians are either respiratory or gastrointestinal — health problems closely related to inadequate shelter, sanitation, and diet — whereas only about 20 percent of non-Indians contract such diseases.

These statistics lay bare the discrepancy between the non-Indian and Indian norms. In the mid-1960's as in the mid-1920's, despite all programs, the American Indians were relatively as underdeveloped as in the past. Even in a statement of averages, as opposed contrasting the Indian minimum to the non-Indian maximum in education, skills, employment, income, and comforts, Indian conditions are extremely low on all measures and suggest extreme deprivation. The *acculturation* has been to rural poverty and, more recently, urban poverty as well. Surprisingly, the Indians of California on all these measures of the quality of life are *much* better off than their counterparts in other states and *much* closer to the standards of living considered adequate for the average United States citizen than their congeners (SACIA 1966).

The Endemic Poverty of Contemporary Indians. To consider the endemic poverty of United States' Indians generally, we shall contrast California Indians with other groups and assess how Indian family household organizations have adjusted to economic deprivation.

The relative "prosperity" of California Indians is partly due to the self-selected migrants to major urban areas, many of whom have some employment, and to generally high welfare standards observed in that state. For the nation as a whole, the average family income of Indians is $1500 per year, $1300 *less* than for California Indian families and about $2000 *under* the currently specified "poverty line." The unemployment rate is between 40 and 50 percent on almost all reservations; that rate is calculated on the BIA's narrow definition of employability. That pegs the employment rate at 50–60 percent; over half represents temporary or part-time employment, i.e., underemployment.

According to the President's Task Force on American Indians (Brophy and Aberle 1966), the present poverty on Indian reservations and among urban ghetto Indians is deplorable. Housing is grossly dilapidated; the incidence of disease, especially upper respiratory and gastrointestinal forms, is seven or eight times the national average; Indian life expectancy is only two-thirds the national expectancy; and one-third of all adult Indians are illiterate. As youthful populations grow on the reservations, many spill off into the ghettos of urban areas replacing rural poverty with urban poverty. Though adequate statistics on urban Indians are not available, particularly from the BIA — the agency responsible for sending many of them to the cities — it is estimated that 200,000 of the 600,000 American Indians currently live in urban areas.

In contrast to California Indians, 38 percent of whom use contaminated water, the national average of such usage by Indians is 74 percent. Forty-eight percent of California Indian families haul all domestic water, whereas 81 percent is the national average. Seventy-three percent of California Indians have unsatisfactory facilities for disposal of excreta; 83 percent is the national average. All Indian households, as well as the California Indian household, average more than five (5.4) occupants. The average size of Indian houses nationally is less than two rooms. The non-Indian household, however, averages only 2.9 occupants and occupies more than four rooms (SACIA 1966; Wagner and Rabeau 1964; SAUS 1966).

The composition of Indian households differs significantly from the nuclear-family, conjugal-pair, and single-person types that predominate in white America. In California 30 percent of all Indian households are composite, including such combinations of kin and non-kin as grandchildren, nieces and nephews, brothers or sisters of the husband or wife, a married child with spouse or children or both, and even more distantly related kin and affines (in-laws). Sixty-one percent of all California household heads are men and 39 percent are women — the latter being widowed, separated, or divorced. The composition of California Indian households is not an anomaly, but is a regular feature of Indian poverty and poverty in the Western Hemisphere generally.[3]

Though there are no national statistics on the subject, the research of Munsell (1967) among the Salt River Pima-Papago of Arizona, Robbins (1968) among the Blackfeet of Montana, and Jorgensen (n.d.) among Shoshones and Utes on five reservations in Idaho, Wyoming, Colorado, and Utah confirms the California Indian household composition distribution. A difference is that these recent studies demonstrate that there are relatively *more* composite Indian households outside of California than in California, and that those outside of California are also larger. This is to be expected, given the greater average family income for California Indians.

The studies cited above clearly demonstrate that household size varies inversely with the amount and stability of income. The less stable and lower the amount of income among American Indian family households, the larger the households. The explanation for this phenomenon is that people with meager means join together to pool resources. It is better to crowd together under a single roof, or adjacent roofs, and share resources than it is to live apart in less crowded households where resources are less predictable. This grouping together characterizes

[3] See, for example, the following analyses of family household organization among people living in poverty who have little access to resources: Black Caribs of Guatemala and British Honduras (Gonzalez 1969); Mestizos of Latin America (Adams 1960); Blacks of the West Indies (Smith 1962; Otterbein 1965); Mestizos in Mexico and Mexican-Americans (Borah and Cook 1966); and Blacks in the United States (Moynihan 1965).

poverty-stricken households among other ethnic and racial minorities within, as well as outside of, the United States (cf. footnote 3).

Through sharing funds from several diverse sources — welfare (e.g., Aid for Dependent Children, Old-Age Assistance, Federal Aid to the Blind), per capita payments from Indian Claims Commission judgments, lease income from land, wages from part-time labor, cash from piece work, goods received as welfare commodities or procured in hunting and fishing — these composite family households have adjusted to their lack of resources. Where nuclear family households occur among American Indians, they usually have a *stable* source of income, males tend to be the household heads, and to a lesser extent, someone in the household is employed.

American Indian family household compositions tend to change in a rather predictable cyclic manner from composite to nuclear. If a son gains regular employment, he and his wife and children move out of his father's home and establish a separate household. In fifteen years or so, this man's nuclear family is likely to become a composite household as his own, or his wife's parents move in to share his resources, or as his own children marry and establish temporary residence in the household.

American Indian composite households and family household cycle are not retentions of aboriginal customs, but are products of their meager and unstable incomes, lack of skills, and lack of control over resources. They do not have money or resources to allow them to cope with life as do the gainfully employed and nonpaternalistically guided lower (working), middle, and upper classes of United States' society. Indian family households change from composite to nuclear to composite as their economic conditions change, making the Indian family similar to other families living in poverty in the Western world. Yet the peculiar niche occupied by the Indians in the American culture of poverty — that of superexploited and paternalistically guided wards of neo-colonialism, the vast majority of whom reside on reservations — separates them, say, from the Mestizo in Mexico, the Callampa dwellers in Chile, the rural poor and the Black urban ghetto dwellers in the United States, and the Black Caribs of Latin America and the West Indies.

Although the major problems of American Indians are rooted

in economy and polity as are the problems of the other groups mentioned, a difference is that Indians often have resources. But the *access* of American Indians to their resources is severely restricted, and the major exploitation of these resources is carried out by non-Indian local, national, and multi-national corporations.

The Political Economic Niche Occupied by American Indians. A brief survey of the niche of reservations in the national economy reveals that reservations generally have land bases that are arid or semi-arid, and because some segments of the land are tied up in heirship, they are not feasible for development of profitable agribusiness. Moreover, most reservations do not have sufficient land, even if all of it were consolidated, to provide decent livelihoods from agriculture for all inhabitants on those reservations (the rural economies surrounding most reservations are basically agricultural). Reservations are generally located long distances from major markets, big cities, and industrial plants, so there are no large job markets. Moreover, the greater distance to market, the less profitable, generally, the agribusiness on reservations. Reservations are also often located considerable distances from railroads and major highways, making transportation expensive and profitable development of heavy industry on reservations unlikely. Industrial development has been further inhibited because Indian populations are undereducated and underskilled (Brophy and Aberle 1966:62–116).

Rural economies adjacent to reservations in most of the western half of the United States have withered, as large farms in the midwest with access to capital and improvements in technology, including hybrid crops, fertilizers, and pesticides, have become more productive and have grown at the expense of small agricultural operations everywhere. Federal farm policies have worked with the large farm corporations to protect them through price supports and soil-bank payments, encouraging further expansion of large farm corporations to gobble up small farms (USPNACRP 1967). In general, the greater the productivity, the greater the government assistance. Since 1920 the farm population of the United States has decreased by two-thirds and its percentage of the total population has plummeted from 30 to 6. Although the average size of all farms has increased, the number of farms has decreased by more than half since 1920. Since 1940 alone the average size of farms in the United States has increased by well over 200 percent (SAUS 1966:613–624, 1967:608). As examples of federal benefits, in 1967, 43 percent of United States farmers with incomes of less than $2500 per year received 4.5 percent of the federal farm subsidies. On the other hand, 65 percent of federal subsidies went to the *top* 10 percent of earners in the farm production pyramid, most of them being large corporations or food processing trusts. (See USPNACRP 1967 for a complete analysis of the subsidy program, especially the programs designed to "encourage, promote, and strengthen the family farm.")

The livestock business has followed a similar course in the past decade as quasi-cartels are beginning to control all aspects of beef production from feeder lots, to packing houses, to supermarket distribution. Grass-fed (range-fed) mature beef is less and less marketable because of the time needed for fattening the animals for slaughter and the difficulty in controlling the size of range-fed beef. Weight can be controlled on feeder lots, yielding animals of standardized size, and greatly easing slaughtering and packing because the animals can also be fattened quicker. In addition, there is a dwindling demand for grass-fed beef by packing houses and distributors (both processes often carried out by the same corporation) because, they allege, the meat is not sufficiently marbled with fat, and the increased production costs, including transportation for range-fed beef, are pushing the producers of grass-fed beef off the market. This squeezes small operators out of business, especially those in the western United States who are long distances from the main markets.

Though the rural economies around Indian reservations are dwindling and farm consolidation is occurring at a rapid rate, there is some money to be made in agriculture on reservations. The BIA (1968) reports that 170 million dollars were grossed from agriculture on all reserves (50 million acres) in 1966. These figures are rather liberal as they include the *estimated* value of all fish and game taken by Indians on their reservations (perhaps 20 million dollars) and consumed by the procurers, but this modest amount of overestimating is not the critical point. Of the 170 million dollars, the Indians realized only 58.6 million, 16 million of which was derived from rents and permits to non-Indians. This means that 127.4 million dollars, or 75 percent of the gross from agriculture, went to *non-Indians* who paid Indians 16 million dollars, or roughly 12 percent of their gross, for exploitation of Indian lands.

The BIA statistics clearly reveal what can happen to Indian resources when Indians have neither access to capital nor the skills or adequate counsel to exploit their own resources. Of the estimated 170 million dollars from agriculture in 1966, the Indian share approximates 58.6 million of which 16 million (27 percent) is from leasing to non-Indians, 23 million (39 percent) is from farming and ranching (this too is an estimate and includes all goods produced *and* consumed by Indians), and 19.6 million (34 percent) is from hunting and fishing for their own consumption. There is no way to know how inaccurate the latter two estimates are.

The BIA statistics on further exploitation of Indian resources are also revealing. In 1967 about 803 million board feet of lumber were cut. Only 100 million board feet, or about 12 percent, were processed in tribal sawmills. Indians were selling their natural resources yet maintaining practically no control over production. Timber sale brought 15 million dollars to Indian tribes in 1967. There are no figures pertaining to the non-Indian gross, non-Indian profits, or the costs to Indian tribes to maintain their resources (see BIA 1968).

As for oil and all other minerals, including uranium, sand, gravel, phosphate, gilsonite, gypsum, coal, limestone, copper, lead, and zinc, the exploitation of these resources by national and multi-national corporations brought 31 million dollars to tribal coffers in 1967 through bids and lease royalties. Again, the tribes do not control production and few jobs are generated for Indian employees. Though there are no figures on corporate profits or gross income, the corporations are generating capital for themselves and offering Indian tribes carrots in the form of lease and royalty incomes, and the Indians are losing their resources.

Finally, since the early 1950's the BIA (1955) has encouraged the location of industries on or near reservations to provide employment for Indians. The emphasis has not been on development of Indian-owned and controlled industries. Tribes have been urged to use their modest amounts of capital from land-claims judgments and mineral royalties to build plants and lease them to private corporations at low rates. The corporations, the Indians have been told, will then move onto the reservations, even though they are a great distance from markets, because they can operate at low costs and use cheap Indian labor.

Nothing much came of this program until 1962 when a few industries moved onto reserves to take advantage of provisions made for them. Between 1962 and 1968, 10,000 jobs were created through the development of industries on or near reserves. Characteristically, 6,000 (60 percent) of these jobs have gone to *non-Indians* (USDI 1968:7). Private corporations are using Indian capital to expand, yet using Indian labor only when it is adequate to the task. Indians do not maintain ownership or control.

"Industrial development" has been mostly talk; development has accrued to industry and not to Indians or Indian-owned and controlled industry. In 1967 private non-Indian development of Indian lands on a lease basis, including all industrial, commercial, and recreational uses, brought 4 million dollars to Indian tribes. Recreation brought 1.9 million dollars of that total (BIA 1968). The irony of this is that whites are paying low-lease fees to exploit Indian lands for white leisure use.

Why are things as they are, even after so much has been done to improve the Indians' lot? From 1955 to 1968 the BIA has grown from 9,500 employees to 16,000 (BIA 1955, 1968). From 1949 to 1969, federal government appropriations for American Indian affairs have increased from 49 million dollars to 241 million (BIA 1949, 1968). In fact, in the 1968–69 fiscal year, about 430 million dollars were spent on federal programs intended to benefit Indians; yet the average annual income for all Indian families was about $1500.

Part of the failure of Indian policies is attributable to mismanagement by the BIA. For example, the BIA has encouraged the development of livestock operations at a time when quasi-cartels have been taking over the industry, and the bureau has advised tribes to allow non-Indian corporations to exploit Indian resources. But the causes of persistent Indian problems cannot be solely attributed to the BIA. Indeed, the growth of the BIA and the federal budget for Indian affairs are indicative of the more important causes of Indian poverty. Federal welfare institutions and funds have increased as exploitation has continued. The growth of the BIA is an effect of the way in which the national political economy has grown. Poverty is perpetually created and welfare measures are used to heal the most gaping wounds.

A HYPOTHESIS ABOUT INDIAN UNDERDEVELOPMENT: THE METROPOLIS-SATELLITE POLITICAL ECONOMY

The Indians of the United States, in my opinion, have been integrated into the United States political economy since they were conquered. As shown above, Indians are currently deprived and have been deprived for the past several decades. This is not a coincidence or a fortuity; Indian poverty does not represent an evolutionary "stage of acculturation" somewhere between the underdeveloped tabula rasa and the developed non-Indian polity, economy, and society. In my hypothesis, Indian underdevelopment is the product of the full integration of United States Indians into the United States political economic society — albeit as super-exploited victims of that society.

With this general proposition in mind, the term "metropolis-satellite" [4] is used here rather than "urban-rural" in a characterization of political economy because the latter implies a city, a locational unit filled with people. "Metropolis" implies *the concentration of economic and political power and political influence.* "Urban" and "metropolis" are not, of course, completely independent, as the directors of the metropolis, their corporations, their research houses, and their liquid capital are located in the great urban areas. But as the economic and political power and influence of the metropolis have grown, especially in the past decade, the great urban centers have withered. Although urban areas have generally grown in number of inhabitants, they have decreased in economic affluence, political influence, social services, and the quality of life. Ghettos have grown through

[4] André Gundar Frank (1967) fully develops the concept of the metropolis-satellite economy.

natural increase and through migration of the rural poor, especially from the south and southwest (Shannon and Shannon 1967:49–75; Shannon 1969:36–56). Moreover, unemployment has risen, and rebellion with subsequent repression is more and more a characteristic of the largest cities (USPNACCD 1968).

This withering of the locational cores of urban areas, too, can be accounted for through the nature of the metropolis-satellite political economic structure. As the satellites, *or the resources and labor of the rural areas or those areas that do not concentrate political and economic power*, are exploited and technological advances are made, fewer and fewer man-hours are required to produce more and more goods on greater amounts of land or from greater areas within mines. Because men who do not control the resources or whose resources are meager can no longer cope, selective migration of the poor and displaced, as well as the upwardly mobile, takes place from the withering rural areas to the urban areas. For many, rural poverty is traded for urban poverty, thus adding to the problems of the urban areas. As a partial effect, middle-income families move to the suburbs of these cities.

To develop the hypothesis, the conditions of the "backward" modern American Indians are not due to rural isolation nor a tenacious hold on aboriginal ways, but result from the way in which United States' urban centers of finance, political influence, and power have grown at the expense of rural areas. The rapid development of urban areas after the mid-nineteenth century brought the Indian social ruin, as measured in status and self-worth; poverty, as measured in access to strategic resources, the distribution of surpluses from one's own region, employment, housing, and general welfare; and political oppression and neocolonial subjugation, as measured by decimation of Indian populations through warfare, the dissolution of aboriginal polities, the loss of self-direction, the lack of access to the locus of political power, the general denial of citizenship (with a few exceptions) until 1924, and the increasing role of the BIA and the Secretary of Interior in approving the conduct of Indian affairs.

These results were brought about by expropriation of Indian land and resources by the railroads, mining corporations, farmers, and ranchers. Economic surpluses were taken from the rural areas, and used for the growth of the metropolis. For instance, from an estimated 16 million bison on the American plains in 1860, the bison population was reduced to about one thousand in 1885 through systematic killing by whites (Klose 1964:79–80) because there was a market for tongues and skins in the eastern United States, and more importantly because the plains could then be farmed and cattle raised without interference from the bison or the Indians who lived off them (Klose 1964:83–84). The railroads, which received vast amounts of right-of-way — i.e., Indian territory — free from the United States government, in turn sold this land to farmers and ranchers. The railroads profited from the sales and later began moving products from these farms and ranches to markets in the east.[5] Indians were the first rural inhabitants to suffer from this development and the first people to be forced into underdevelopment from their previous condition of self-support and self-governance. Mining industries expanded throughout the west from the 1850's to the turn of the century, and they too expropriated Indian land and resources.

With the growth of technology influenced and controlled by the metropolis, particularly as it affected agribusiness and the mineral industries, non-Indian ranchers, farmers, and miners in rural areas, too, became "underdeveloped." For instance, the beef production industry, once based on range-fed cattle, has been revolutionized by development of hybrid crops, feeder lots, mechanized packing techniques, and the growth of large supermarket quasi-cartels which are beginning to control all aspects of production. Since 1935 the man-hours (labor-time) to produce beef (measured in live weight) has been cut nearly in half, and it has been cut by one-fourth since 1959 alone (SAUS 1967:629). Only those producers who control the greatest amount of capital are able to survive. Technology has influenced the grain, vegetable, and cotton industries through mechanization and fertilizers. Again, only the largest producers are able to survive. The small producer is losing his land due to costs or taxes, or both. He

[5] The transcontinental railroad, completed in 1869 with the extensive use of Chinese labor, was such an expensive project that the railroads could not foreseeably pay off their loans from the federal government. The government, in turn, cleared the loans without payment and left ownership in the hands of the railroad "financiers."

cannot get loans because he is a bad risk, and the large producer, in turn, is consolidating the land made available through the former's liquidation. But this trend is not solely a product of technology and capital: political influence and power, too, are critical in maintaining this trend.

Underdevelopment of rural areas is a product of the development of urban centers of finance, and the latter wield considerable influence in enacting legislation to maintain their growth. The mineral industries have long lived under special tax-privilege umbrellas; they have profited from the special-use tax (allowance) applicable to the exploitation of Indian lands, as well as the tax-depletion allowances offered to oil, gas, and mineral producers generally. The influence of the mining lobbies prior to the General Allotment Act and of the multi-national oil and mineral corporations in maintaining the privileged tax-depletion and protective import laws that have sheltered them for decades is solid evidence of the relationship between polity and the growth of the metropolis.

Agribusiness, too, has had long-term special federal privileges in the form of price supports, soil bank, and government-sponsored research which benefits huge producers but displaces the small operator. A recent investigation (USPNACRP 1967:142) reports that farm policy is not only dominated by acreage and price supports, but about 70 percent of the federal cost of assistance to farmers is correlated with attempts to bring supplies in alignment with demands for farm commodities. Farmers receive benefits from this assistance in proportion to their production or contribution to total farm output. This is not a policy to alleviate rural poverty; it is a commercial farm policy.

This internal contradiction of capitalism in the development of the metropolis, or the urban financial center, at the expense of the satellites, or the rural areas, was as apparent in the 1960's as it was in the 1860's. But it is more poignant now, perhaps, because the progeny of non-Indian pioneers — farmers, cattlemen, miners, and shopkeepers — are feeling the sting of underdevelopment which the Indians felt because of their pioneering forefathers.

As the metropolis grows and the resources of the satellites nourish that growth, many people living in rural areas choose to better their conditions by moving to urban areas. Some are successful, especially if they are white, yet many trade rural poverty for urban poverty. For Indians who stand in a special neocolonial relationship to the rest of society, the latter is usually the case (Price 1968; Hodge 1969; and Graves in this volume). This is not to say that all Indians are doomed to poverty. Just as some native Africans once living in colonial Kenya can, for example, be educated at Oxford and through help open businesses in London or Nairobi or even enter the British colonial service, so can some United States Indians move from reservations, gain university educations, and become popular authors or high ranking officials in the Indian Service. But the odds and the context in which both colonial Africans and neocolonial Indians live weigh heavily against such happenings. In both colonialism and neocolonialism, however, some subjects have made their way out of their native predicaments, just as some non-Indian ghetto dwellers and rural whites have.

To distinguish between Indians and non-Indians in the rural milieu is critical. The immediate local economies including banks, shops, farms, and ranches are controlled by non-Indians — usually the progeny of those non-Indian pioneers who "settled" the west. In the rural areas, too, the non-Indian populations control the churches, the education system, and the local government. The representatives from these areas to state and federal governments are almost always non-Indian. The obvious generalization from these and earlier generalizations is that whereas the satellites are exploited so that the metropolis may grow, the rural areas are in the immediate economic, political, and social control of non-Indians.

The Indian lives on or near reservations, agencies, colonies, or rancherias in a special wardship status not enjoyed by non-Indians. His tribal government has only limited control over tribal resources and tribal affairs. Ultimate authority is invested in the Secretary of Interior, with local BIA employees having lesser authority over scores of aspects of the personal lives of Indians, such as the disposition of funds in their Individual Indian Monies accounts. The average Indian, then, is subject to local, state, and federal governments like everyone else, plus special neocolonial institutions such as tribal governments which exercise only a modicum of control over their affairs, and the

BIA which serves as a caretaker of these tribal governments. Also, the Secretary of Interior and the House Committee on Interior and Insular Affairs can and do intervene in the lives and affairs of Indians, having decision-making powers which they do not have over any other race or ethnic group.

To summarize the hypothesis presented here, the growth of the metropolis caused the Indians of the United States to be underdeveloped; Indians did not begin that way. Non-Indians who originally settled in rural areas, expropriated Indian land and the resources thereon, and manned the satellite sector of the economy, met with some success. Yet the past four decades have brought economic reversals for their progeny. Only the largest producers have been able to cope, profitably, with the changes in their industries as the metropolis has grown. As a consequence, out-migration of rural non-Indians has been substantial since 1920, farm and ranch consolidation has been enormous, and rural labor needs have been greatly reduced.

As the satellite economies, especially in the western states, have withered and the threat of economic demise has become more pressing, the non-Indians who own the shops, manage the banks, and operate the ranches and farms in rural areas have hired non-Indians rather than Indians for the permanent and temporary jobs they control. They tend to provide jobs for kin, friends, and others of the same race as the owner or manager. The Indian is most generally a consumer, seldom a wage earner, almost never an owner or controller of the production of any-thing in the economic satellites. Just as in the initial westward expansion of the metropolis-satellite economy, the Indians have been the first to suffer in the subsequent growth of the economy.

As a corollary, the greater the contribution of a producer to the national farm, ranch, or mining economy, the greater the federal benefits accruing to the producer. Those that have, get. Though the rural areas exert little political influence, any influ-ence that is felt, especially in state government, is that of the non-Indian. Another corollary is that as satellites have withered and small producers have gone bankrupt, those people who contribute least to the economy also exert the least political influence and receive the fewest benefits — usually only welfare assistance. The Indian, who has almost never produced anything, has the least influence and the least control over his own resources and the federal welfare he receives.

Finally, because Indians have few skills, little education, no capital, poor housing, poor health, and no influence or power, they are discriminated against by local non-Indians. The people who took their resources have denied status to Indians and have rebuked their morality because they have not been productive members of the society and because they have been special wards of the federal government. The cycle is vicious.

A brief exposition of the case history of the Northern Ute Indians of eastern Utah serves as an example of my concluding hypothesis: the development of the metropolis-satellite economy through technology, capital, political influence, and power has locked the Indian into poverty conditions. Over the past century, the Northern Utes have become more, rather than less, dependent on federal welfare as their own resources have been exploited by local non-Indians and multi-national corporations. The enduring endemic poverty among American Indians has been epidemic among the Northern Utes; this culture of poverty is not a fortuity, not a product of lazy people with low "need achievement" (a popular tautology for people who have or have not achieved), and not a product of slavish retention of native traits.

A detailed analysis of the Northern Utes as well as four other Shoshonean groups can be found in a previously cited manuscript (Jorgensen n.d.). The following account excludes a substantial amount of data, tests, and generalizations about the causes and the nature of deprivation among the Northern Utes.

A CASE STUDY OF INDIANS VIS-À-VIS
THE METROPOLIS: THE NORTHERN UTES

A Brief History. The Utes have been the victims of a process of expropriation, exploitation, domination, and dole, promoted primarily by the metropolis which has used the BIA as an instrument and secondarily by local, small-scale entrepreneurs such as farmers and herders. In 1830 there were perhaps 12,000–15,000 Utes in Colorado, Utah, and New Mexico. Figure 2.1 shows the approximate range of the Ute bands at that time. For the one hundred and fifty years prior to that date, the Utes had been organized into equestrian bands which subsisted on bison,

Figure 2.1 Distribution of Equestrian Ute Bands (Summer Residential Groups) circa 1830

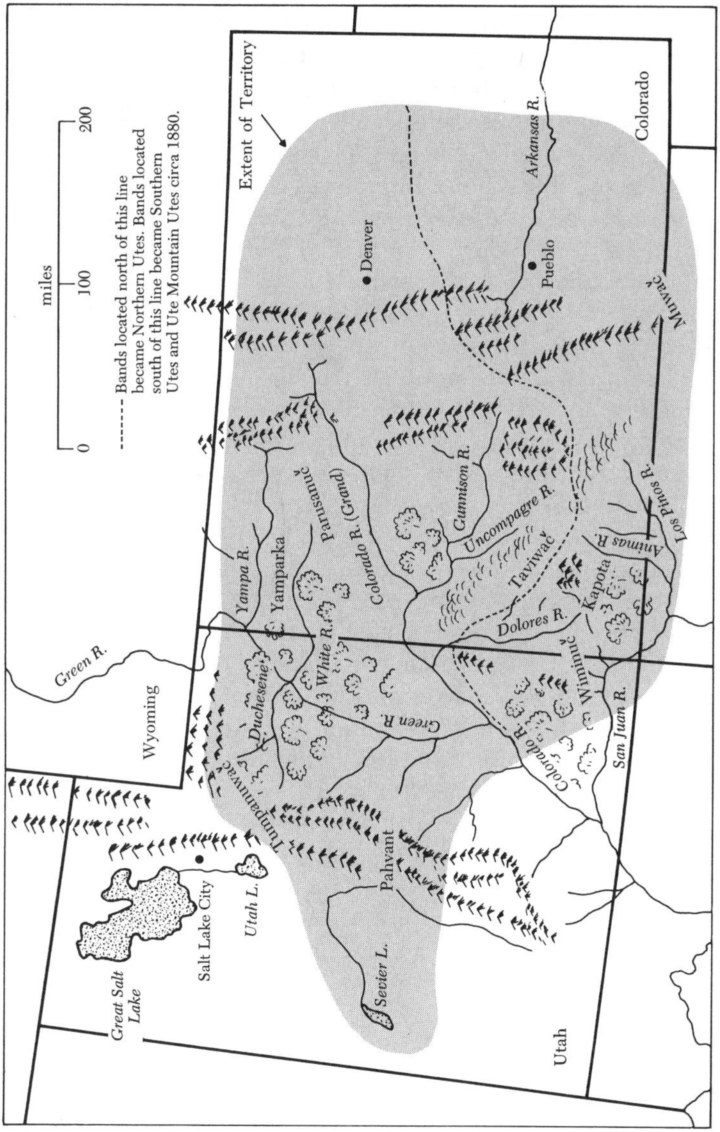

Source: Adapted from Jorgensen (1964).

deer, elk, and mountain sheep, as well as rabbits, fish, sage hens, nuts, seeds, roots, and berries. They periodically raided eastern and western Pueblo villages in what is now Arizona and New Mexico and Spanish towns and haciendas in the same areas plus California; they also raided travelers along the Santa Fe Trail when this opened in the early nineteenth century. Bands of Utes also traded with many people in these areas, swapping game for corn, beans, squash, and European goods.

In quest of bison, Utes regularly ventured east of the Rocky Mountains where they often battled Comanches, Kiowas, Arapahos, and Cheyennes. When they went north to hunt, trade, or raid, they often fought Wind River Shoshones and, less often, Dakotas. The Utes intermittently raided the people to their west — Gosiutes, Paiutes, and Western Shoshones — for women and children for slave trade in Spanish and Pueblo villages.

In 1847 Mormons (members of the Church of Jesus Christ of Latter-Day Saints) established themselves east of the Great Salt Lake. By 1867 they had entered into two prolonged wars with the Ute populations in Utah, one in the early 1850's and the other in the early 1860's. The Mormons displaced the Utes from their territory west of the Wasatch Mountains and from the federal farms that had been established for them in the 1850's near Utah Lake in what is now Sanpete County. With federal help, the dominant Anglos removed and restricted the Utes to the 2,039,000 acre Uintah reservation in eastern Utah, an area considered valueless for farming or ranching.

Between 1847 and 1867 many Utes died from disease, starvation, frostbite, and warfare; these deaths were due partly to loss of access to the resources that they once subsisted on, partly to their lack of protection from white-carried disease, and partly to the failure of the federal government to deliver annuities promised them as treaty *obligations* and payments for relinquishing their territory which would have warded off starvation. Attempts to induce the Utes in Utah to farm were unsuccessful; they preferred to hunt and continued to do so.

In 1870 the Ghost Dance religion swept out of Nevada and was introduced among the Utes in Utah and Colorado by their Shoshone congeners to the north. The Ghost Dance religion prom-

ised that the world would be radically and imminently transformed, that deceased Indians would join with living Indians in
the here and now, and that the old and preferred way of life
would be restored and practiced to the exclusion of whites. It
was an appeal to supernatural means to accomplish what fighting
and fleeing had not, namely, to bring about the removal of whites
and the reestablishment of Indian ways. Utes sponsored Ghost
Dances for a few years, but seemed to lose faith when the magical
transformation did not occur.

Throughout the 1870's the Utes in Utah were more and more
restricted to the Uintah reservation as settlements grew around
their territory and as their Ute counterparts in Colorado were
confined to areas west of the Colorado Rockies. By 1879 some
Utes had begun to farm and raise livestock in addition to their
huge herds of horses. But just as the Utes were being forced into
a rather sedentary existence, white ranchers illegally began
grazing their cattle on the western portion of the reservation,
and white prospectors discovered huge deposits of asphalt, gypsum, and gilsonite on the southern and eastern portions. These
were harbingers of worse things to come.

The Utes in Colorado and New Mexico were not conquered
and corralled as early as the Utah Utes. From the 1860's on, they
came increasingly into conflict with Indians of the Plains as they
both competed for the rapidly dwindling bison herds, and with
miners and prospectors who had discovered gold, silver, and lead
as far west as the southern Utah-Colorado border. Between 1863
and 1873 some Utes were successfully coerced and enticed to
sign three separate treaties relinquishing most of the Colorado
Ute territory in the Rocky Mountains. In 1880, following a battle
between the United States Army and the Yamparka and Parusanuč bands of Utes (White Rivers) near Meeker, Colorado, in
the northwest, the Utes in Colorado, both participants and nonparticipants in the battle, were forced to relinquish all but a few
thousand acres of the territory previously ceded to them.

Governor Frederick Pitkin of Colorado had extensive mining
interests in the southwest, and along with many other mineral
speculators desired to exploit Ute territory. Following the battle
near Meeker, Pitkin called for a war of extermination against the

Utes. That prompted the federal government to hastily remove 2,026 Taviwač (Uncompaghre Agency), Yamparka and Parusanuč (White River Agency) Utes from Colorado and locate them in Utah. The Wiminuč, Kapota, and Muwač Utes, numbering 1,150, were restricted to a narrow strip of land about fifteen miles wide and one hundred miles long on the Colorado–New Mexico border.

Between 1850 and 1880 the Ute population had been reduced from 12,000–15,000 to 3,975. The Southern and Ute Mountain Utes in Colorado totaled 1,150, and 2,825 Northern Utes were located in Utah. Their aboriginal territory of about 60–70 million acres had been reduced to about 4.5 million reservation acres of which about 4 million were located in the high, desolate canyonlands and basins of northeastern Utah — 150 mountainous miles from Salt Lake City and 350 from Denver. Indians had been moved by force and were required to stay on their assigned reservations. Military posts were established to control the Indian populations. Their aboriginal territory had been commandeered by farmers, ranchers, and miners and the once independent Ute Indians had become subject populations. They no longer could administer their own affairs, no longer had access to their resources; in their status as non-citizens and as dominated people controlled by the United States Army and a bureau of the federal government, they had no access to the locus of political power.

The Northern Utes experienced even more deprivation. The 665 Utes from the White River Agency in Colorado were re-located on the 2,039,000-acre Uintah reservation, joining the 800 Uintah Utes who were already there. The 1,361 Utes from the Uncompaghre Agency in Colorado were relocated on a new reservation, the Ouray, which bordered the Uintah reserve and was comparable in size. By again forcing these populations to relocate, the federal government exacerbated their unhappiness. Although the Uncompaghres had not joined the insurrection, they had been forced away from their agency because precious minerals were located on their Colorado reserve. In addition, they were angry at the White Rivers for precipitating the removal of both groups in 1880. The White Rivers, on the other hand, were angry about having been chased from their territory simply because they had defended it, and were furious with the Uncompaghres because they had refused to join in a common defense.[6] The Uintah Utes, who had to relinquish about half of their territory to accommodate the displaced White Rivers, received no immediate compensation for their "generosity."

The Ute Indians were not consulted; they were merely corralled like bison against their will. Within six years a group of about a hundred Utes of both sexes and all ages, formerly assigned to agencies in Colorado, slipped off the Ouray reservation and returned to Colorado; they fled Utah because miners were encroaching on the Ouray reservation, and hoped to dissociate themselves from whites and to restore their old ways. White settlers in western Colorado, who feared and hated the Utes, attacked and killed some of them; they also stole 5,000 pounds of dried meat, 500 horses, 2,500 sheep and goats, and 37 cattle. Most of the Utes escaped and returned to the Ouray reservation under the protection of a small party of United States cavalrymen and Utes who had found the beleaguered recluses and had escorted them out of Colorado. No reparations were received for the stolen goods; no whites were brought to trial for the Ute slayings.

In the mid-1880's, cattle, sheep, and mining interests pressed the United States government to open Uintah and Ouray reservation lands to white exploitation. The Utes adamantly opposed this action, but in 1887 the General Allotment Act was passed and, regardless of Ute opposition, the lands were allotted.

In 1890, before Northern Ute lands were allotted and at a time when the Utes were trying unsuccessfully to sue the United States government for broken treaty rights and for land stolen from them in Colorado, the Uintah Utes began performing the Sun Dance religion, a modified version of the Plains ritual. The Sun Dance had been reworked by several Wind River Shoshone shamans who had lost faith in the imminent transformation of the world promised by the Ghost Dance religion. The Sun Dance religion only promised that men could be redeemed so that they

---

[6] Other factors were involved, particularly two treaty signings in the 1860's, entered into primarily by the Uncompaghres, who gave away territory exploited by the White Rivers. Also, the White Rivers were forced to pay reparations to the families of all whites killed in the battle at Meeker out of the scant funds made available by the government, in recompense for extinguishing their rights to their land in Colorado. Nothing was deducted from the Uncompaghre funds.

could cope with daily life, and was intended to bestow super-natural power on shamans and other participants to cure ill health and to alleviate suffering. The White River and Un-compaghre Utes soon joined the Uintahs in sponsoring the new religion.

Regardless of Ute resistance, the Ouray reservation was al-lotted in 1897. Because of its vast asphalt, gilsonite, gypsum, oil, and shale oil deposits, it was the first part of the Northern Ute reserve to be allotted. To add to Northern Ute problems, the majority of Utes who had resided on the Ouray reservation were allotted land on the Uintah reservation. Some received their al-lotments along the rivers on the Ouray reserve, but the majority of all Ouray reserve land was returned to public domain. The Uintah and White River Utes refused to comply with allotting procedures; the latter threatened to flee from the reserve if their land was taken. In late 1905 the federal government al-lotted the Uintah reservation against the will of the inhabitants, and 365 White River Utes left the reserve and headed northeast intending to restore their old hunting way of life and to dissociate themselves from whites. The White Rivers were eventually rounded up by the United States Cavalry and placed on the Cheyenne River Sioux reservation in South Dakota. By 1908 the White River Utes had eaten the cattle given them by the government when they were relocated; hungry and unhappy, they asked to be returned to the now consolidated Uintah and Ouray reservation. Their request was granted, and when they moved back to Utah, they received allotments of land not al-ready claimed by whites.

The following decades were miserable for the Northern Utes. The population of 2,826 in 1880 had plunged to 917 full-bloods by 1930. The joint Uintah and Ouray reservation territory of nearly 4 million acres in 1880 was reduced to 355,000 acres after allotment. Of these acres, 113,000 were awarded to Ute in-dividuals (allottees), but by 1930 about 30,000 of the allotment acres had been alienated through sales and 64 percent of the non-alienated allotment acreage was tied up in heirship status.

Several extended families developed cattle and sheep enter-prises on the reservation. Though there was little surplus for market sales, Utes contributed to their own subsistence by raising and consuming cattle and sheep, by leasing and selling their allotments to whites, by working for the federal government or, on a temporary basis, for white ranchers and farmers — averaging about 10 percent full-time employment — and by hunting deer, elk, rabbits, and sage hens, fishing, and collecting nuts and berries. The federal government assisted them with rations.

Ute health problems can be inferred from the decimation of the population. Some diseases, especially those clearly correlated with poor nutrition, inadequate housing, and poor sanitation, were epidemic on the Northern Ute reserve. About 30 percent of the population suffered from either tuberculosis or trachoma or both during the 1910–1930 period; tuberculosis, pneumonia, and several gastroenteritic diseases were the major causes of death.

Prior to the late 1930's about 40 percent of the Northern Ute houses had dirt floors. Most houses with flooring were either frame or clapboard shacks which were invariably overcrowded. The majority of the population was illiterate; the literate ones who had attended school had not gone beyond the eighth grade.

In this context the Sun Dance religion flourished, as did the Peyote religion which was introduced in 1914 on the reservation and which, like the Sun Dance, promised redemption for the participants so that they could cope with life. During the 1930's practically all Northern Utes adhered to both religions.

In the late 1930's the Northern Utes established a tribal government under the provisions of the Indian Reorganization Act (IRA). Only 30 percent of the eligible voters ratified the tribe's charter, which provided for the establishment of a business committee to conduct the economic, legislative, and judicial affairs of the tribe. There is some evidence that ratification was greatly influenced by local BIA officials who turned out favorable votes among the mixed-bloods and the Uncompaghre full-bloods. The first committeemen to be elected were mixed-bloods and Uncompaghre full-bloods, and their actions created considerable animosity among the White River and Uintah full-bloods who for decades had scores of disputes with both subgroups.

Figure 2.2 juxtaposes the Indian-owned acreage of 1880 with that of 1937. After 1937 the federal government, as part of its obligations under the IRA, began purchasing acreage that had

Figure 2.2   Uintah and Ouray Reservation

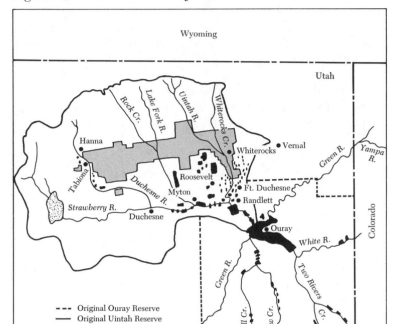

Ute-owned lands as of 1880 = approximately 4,000,000 acres, while
Ute-owned lands as of 1937 = approximately 360,000 acres.

Source: Modified from Wright (1948:329), and adapted from Jorgensen (1964).

been sold to non-Indians following earlier passage of the General
Allotment Act. Much of the Uintah Basin area had become
saturated with alkali from unintelligent irrigation and land exploitation. Many Basin non-Indians sold their holdings to the
government because their farms and ranches were no longer
profitable, because they were in arrears on property taxes, and
because they needed cash during the Depression. Other acreage
that had never been deemed valuable nor claimed by farmers,
ranchers, or mineral developers was transferred to tribal ownership by the federal government. Since 1950, the tribe has owned
about a million acres, one-fourth of their 1880 acreage, but nearly

three times as much as they owned between 1907 and 1950. Figure 2.3 shows the approximate current reservation boundaries.

The Modern Period. The period following organization and incorporation has seen few beneficial and lasting changes in Ute life. Ute life has worsened a little as their expectations have risen and their economic circumstances have fluctuated and become oppressive. More allottees have died and more acreage has gone into heirship status. Farm technology, especially machine equipment, has liberated many people from farm and ranch labor, causing rural whites, especially the youths, to move out of the Uintah Basin, and has made fewer part-time farm and ranch jobs available for Indians.

The tribal business committee began purchasing heirship allotments from joint heirs and from allottees who were in arrears in water-use taxes and subjugation assessments,[7] using tribal funds won in a judgment against the government and IRA funds. By 1968 all but 33 percent of the original allotments had been sold to non-Indians or purchased by the tribe. Of the 38,000 allotment acres that had not been alienated, 97 *percent* were tied up in heirship status, and neither heirs nor allottees had capital to work their land.

The small farm or ranch operated by anyone, especially an Indian, has been a bad business risk for years. Non-Indian lessees have always out-produced Indians on Ute lands, so it is easier for the former to borrow capital to work Indian lands than for the Utes to acquire capital to do the same. This is only part of the story, however. Generations of paternalism, unemployability, unemployment, and undereducation coupled with bigotry, apathy, poor land, and distant markets have coalesced with other underlying economic causes to keep the Utes from enjoying solvent, agrarian-based livelihoods.

---

[7] In 1906 the Uintah Irrigation Project was initiated by Congress against the will of the Northern Utes. The project continued intermittently for over thirty years. All allottees were assessed for the costs of the project, and by 1937 many allotments were as much as $1,600 in debt. The Utes had no capital to pay these debts, and were not allowed to farm until the debts were paid. In 1946 the Uintah and White River bands filed a suit in the U.S. Court of Claims for "compensation for wrongful and wasteful use of tribal trust funds [in the] Uintah Irrigation Project." The grievance was not satisfied.

Figure 2.3   Uintah and Ouray Reservation, 1969

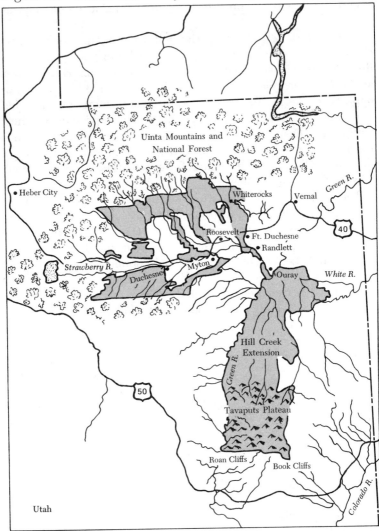

Source: Adapted from Jorgensen (1964).

In 1948 the tribe began receiving royalties from oil, phosphate, and gilsonite leases. By June, 1951, $1,500,000 had been received and $1,453,000 had been spent by the business committee to pay salaries, purchase allotments, and pay for some land subjugation costs. In 1951 the Northern Utes received $18,000,000 of a $32,000,000 judgment awarded to the Confederated Utes (Northern, Southern, and Ute Mountain) in the Indian Court of Claims. In the following fifteen years they received another $12,500,000 in claims judgments. After the first award, the tribe requested immediate relief for food, clothing, and household repairs, and received some help after Congressional approval. Indeed, all funds in the judgment were allowed to be expended only when the business committee submitted a plan to the BIA and the Secretary of Interior which was approved by the House Committee on Interior and Insular Affairs.

From 1951 the Northern Utes quickly moved from a semi-self-sufficient population of about 1,200 full-bloods subsisting on farming, ranching, hunting, gathering, part-time labor, government employment, and welfare, to a population almost completely dependent upon unearned income. Unearned income was distributed to each enrolled Ute, first as per capita payments and later as "family plan" funds. Between 1951 and mid-1959, over $11,000 was awarded to each Northern Ute. During the same period the population, on the upswing since the nadir of 917 in 1930, grew from 1,200 to about 1,500 full-bloods, household size decreased from about 6.2 to 4.4, and household *apparent* income increased annually from about $1,500 to $6,750. Thus, apparent per capita income jumped from about $240 per year in the 1945–51 period to $1,535 in the 1952–59 period.[8] Yet even in

---

[8] The income is deemed "apparent" because parents did not have access to their children's funds except in dire circumstances; they did not even have direct access to their own funds from 1957 through 1959 while the family plan was in force. Indeed, 21 percent of *all* family plan funds went to pay off loans and debts (Uintah Irrigation Project and other debts incurred prior to 1950, or more recent debts incurred against the prospect of per capita distributions). All other funds from the family plan were administered by the BIA which granted Ute families monthly allowances for each child, paid for home improvements, allowed for the purchase of home appliances, and so forth. Checks were drawn to the supplier, not the Indian, as the BIA did not trust the Indian to control his own money; the argument for this procedure was that the Indian had squandered his per capitas be-

1959, Indian housing was way below state standards and generally lacked running water, indoor toilets, telephones, gas heaters, and stoves; in fact, electricity was not available to a substantial number of homes.

In 1954 the full-bloods were successful in dissociating the 490 mixed-bloods from the tribe. The mixed-bloods (Affiliated Ute Citizens) were terminated by the federal government, but they took 27 percent of all judgment funds and about 25 percent of the reservation land with them. The full-bloods, on the other hand, assumed full control of the business committee and terminated their relations with the mixed-bloods. The Uncompaghres, who had practically no mixed-bloods on their membership rolls, were especially pleased to terminate the relationship.

The new business committee had some continuity with the old because a powerful Uncompaghre committeeman and his nephew served on both. The nephew soon had control of the new business committee and led the way in hiring advisors and drawing up plans, in conjunction with the BIA, for the expenditure of land-claims funds. The major plans called for reducing per capita distributions and increasing tribal expenditures after 1956. These expenditures primarily went for recreation, education, counseling, and tribal staff maintenance. Expenditures were also made to purchase allotments and to develop a tribally owned farm through a costly subjugation project.

In short, the business committee had some voice in the manner in which their land-claims funds would be expended. Practically all funds were allocated toward meeting individual living expenses or to noninvestment ends. To recapitulate: individuals did not have absolute control over funds allotted to them; jobs opened by the tribe expended, rather than produced, capital; even the subjugation farm always operated at a loss. In addition the tribe, following the advice of non-Indians, did not gain control over mineral production on the reservation; it settled for lease income and royalties offered by multinational corporations.

---

tween 1951 and 1956 so he had to be taught how to allocate his scarce resources, i.e., how to consume. Between 1951 and 1959 the monies made available to Utes went for daily subsistence needs.

In 1960 per capita distributions were greatly reduced, and in 1962 they were terminated completely as the tribe spent money on collective projects. A political faction — the True Utes — emerged and challenged the business committee to dissolve at one point, through an armed attack on tribal headquarters. The True Utes wanted tribal spending to be stopped immediately along with an abrupt termination of the land-collectivization program wherein allottees and heirs were forced to sell their acreage; instead, they wanted the funds to be used exclusively for per capita payments. The True Utes were incarcerated by tribal police; when they were freed from jail they were periodically intimidated by the dominant Uncompaghre member of the business committee. The dispute was not a simple factional affair between Uncompaghres and Uintah–White Rivers. Members of the Uintah–White River bands made up the core of the True Utes, but the group gained membership from all bands, especially as conditions worsened and as the discrepancy between what the Utes had and what the Utes thought they ought to have widened.

In 1964 the tribe went through a fiscal crisis. The 1951 judgment funds had been expended, the subsequent awards were tied up in litigation over the federal government's claim to some funds as compensation for costs incurred while running the reservation, and the vastly increased and youthful Ute population was without individual allotment land, skills, education, jobs, or access to jobs. There was no viable economy on the reservation and no market for unskilled labor near the reservation.

The tribe pulled back its activities as the dominant Uncompaghre committeeman, who had become persona non grata, left the reservation. As more judgment funds became available, the tribe on the advice of BIA and other non-Indian specialists increased their investment in their cattle enterprise, but it has never shown a profit, has created few jobs, and was developed when grass-fed beef began to lose its profit margin. Other funds went into a small recreation hunting enterprise which attracted wealthy non-Indians to the reservation; though the endeavor showed a small profit, it created few jobs and gave whites privileged access to tribal game. In 1969 tribal members voted to end this business at their annual General Council because they did not want non-Indians killing game upon which they relied for their livelihood.

From 1962 on, Indian families became destitute as their access to relatively adequate sources of unearned income was curtailed. A few families moved to Oakland, Los Angeles, and Denver under the Employment Assistance Program, but practically all returned to the reservation before a year had passed. Many families — 25 percent of all Northern Utes residing on the reservation — began receiving state welfare.[9] Other individuals received tribal assistance and federal commodities. Family household incomes plunged to about $2,600 per year in 1965, while the average household size increased to 6.6 people. The per capita annual income of about $390 represents an apparent decrease of over $1,100 from the 1951–59 period; the increase in household size over the same time is by 2.2 people. By 1969 Ute household incomes had plunged even further and the per capita income was less than one-fifth of the average for the state.

Table 2.2 shows the average household size, sources, and amount of income for the 1945–66 period. Household size varies inversely with amount of income: Ute family households changed from large units based on predominantly earned but extremely low income, to smaller units based on predominantly unearned and relatively high income, and back to large units based on predominantly unearned and very low income. In a brief fifteen-year period Ute families became dependent on unearned income, their population grew, the economy around them withered, and they spent their funds paying old debts and for

[9] How the Ute welfare recipients are treated can be seen in the following example. In late 1968 the Utah State welfare office in Vernal decided to withhold the Ute welfare checks for December because the Utes were to receive an annual dividend of $150 through a recently initiated program wherein some Ute judgment funds were placed in a local bank to accrue interest. The interest was paid to each Ute. The Utes were furious with the welfare officer and formed a pressure group to get their welfare checks. After consultation with state officials in Salt Lake City, the welfare department decided to let the Utes keep their dividends and their welfare payments so long as they could prove that the dividend money was spent for clothes, home improvements or the like.

TABLE 2.2

Average Household Size and Income (All Sources),
for Selected Periods, Northern Ute Reserve, 1945–66

Years	Major Sources of Income (Listed in Order of Importance)	Average Household Income per Year	Average No. of Persons in Household
1945–50	Part-time labor; piece-work; "self-employ-ment"; state welfare; regular employment; lease income	$1,500	6.2 (1950)
1951–59	Unearned income from land claims, leases; regular em-ployment; part-time labor; "self-employ-ment"; piecework	$6,750	4.4 (1957)
1960–62	Unearned income from land claims, leases; part-time labor; piecework; regular employment; tribal assistance	$4,000	
1963–66	State welfare; un-earned income from land claims, leases; part-time labor; piecework; regular employment	$2,600	6.6 (1965)

daily needs. When unearned income was dissipated, households had to combine and to pool resources, such as lease-income, wages from part-time labor, and welfare payments, in order to exist. The movement from large to small and back to large households can be understood in this light.

Seventy-five percent of all Northern Utes live in houses where there is more than one person per room. These figures are *reversed* for the general Utah population. Moreover, the median number of persons per room is .80 for the overall state, but 1.5, nearly double that figure, for the Northern Utes. The Utes live in crowded homes with few conveniences. They suffer and die from all the diseases that have been endemic among them for nearly a century — diseases that occur at rates up to one hundred times greater than those for the white population. Indians die from accidents — household fires, for instance — at unbelievably greater rates than the local whites or the general population of Utah.

These effects of Indian integration into the United States political economy are appalling. An assessment of recent Ute employment and its pattern in the past decade is instructive. Table 2.3 shows that of all Northern Utes aged 18 to 55, only about 45 percent have been considered employable.[10] By contrast, the non-Indian employability rate has been around 75 percent. The figures in columns *D* and *G* show that permanent employment has hovered around 20 percent of the employables, whereas the unemployed, underemployed, and unemployable comprise about *90 percent* of the adult population.

Who are the employers? Until 1959 the tribe and the BIA were the major employers of both permanent and temporary personnel, though about thirty men continued to raise sheep and cattle (i.e., were self-employed) through about 1955. By 1962 the tribe supplied 60 percent of all jobs, the BIA 32 percent, and self-employment and other federal sources (mainly the armed forces) 8 percent. By 1964, during the tribe's fiscal crisis, the BIA had become the major employer, providing 53 percent of all jobs to the tribe's 40 percent, with 7 percent from self-employment and part-time ranch labor. By 1966 the BIA and the tribe each supplied only 35 percent of the jobs because new jobs had been opened by the Office of Economic Opportunity and the Community Action Project, two arms of the federal welfare bureaucracy, and the poverty program through these appendages was providing 23 percent of all employment.

Beside the shocking instability of jobs and the instability of the employment structure itself, overall it is clear that Utes are dependent for their livelihoods on federal government funds. Jobs that provide earned income from the Ute point of view are

---

[10] This follows the "narrow" definition explicated above.

TABLE 2.3

Employment, Northern Ute Population, Aged 18–55 for Selected Years, 1956–66

Year	A Total (Males and Females)	B Unemployable Percentage of A % No.		C Employable Percentage of A % No.		D Permanently Employed Percentage of C % No.		E Temporarily Employed (Underemployed) Percentage of C % No.		F Unemployed Percentage of C % No.		G Underemployed (E), Unemployed (F), and Unemployable (B) Percentage of A % No.	
1956[a]	466	52	242	48	224	50%	113			50	111	75	353
1962[b]	547	57	310	43	237	18	44	35	83	46	110	91	503
1964[c]	598	57	338	43	260	17	45	44	115	38	100	92	553
1966[d]	641	54	341	46	300	27	83	16	48	56	169	87	558

[a] Data are adapted from Ute Tribe (1956:81). Age intervals are adjusted to exclude people over fifty-five years of age. Temporary and permanent employment are lumped together in these data.

[b] Data are adapted from Indian Unemployment Survey (CHCIIA 1963:440–443).

[c] Data are from Jorgensen (1964:chapter 4; 1964 unpublished field notes).

[d] Data are adapted from Uintah and Ouray Agency Report of Labor Force (1968), Bottenfield (personal communication), and Jorgensen (unpublished field notes).

dependent on federal budget allocations to the BIA, or the welfare bureaus of the War on Poverty, or funds made available through the Indian Court of Claims. Unearned income, too, is provided by federal and state government. White shopkeepers in the area, although partially dependent on the Utes as consumers as well as on other Ute resources, do not employ Utes. The white-controlled industries in the area including those on Indian land do not employ Utes. Mineral industries developed on Ute lands have been controlled by national and multi-national corporations, with Utes receiving lease and royalty income only.

As agribusiness has pushed the small producer out of production and technology has replaced much farm labor, the remaining available jobs go to whites. Almost the only Indian laborers employed by non-Indians hold temporary jobs during the haying season. If an Indian male is jailed in a white town for drunkenness, his fine of from $15 to $30 is often paid by a local rancher. In turn, the Indian must work for a week or two in the white man's hayfield, which is often leased from Indians. Shopkeepers employ their families in their stores, restaurants, and gas stations; the mining industries require little labor, and this must be highly skilled.

The lack of employment can be partly attributed to lack of skills. Less than 50 percent of adult Utes have skills or semi-skills, and that classification uses a definition of semi-skills so loose as to include the ability to drive a truck or erect a barbed-wire fence. Moreover, as of 1969 there were only four Northern Ute college graduates, and the median years of school completed for all adults equalled 8.7. The median for all of Utah was over 12 years. These figures say nothing about the contexts in which education is acquired, nor the quality of the education received. Utes have attended local white schools intermittently since 1951 from funds paid to local county school boards through provisions of the Johnson-O'Malley Act. But Utes have not received educations comparable to whites (Jorgensen n.d.).

No matter how the situation is analyzed, lack of skills and education are causal effects rather than the causes of Ute unemployment and Ute poverty. Utes have never had complete control of their own resources nor the capital and advice needed to exploit their resources profitably. When their land or the resources thereon have been desired by an expanding economy, they have been taken. When Ute labor has been useful, it has been exploited. When Utes have had cash they have been welcome in white-owned stores and have received credit. When Utes have needed cash, white-controlled banks have not had money to loan them, nor has credit been extended. When the land taken from the Utes could no longer be exploited profitably and the agricultural satellites themselves began to wither, Utes reacquired some of this alienated land — they are still purchasing and consolidating acreage.

The federal government, through the BIA, has overseen Ute "development"; that development has resulted in generations of apathetic and disillusioned Utes. A viable economy has never been generated and the Utes have more and more become buried in the depths of a welfare enterprise — BIA, state welfare offices, OEO and CAP — which has been the political response toward solving their economic deprivation. The solutions have, of course, treated symptoms, not causes, and as conditions worsen, the welfare establishment grows, providing jobs for non-Indians and some Indians, as well as handouts. Without skills, education, or adequate advice, and with limited control over their own resources and practically no influence over the people who make decisions for them, Utes are, de facto, trapped. It is true that a Horatio Alger type *could* move off the reservation and become a dentist or the president of a railroad, but it is not very probable.

It is unfortunate that as Ute conditions of poverty have persisted, the pervasive factionalism in Northern Ute society also has continued. The mixed-bloods have been dissociated from the tribe, the composition of the business committee changes regularly, and the legislative acts of that committee have constantly brought criticism. Factionalism, like Ute poverty, is a phenomenon of mid-nineteenth century origin: both were caused by the manner in which the metropolis-satellite political economy grew.

Not surprisingly, when the Northern Ute responses of fighting whites, fleeing from whites, and signing treaties with whites failed to have their intended and, in the case of the treaties, their *promised* effects, Northern Utes turned to a transformative social movement, the Ghost Dance, to bring radical and imminent changes to the world.[11] When the transformative movement failed, Utes turned to the redemptive promise of the Sun Dance and the Peyote religions. Both have allowed the Utes to cope with daily life, and both have persisted since they were introduced on the reserve. Indeed, the Sun Dance religion is participated in, and adhered to, by all but a tiny handful of Northern Utes. The persistence of these movements obviously marks the continual response of Northern Utes to their neocolonial lives, their lives in programmed poverty.

SOME BRIEF CONCLUSIONS

In summary, modern American Indian "underdevelopment" has been caused by the "development" of the metropolis-satellite political economy. "Underdevelopment," "backwardness," and other similar designations are euphemisms for poverty. Indians have lived in neocolonial settings without access to their own strategic resources and without direct access to the locus of power. Thus Indians have relied on kin for help in coping with daily life, and this has meant pooling their meager educations and few skills in a context of poor housing, poor health, and unstable employment. They are in the whiplash of economic growth, barely hanging on. Their special political sector of the dwindling agricultural satellites represents a special form of a welfare response to deprivation.

The modern American Indians are the progeny of the super-exploited Indians of the nineteenth century who were forced to relinquish their territory, their self-governance, and their self-esteem so that the metropolis could grow. Some Indians have worked their way, through one means or another, to regular employment, even to positions of prestige. The average Indian has not. The reasons why he has not have been explicated here: simply enough, the modern Indian, too, is super-exploited.

[11] I urge the reader to consult Aberle (1966); Part V of his book is a major analysis of the types and causes of social movements. I follow Professor Aberle's typology of *transformative* and *redemptive* movements here.

BIBLIOGRAPHY

Aberle, David F.
    1966   *The Peyote Religion among the Navaho.* Viking Fund Publications
            in Anthropology, no. 42.
Adams, Richard N.
    1960   "An Inquiry into the Nature of the Family." In *Essays in the Sci-
            ence of Culture,* Gertrude E. Dole and Robert L. Carneiro (eds.).
            New York: Crowell, pp. 30–49.
BIA (Bureau of Indian Affairs)
    1949   *Answers to Your Questions about American Indians.* Washington,
            D.C.: U.S. Government Printing Office.
    1955   *Answers to Your Questions about American Indians.* Washington,
            D.C.: U.S. Government Printing Office.
    1968   *Answers to Your Questions about American Indians.* Washington,
            D.C.: U.S. Government Printing Office.
Borah, Woodrow, and Sherburn F. Cook
    1966   "Marriage and Legitimacy in Mexican Culture: Mexico and Cali-
            fornia." In *The Law of the Poor,* Jacobus tenBroek (ed.). San Fran-
            cisco: Chandler Publishing Company, pp. 622–684.
Brophy, William, and Sophie D. Aberle
    1966   *The Indian: America's Unfinished Business.* Norman: University of
            Oklahoma Press.
CFEPC (California Fair Employment Practice Commission)
    1966   "Minority Groups in California." *Monthly Labor Review.* Bureau
            of Labor Statistics, U.S. Department of Labor.
CHCIIA (Chairman, House Committee on Interior and Insular Affairs)
    1963   *Indian Unemployment Survey.* Committee Print no. 3, 88th Cong.,
            1st sess.
Deloria, Vine, Jr.
    1969   *Custer Died for Your Sins: An Indian Manifesto.* New York: Mac-
            millan.
Frank, André Gundar
    1967   *Capitalism and Underdevelopment in Latin America: Historical
            Studies of Chile and Brazil.* New York and London: Monthly Re-
            view Press.
Gonzalez, Nancie L. Solien
    1969   *Black Carib Household Structure.* Seattle: University of Washing-
            ton Press.
Haas, Theodore H.
    1957   "The Legal Aspects of Indian Affairs from 1887 to 1957." In
            *American Indians and American Life. The Annals of the American
            Academy of Political and Social Sciences,* vol. 311, George Simp-
            son and Milton Yinger (eds.).
HCIIA (House Committee on Interior and Insular Affairs)
    1953   *Investigation of the Bureau of Indian Affairs.* United States Con-
            gress House Report.
    1954   *Investigation of the Bureau of Indian Affairs.* United States Con-
            gress House Report.

Hodge, William H.
    1969   "The Albuquerque Navahos." *Anthropological Papers of the University of Arizona*, no. 11.
Indian Record
    1968   "Special Issue: Economic Development." *Indian Record.* October, 1968. Department of Interior. Washington, D.C.: U.S. Government Printing Office.
Jorgensen, Joseph G.
    1964   "The Ethnohistory and Acculturation of the Northern Ute." Ph.D. dissertation, Indiana University, University Microfilms.
    n.d.   "Conquest, Neo-colonialism and the Modern Sun Dance Religion of the Shoshones and Utes." Mimeographed.
Klose, Nelson
    1964   *A Concise Study Guide to the American Frontier.* Lincoln: University of Nebraska Press.
Lurie, Nancy O.
    1957   "The Indian Claims Commission Act." In *American Indians and American Life*, pp. 56–70. *The Annals of the American Academy of Political and Social Sciences*, vol. 311, George Simpson and Milton Yinger (eds.).
Meriam, Lewis
    1928   *The Problems of Indian Administration.* Baltimore: The Johns Hopkins University Press.
Moynihan, Daniel
    1965   *The Negro Family — the Case for National Action.* Office of Policy Planning and Research, United States Department of Labor.
Munsell, Marvin
    1967   "Land and Labor at Salt River." Ph.D. dissertation, University of Oregon, University Microfilms.
Otterbein, Keith F.
    1965   "Caribbean Family Organization: A Comparative Analysis." *American Anthropologist* 67:66–79.
Price, John A.
    1968   "The Migration and Adaptation of American Indians in Los Angeles." *Human Organization* 27:168–175.
Robbins, Lynn A.
    1968   "Economics, Household Composition, and the Family Cycle: The Blackfeet Case." *Proceedings of the American Ethnological Society,* Spring, 1968.
SACIA (State Advisory Commission on Indian Affairs)
    1966   "Indians in Rural and Reservation Areas." Submitted to the Governor and Legislature of California. Sacramento.
SAUS (U.S. Bureau of the Census)
    1966   *Statistical Abstract of the United States: 1966.* Washington, D.C.: U.S. Government Printing Office.
    1967   *Statistical Abstract of the United States: 1967.* Washington, D.C.: U.S. Government Printing Office.
Shannon, Lyle W.
    1969   "The Economic Absorption and Cultural Integration of Immigrant Workers: Characteristics of the Individual vs. the Nature of the System." *American Behavioral Scientist* 13:36–56.

————, and Magdaline Shannon
   1967   "The Assimilation of Migrants to Cities: Anthropological and
           Sociological Contributions." In *Urban Affairs Annual Review,* Lyle
           W. Shannon and Magdaline Shannon (eds.). New York: Sage, pp.
           49–75.
Simpson, George, and Milton Yinger (eds.)
   1957   *American Indians and American Life. The Annals of the American
           Academy of Political and Social Sciences,* vol. 311 (May, 1957).
Smith, M. G.
   1962   *West Indian Family Structure.* Seattle: University of Washington
           Press.
Uintah and Ouray Agency
   1968   "Report of Labor Force." Submitted to Bureau of Indian Affairs
           and Department of Labor.
USPNACRP (United States President's National Advisory Commission on
Rural Poverty)
   1967   *The People Left Behind.* Washington, D.C.: U.S. Government
           Printing Office.
USPNACCD (United States President's National Advisory Commission on
Civil Disorders)
   1968   *Report of the National Advisory Commission on Civil Disorders.*
           New York: Bantam Books.
Ute Indian Tribe
   1956   "Ten-Year Development Program." Fort Duchesne. Mimeographed.
Wagner, Carruth J., and Erwin S. Rabeau
   1964   "Indian Poverty and Indian Health." *Health, Education and Wel-
           fare Indicators.* March, 1964.

CHAPTER 3 the reservation community
and the urban community:
hopi indians of moenkopi

SHUICHI NAGATA

INTRODUCTION [1]

Since the beginning of this century when the majority of the
present Indian reservations were established in the Southwest,
the Indians have never totally resigned themselves to the economic

[1] The data for this chapter were collected during my two years of fieldwork in the Tuba City–Moenkopi–Flagstaff area between 1962 and 1965.
While the description of the area is generally applicable to this period, significant changes after that period have been incorporated. Special thanks
are due Julian H. Steward, who generously supported my work through the
Studies of Cross-Cultural Regularities at the University of Illinois. I also
thank a number of individuals for providing the information regarding
developments in Tuba City since I left. J. W. Bosch, D. M. Brugge, W. P.
Carstens, R. E. Kelly, J. E. Levy, J. A. Nagata, and B. A. Wright kindly
helped me with facts, theory, references, and the English language. All the
personal, brand, and company names in the text are pseudonyms.

stagnation of the reservations. Early in the century, off-reservation migration took place in the form of seasonal agricultural labor, railroad work and, in the case of females, domestic service. A great number of Indians in Arizona participated in cotton picking shortly before the Depression. During World War II and the Korean War, Navajo and Hopi Indians migrated off their reservations to take up the slack in unskilled labor. As economic opportunities remained limited on the reservation, there seemed to many Indians little alternative but to leave home in search of a better life.

Partly to alleviate the depressing condition of so many reservations, particularly those of the Navajo and Hopi, the Bureau of Indian Affairs (BIA) established the Branch of Relocation in 1948, with the aim of assisting Indian migration to distant urban centers. In such recipient cities as Phoenix, Los Angeles, Denver, San Francisco, and Chicago, various state and civic organizations were created to assist new Indian arrivals there.

In spite of these institutional supports, urban migration of the Indians in the Southwest is still beset with problems of adjustment, some of which are discussed in this volume. The Indians are confronted with the alternatives of staying on the reservations which are economically underdeveloped and yet secure in legitimately maintained, if greatly truncated, tradition, or of migrating to cities which provide possible access to material comforts and freedom from conservative constraints, yet also can cause personal disorganization and a feeling of uprootedness among anonymous strangers.

The dilemma of city "exiles" (so eloquently stated in Kent Mackenzie's film, 1959–61) and of "stay-at-homes," however, glosses over some serious changes in progress on a number of reservations in the Southwest for the last two decades. Two such developments are significant. First is the growth of tribal governments as a mediating link between the interests of Indian tribesmen and external agencies, including federal and local governments, private business, and industries. As the tribal councils have assumed a greater role in promoting the economic interests of the reservations, the reservations have been assuming the character of economic corporations (Dobyns 1968, Woodbury and Woodbury 1964). Second is the increasing role of the federal and tribal governments in providing social services on the reservation in the form of welfare payments, education, medical protection, and public works projects. These two factors have contributed to considerable improvement of reservation life, which, in turn, appears significantly to alter the meaning of the above alternatives. Although the quality of life on many reservations still falls far short of the average national standard, the economic development of the reservation is regarded as an important and perhaps more meaningful strategy than off-reservation migration, to eliminate the material deprivation and spiritual degradation of the American Indians.

Along with the reservation development, a new type of community has begun to emerge, frequently around the sites of the BIA and tribal governments and sometimes around on-reservation boarding schools, mission stations, and trading posts — indeed, wherever enough stable jobs were available to call for prolonged residence of Indian and non-Indian employees. In origin, most of these communities are administrative centers dominated by the Anglo employees of the bureau, and constitute what Spicer called "reservation communities" (1962a:353–357). As reservation development progressed, a number of these communities grew in size and complexity. In contrast to small and isolated reservation communities, they comprise a population of a thousand or more having ethnic (both Indian and non-Indian) and occupational heterogeneity, engage in concentrated production of various services for the outlying rural bases of the reservation, and are provided with basic utilities and recreational facilities. The standard of living in these "agency towns" compares favorably with an average small town in the United States. Further, since these towns exist on the reservations and are numerically dominated by the Indians, the Indians are exposed to less risk of psychological alienation. They represent, in short, "urbanism" on the reservation.

Whether or not this new style of life can eliminate the need of urban migration for the Indians is a moot question. The number of reservation Indians to whom this option is open is greatly limited. In considering a better future for the American Indians, however, the preoccupation with the choice between underdeveloped reservations and impersonal city environments should not preclude the possibility of combining the best of the two alternatives. The present chapter is concerned with this possibility.

MOENKOPI, TUBA CITY, AND FLAGSTAFF

The Hopi Indian community of Moenkopi for many practical purposes belongs to the agency town of Tuba City and yet depends for the acquisition of consumer goods upon the off-reservation town of Flagstaff.

A settlement of about six hundred residents, Moenkopi is unique among the Hopi villages of northeastern Arizona. It originated as a "colony" of Old Oraibi toward the end of the last century and grew under the protection of the Mormon settlers who established Tuba City in 1875. Moenkopi is located in a tiny oasis of the Painted Desert; the main subsistence of the village was derived from extensive irrigation farming. When a reservation was established for the Hopi Indians in 1882, Moenkopi found itself outside the reservation boundary. In 1900, the area around Moenkopi was set aside as Western Navajo reservation, which was later consolidated into the rest of the Navajo reservation in 1935. When the Mormons withdrew in 1903, Tuba City became the site of the Western Navajo agency of the BIA. Since 1955 it has been the location of Western Navajo subagency, a branch of the Navajo agency of the bureau at Window Rock. Today, therefore, Moenkopi is situated upon the Navajo reservation.[2]

Since 1936 when the Hopi tribal council was established through the implementation of the Indian Reorganization Act, Moenkopi has been divided between Upper Moenkopi, now a part of the tribal council for which Upper Moenkopi village council sends a representative, and Lower Moenkopi, which still retains the traditional chieftainship and refuses to go along with the tribal council. In spite of its location on the Navajo reservation, Moenkopi comes under the jurisdiction of the Hopi agency of the bureau at Keams Canyon, mainly for welfare and education. In the early 1960's, Upper Moenkopi installed systems of domestic water supply and sewage disposal through the assistance of the U.S. Public Health Service at Keams Canyon and paved its major streets with the help of the Hopi agency.

[2] The reality of the reservation status of Moenkopi is far more complex than discussed here. There are a number of Hopi land allotments in Moenkopi, two of which cover half the present village site (Nagata 1970).

Moenkopi's ties wth the villages of Hopiland proper remain strong. Intermarriage between Moenkopi and Hopiland residents is still frequent, and due partly to the decline of ceremonial activities in Moenkopi, the people of Moenkopi often take part in the religious practices in Hopiland. On the other hand, some people from Hopiland temporarily migrate to Moenkopi to commute from there to work in Tuba City.

The style of life in Moenkopi can best be described as a wagework reserve of Tuba City. Although farming and raising livestock are widely practiced, their contribution to the total income of Moenkopi is secondary to wagework. There are two stores, one shoe-repair shop, and one garage, all run by the Hopi. Except for one store and the garage, their existence is hardly apparent, although many clients of the garage are the Navajo from the environs of Moenkopi. The active store in Upper Moenkopi is run by a man who is a wage earner in Tuba City and who operates the store after his job hours and on weekends, i.e., when the stores in Tuba City are closed. Most of the active labor force in Moenkopi is engaged in wagework in Tuba City and there is a minor rush-hour traffic jam on the two-mile stretch of the highway between Tuba City and Moenkopi every weekday.

The scope of communitywide activities is limited. Kachina ceremonies (see page 145) and social dances are given annually by both Upper and Lower Moenkopi, and the initiation ceremony to the Kachina society occurs once every two years. Although the number of ceremonies in Moenkopi has declined in recent years, as has the number of participants, initiations occupy the most important aspect of community life at present. Otherwise the only institution of communitywide significance is the Moenkopi Day School, whose function, however, was recently curtailed to the first four years of grade-school, the remainder of schooling being given in Tuba City. The influence of the two churches in Moenkopi is minimal. The Upper Moenkopi village council has been active in a number of community projects, in which participation is limited to a small core of supporting households. Due to the predominance of wagework and the decentralization of irrigation systems (Nagata 1970:135–137), one project in particular — cooperative labor for the maintenance of irrigation reservoirs and canals — has degenerated into a token activity of a few politically conscious members of the community. A major burden of social control in Moenkopi is now carried by the Navajo tribal police in Tuba City.

There is, therefore, an overall tendency for the people of Moenkopi to withdraw to their own households, limiting their interactions within the community to small circles of their own relatives. Disregarding the difference between the two segments for the moment (Kunitz, *et al.* 1970), what stands out in contemporary Moenkopi is the increase in domestic consumption directed toward household improvements. Most households are equipped with refrigerators, gas ranges, and — in a majority of Upper Moenkopi homes and in half the Lower Moenkopi homes — electric lights. Running water is available for all households, and in Upper Moenkopi, inside water supply and bath and flush toilet facilities are common. A majority of Upper Moenkopi houses have two rooms or more, some two-storied, while others are being added to. Automobiles, though still the single major item that strains household finances, are considered by most Moenkopi Hopi as indispensable. Vacuum cleaners, washing machines, gas heaters, and radio-phonographs, sometimes even stereo-phonographs, have been purchased by a number of households. One Upper Moenkopi family subscribes to a telephone service and a small number receive off-reservation newspapers.

At the same time as people are endeavoring to improve their home life, they are being drawn into social activities in Tuba City. Many are regular clients of the weekly movie shows at the Navajo community center, Moenkopi teenagers frequent dance parties there, and both adults and children take part in sports events conducted at a playground and the community center. Rummage sales, bake sales, and other social events given by churches, public schools, and numerous occupational groups attract the Hopi to Tuba City. Thus, while the life in Moenkopi is less exciting, Tuba City appears to compensate for its lack of activities.

The suburban type of living in contemporary Moenkopi is largely determined by its relationship to Tuba City and Flagstaff. In the early decades of this century, when the agency ran a school farm, many Hopi commuted the two miles from Moenkopi to Tuba City on foot to earn wages as farm laborers. Since

1950, Tuba City has assumed a critical position for the development of the western part of the Navajo reservation through the implementation of the Navajo-Hopi Rehabilitation Act. The agency at Tuba City was charged with the task of developing not only the community at Tuba but also a number of newly emerging small communities in the outlying area. The growth of Tuba· City was accelerated further by the U.S. Public Health Service, the Navajo tribe, state public schools, church missions, and private businesses. Tuba City's location is strategically close to such tourist spots as Monument Valley and Betatekin ruins, and the Navajo Trail passes close by. Another highway, leading to Hopiland proper and Keams Canyon, starts at Tuba City. The community also possesses a plentiful supply of underground water. All these factors have contributed to the current expansion of service industries in Tuba City, from which the Moenkopi Hopi have doubly profited: they are not only the recipients of most of these services but are also hired to provide them.

Flagstaff (population, 25,000) is about seventy miles from Moenkopi on State Highway 64 and U.S. Highway 89, or approximately two hours' drive by automobile. In contrast to the Hopi of Hopiland proper, to whom the towns of Holbrook and Winslow on U.S. Highway 66 have been important, the Moenkopi Hopi and the agency at Tuba City have depended on Flagstaff for provisions and mail delivery. Flagstaff is now known for its tourism and as an access point to the Grand Canyon, although it also contains lumber and ranch industries (Kelly and Cramer 1966:11), a state university, a museum, a well-known observatory, and a NASA laboratory. A number of Moenkopi Hopi families migrated to Flagstaff and particularly to Bellmont, about ten miles west of Flagstaff, where the Navajo Ordnance Depot, an army establishment, hired a large number of Indians during World War II and the Korean War.

To the people of northeastern Arizona, Flagstaff remains important as a supply center; it is in this context that the Moenkopi Hopi most frequently visit the city. Flagstaff has made it possible for them to avail themselves of numerous material comforts with the wages they earn at Tuba City. In the following sections, the relationship that the Moenkopi Hopi maintain with the two communities is examined in greater detail.

MOENKOPI AS PART OF "GREATER TUBA"

Because Tuba City is unincorporated, it is almost impossible to assess its population. Broadly, the land basis of this agency town is under control of the federal government, the Navajo tribe, and a few Anglo individuals. No Indian-owned land allotment exists in Tuba City. A majority of the private business establishments in the town operate through lease arrangements with the Navajo tribe.

The pattern of residential distribution in Tuba City closely parallels the distribution of service agencies. On one major street, about half a mile long, that runs through Tuba City, the important public and private establishments from north to south are: public schools, U.S. Public Health Service, BIA, churches, a trading post and other private buildings, a post office, and a complex belonging to the Navajo tribe. Both the bureau and U.S. Public Health Service, along with their respective housing areas, stand on government land and are referred to as the "government compound." At the junction of State Highways 64 and 264, which the main street eventually joins, are a supermarket and two gas stations and garages. Except for the bureau, which maintains housing scattered throughout Tuba, all housing for employees is within walking distance of their places of work.

A large tract between the tribal complex and the highway junction, especially on the east side of the street, has been dotted with the homes of Navajo wage workers at Tuba City. The settlement in this part of Tuba City is a postwar development, generally referred to as South Tuba (Levy 1962a, 1962b). It is characterized by various house-types (Bosch 1961:19), lacking an overall design. Aside from its land status, this is the only significant area of private housing in Tuba City.

The area in and around the government compound is fairly densely built up. Many families of the public school and U.S. Public Health Service employees live in single-storied multiplex buildings. House trailers, one of the common types of dwelling, are used by the public school and bureau employee families in two delimited blocks in the north of the town. A trading post maintains a trailer court, whose serviced lots in 1963 were mostly taken up by the families of construction workers for a complex of new Navajo boarding schools. Large, single-family dwellings are limited to the Public Health Service medical doctors living along two short, back streets and a small number of bureau employees scattered along the major street. While housing in Tuba City is certainly not sufficient, there does not seem to be acute over-crowding in any living quarter in the town.

Although automobile traffic is rather heavy at certain times of the day, there are no parking meters nor traffic signals, but there is a low speed-limit zone in the core section of the town. Except for a white bureau officer and a Navajo judge, the car commuters are generally the South Tuba Navajo and Moenkopi Hopi workers.

The size of the present population in the government compound numbers approximately 2,000, while that of South Tuba in 1960 was counted to be 360 (Levy 1962a:797). If the 650 persons in Moenkopi are included, the population of Tuba City and Moenkopi reaches about 3,000. Spicer remarks that the population of the agency town varies from several hundred to two thousand or more (1962a:469). The population of Tuba City and Moenkopi thus reaches the upper limit.[3] Disregarding the land in use by the residents of Tuba City and Moenkopi for grazing and farming purposes, the area on which the two settlements stand may not amount to more than ten square miles. Although this is a tentative estimate, the population density of 300 per square mile is almost a hundred times as large as that of the Navajo Reservation as a whole (Shepardson and Hammond 1970:13). Admittedly, these figures far from qualify Tuba City as "urban" (Anderson 1968); however, Tuba City possesses other characteristics of the "urban way of life."

Heterogeneity. One of the remarkable urban features of Tuba City is the racial, ethnic, and occupational heterogeneity of the population. Against the majority of Indian and white residents, in 1962–63 there were Negroes, Spanish-Americans, Orientals (Japanese and Filipino), and one Eskimo. The ethnic diversity is

---

[3] The exact population is difficult to determine for agency towns. In 1959, a total of 1,721 was reported for Fort Defiance (Bosch 1961:13). Fruitland, whose relationship to the border town of Farmington is somewhat similar to Moenkopi's relationship to Tuba City, had a Navajo population of 1,182 in 1955 (Sasaki 1960:6). Further, Wilson reports that about half the population of the Jicarilla Apache live in company with non-Indians in the agency town of Dulce, New Mexico (1964:317).

striking, and the tribal origins of the Indian residents are disparate, e.g., Choctaw, Comanche, Sioux, San Juan, and Zuñi. Among the whites, there were Jewish,[4] Irish, Portuguese, and Dutch origins represented, if only by a single individual or family. Indeed, the racial-ethnic diversity of Tuba City is so complex that to call it a small town with the current image of a homogeneous, rural community is a misnomer.

As in any reservation community, Tuba City has a number of churches (Catholic, Presbyterian, Baptist), which both Indian and non-Indian residents attend. Others commute to Mormon and Mennonite churches in Moenkopi. In 1962–63, the family of a Bahai public schoolteacher was resident and active in mission work.

The numerous occupations in Tuba City include those of schoolteacher, doctor, clergyman, policeman, judge, postmaster, engineer, agronomist, trader, restaurant and supermarket manager, cattle dealer, garage mechanic, nurse, secretary, store clerk, school matron, bus and truck driver, gas station and laundromat attendant, cook, barber, janitor, night watchman, and an assortment of construction tradesmen and others among the bureau employees. Although not clear in the above enumeration, it first is noteworthy that a majority of these occupations are civil-service positions, the inevitable result of Tuba City's being an agency town. Contemporary Tuba City differs significantly from that of the old days, however, in that the bureau is no longer the single major agency; the U.S. Public Health Service, the Navajo tribe, and state public schools vie as employers with it. Second, the list of occupations shows the preponderance of service trades and professions. In striking contrast to the Tuba City of the Mormon period, there are no farmers or ranchers, the occupations that today constitute the "rural" base of Tuba City on the reservation. In recent years the image of Tuba City as a "dispenser of charity," in the words of the geographer Herbert E. Gregory (1915:117; also see Nagata 1970:36), has been accentuated.

---

[4] During my fieldwork, thanks to an anthropologist in Tuba City, I took part in a passover rite given at the home of a Jewish doctor. During my residence in Tuba, I rented a trailer from an Irish Catholic priest, and then moved to a house trailer next to the families of a Baptist preacher and a Spanish-American lather.

In spite of these heterogeneities in the Tuba City population, there is an overall simplicity in the system of social stratification. It consists mainly of non-Indian professionals earning salaries and Indian laborers earning wages. This division broadly coincides with what is here called the division between professional and client populations. The former is generally transient; the latter is not.

This stratification is being modified in two directions. One change involves a small group of business-operating "Anglo" families who have been long resident in Tuba City. One family runs the oldest trading post, a motel, a trailer court, and a gas station; the head of the family is a postmaster, and the wife was a member of the Tuba City school board. If Merton's typology of community leadership (1957) is applied to Tuba City, this family occupies the position of "locals" in contrast with government professionals who are "cosmopolitans."

The second source of modification comprises those Navajos who enter the rank of professionals, such as the Navajo officers of the Land Board, Grazing Committee, Tuba City Chapter, Community Center, and tribal council, and members of the Navajo school board and Lions Club. In contrast to the simple Indian/non-Indian stratification of the past, the present system is characterized by the emergence of Navajo bureaucratic elites and "local" leaders, Indian or non-Indian. The future of Tuba City as an autonomous town depends much on the growth of the Indian leaders.

Division of Labor. Related to the occupational diversity is the degree to which the people depend on others in their daily activities. No resident in Tuba City is self-sufficient, whereas the Mormon pioneers a century ago were, to a large degree. The average family in town sends children to the public schools, worships in a church, obtains daily provisions at a store, occasionally eats at a restaurant, finds entertainment at the community center, borrows books at a public library that visits Tuba City twice a week, and goes to the public health service hospital. The head of the family may work in one of the government agencies. The family may use a Laundromat, and its refuse may be disposed of by the bureau. Social control is no longer based upon a deep sense of community solidarity nor on an internalized set of norms cultivated through a slow process of socialization. The Navajo tribal police enforce the law.

While the interdependence of the people is considerable, the town far from satisfies all their needs. Commodities for daily consumption are not unlimited in Tuba, and sometimes one has to drive out as far as Flagstaff, for example, to get a fresh piece of pork. The legal restriction of liquor on the reservation sets the tone of town life. Some of the existing services are not easily available nor of an acceptable standard, and many whites go to Flagstaff and other off-reservation cities to get their cars serviced or to dine out.

Unlike the Mormon pioneers, who depended greatly on their own forbearance and improvisation to live self-sufficiently in Tuba City, today's residents readily travel to Flagstaff to make up the shortcomings of the agency town. Unlike peasants who may regard cities with fear and suspicion, they tend to be weary of isolation in the small town and to seek recreation in visits to border towns and more distant cities.

Segmentalization of Roles. Occupational heterogeneity and interdependence contribute to the fragmentation of an integrated, total "status" into a bundle of simplex roles and "contracts" between persons. This aspect of life in Tuba City is obvious from the foregoing. On the other hand, social relationships in the community are largely stereotyped and categorized by race and occupation. Contexts of interaction, rather than subjects, determine the quality of relationship, which is generally superficial. Except for occupational circles, people seldom know other residents by name. Many Moenkopi Hopi, who have much to do with daily Tuba City life, are ignorant of the name of the subagency superintendent, though they all not only know the Hopi agency superintendent's name but also passionately like or dislike him.

A few individuals in Tuba City have become well known among the residents. Both Indian and non-Indians are familiar with the long-resident family that runs the trading post and a supermarket manager who makes his home in Sedona. But the superintendent, hospital administrator, and public school principals, all holding the highest governmental positions in Tuba City, are not well known except in their occupational circles. The Moenkopi Hopi often refer to the doctors at the public health service hospital by name in contrast to their unfamiliarity with bureau officers.

The superficiality of human relationship is compounded by the high mobility of a majority of Tuba City residents. They are transients serving a hitch in the town. Due partly to the legal restrictions on land ownership, home ownership is almost nil and Louis Wirth's statement is directly applicable to Tuba: "Overwhelmingly the city-dweller is not a homeowner" (Reiss 1964:76). Except in South Tuba, homes, where owned, are mostly trailers.

The impression of impersonality must not be exaggerated, however. First, the division between client Indians and professional non-Indians introduces a bias in favor of the Indians regarding certain services available. Land use, livestock ownership, and free medical care are the major services either restricted or inaccessible to non-Indians. As one white resident remarked, the non-Indians are discriminated against in Tuba City. Client status is legally closed to non-Indians. Finally, for certain labor contracts, preference is given to the Navajo Indians (Nagata 1970:190). Consequently there is a tendency for emerging new roles to be concentrated among local Navajo residents. Among the non-Indians, the trading post family, mentioned above, alone appears to play multiplex roles in Tuba City. This suggests that while the old agency community, in which a small corps of the bureau personnel assumed multifarious roles, is being disintegrated by the differentiation of service agencies and intrusion of specialist groups, the local Navajo residents are being recruited to a few areas of community leadership, and provide the locus for the continuity and solidarity of a new community.

The bias against the professional non-Indians does not bring about solidarity among them, and occupational differences tend to divide them further. This is one reason why the term "Anglos" in reference to white residents, seldom used in Tuba City, is wrong. The solidarity of each occupational group is indicated in the pattern of residential distribution. Sports teams (basketball and baseball) and evening social events are often organized independently by the people working for the public health service, or the bureau, or the public schools. Between the Indians and non-Indians, informal friendships and marriage — though this is rare — result from occupational contexts. These small professional "communities" are a potent factor in mitigating the cleavage between the Indians and non-Indians.

A number of voluntary associations have memberships that minimize occupational cleavages and the division between client and professional populations: the Sportsmen's Club, Boy Scouts, 4-H Clubs, church and hospital auxiliaries, and the Lions Club. Generally, white residents dominate these associations in membership as well as in leadership. Although the degree of Indian participation is still limited, the associations play an important role for the promotion of community solidarity.

Tuba City subagency serves Land Management districts 1, 2, 3, 5, and 8, covering six million acres of the Navajo reservation. For its location in district 3, outside of the Hopi district (district 6), land matters pertaining to Moenkopi (farm land except land allotments and grazing) come under the jurisdiction of the Tuba City subagency and the Navajo tribe. Public school education beyond the first four years is available for Moenkopi children only at Tuba City. Navajo tribal police in Tuba deal with the cases of misdemeanor and traffic violation of the Hopi in Moenkopi. In addition to these, the Navajo tribal court at Tuba handles disputes involving the Navajo and Moenkopi Hopi, cases that could also be heard at the Hopi court at Keams Canyon. Finally, the public health service hospital at Tuba City deals with Moenkopi for certain immediate and practical public health problems, including mass inoculation. These are the formal linkages between Moenkopi and Tuba City.

More pervasive is the informal nexus of Moenkopi to this agency town. Because of this special connection of Moenkopi, it seems appropriate to call the social sphere consisting of the two communities "greater Tuba." [5] First, Moenkopi is a labor reservoir for the service industries of Tuba City. Members of the Moenkopi labor force have certain advantages over that of the Navajo on the reservation "rural" base: they are relatively stable and concentrated in proximity to Tuba, they have a higher

[5] The expression was used by the public health service staff on the occasion of mass inoculation in 1963 and was meant to include not only Moenkopi but also Moenave, a small community fifteen miles west of Tuba City. For the present purpose, Moenave, which is not particularly different from other "rural" Navajo communities in the environs of Tuba City, is excluded.

quality of education and reliability, and they are somewhat more aggressive, partly because of their minority position on the Navajo reservation. Currently, more than half the active laborers of Moenkopi are engaged in wage work in the agency town.

In addition to being clients of the governmental services in Tuba, the Moenkopi Hopi patronize private businesses there for their daily needs. A portion of their wages, therefore, flows back to Tuba, but not all.[6] Already noted is the participation by the Moenkopi Hopi in recreational activities of Tuba City that involve cash expenditures. In short, the Moenkopi economy is closely tied to Tuba's through production and, to a lesser extent, through consumption.

Secondly, Tuba City has absorbed a number of community functions from Moenkopi, apparent in the formal linkages of the two settlements. Important life-cycle events of the Moenkopi Hopi occur in Tuba City: birth at the hospital, graduation from school, death at the hospital, and burial at the community graveyard. Only the initiation ceremony to the Kachina society and a series of Kachina ceremonies remain unique and important to Moenkopi, although many Moenkopi Hopi now go to other villages of Hopiland proper to take part in these and other rituals.[7]

As a consequence of this socioeconomic dependence upon Tuba City, Moenkopi is no longer a self-sufficient and autonomous "community" but a settlement in which the communal spirit of cooperation is low and individual households are somewhat atomized. Can Moenkopi be regarded as a peasant community, since it is part of "Greater Tuba" and a majority of Moenkopi wage laborers are also engaged in small-scale farming? Probably not, since Moenkopi agriculture is not productive enough even for subsistence. The land basis of Moenkopi is excluded from the national money economy by reservation control of the land. Finally, Tuba City controls not the agricultural products of the Moenkopi Hopi, but their labor.

[6] This is a sore point between the Navajo and Hopi tribal councils. The Navajo tribe receives royalties from these business establishments in the form of permits and land leases, but the Hopi tribe does not, in spite of Moenkopi's contribution as clients to these establishments.

[7] Hair-washing ceremonies at the first naming of babies are still frequently conducted within Moenkopi. As for burial, there is a division — the Moenkopi graveyard serves only those whose deaths occurred within Moenkopi.

A previous work (Nagata 1970:291–295, 314–315) describes the integrative pattern of contemporary Moenkopi to Tuba City as "suburban." Intensive participation in wage labor and administrative services in Tuba City has resulted in Moenkopi's surrender of many of its community functions, the increasing importance of individual households, limited specialization of economic skills and occupational diversity, indifference to community interests and weakening of community solidarity, and growing reliance upon the means of social control outside Moenkopi. These are the features of social life shared by many city suburbs.

These characterizations, however, miss one significant aspect of Moenkopi. Whatever surface similarity may exist between Moenkopi and any city suburb, the village is the product of a series of administrative decisions that have been coerced upon it through the control of the reservation by the government. In this respect, the present socioeconomic status of Moenkopi is essentially determined by the institutional linkages that the larger society extends to Tuba City and from Tuba to Moenkopi. This administrative integration of Moenkopi to the larger society by the federal government, through the instrument of the reservation, places the village in a position of powerlessness and dependence vis-à-vis American society. The result of this dominance by the larger society is the present "suburban" or "post-peasant" life of Moenkopi (see Jorgensen in this volume).[8]

The dependence of Moenkopi upon the larger society is also seen in the way the Hopi villagers spend money to buy household necessities in Tuba City and Flagstaff. Of the two places, Flagstaff has been assuming greater importance as a shopping center for the Moenkopi Hopi. Especially since it has become accessible by automobile, an increasing number of Hopi have been attracted to this border town and exposed to its way of life.

MOENKOPI AND FLAGSTAFF

Moenkopi has been a migration-oriented settlement since its origin. As a "colony," it has received immigrants from Hopiland

[8] For this view of reservation society I am indebted to Steward (1950, 1955:53), Spicer (1962b:526), and Carstens (1966, 1968, 1970, 1971).

proper, but it has also produced many emigrants to off-reservation cities and recently to new reservation communities. Flagstaff is one city where a number of Moenkopi Hopi have settled since World War II. Kelly and Cramer have already given a general outline of the life of the Indians, including Moenkopi Hopi, in this city (1966). This section, rather than showing the pattern of migration from Moenkopi and the life of the Moenkopi migrants in Flagstaff, concentrates on how the Hopi who remain and live in Moenkopi view Flagstaff and how they utilize the institutions in Flagstaff.

The Image of "Town." To the Moenkopi Hopi, Flagstaff is their "town." One of the first Hopi expressions I learned is, *"Um ka town aoni"* ("Aren't you going to town?" i.e., Flagstaff). Such English phrases as "going to town" and "shopping in town" are also in common usage.

In the minds of many younger Hopi, Flagstaff is a place of fun and excitement with movie shows, restaurants, bars, and the annual powwows, and a place where they can escape the scrutiny of their relatives and meet friends and old acquaintances. In contrast, life in Moenkopi is unexciting. One Moenkopi nurse confided why she wanted to leave Moenkopi: "It is boring, sweeping the house, doing laundry, and cooking."

Flagstaff is a meeting place for the Indians. Especially during the powwow season, the Hopi run into old classmates from off-reservation boarding schools, army "buddies," and former colleagues in migration labor camps. While meeting these people and exchanging gossip in bars and the powwow grounds, the Hopi learn what is going on among other Indians and reaffirm the value of their reservation life. The following story serves as an illustration:

> Several years ago, Anita went to the powwow and was surprised to be called by a miserable-looking Indian woman resting in the shade of a tree. "How are you, Anita? Don't you remember me?" she asked. As it turned out, she was Anita's close Ute schoolmate when they were both in the Sherman Institute in California. Giving the reason for her present miseries, this friend explained to Anita how her tribe had lost its land to the white man and how quickly the money obtained through the land was

gone. "So, Anita, don't sell that land!" she said. Anita remarked that a once beautiful girl now looked horrible. This girl was now making a living as a prostitute.

To the younger Moenkopi Hopi, Flagstaff is an open arena for individual escapades and adventures and where the Hopi cease to be Hopi and are simply "Indian." In this urban environment, the finer differences of tribal customs and practices among the Indians are not given meaningful expression, but all the Indians merge into a single category (Indian), irrespective of their tribal origins. The Hopi, who are aware of such a shift in their identification, take advantage of this fact and amuse themselves by playacting a "dumb Navajo" or a "drunken Paiute" in Flagstaff. The ease of crossing tribal boundaries in town because the significant audience, the whites, are unaware of these, also encourages the Hopi to make closer contacts with other Indians. These contacts are often colored with a touch of adventure: one of the frequent topics about "town" among the young males of Moenkopi is the sexual and trading exploits of non-Hopi Indians on their visits to Flagstaff.

The suspension of rigid tribal identities in Flagstaff is related to another view of "town" commonly held among the migrants. Many migrants and young Moenkopi Hopi remarked, "You don't have to fight always when you are in town," or "Your relatives don't bug you in Flagstaff." During my visits to Flagstaff with Hopi families, it was surprising to see how often the Hopi who were not on easy speaking terms in Moenkopi exchanged greetings gracefully and chatted in a friendly manner. Political antagonists, who are afraid of being seen together in Moenkopi, drink in the same company at a bar in Flagstaff. The urban context thus appears to relax hostilities and political differences maintained in Moenkopi.

This loss of Hopi identity and lack of customary constraints over certain types of behavior in Flagstaff is the reason for the negative image of "town" held by the older people of Moenkopi. The main ingredients of this image are liquor, sex, fights, thefts, police, and jail. This image reflects misgivings about a place where vice often defeats virtue, and license affronts status integrity.

While Flagstaff is viewed with varying moral connotations, the prevalent outlook among the Moenkopi Hopi is practical and determined by Flagstaff's economic function as a town for shopping. The Hopi attitude toward the town in this respect is sophisticated: major shops are noted by names, and information regarding their relative merits and special sales is constantly exchanged by Moenkopi housewives. The Hopi do not conceive of the whites there as a stereotype, but as differentiated groups of individuals, some of whom are friends (*pahankwachi*). In particular, there seems little evidence to indicate the Hopi view of Flagstaff as the white man's town. In the synthesis of their image, they include the institutions and contexts of the city that they frequently use, and avoid including in it the other aspects they do not participate in because they fear prejudice (Aberle 1969:242). Thus their image is relatively inarticulate regarding tense race relationships in Flagstaff, expensive restaurants and hotels, certain cultural activities, and new public developments. In short, the separateness of the Indian-white relationships in Flagstaff contributes to the absence of the whites as an ever-recurring element in the Hopi image of Flagstaff.

Visiting Town. No Hopi, living in Moenkopi, commutes to Flagstaff for a regular job. Occasionally some Hopi may be seen standing outside the bars and on the street corners of Flagstaff peddling Kachina dolls or Hopi sashes among the Indians and white tourists. This peddling seems especially common around the period of the Kachina initiation ceremony, which usually incurs a considerable financial outlay and yet is limited to the Hopi from Hopiland proper. The Moenkopi Hopi seldom engage in peddling in Flagstaff (Nagata 1970:200).

While Flagstaff performs a number of functions other than economic, the single major context in which most Moenkopi visit the town is for the purpose of shopping. The frequency of visits varies according to the individual family, the season of the year, and, of course, the availability of cash. A few families, including the one I lived with, go to town almost every weekend during the warmer part of the year. This is the maximum amount of visits; the majority of families make one or two visits a month. Older residents tend to venture out to town only occasionally (for instance, for Christmas shopping). Some young householders are prudent enough to calculate the advantage of shopping in Flagstaff over Tuba City where prices are usually slightly higher. Most people shop in town soon after payday and have their checks cashed at various supermarkets. Saturday is the favorite shopping day because husbands can drive their wives to town. Moenkopi becomes strikingly empty of people during the weekends since their major activities consist of shopping in Flagstaff, attending ceremonies in other villages, or tending farms or livestock.

Apart from shopping, the Hopi have little to do in Flagstaff. Visiting bars is strongly disapproved of by the Hopi as a whole, and because shopping is usually a family affair, Hopi shoppers seldom drop in bars. Drinking and disorderly conduct have been reported to be caused not so much by the resident Indians as by visiting Indians from the reservation (McPhee 1953:11, 49, 57). While there are no quantitative data to confirm this report about the Moenkopi Hopi, most of the drinking troubles at Flagstaff that I encountered or heard about were committed by the young male Hopi, married or unmarried, who had come individually to town because they felt frustrated at home or at work.

While on shopping trips in town, the Hopi usually park their cars at a supermarket lot in the center of the downtown section. On Saturdays in better seasons of the year, this lot becomes a point where the Hopi shoppers and their families converge; the men idle in their cars, gossiping with other Hopi while waiting for their wives. In contrast to the cities of Winslow and Gallup which have rest places for Indian visitors from the reservation, Flagstaff maintains a campground where both Indian and non-Indian visitors can stay for visits of more than a day. An Indian rest house in Flagstaff is still in the planning stage. Although there are a public library and a movie theater in the downtown district, the Moenkopi Hopi seldom take advantage of them.

The only public facility the Hopi use in town is the restaurant. Eating out during a shopping day is a popular pastime among the Moenkopi Hopi, who patronize reasonably priced restaurants, know them by name, and use them as meeting places. The majority of them serve either Chinese-American or Mexican-American dishes, the latter being the Hopi favorite. Indians seem to shy away from the numerous fancy hotel or motel restaurants in

Flagstaff.[9] There does not seem to be a tendency for certain restaurants to be patronized by particular tribes.[10]

Hopi shoppers also frequently visit relatives and white friends in town. These visits are often announced ahead and appear to be a source of embarrassment to the hosts. Perhaps because the Moenkopi Hopi are aware of this, their visits are usually brief and consist mainly of exchanging gossip, drinking coffee, and watching television. The Hopi visitors also bring such farm products as corn and melons to their relatives in town and, when there are children in the hosts' homes, give a little money to them. On these visits, the Moenkopi Hopi inquire about jobs in town and admire home furnishings not seen on the reservation. These visits provide an opportunity for the Hopi to learn more about urban living.

Thus, shopping in Flagstaff is a practical business to the Moenkopi Hopi. They may eat at restaurants or visit relatives, but their main excitement in coming to town is being treated on equal terms with white shoppers as an individual consumer amid the affluent display of department stores. For a family of five, the average amount spent on a shopping trip is fifty dollars, covering groceries, hardware, household equipment, and occasionally automobile parts. Although groceries and small household items, to a lesser extent, are also purchased at the trading posts and the supermarket in Tuba City, such commodities as automobiles, which call for large expenditures, are available only in Flagstaff. Payment for these goods is seldom made out of household savings, usually too small in the average Moenkopi household to cover this type of expenditure. Instead, the Hopi obtain loans from financing institutions in Flagstaff, so in this context Flagstaff assumes its unique position in the economy of Moenkopi.

[9] For a treat I once took a young couple to such a restaurant; the Hopi wife said that the only time she had been there was when she came to town with a white public school teacher for whom she had been babysitting. Quite by accident, her mother passed by, spotted us in the restaurant and came in. She remarked, "I was wondering if this could be a place Indians could go in."

[10] Racial and ethnic segregation is noticeable in the two bars on the south side of the Santa Fe Railway, which are mainly patronized by Indians and Negroes.

The Moenkopi Hopi use finance companies in Flagstaff mostly to borrow funds for automobiles, tractors, refrigerators, washing machines, and (less often) tuition to send children to higher educational institutions. Occasionally white salesmen drift into Upper Moenkopi and sell consumer durables like vacuum cleaners on installment plans.

The use of off-reservation financial loans by the Indians of Arizona did not begin until the mid-1950's. Before this, the Hopi had access to a system of revolving funds set up with government assistance at the time of the Indian Reorganization Act; otherwise they were under the credit control of local stores and trading posts. With the general improvement of economic conditions on the reservation, however, the level of economic aspiration of the Hopi and Navajo Indians rose higher and the need for cash grew stronger. To meet this need, the credit restriction against the Indians was relaxed; off-reservation finance institutions now extend loans against the securities of regular employment or livestock (Nagata 1970:201). As these loans became possible, credit control by local trading posts for Indians has been gradually replaced by that from off-reservation finance institutions. For the Hopi and the Navajo, this control is exerted by the institutions in the border towns along U.S. Highway 66.[11]

While the use of off-reservation loans is common, it appears to be accompanied by many problems. Kelly and Cramer report that their sample of loan companies in Flagstaff regard the Hopi as better credit risks than the Navajo, and the reservation Indians as riskier than the resident Indians in town (1966:39–40). On the other hand, I heard a few bank and finance company managers report favorably on the credit standing of the Moenkopi Hopi. Pressure is exerted in a number of ways to maintain good credit records among the Hopi. First, finance companies to which both the Hopi and Navajo resort for loans are well aware of the credit standing of Indians in the major towns along

[11] It is doubtful if on-reservation banks could improve the financial standing of the Navajo and Hopi Indians. As of 1970, there were at least three banks at Window Rock, Shiprock, and Tuba City. These three are branches of off-reservation banks with controlling interests in the hands of non-Indians. A mutual savings association based on voluntary subscription, however, operates in Tuba City; its members include not only Indian and non-Indian residents of Tuba City, but some Hopi as well.

Highway 66. Secondly, the Moenkopi Hopi fear the consequences of delinquent accounts that may take the form of gossip and slander. When one is in financial trouble, therefore, much effort is made to avert it, and mobilization of the kinship network occurs. To illustrate these points, an extended account follows from my fieldnotes about a young Hopi from Shongopavy who married a Moenkopi girl and resided at her parents' home. (For the genealogical relationships of the personalities in the episode, see Figure 3.1.)

October 2, Wednesday

Toward the evening, Bill Watson came up to my trailer in Tuba City and asked me to bring John Scott (his son-in-law) and his wife Mary back from Shongopavy. While working at school today, Bill had a telephone call from a finance company in Flagstaff about the delayed payment of John's loan. About 8 P.M., when I was preparing to leave for Shongopavy, John suddenly showed up and said Bill had told him to come up here right away when he returned. I invited him in and he started telling me about his frustrations with his in-laws: they did not believe in Hopi religion, though they talk about it; they have not "washed" the hair of any of Jim's kids and yet they were already "teasing" them, etc. I told him why Bill wanted me to go after him, and John said he now understood what it was all about; he said when he went to Bill's, his father-in-law was talking about some policeman coming in.

John's explanation of the problem was not quite comprehensive, however. He had bought one car, a Buick, but he later turned it in for a 1956 Plymouth station wagon with the money financed by the Friendly Finance Co. of Flagstaff around August. The amount loaned was about $700, used to pay for the insurance, the title, and the car itself. He bought both cars at Sinclair Autos of Flagstaff.

John said that there were two back payments amounting to $80, and that the Friendly Finance Co. was after this. But there was a complication: soon after the purchase of the Plymouth, the Scotts, John's parents, borrowed the car because their unpaid-for pick-up truck had been disabled, and took it to Flagstaff. Then a piston broke down and they got it fixed at Sinclair's. John went in later and found that the repairs cost $267.64, and the bill, which he showed me, was dated April 16. Sinclair had overhauled the engine and put in a "new used

Figure 3.1

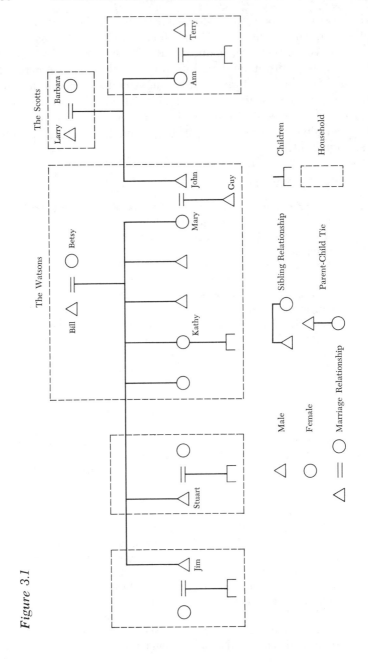

one." Now John couldn't pay, and so he had come back without the car, which is still at Sinclair's.

After John told me all this, we decided to go down to the Watsons to discuss the matter. Everybody was there and Bill said that he was prepared to cover the back payment and that Stuart, one of his sons, could continue the rest on the condition that the car belong to the Watsons and the repair bill be paid by the Scotts or John, or both. I suggested the possibility of giving it up, but Kathy, John's sister-in-law, said it might hurt John's credit standing. Bill added that he did not want to lose close to $400 already paid and that Stuart thought his car was getting too old and wouldn't mind having a new one. John and I then decided to go to Flagstaff tomorrow anyway just to find out what we could do. I came back to my trailer with John and Mary and suggested to them that I was willing to loan $40 to John if it was of any use and if John could return it by October 11. Mary was willing to borrow and said that it would at least please Bill, but John was reluctant and said he thought he would not be able to return it so soon. I told them to think it over till tomorrow and took them back to Moenkopi.

October 3, Thursday

In the morning, I picked up Mary in Moenkopi and went to a gas station in Tuba City, where John's father, Larry,[12] works. John was there, working with Larry and another Upper Moenkopi man on the car that belongs to Terry, John's brother-in-law, and that John has been using. When we were about to leave, Larry said he would be able to pay $40 and took out two $20 bills from a wallet, but John said he should wait and so Larry gave John a $5 bill instead.

We got to town a little past noon and ate first at a restaurant. Then we went to the Friendly Finance Co., but Mr. Parsons, who made the loan, was "out at a Lions meeting" and we were received by another man, who had placed the call to Bill. He told us little, however, asking us to come back at 1:30 P.M. for Mr. Parsons and refusing to explain what he himself spoke of as "further actions." So we decided to see about the repair bill at Sinclair's.

The sales manager was there and John explained the purpose of our visit. Perhaps encouraged by my presence, the manager gave a tedious lecture on the Indian people who refuse to take

[12] Larry and his wife Barbara are from Shongopavy, temporarily residing in Moenkopi for Larry's work.

responsibilities, while accepting the white man's convenience; John remained mute. Then the manager asked John about his prospect of employment, which was none. I asked if the manager could make some arrangement for an installment payment, suggesting $80 down and $25 a month to be paid in full within ten months. I had in mind Larry's $40 and my $40 loan. A fat, aggressive looking salesman was standing by us and eavesdropping on our conversation. At John's mention of his father's name, he suddenly butted in and said Larry Scott's credit standing was very poor, to which I countered by pointing out that Larry had been carrying a loan from a Winslow bank, had only $150 to go, and had been a regular employee at a gas station in Tuba City. But the fat man said that Sinclair's had inquired in Winslow about that, and there Larry also turned out to be bad. Luckily for us, the manager came out on our side and accepted the installment plan anyway. He said that Larry must come in to sign for the contract and that then we could take the car — with no storage charge.

We went back to the Friendly Finance Co. On the way, Mary bought a local newspaper. Mr. Parsons was there. He was young, friendly, but spoke too fast. Besides, I could not understand complicated subjects like "prerogative of transferring a loan to the interest bearing," etc. I remained as silent as John, who was clutching the newspaper in his hand. Guy, their adopted baby, began crying and Mary had to go out to calm him. I gathered my courage and bluntly asked about the consequence of giving up the whole thing. Parsons said the company would pay Sinclair for the repair bill out of the money obtained through the auction sale of the car and collect whatever deficit remained from the co-signer, who was Bill.

"But, John, couldn't you find a job?" asked Parsons.

"You see the paper in his hand?" I retorted.

"Oh, you're looking for one," he said.

I then explained to Parsons the possibility of paying $80, the back payment. He seemed to be relieved but told us that (for some reasons beyond my comprehension) the $80 would not cover the back payment which amounted to $129 or so. I gave up and suggested to John that we should come back tomorrow.

Back at Tuba, John and Mary asked me to take them to Bob's supermarket, where they wanted to see the manager about a job, but he was not there. I took them to the Scotts, who served us supper. John explained to Larry what happened, but Larry said he could not provide $40 any more because a man from a

Winslow bank had come in today and he had to give him fifty odd dollars for his back pay. Barbara, John's mother, made an insinuating remark: "Terry throws money at Ann [John's sister] when he comes back from work." [13] Mary brought up the possibility that Jim, another of her brothers, might take over the repair bill, for he had not gotten a car, but since he had already left for Kayenta, Jim was not available to agree to this.

I asked John if he could get some help from Ann, but Barbara said she had too many bills to pay. I asked Larry when he thought he could make some money, but he remained silent. His present loan is for the pick-up that has been in a Moenkopi man's garage since last winter when "a piston was broken." To encourage the company, Barbara said she would make a hundred baskets and pay off all the debts, and a woman in Moenkopi had already asked her to make fifty baskets for sale. I asked John and Mary to show me their loan book and contract papers, but they said they were in the car; all they could produce was the repair bill. We seemed to get nowhere, and I decided to leave for the Watsons.

Bill was already in bed but Betsy, his wife, woke him up. I told him that Larry could not cover the repair bill, and Bill said he had expected that; for he had known Larry was unable to get a loan from just about anywhere, and now Larry had to make payments not only to the bank in Winslow but to a Tuba City trading post and a store at Shongopavy. However, Bill's credit is impeccable in Flagstaff, and as I found out today, his loan from the Friendly Finance Co. in 1958 was paid in full. I told him what happened in Flagstaff and said there was no prospect of bringing the car. Bill said that it was all right as long as the Scotts were to answer for the bill. John, who presently joined us, said they would. We then decided to go to town tomorrow afternoon.

October 4, Friday

In the late morning, we left for Flagstaff, Bill and his family in their pick-up and John and myself in my car. As soon as we got to town, Bill said the pick-up's battery was not charging, so we left it in a trailer court I knew and drove in my car. First we ate at a cafe; then the Watsons left for the Family Finance Co., Bill's finance company. John said he wanted to go to Sinclair's. I was rather surprised at the spontaneity of his decision, and we

[13] Terry and Ann live in Shongopavy.

all agreed to go with him. We did not have to wait long this time, and as soon as John, Mary, and I were settled there, the sales manager appeared. At the sight of the manager, however, John appeared to lose his courage and, nervously holding a cigarette in his fingers, started to speak. After John's halting story, the manager asked, "What can I do for you, then?" John sat silent. "We want the whole deal postponed," I said. The manager asked when the Scotts could make a down payment, and John said Larry would come around the fifteenth. The manager agreed to wait till then, and we left Sinclair's.

The Watsons were not at the Friendly yet, so John and I decided to walk around the town, leaving Mary and Guy at the car. While we were walking, we heard a siren, which reminded John of the forest fire-fighting. He said that although they had given him a fighter's card, there was not any fire and they had not called him yet. Crossing a street, John bought a local newspaper and a pack of cigarettes at a blind veteran's booth. We went back to the car; John found a want-ad for a janitor in the paper and went to a hotel to make a phone call. The call was unproductive as the advertiser wanted a local man who had lived in town for six months at least, but he told John that he might contact him if local recruitment failed. John said he left his post office box number with him. I asked John if he did not prefer a job around Tuba, but he said if he could not find a job there, he would go anywhere. While waiting for the Watsons, John spotted three young Hopi standing by a furniture store across a street and went to chat with them. They were waiting for a ride to Phoenix. John came back and told me that they had the same problem as John since they did not belong to the bricklayers' union and were about to be expelled from a current job. John has been unable to join the construction laborers' union in spite of his repeated attempts. It was already 4:30 P.M. when we finally sighted the Watsons walking toward the Friendly Finance Co.

At the Friendly, Bill began the talk by telling Mr. Parsons about Stuart and the possibility of his continuing the payment with a new record, which Parsons said might be too expensive. Bill also wanted to know if the title of the car could be transferred, but Parsons said it was not an immediate question. This time Mr. Parsons tried to impress upon Bill his responsibility as a co-signer but the conversation seemed to end in non sequitur. Bill brought up the question of adjusting Stuart's monthly payment. Parsons said he would rather do it when Stuart came in, and handed to Bill his card, suggesting that he make a collect call as soon as the trip was arranged. The transaction went on, but I left the tiny office, wishing the Watsons the best. Shortly afterward, Bill and the others came out but without having made the payment of $80, which his wife Betsy discreetly pointed out to Bill. The $80 in cash was part of a loan he had obtained from the Family Finance Co. — that was why he had taken so long to meet us.

Back at the trailer court, we worried whether Bill's old GMC pick-up truck would start. Somehow it did, and Bill drove it to a nearby garage to fix it. A white mechanic told Bill of trouble with the generator and suggested he overhaul it; Bill told him to go ahead and fix it. I was shocked and immediately asked the mechanic how much the whole thing would cost. "About $28." I looked at Bill, who nodded understandingly. When the repair was done, Betsy paid for it out of her purse, and then we all went to her sister's house in East Flagstaff. Only the children were there, and we watched TV briefly. After a while, I bade them goodbye; Bill insisted that I go to see a movie with them, but I declined. He said they would stay overnight in Flagstaff and then, tomorrow morning, take the Fort Valley Road to the Grand Canyon to see if the piñons were ready to be collected. John remained silent all this while.

November 16, Saturday

Finally Stuart brought John's Plymouth. Mary said the deal was concluded as follows: Stuart paid $100, Bill $30, Larry $30, and John $40. John made $40 out of three weeks' work in October repairing the roof of a home belonging to the Watsons' relatives in Flagstaff. When Stuart went to town today, however, the people John worked for could give only $10 in cash. So Stuart had to get an additional $100 from a finance company in Flagstaff. In any case, the Sinclair agreed to let the car go if they paid $200 within thirty days and to cancel the rest of the bill. John now owes $30 to Stuart. How much Stuart owes to the finance company, I do not know.

MOENKOPI AS HOME FOR EMIGRANTS

What significance the home communities on the reservation hold for their emigrants is important in a comparison of urbanization on the reservation with migration to cities when the former is suggested as the preferable alternative. A variety of circumstances causes emigrants to return to Moenkopi, and the frequency of returning emigrants naturally varies with geographical distance. Seldom, however, do they abandon Moenkopi for good.

Among the factors causing return are the emigrants' familiarity with the social environment and their readiness to recruit assistance of relatives. A young wife, who had moved into a rented house in Flagstaff with her children in order to care for her Shipaulovi husband who was working for the state highway department, could not take the lonely hours in town; she often went back to Moenkopi during the weekdays after sending her husband to work and would get back to town in time to pick him up after work. In order to alleviate such loneliness, it is common for emigrant families to have some kin from Moenkopi living with them, as this particular family did later.

Life in Moenkopi possesses certain economic advantages: the Indians on the reservation are exempt from land and property taxes and receive free medical services from the U.S. Public Health Service. Some emigrants in Flagstaff visit the Tuba City hospital for this reason. A young man who had an auto accident in Phoenix returned to Moenkopi with his wife and children for treatment; soon after recovery, he took his family back to Phoenix. Thus Moenkopi provides a refuge for young emigrants in temporary distress.

Some emigrants return to Moenkopi to tend their farms. Sale of farmlands is not customary among the Moenkopi Hopi; consequently, when they leave Moenkopi, many emigrants either make arrangements to have friends and relatives work their land, or simply leave it uncultivated. Those emigrants living in the environs of Moenkopi, however, come back to plant and to harvest crops. A similar situation prevails regarding the emigrants' house property; no house, to my knowledge, has been sold to other Moenkopi Hopi by emigrants, who either rent their houses or leave them vacant in readiness for their return to the community.[14] Thus, the emigrants seldom surrender the material basis of their residence in Moenkopi.[15]

[14] Some houses in Lower Moenkopi were sold, however, by people who moved to new houses in Upper Moenkopi.

[15] In contrast to other ethnic migrants (Manners 1965, Philpott 1968), the Hopi emigrants do not send regular remittances to their relatives in Moenkopi. The absence of this remittance custom among the Hopi is due mainly to their tendency to migrate as individual families and to the fact that a married couple is the unit of cash disposal (Nagata 1970:204). According to a recent and reliable estimate, out of 150 money orders handled at the Tuba City Post Office, about 95 percent more are deposited than are received, and these are mostly for payments and mail-order purchases by both

By far the most important context for the emigrants' return is ceremonial. Hopi religious practices act as a powerful magnet to attract widely dispersed emigrants. During the early summer when the Kachina ceremonies are given, emigrants return to Moenkopi; they stay with their relatives, exchange gifts, and watch dances at the plaza. Partly to accommodate the demands of wagework, many religious activities are held on weekends, and some ceremonies during the tourist season are announced by local newspapers.

Many emigrants also take part in the ceremonies. Extended time is necessary for preparation, so their participation is limited to those who can afford to travel to Moenkopi in the evenings after work or those who are taking long vacations there. The Moenkopi Hopi show little reluctance to let them in, and, on the whole, welcome their participation. An example of this took place one weekend in the early fall of 1962. A group of male emigrants in Flagstaff and some Hopi of Upper Moenkopi formed two troupes for the performance of an unmasked social dance; then they presented a series of dances, each troupe appearing alternately. As the dances progressed, an element of competition emerged between the two groups, and the songs and dances became increasingly enthusiastic. This type of "ceremonial exchange" has not been observed in either Lower Moenkopi or Hopiland proper. Whatever occasioned this form of exchange,[16] it has been a common practice for some emigrants in Flagstaff to cooperate with Upper Moenkopi in social dances (Nagata 1970:75). The people are concerned with maintaining ties between Moenkopi and its emigrants, and acknowledge this in their ceremonial activities.

Of all the ceremonies, initiation to the Kachina cult bears a special significance to the emigrants. This *rite de passage,* at present given once every two years toward the end of January

---

the Navajo and Hopi Indians. One family in Upper Moenkopi used to send monthly allowances to a son in a college, and during my fieldwork, another family mailed remittances to a daughter; sometimes the Moenkopi Hopi send money orders to their emigrant relatives to help in an unexpected financial outlay. But such instances are not common.

[16] It was rumored in Moenkopi that this was to make up for the fact the Hopi had not taken part in the powwow in Flagstaff that year. Whatever the reason, the participants were active supporters of the Upper Moenkopi Council.

and beginning of February, initiates the Hopi children to the Kachina and Powamu societies and confers upon them the privilege of participating in the rituals of the Kachina cult. In the traditional religious system, the tribal initiation (Titiev 1944, Eggan 1950) legitimated full adult status for the Hopi by initiation to the Wuwuchim society. Recently the tribal initiation has been suspended in many major villages, and there is a tendency for the Kachina initiation to take over the legitimating function of tribal status. While this is a complex problem, factionalism between the tribal council and those against it appears partly responsible for the shift. Many council people condemn a number of traditional cults as dangerous and destructive (*Navajo Times* July 22, 1965) and hold the Kachina cult as the only admissible religious practice. By this assertion they counter their antagonists' argument that the council is deserting the Hopi way of life by abandoning religion. Consequently, both the council and its opposition now place a renewed emphasis on the Kachina initiation.

Emigrants even from such distant cities as Los Angeles and Oakland return to Moenkopi so their children can be initiated. They arrange their work schedules to make this visit, write their relatives in Moenkopi to have godparents selected for their children, and sometimes send money to relatives to prepare ceremonial foodstuff. For many children, the occasion provides their first opportunity to visit Hopiland and experience Hopi life; since they were born and brought up in off-reservation cities, their first language is often English and they often cannot speak Hopi. For example, at Hotevilla in 1963, two daughters of a Hopi mother and an Apache father, who were brought up as Christians in Phoenix, were initiated along with two half-Navajo children. During the initiation period, children are given new Hopi names by godparents after a hair-washing ritual, are introduced to the tribal mysteries in a kiva, or subterranean ceremonial chamber, and are whipped by *hö:kachina's*. After this, as a boy remarked to his younger sister who had just been initiated, "*Um pai ka piu kahopi*" ("You are no longer *kahopi*"). The initiands are reborn as Hopi.

The ceremony lasts about a week if one attends the kiva feasts after the initiation ritual, the parade of Kachinas, and the

Powamu dances in the kivas at night. Usually, however, visitors leave as soon as the initiation ritual is over. During this week, all Hopiland stirs with activities. It is as if the Hopi, scattered in many parts of the United States, gathered in their respective villages for a brief moment and experienced the value of being Hopi. Emigrants, who otherwise may be lost in the white man's cities, renew their identity and pride in being Hopi and transfer these values to their offspring through the initiation ritual.[17]

Perhaps because the home community continues to hold such meaning, many emigrants are actively concerned with the political condition of Moenkopi. Moenkopi emigrants seem to compensate for their alienation from local politics in alien communities by having arguments on tribal politics among themselves. The emigrants' interest in reservation politics as a whole is further encouraged when the tribal council proceeds with plans to receive royalties from industries invited onto the reservation. Upper Moenkopi village council meetings are often convened in the presence of visiting emigrants (Nagata 1970:75), some of whom return expressly to attend these meetings.[18]

URBANIZATION ON THE RESERVATION

In conclusion, there seems little doubt that the major reason for urban migration of Hopi Indians is the economic one. In spite of relative improvements in recent times (Kennard 1965), Hopiland proper is no exception to the general pattern of economically underdeveloped Indian reservations throughout the country: "a growing population but a young one, a decreasing and already inadequate land base . . . , high unemployment, low incomes"

[17] Although infrequently practiced at present, there is also a complex of passage rites for a Hopi about to embark on a journey. A prayer feather is made for a Hopi leaving the village, and corn flour is sprinkled in the direction of his destination. Upon his return, he has his hair washed by the women of his paternal clan, and worships the sun at dawn. A Hopi village is thus not only a place of residence but a moral community.

[18] For example, a Hopi journeyman plumber, who lived in Phoenix many years and worked as a foreman in a number of construction projects both on and off the reservation, was elected as chairman of the Hopi tribal council in 1963. A somewhat similar case was the election to chairmanship of the Navajo tribal council of a man who used to be an off-reservation resident. Active participation by returning emigrants in reservation politics is not limited to these two cases.

(Brophy and Aberle 1966:67).[19] In spite of the growing demand for money, acquired through limited contacts with the national economy and encouraged by the government to "civilize" the Hopi, cash-producing opportunities are so limited on the reservation that they have little alternative but to migrate. To the Hopi, urban migration is not a matter of choice but a necessity forced upon them.

Urban migration also entails the abandonment of the Indian identity when the emigrants submit to the domination of the white American culture and economy. A Shongopavy song, composed by the women of the Marau society as a jest toward their male counterparts in the Wuwuchim society and sung in public, states the problem succinctly:

> Sikyapki no longer wants to go back to Sedona
> For he wishes not to live the white man's way
> But he is still working for the white man
> To pay the bills he has made on credit.

Cultural and economic degradation, an outcome so frequently attendant to Indian migration to large cities, may give an added urgency to the possibility of developing the reservation economy. Urbanization on the reservation must be considered from the perspective of eliminating poverty and restoring the dignity of the American Indians.

The preceding discussion has explored the case of Hopi Indians in Moenkopi and their relationships to Tuba City, Flagstaff, and emigrants from Moenkopi. Tuba City and Moenkopi, called "Greater Tuba," have been presented as a new type of reservation community with a few characteristics of urban life. Shiprock (the site of the Northern Navajo subagency), Fort Defiance–Window Rock (where the Navajo tribal council and the

---

[19] The 1968 survey of income distribution, conducted by the Hopi tribal council, gives 44.6 percent of 1,755 Hopi on the reservation, sixteen years or older, as earning less than $1,000, while 83 percent of this population earn less than $1,600 (Hopi Indian Agency, personal communication). The infant mortality rate for the Keams Canyon Service Unit (Hopi) of the U.S. Public Health Service between 1964 and 1968, is reported to be 28.8 per 1,000 (Indian Health Area Office, U.S. Public Health Service, personal communication). This seems close to the national rate (27.1 in 1958) and very low in comparison to the national Indian rate (58.5 in 1957–59) (Brophy and Aberle 1966:163, 227). I suspect the Keams data are based only on the births that occurred in the hospital.

general Navajo agency are located), and probably Chinle and Crownpoint are further examples of this type of community on the Navajo reservation. Still more examples may be found on other reservations;[20] they are what Spicer called "agency towns" (1962a:468) and what Levy (1962a) and Shepardson and Hammond (1964) called "transitional reservation communities."

All these communities are the sites of federal, state, and tribal agencies and include an assortment of Christian missionaries and private enterprises. Their industry is service-oriented (administrative, medical, and educational), from which a majority of residents derive their primary income. The resident population is heterogeneous in race, ethnicity, and occupation, and a considerable portion of it is transient. In spite of the heterogeneity of the population and the decentralization of administrative power in these communities, the division between the client population of Indians and the professional population of mainly non-Indians permeates many aspects of community life.

Living conditions in these communities are relatively better than in the reservation hinterland. Basic utilities of electricity and running water are available. There are garbage and sewage disposal services. Various programs of public entertainment are also provided. Lured partly by the better condition of life and partly by the availability of more economic opportunities, settlements of Indian wage earners have emerged close to the original agency complexes and now constitute satellite components of these agency towns. More important is the fact that a number of Indian emigrants to off-reservation cities returned to these towns on the reservation as they saw an opportunity of combining the material advantages of cities within their own cultural context (Hodge 1969:5, 27). This is particularly true in Upper Moenkopi where a few returnees tended to spread the urban style of life to other residents. There is a strong likelihood that should the economic opportunities of these communities expand, the influx of migrants from the reservation hinterland will be as much as that from off-reservation cities.

The characteristics of the agency towns contrast sharply with those of agency communities of the past which consisted of a small corps of Anglo bureau personnel, "agency Indians" (Kluck-

[20] See footnote 3.

hohn and Leighton 1948:106; Spicer 1962a:356), a trader, and a missionary. These communities were under the domination of superintendents who were the sole loci of authority. Out of paternalistic concern to protect their Indian wards, the super-intendents generally discouraged contact with non-Indians off the reservation; hence, the agency communities tended to be tightknit outposts of civilization, isolated from off-reservation cities except for mail delivery and acquisition of agency provisions. Employment opportunities were extremely limited for the Indians, whose primary productive activities were directed toward subsistence. Aside from Indian employment, in which Tuba City agency was unique (Nagata 1970:176–178), the agency community of Tuba City continued to be characterized by these traits until World War II.

To the Hopi and Navajo Indians of today, the agency towns occupy only one segment of their social orbit (Hodge 1969:25ff.). On the western part of the Navajo reservation, the hinterland or "traditional" communities are exemplified by Navajo Mountain and Shonto. The Navajo Mountain community (Shepardson and Hammond 1964, 1970), about eighty-five miles north of Tuba City, consists of two trading posts, a day school, and a mission station which act as contact agents in the community, with about six hundred Navajos engaged in sheep-herding, subsistence farming, and occasional wagework. Due to extreme isolation, the people of Navajo Mountain live in a kinship-based system of interaction and derive more than half their income from sheep-herding. Wagework is limited to a small number of full-time positions in the school, the Navajo tribal council, and occasional projects introduced by outside agencies (Shepardson and Hammond 1970:114–115).

Shonto lies about forty miles northeast of Tuba City (Adams 1963). Initially a trading post, today Shonto includes a day school, a mission, and a half dozen Navajo employee families that form the core settlement of the community. Except for occupational contexts, the white residents seldom interact with the Navajo; for social activities, the whites usually go to off-reservation towns. For them, "Shonto is not a community but a job" (Adams 1963:166). The Navajo around the settlement make their living by sheep-herding on the reservation and by seasonal railroad work off the reservation, which accounts for more than half their income. Their earnings are tied to the Shonto trading post through its credit control. The flow of Indian incomes in Shonto, therefore, is the reverse of that in Tuba City: income is derived from outside the reservation and consumed within it. Because of the paucity of spending opportunities and the isolation from the regional market centered in Flagstaff, consumption in Shonto takes the form of luxury spending (Adams 1963:140; Nagata 1970:208). These conditions, coupled with the lack of occupational differentiation, tend to reinforce the undifferentiated, "rural" character of Shonto.

As Tuba City grows and the trip becomes less difficult, the Navajo and the Hopi in the reservation hinterland visit Tuba City more frequently and tend to be less dependent upon local trading posts.

Outside the reservation, the agency towns are tied to border towns and the more distant cities of Arizona and New Mexico. In spite of relative improvements in economic conditions, Greater Tuba, Shiprock, and Fort Defiance-Window Rock, all depend upon Flagstaff, Farmington, and Gallup, respectively, for purposes of shopping, financing, and "drinking" (Bosch 1961:28–31). The economy of these border towns depends on Indian clients or tourists. Aside from a small number of extractive industries, therefore, the border towns are as much service-oriented in their economy as agency towns, and the businessmen of the two communities compete for Indian income (Aberle 1969:242).

Further away from the reservation are the white man's cities, where the Indians may go to high schools or work as more-or-less permanent residents. In both the state capitals of Albuquerque and Phoenix, the bureau and U.S. Public Health Service maintain area offices that deal with the overall administration of the Indians of the Southwest and issue directives to respective offices in the agency towns.

Along this chain from the isolated, "traditional" community on the reservation to the state capital, and finally to Washington, D.C., the agency communities occupy a position that connects the reservation society to the larger American society. As Spicer states, they "constituted a level of integration intermediate between the Indian and the nearest cities" (1962a:468).

Growth of agency towns is mainly a result of the administrative fiat by federal government and tribal councils for reservation development. In contrast to off-reservation cities, therefore, these towns have an air of artificiality, of an externally forced design for living. Such an atmosphere is already apparent in some of the economic and political characteristics of the towns.

First, in Greater Tuba there is no large commodity-producing industry. A uranium mill, which opened about ten miles east of Tuba City in 1958, was recently shut down. The significant Indian private industry is raising livestock, which is, however, restricted from expansion by conservation measures of the Navajo tribal council and the poor forage of the grazing land. Secondly, in the variety of private service occupations of Greater Tuba, the number of Indian entrepreneurs is extremely small in comparison to that of non-Indians. In Tuba City proper, a restaurant and a barber shop are the only Indian private enterprises. It may be argued that this is due to the lack of entrepreneurial initiatives among the Indians, but this is not the case (Nagata 1970:198, 297–298). The more important factors are lack of sufficient commercial capital and managerial skills that can effectively compete with non-Indian businesses.

To supply these missing factors, the Navajo tribal council has assumed a greater responsibility; it now runs motel-restaurants in Window Rock, Shiprock, and Chinle, and the tribal sawmill near Fort Defiance, the Window Rock Coalmine, the Arts and Crafts Guild, and the Monument Valley Tribal Park (Young 1961:183, 190, 347; Aberle 1969:254–255, 259). However, the general policy of the Navajo tribal council has been to withdraw from direct investment in, and management of, enterprises and to attract private industries to the reservation through mutually satisfactory arrangements (Young 1961:191). This orientation of the tribal council appears to depress the initiatives of potential Navajo entrepreneurs who are further confronted with the maze of tribal bureaucracy to obtain support and financial backing (Brugge and Levy, personal communication).

The Navajo Tribal Utility Authority was created in 1959 with the aim of providing utility services on the reservation and bringing industries into it. Except for the Shiprock area where the tribe maintains an extensive irrigation system and many Navajo engage in cash farming (Aberle 1969:264), individual Indian enterprise is almost nonexistent on the Navajo reservation. In the western part of the Navajo reservation where industrializa-

tion lagged behind the eastern and northern parts, even the tribal
enterprise is limited to a branch office of the tribal utility
authority and a warehouse of the tribal sawmill. Although there
are still a dozen or so small Hopi stores and white trading posts
in Hopiland proper, their number will probably be reduced as
the Hopi tribal council, following the general strategy of the
Navajo, invites private industries to enter Hopiland [21] and as the
Hopi prefer to spend an increased income in larger commercial
centers.

As Aberle pointed out (1969), this strategy of "leasing" cannot
be regarded as either optimal or equitable to the Indian interests.
Perhaps the most questionable of all is the lack of Indian control over industries invited to operate on the reservation. These
industries consist mainly of gas, oil, and electric companies and
a number of defense-oriented light manufacturing plants. The
operational needs of these large corporations are basically determined without much concern over the long-term future of the
Indians so that, in the case of mineral companies, the exploitation of the reservation natural resources may come in serious
conflict with Indian welfare. Further, these and perhaps the
defense-oriented plants receive certain tax incentives to operate
on the reservation (Aberle 1969:240, 256). In spite of these in-
equities, Aberle suspects that the federal government is unwilling
to encourage tribal industries that may compete with large
private corporations (1969:240).

The near absence of Indian entrepreneurs on the reservation is
related to the predominance of wagework in Indian productive
activities. The service industry of Greater Tuba employs Indian
wage labor. However much occupational differentiation there is
among Indian workers, it is limited to blue-collar occupations.
Further the tribal law prohibits the unionization of Indian labor
on the reservation (Aberle 1969:257); hence, in Greater Tuba,
unionized labor is confined to private construction trades in
which the Moenkopi Hopi are numerous. Indian labor in Greater
Tuba is thus not as mobile as unionized labor but is tied to the
government and dependent upon it (Nagata 1970:190). In spite
of the unitary class position of Indian workers in the agency

[21] Contracts have recently been made with the Brown Co. to hire the
Hopi in an underwear manufacturing factory and with the Black Coal
Co. to strip mine in Hopiland (Clemmer 1969:26).

town, they are isolated from the working-class people of the nation.

Greater Tuba has no government of its own but a patchwork of various administrative agencies. For example, consider the utility services. The bureau supplies water to itself and the public health service hospital and the residence of their employees in the government compound. The public school has its own wells and distribution system which can be connected with the bureau if necessary. The Navajo tribe operates its own system for the tribal complex and South Tuba. Private residence and business establishments are dependent on either of the two systems, while the Catholic and Mormon churches and a trading post use their own wells. The system of sewer canals is divided between the bureau and the tribe, although all the sewage is eventually disposed of in the lagoons maintained by the Navajo Tribal Utility Authority.

Moenkopi, on the other hand, has its own water and sewer systems. As for electricity, a private utility company services the government compound, private establishments, and Moenkopi, while the tribal utility authority covers the tribal complex and South Tuba. Garbage disposal is handled by the bureau for Tuba City but not for South Tuba and Moenkopi. The confusing state of the present utility services in Greater Tuba may be a passing phase and, as with Fort Defiance and Window Rock, the Navajo Tribal Utility Authority may assume the full responsibility for all segments of Greater Tuba in the near future. However, this is unlikely as the Hopi village of Moenkopi will strongly resist such incorporation into the Navajo tribe.

Greater Tuba is thus confronted with the need for a "metropolitan government." However, this is made extremely difficult because of diversity in the land control of the area and of Moenkopi. The administrative problem of Greater Tuba is further compounded by the fact that its development has largely been directed by the bureau and Navajo and Hopi tribal councils, whose jurisdictional responsibilities are not confined to Greater Tuba alone. While this pattern permitted a relatively balanced development throughout the Navajo and Hopi reservations, it is doubtless discouraging the rise of grass-roots concern with the town (Aberle 1970:273).

A still incipient growth of community leadership is related to the foregoing comments. A majority of the leadership positions occupied by Navajo individuals in Tuba City are "intrusive" roles in the political system of the reservation (Shepardson and Hammond 1970:21). The officers of the community center, the judge of the Navajo tribal court, and the captain of the tribal police are all appointed by the tribal council. The officers of the Tuba City chapter, land board, and grazing committee are elective. However, the constituencies of these political positions are not restricted to the people of Greater Tuba but include the "rural" Navajo in the environs. The Moenkopi Hopi are subject to the jurisdiction of the land board and grazing committee but cannot vote in the election of their members (Nagata 1970:59–60). Thus it is difficult to see these offices as being rooted in the community.

Further, there is a potential conflict over available leadership positions between the local Navajo, who have been long settled in Tuba City or its direct vicinity, and those who migrated to the town to assume government or tribal posts. Generally the latter group of Navajo are more acculturated and often have some experience in urban living. Hodge characterizes them as "Anglo-modified" (1969:4–5). Many are as much transients as non-Indian professionals. Perhaps because of their better educational background and technical competence, these "cosmopolitan" Navajo tend to dominate such local positions of the tribal bureaucracy as the directorship of the community center (Levy, personal communication). The chapter leadership thus far comes from the people of the "rural" area (Levy 1962a:796, 798). The lack of leadership from the grass roots of Greater Tuba is also apparent in the composition of the school board.

Perhaps the Tuba City school board is the only administrative organization relevant to Greater Tuba as a whole. In theory, all school board members are elected by the registered Indian and non-Indian voters of the district, whose overwhelming majority consists of Tuba City and Moenkopi residents. In the early 1960's, however, three non-Indians were appointed to the board. They were one uranium mill worker, a wife of the local trader, and a captain of the Navajo police. At present, the board members consist of three Navajos and two non-Indians. The Navajo members are not officers of Tuba City chapter but one of them is a former tribal employee with a college degree, while another is a "traditional" from the rural environs of Tuba City. The last Navajo member is a former bureau employee, who lived in Tuba City presumably before the Depression and yet appears to have little connection with the "rural" Navajo. The non-Indian members are a trader and a school superintendent. It appears, then, that the present board consists of two "cosmopolitans," Navajo and non-Navajo, one rural Navajo and two Tuba City "locals," Navajo and non-Navajo. It is obvious that Indian leadership, based on the community of Greater Tuba, is yet to emerge.[22]

In sum, the administration of Greater Tuba is executed by mutually uncoordinated agencies, the jurisdictional powers of which are externally derived. In contrast to small rural towns, Greater Tuba, like other agency towns on the reservation, depends for its existence upon multifarious institutional linkages with the outside world. In spite of their small size, therefore, all the agency towns possess a touch of cosmopolitan atmosphere.

The concentration of industry on welfare service and the ad hoc administration by the "intrusive" agencies place the agency towns in a class similar to the administrative cities of the ancient Orient (Weber 1950:90, 128, 272; 1962:91; 1964:13ff.) and, more recently, Washington, D.C., where some years ago the people had no franchise nor organization to determine their operation. The Indians' life is largely dictated by the demands of the larger society, which are mostly unknown to the Indians and seldom relevant (Shepardson and Hammond 1970:163).[23] Since they are unable to mold the community by themselves, the Indians are uncertain of its future and afraid to commit themselves to it.

The overall consequence of the development of Greater Tuba was to displace the Hopi and Navajo Indians to the position of wage laborers. It is not a secure position, however. Layoffs and unemployment are fairly common and the Hopi income is often characterized by the diversity of its sources (Nagata 1970:194; Carstens 1966:60ff.). The insecurity of political and economic

---

[22] The situation appears fairly similar in other school boards on the reservation. Although the exact backgrounds are obscure, the board in Window Rock includes three Navajo residents in the town. What clearly emerges in the board membership is the almost invariable presence of local non-Indian traders (Brugge, personal communication).

[23] ". . . the very existence of Indian organizations is now dependent on the pleasure of Congress" (Price 1969:192).

conditions in the agency town reinforces Hopi adherence to subsistence farming and unprofitable grazing (Nagata 1970:219),
thus making "occupational versatility" an indispensable survival
strategy (Carstens 1970) and "efficient specialization . . . impossible" (Aberle 1969:245). The stage that urbanization has
reached in Greater Tuba is one in which the Indians relate to
the town as proletarian peasants without the right to decide its
future. If the Moenkopi Hopi have succeeded in evading either
the material deprivation of the reservation hinterland or the fate
of being an uprooted urban minority, they have yet to achieve
the freedom and independence often characteristic of urban
citizens.

BIBLIOGRAPHY

Aberle, David F.
    1969   "A Plan for Navajo Economic Development." In *Toward Eco-
            nomic Development for Native American Communities.* Joint
            Economic Committee, U.S. Cong., 91st sess., vol. 1. Washing-
            ton, D.C.: U.S. Printing Office.
Adams, William Y.
    1963   *Shonto: A Study of the Role of the Trader in a Modern Navajo
            Community.* Washington, D.C.: Bureau of American Ethnol-
            ogy, Bulletin 188.
Anderson, Theodore R.
    1968   "Comparative Urban Structure." *International Encyclopaedia of
            the Social Sciences.* Vol. 2. New York: Free Press of Glencoe.
Bosch, James W.
    1961   *Fort Defiance: A Navajo Community in Transition.* Vol. 1.
            Window Rock, Ariz.: Navajo Tribe.
Brophy, William A., and Sophie D. Aberle
    1966   *The Indian: America's Unfinished Business.* Norman: Univer-
            sity of Oklahoma Press.
Carstens, Peter
    1966   *The Social Structure of a Cape Colored Reserve.* Cape Town:
            Oxford University Press.
    1968   "Mission Station to Small Town: The Development of a Rural
            Cape Colored Community." Paper delivered at the annual
            meetings of the Rural Sociological Society, Boston.
    1970   "Hobson's Choice and Poverty with Particular Reference to a
            South African Reserve." *Canadian Journal of African Studies,*
            vol. 4, no. 1.
    1971   "Coercion and Change." In *Change and Conflict in Canadian
            Society,* R. J. Offenberg (ed.). Scarborough, Ont.: Prentice-Hall
            (in press).

Clemmer, Richard
  1969   "The Fed-Up Hopi: Resistance of the American Indian and
            the Silence of the Good Anthropologists." *Journal of the
            Steward Anthropological Society* 1:18–40.
Dobyns, Henry F.
  1968   "Therapeutic Experience of Responsible Democracy." In *The
            American Indian Today*, Stuart Levine and Nancy O. Lurie
            (eds.). Deland, Fla.: Everett/Edwards.
Eggan, Fred
  1950   *Social Organization of the Western Pueblos*. Chicago: University
            of Chicago Press.
Gregory, Herbert E.
  1915   "The Oasis of Tuba, Arizona." *Annals of the Association of
            American Geographers* 5:110–119. Chicago.
Hodge, William H.
  1969   "The Albuquerque Navajos." *Anthropological Papers of the
            University of Arizona*, no. 11. Tucson.
Kelly, Roger E., and John O. Cramer
  1966   "American Indians in Small Cities." *Rehabilitation Monographs*,
            no. 1. Flagstaff: Northern Arizona University.
Kennard, Edward A.
  1965   "Postwar Economic Changes among the Hopi." *Proceedings of
            the 1965 Annual Spring Meetings of the American Ethnological
            Society*. Seattle.
Kluckhohn, Clyde, and Dorothea Leighton
  1948   *The Navajo*. Cambridge, Mass.: Harvard University Press.
Kunitz, Stephen J., *et al.*
  1969   "Effect of Improved Sanitary Facilities on Infant Diarrhea in
            a Hopi Village." *Public Health Reports* 84:1093–1097.
Levy, Jerrold E.
  1962a   "Community Organization of the Western Navajo." *American
            Anthropologist* 64:781–801.
  1962b   "South Tuba: A Western Navajo Wage Work Community."
            Paper presented before the annual meeting of the American
            Anthropological Association, Chicago. MS, Ethnology Papers,
            Window Rock, Field Office, USPHS.
Mackenzie, Kent
  1959–61   *The Exiles* (a film). Los Angeles: University of California.
McPhee, J. C. (ed.)
  1953   *Indians in Non-Indian Communities*. Window Rock, Ariz.:
            Welfare-Placement Branch U.S. Indian Service. Mimeographed.
Manners, Robert A.
  1965   "Remittances and the Unit of Analysis in Anthropological Re-
            searches." *Southwestern Journal of Anthropology* 21:179–195.
Merton, Robert K.
  1957   *Social Theory and Social Structure*. Glencoe, Ill.: Free Press.
Nagata, Shuichi
  1970   *Modern Transformations of Moenkopi Pueblo*. Urbana: Univer-
            sity of Illinois Press.
Navajo Times
  1965   July 22, 1965, vol. 6, no. 29. Window Rock, Ariz.

Philpott, Stuart B.
 1968 "Remittance Obligations, Social Networks and Choice among Montserrat Migrants in Britain." *Man* 3:465–476.
Price, Melvin E.
 1969 "Lawyers on the Reservation: Some Implications for the Legal Profession." In *Toward Economic Development for Native American Communities.* Joint Economic Committee, U.S. Cong., 91st sess., vol. 1. Washington, D.C.: U.S. Government Printing Office.
Reiss, Albert J., Jr. (ed.)
 1964 *Louis Wirth on Cities and Social Life.* Chicago: University of Chicago Press.
Sasaki, Tom T.
 1960 *Fruitland, New Mexico: A Navajo Community in Transition.* Ithaca, N.Y.: Cornell University Press.
Shepardson, Mary, and Blodwen Hammond
 1964 "Change and Persistence in an Isolated Navajo Community." *American Anthropologist* 66:1029–1050.
 1970 *The Navajo Mountain Community.* University of California Press.
Spicer, Edward H.
 1962a *Cycles of Conquest: The Impact of Spain, Mexico and the United States on the Indians of the Southwest, 1533–1960.* Tucson: University of Arizona Press.
 1962b *Perspectives in American Indian Culture Change.* Chicago: University of Chicago Press.
Steward, Julian H.
 1950 *Area Research: Theory and Practice.* New York: Social Science Research Council, Bulletin 63.
 1955 *Theory of Culture Change.* Urbana: University of Illinois Press.
Titiev, Mischa
 1944 "Old Oraibi." *Papers of the Peabody Museum of American Archaeology and Ethnology* 22:1–277. Cambridge, Mass.: Harvard University Press.
Weber, Max
 1958 *The Religion of India.* Glencoe, Ill.: Free Press.
 1962 *The City.* New York: Collier Books.
 1964 *The Religion of China.* New York: Free Press of Glencoe.
Wilson, H. Clyde
 1964 "Jicarilla Apache Political and Economic Structures." *University of California Publications in American Archaeology and Ethnology* 48:297–360. Berkeley and Los Angeles: University of California Press.
Woodbury, Richard B., and Natalie F. S. Woodbury
 1964 "The Changing Patterns of Papago Land Use." *Proceedings of the XXXVth International Congress of Americanists,* Mexico, 1962. Mexico City.
Young, Robert W. (ed.)
 1961 *The Navajo Yearbook, Report No. 8, 1951–61: A Decade of Progress.* Window Rock, Ariz.: Navajo Agency.

PART 2   **life in the city**

INTRODUCTION

While Part 1 of this book concentrates on the influences of an urban society upon Indians living on reservations or in other nonurban communities, the five chapters in Part 2 are concerned with the quality of the lives of those Indians who live in cities. These chapters employ various approaches to describe American Indians in urban settings and focus on various aspects of city life. Merwyn S. Garbarino gives an impression of Indian life in Chicago. The chapters by Peter Z. Snyder, Robert S. Weppner, and Theodore D. Graves utilize rigid research design and quantification of data, and each concentrates on some particular aspect of the lives of Navajo migrants to Denver. Frank C. Miller deals with a unique case in education, the development of the De-

161

partment of American Indian Studies at the University of Minnesota in Minneapolis.

In "Life in the City: Chicago," Merwyn S. Garbarino draws upon her experience as a volunteer case worker for the American Indian Center in Chicago. Her aim is not to concentrate on any particular tribal group or any specific problem or process of adjustment to urban life, but to show the flavor of life as it is lived by American Indians in a major American city.

In contrast to the three chapters that follow, Garbarino's approach is impressionistic and nonstatistical, but one which, in her words, "will hopefully be an accurate impression, based upon long-time, intimate contact and friendship, as well as scheduled interviews and pointed discussions." Instead of testing hypotheses or presenting probabilistic models of behavior, Garbarino prefers to let the Indians of Chicago speak for themselves, and as a result her essay is liberally laced with quotes gleaned from interviews and conversations with Indians in Chicago.

With ninety to one hundred tribal groups of American Indians contributing approximately 12,000 individuals to the population of Chicago, Garbarino feels that it is useless to generalize about the "urban Indian" and his way of life, but writes that "the adjustment patterns, recreation behavior, employment, and education expectations vary as much for people classified as Indians as similar expectations vary for the general population moving from nonurban to urban life." Indeed, the question of the existence of an "urban Indian way of life" is one of the issues raised by this book. We urge the reader to ask himself, as he reads Garbarino's description of Chicago Indians, whether or not they react any differently from Blacks, Puerto Ricans, Poles, Italians, or Appalachian whites in their problems with housing, education, and marriage.

Peter Z. Snyder's chapter, "The Social Environment of the Urban Indian," focuses on the associational networks of Navajo Indians in Denver, and is based on both survey and ethnographic research. Snyder is concerned with documenting the interpersonal contacts made by Navajos in Denver, and the roles played by these contacts in adjustment to the urban milieu.

Snyder notes that the literature on urban migration makes frequent reference to the proximity of the city to the potential mi-

grant's home and the presence of a group of kinsmen and friends
in the city as being important factors in choosing an urban area
to which to migrate. Yet, he finds that the Navajo choice of
Denver "is *not* predictable on the basis of closeness to home nor
upon kin and friends in the city prior to migration." In accounting for this apparent anomaly, Snyder develops the idea of the
"Following Reference Group," which has to do with a migrant's
knowing that friends or kin will be joining him after his arrival
in the city.

Snyder also investigates the presence of an "urban ethnic enclave" of Navajos in Denver which would be comparable to a
Black ghetto or a Mexican-American *barrio*. Although evidence
indicates that such an enclave of Navajos does not exist in Denver, Snyder makes the interesting observation that the Bureau of
Indian Affairs Relocation Office in Denver performs many functions attributed to ethnic enclaves including amelioration of
problems of adjustment by providing initial lodging, employment assistance, and moral support. The idea that Navajos in
Denver have an urban enclave composed of government bureaucrats is an intriguing one, and serves to dramatize the impact of
the BIA on the lives of American Indians.

Several of Snyder's other findings are interesting and, in some
cases, surprising: Navajos have as many interactions with non-
Indians in private settings as they do with other Navajos;
Navajos interact with a larger percentage of non-Indians than
Navajos in a public setting; Navajos meet in bars and drink least
with other Navajos and most with other Indians; members of a
Navajo clique who displayed the least alienation and stress, who
had the highest economic value orientation, and who perceived
the future advantage of living in Denver, also displayed a high
rate of drunkenness.

Robert S. Weppner, whose chapter "Urban Economic Opportunities: The Example of Denver" is next, uses data gathered
from interviews with Navajo workers, an Anglo comparison
group, and the employers and supervisors of these workers in
order to describe the economic factors that are operable in determining the adjustment of Navajos to urban life. Economic factors
are generally important to consider in any analysis of American
Indian urban migration because (as Snyder mentions in his

opening section) virtually all researchers agree that economic necessity is the prime consideration in making the decision to leave the reservation. These factors are especially important in relation to the Navajo, however, as the Navajo reservation is becoming economically more and more inadequate to meet the needs of a rapidly expanding population. Further, as Weppner points out, studies have indicated that if a migrant's initial economic experiences in the city are disappointing, his urban adjustment and assimilation are greatly hampered.

Weppner investigates several characteristics of Navajo migrants to Denver that militate against their economic adjustment in the city (for example, poor or incomplete job training, inadequate English language skills), and finds that the most potent predictor of success or failure is a combination of two factors: vocational experience and initial job experience in the city. As Weppner says, "The Navajo migrant who comes to the city with poor background and has had a bad experience in obtaining a job (long wait and low wages when he gets one) is not going to become economically absorbed or culturally integrated."

In looking at the Contents of this book, the average reader would first notice Theodore D. Graves's "Drinking and Drunkenness among Urban Indians." Perhaps nothing is associated more with Indians in the American popular mind than alcohol. The association evokes images of Plains Indians, noble and proud on their horses, who eschew their dignity and trade their souls and their lands for a little firewater, or of rows of Indians lying in a drunken stupor around a tavern bordering some reservation. Unfortunately, the evidence presented by Graves in his essay does little to dispel this stereotype.

Graves finds that in comparison with other groups, American Indians exhibit an extremely high arrest rate for drunkenness and drinking-related offenses. Even when controls to prevent bias are introduced, the data for Denver Navajos show that they still have an arrest rate significantly greater than that for Anglos or Spanish-Americans.

Granted, then, that drinking is a problem for American Indians, Graves seeks to relate drinking to various social and psychological variables in his study of Navajos in Denver. His chapter is essentially concerned with the testing of hypotheses that relate drunkenness with economic rewards, opportunities for acquiring job skills, personal goals, and social pressures and controls.

Graves rejects cultural explanations for Navajo drunkenness: "the vast majority of Indian drunkenness can be explained purely in terms of structural and psychological variables relatively independent of their particular cultural tradition." The majority of Navajo drunkenness in Denver, Graves feels, can be accounted for without recourse to the fact that the subjects are Indians. We can accept Graves's notion that anyone, Indian or not, given a certain constellation of social and psychological variables, is likely to have problems with alcohol. But we would remind our readers that there is a possibility that Indians, due to the position they occupy in our society, are more likely to be subject to those factors that are correlated with high rates of drunkenness.

Lack of formal primary and secondary education has been cited in earlier chapters as being one of the factors that sometimes preclude an Indian's facile adjustment to urban life, but Frank C. Miller's chapter, "Involvement in an Urban University," deals with formal education on a different level and in a very unusual way. Miller presents a case study of the creation of the Department of American Indian Studies at the University of Minnesota, the first such department to exist anywhere.

Miller describes how several facts and ideas led to the Department of American Indian Studies. The fact that American Indians are Minnesota's largest minority, the growing awareness of Indians that the essence of the "Indian problem" is Anglo ignorance, the increasing public interest in, but incomplete understanding of, Indian culture — all were factors that, in their interplay, had a role in creating the department.

Miller, who served on the committee responsible for the formal development of the department, writes from the point of view of an "observant participator" in documenting the creation of the department. He describes the growth of the concept of such a department from the first committee meetings in the mid-1960's to the official approval of the department by the Board of Regents of the university in June, 1969. The Department of American Indian Studies officially opened in September, 1970.

Part 2 aims at giving the reader a view of life for the Indian in the city and the concomitant adjustments and realignments he must make to succeed in an urban setting. Part 2 also suggests that in some ways American Indians are a unique urban minority and that in other ways they share traits of other "culturally disadvantaged" minorities.

With the specific nature of these five chapters as a frame of reference, several questions are raised. Is life in the city for an Indian in Chicago much the same for an Indian in Boston or Los Angeles? Do Navajos in San Francisco have similar problems with drinking or employment as Navajos in Denver, or Papagos in Tucson, or Chippewas in Minneapolis? These are obviously important issues that must be resolved before we can speak with authority about American Indians in an urban society.

CHAPTER 4

life in the city:
chicago

MERWYN S. GARBARINO

INTRODUCTION

One day I was talking to a friend who had lived in Chicago for
several years but who had been born and spent his early life on a
Sioux reservation. "Did you see that article in the paper about
Indians in Chicago?" he asked. "All those reporters do is try to
find someone who will say what they want to hear, who will say
something to attract the readers. They always find someone who
will talk about 'cement prairies'. How many people do you know
who really talk about the city being a 'cement prairie'? I never
heard anyone say that except someone talking about what is
printed in the papers." I agreed that I had never heard anyone
actually use the term either. He went on, "And, 'Red Power'.

169

Who used that? Only whites. Most Indians don't even think in such terms. Even the young ones who wear those buttons call it 'Indian Power'. 'Red Power', ha! And alcoholism. There's another good one the reporters get a hold of. Do they ever talk about the Indians in the city who keep jobs for years and years, or who go to college, or send their kids to college, or who never get into trouble? No, it's always how Indians can't adjust to city life, how they only want to get back to the reservation, how much they drink. No one ever talks about all the different kinds of Indians here and all the different ways they behave."

I report this conversation because my friend was making a good point, and feel some views about Indians in Chicago should be counteracted, views that are popular but not founded in fact or that give only a part of a much more diversified picture. The topics my friend raised and more will be discussed below, but I will not generalize about Indians in cities, for I do not know enough. Nor will any attempt be made to draw conclusions or suggest solutions to problems Chicago Indian people face, because to do that would be as difficult as drawing conclusions and making generalizations about the total Chicago population, or as difficult as solving all the city problems for the mayor and city council. Rather, on the following pages, many Indians will speak for themselves. There will be as few of my own opinions as possible.

Because there are real difficulties in talking about a population with a wide range of behavior and experience, such qualifying terms as "often," and "occasionally" must be employed, and because no attempt has been made to quantify this material, exact numbers of percentages will not be used. What I have to say, therefore, will instead be impressionistic, but it will hopefully be an accurate impression, based upon long-time, intimate contact and friendship, as well as scheduled interviews and pointed discussions.

For the reader interested in the changes that have occurred during the past decade or two in the responses of Indians to urban life, the following selections are suggested: Ablon (1964), Garbarino (1970), Hurt (1961), Lovrich (1951), Ritzenthaler (1955), Sasaki (1960), Verdet (1959), and White (1959). Any of these works will add to the comparative perspective even though only one of them, the Verdet report, deals with Chicago itself.

ARRIVAL IN THE CITY

No one arriving in the city from rural areas today can be completely naive about urban life. Education and television have both been instrumental in giving at least some information about cities to people from small towns and reservations. In addition, the general mobility of the Indian population has always meant some contact with people who have lived in a city, so that there do not appear to be expectations that are grossly unrealistic on the part of new migrants to Chicago. Much of what has been written about the government's relocation program during its first decade — when television sets were rare on reservations and when the urban Indian population was much smaller and therefore less apt to spread accurate information about urban life to a wide reservation audience — is no longer true, at least as far as Chicago is concerned. Some of the earlier conclusions, that Indians in the city felt as though they were serving time or were virtually at the mercy of government administrators who did not really care, are not supported by the experience reported by the people with whom I talked at the end of the sixties.

> I more or less knew what to expect. I had relatives who had moved to the city, and they came home and talked about it. I needed work, and the relocation program seemed like a good idea to me. Sometimes I got mad at the BIA. Seems like they tried to confuse me sometimes. But I finished the training and got a job, and then I changed jobs on my own, and I still have that job — four years almost — and I think it is a good idea to help people make it to the places where there are jobs. We could have used more money, though, while I was in training. — *Male, age 37.*

The early reports on Indians in the cities seemed to find a single urban way of life for Indians. Today, it is not only useless but absurd to talk about "the urban Indian" in the singular. The adjustment patterns, recreation behavior, employment, and education expectations vary as much for people classified as Indians as similar expectations vary for the general population moving from nonurban to urban life. Some come from other cities or very large towns or from villages, others are rural but not from reservations, and many, of course, are from reservations. It is therefore as difficult to talk about the urban Indian in Chicago as a generalization as it is to talk about the entire population of Chicagoans as a generalization.

Population Size. Accounts of the population size of Indians in Chicago usually range around 15,000 to 16,000, but the fact is that there are no hard statistics on this population. For 1969, the Bureau of Indian Affairs (BIA) estimated the population at 12,000 in the urban area that includes more than just Chicago. It would be safe to say that the population at any one time lies between 10,000 and 20,000, but a range of this magnitude, while safe, is rather meaningless.

There are many problems in assessing the population. The people involved represent an extremely mobile population so that any individual in the city for one count might very well be away for a count made the week before or the week after. It is not only the mobility between the city and other regions that complicates census taking, the mobility within the city also is an unknown factor. An additional problem in making a count of people of Indian extraction is that their visibility is low, as compared to the visibility of the Black population for example, and people who consider themselves to be Indians, unless asked about their ethnicity, may not be included in that category. It often depends on the individual who is making a point of being Indian. The schools, for instance, no longer keep records that categorize students by race. There are no wards or neighborhoods that are predominantly Indian. Indians are scattered throughout the city and live in the Chicago suburbs as well as in nearby Indiana. The heaviest concentration of Indian people is in the north area called Uptown; other ethnic groups prominent in this district are Puerto Ricans and Appalachian whites. Additionally, Mexican Indians are usually classified as Mexicans or Spanish-Americans rather than Indians, although some of them count themselves as part of the Indian population, and technically they are a part of the Indian category. Therefore, population estimates often come down to hair-splitting, division into artificially drawn categories, and guesswork.

Indians have been living in Chicago since early frontier times, but because there are no reliable records available on their lives in the early years of the city or their numbers there during the nineteenth century, it is impossible to talk about the first Indians to live there. For recent populations, it was unquestionably the job opportunities resulting from the industrial build-up during World War II that enticed a number of individuals and families to Chicago and its suburbs. Also many Indians in the armed services trained at bases close to the city or passed through the city where they sought entertainment and relaxation. At the present time, there are people from these two groups who either remained in Chicago after the war or who returned to live in the city after demobilization. They are long-time city dwellers; interviews with their children often indicate that they consider themselves a part of the general urban population and not members of any Indian tribe or group.

> Well, you know I was born here thirty years ago, and Chicago is the only place I've ever lived except when I was in the service. My mother and father are both enrolled members of Indian tribes, but I don't really think of myself as an Indian. Once in a while I have gone to the Indian Center with my mother, but I would never go there myself. My friends are not Indian, not because I don't like Indians, but because in my business I do not meet any Indians, and my friends are almost all from my business associates. I have been to my mother's reservation to visit my grandmother. I think you could say it would be just like anyone going to visit a grandmother. It didn't make me feel like an Indian; I just liked to see my grandmother because she was nice to me, and I had fun playing there in the summer when school was out.

> I went to the University of Illinois, and there were no Indians there to my knowledge. Sometimes people have asked me if I am Hawaiian. Practically nobody ever says I look like an Indian. Of course, neither my mother or father were purebloods, but they were enrolled, and that means "Indian." I think it is something you can choose, whether to be an Indian or not. I mean you can choose if you have grown up in the city. It's prob-

ably not the same thing if you are reservation-bred because there would be stronger ties to Indian identity, whatever that is. But anyhow, in my case, you can say that I am just a Chicagoan.

Indians come to live in Chicago from all over the United States, but especially from the Great Lakes region and the northern plains. Talking with Indians and reviewing the membership of the American Indian Center reveals there are between ninety and one hundred different tribes represented in Chicago. A common question asked when one Indian meets another is, "What kind of Indian are you?" The question, however, appears to be more a matter of curiosity than a matter of importance, as far as relationships are concerned.

There ain't many Oneidas down here you know, mostly a lot of Sioux, Chippewa, and Winnebago. There's lots of old-timers, real old, who fought for the tribes and stuff like that, but why should we do it now? If any other Indian and me were in Chicago and we was to meet up, we would still be buddies if we liked each other as a person. But here's another thing. I'm Oneida and we lived just a little ways from the Menominees. About forty miles, you know. But every time Oneidas go to Keshena a bunch of us guys would go to the bars and we'd get in a great big fight. Everybody would end up fighting and probably they'd beat us up. Same way with the Menominees, if they came to the Oneidas and they'd be drinking in a bar, pretty soon it wouldn't be very long before they'd get in a fight and they'd get beat up. But we all come here in Chicago, and we're all good friends. When we get to the city we begin to think of ourselves more as Indians. Here we all stick together. — *Male, age 33.*

Well, we have the tribal clubs, but not everyone belongs to a club. I don't think your tribe is really very important in the city. Maybe if you knew people back on the reservation, then you are with them more if you are both in the city. But that's because you are already friends. It depends on the individual. Of course I always ask about the tribe, but then it doesn't mean much, I mean, it's like asking if you're Irish or something. You just know who is what, but it's the person that counts. Lots of people have a mother who is one thing and a father who is from another tribe, or maybe all four grandparents are from different tribes. What do you call yourself then? And almost everybody has white blood some place. I bet there aren't a dozen full-blood Indians in all Chicago. Some people say they are, but I bet if you could trace back far enough, you'd find they were wrong. — *Female, age 29.*

Indian Contact with Non-Indians. Today, association between Indian and non-Indian is common on the basis of genuine friendship. Many Indians say that they have more contact with non-Indians than with other Indians. Most Indians are surprised to be asked whether they consider it possible to be friends with a non-Indian. "I don't care whether he's an Indian or not. It's the person that's important." However, once in a while, one hears a denial that it is possible to have a real friendship with a non-Indian. "I couldn't be real friends with no white men, that's a fact," but that attitude is rare. Frequently among the Indians who are in the lower socioeconomic class, there is antagonism toward certain ethnic groups, especially the Puerto Rican, although within the Indian community as a whole there is also a noticeable unfavorable reaction to Negroes. However, since the Indians in general do not live in areas with heavy Black concentration and they do live where there are sizeable groups of Puerto Ricans, Mexicans, and Appalachian whites, these latter groups are usually the targets of ethnic prejudice. "I just can't get along with hillbillies."

> Every time you see an Indian and a hillbilly, you can expect a fight. Most of them will try to lick us. They'll knife you too, right quick. There's good and bad in all of us, so I cannot say nothing that means all people, even Niggers, there's good in them, there's good and bad. And the Indians, there's good in Indians too, but I wouldn't trust some Indians myself, and I wouldn't trust some whites. But most of them I'll trust all the way. But when you get to hillbillies, you can't get along with them. — *Male, age 49.*

> The older hillbillies are all right. I got some are good friends. They'll go to hell for me. You want a drink or you want to get something to eat, and they'll give it to you. But these younger guys, them's the ones that you got to watch. It's like these Puerto Ricans on Montrose. I wouldn't walk down that street after it's dark. You couldn't give me money to walk down that street. — *Male, age 53.*

I've heard some Indians talk about Puerto Ricans and hill-billies. It's mostly the men who talk, the men who drink a lot and fight a lot. They're usually looking for trouble and they find it. I have never had any trouble in the public housing unit where I live. We're all mixed up racially there, and my children play with Negro children, and Puerto Ricans, and whites. And it depends on the individual, and I have never had any group of people that I have told my children to stay away from. It depends how you've been raised. And some women keep neat apartments and some don't, and you can't say it's because they're Indian or Puerto Rican or anything else. — *Female, age 36.*

Indian contact with non-Indians in Chicago is really a matter of choice. If they wish to mingle with other ethnic groups, they are free to do so. It is almost chic to know an Indian today; they are "in" right now. Therefore, since it is fashionable to know Indians, there appears to be little discrimination against them as a group.

Employment and Relocation. Word gets around about job opportunities, or people decide to move to the city after visiting friends and relatives there. These are often individual decisions made by people both from reservations and from rural villages and towns not on reservations. For instance, the termination of the Menominee reservation resulted in a large number of Menominees moving into the city. However, by far the largest influx of Indians into Chicago in the past two decades has resulted from the so-called "relocation program" of the BIA.

This program, now called "employment assistance" but still referred to popularly as "relocation," was started in 1951 as an effort by the government to move Indians from the low employment reservation areas to various cities where employment opportunities were greater.

The Chicago Field Employment Assistance Office opened in 1952. Under the program, a move to the city must be initiated on the reservation through the BIA, which means that individuals already in the city and any who are not enrolled members of tribal groups are not eligible for aid or services. Ideally, there is an attempt at the reservation level to screen out individuals who are obviously ill-equipped for city life. In an attempt to assess the potential of individuals and families, counseling is provided; the background of the possible relocatee is presumably examined for his work history, emotional stability, military service, and experience off the reservation, and some aptitude tests may be administered. Although vocational interests are supposed to be taken into consideration and counseling about life in the city and its problems is presumably available — both at the reservation and at the city field office — Indians frequently express discontent with the program. Some of the dissatisfaction arises from the fact that at one level or the other, the ideal information system does not operate, i.e., either adequate information about city life is not made available before the persons concerned leave the reservation, or advice and help are not forthcoming after arrival in the city. There have also certainly been frequent misconceptions about the amount of aid which the bureau is authorized to give the relocatee. Many problems in relocation, besides the purely financial problem of learning to live with the higher prices in the city, are simply due to the lack of adequate communication.

If the BIA has brought in a person or family under the employment assistance program, the agency aids them in finding housing and, in addition, periodically contacts them to aid in adjustment. In the case of an individual in an educational training program, the bureau offers limited funds for tuition, subsistence, and clothing. There is also some help in these areas for people placed in jobs. A living allowance and money for moving to the city and for medical needs are allocated to the relocatee. The bureau makes an effort to find housing convenient to work or school as well as within a realistic financial range. Some complaints have been voiced that the bureau does not keep in touch to help out during the first year of adjustment as presumably was promised. However, these complaints are often made by relocatees who have moved to another address without informing agency personnel. There is a lack of communication from both sides.

Many people are brought in under relocation who change jobs, dwellings, or schools after they have become familiar with the city. Sometimes these changes are made on their own initiative; on other occasions, the bureau has aided in making changes more agreeable to the people concerned. As the program has matured, there appear to be more satisfied individuals, or perhaps it would be more accurate to say that there are fewer complaints about the program. The economic recession at the end of the 1950's worked severe hardship on many relocatees who were, for the most part, in unskilled or semi-skilled employment. A large percentage of those people doubtless would have been more successful and satisfied under other circumstances, but the bureau can hardly be held responsible for the national economy. Most complaints are not about the goals of the program, but rather they express concern about whether it actually works on the local scene.

To avoid generalizing, statements from a number of people with various experiences under the relocation program follow below. The range of experience is wide, and the factors involved are extremely complicated. I do not attempt to draw conclusions or present solutions to problems of city living, but merely hope that the histories and individual statements will speak for themselves to indicate the tremendous complexity involved in relocation, regardless of whether or not the move to the city was sponsored by the bureau.

To call one man's urban experience successful and another's a failure must to some degree be an arbitrary classification, for some people who stay in the city apparently adjust well, but claim that they hate urban life. On the other hand, some leave the city for reasons that do not involve a dislike of urban living, reasons such as kinship responsibility or a desire to participate in and hopefully improve conditions at the reservations or home towns. Therefore, the categories of "successful" and "unsuccessful" are not presented as objective reality, but involve making a subjective judgment with which others might disagree. The "successful" examples that follow are individuals or families who (whether they stay in the city or not) have, in my opinion, adapted to urban conditions with no greater trauma than one would expect to find within the general population of those who move to the city from rural areas. Conversely, the "unsuccessful" examples are people who appear to have failed in adjustment to a greater degree than those of the general population in a similar situation.

Successful Adjustment to Urban Conditions

I didn't come because the BIA or anyone else helped me. We heard in Wisconsin that there were jobs in Chicago. I knew something about welding, so I came, and I've been here ever since — except I go back to visit and I travel around some. I like it here. I raised my kids here. Sometimes they got in with the wrong crowd and there was some trouble, but they're all grown now, and everything worked out OK. My children are real city kids. They like to visit in Wisconsin, but Chicago is their home. One boy even went to junior college — Wilson. All of them married whites. I don't care and my wife doesn't care either. That's their business. We have seven grandchildren, and I don't think they consider themselves Indians at all. Oh, they know where their grandparents came from, but they're all just part of the city. There's a lot of dirt and noise, and when the children were little, I used to worry about the traffic, but I think they got a better education here than they would back home, and I like the things to do in a city, lots of people, and much better jobs. It may cost more to live in the city, but with a job you can afford it. What is there back home? When I go back I see no jobs, nothing to do, everyone just drinks. — *Male, age 53.*

I heard about relocation on the reservation. It's a good idea. Sometimes it doesn't work too well. When I first came, I had some training, and then things got bad and I lost my job. The BIA helped me get another one, but it didn't pay too good, and we had a hard time making out. We had to get some welfare at times. That sort of embarrassed me at first, but then in those days lots of people were out of work. At first it was just my wife and me. That wasn't so bad. She did some day jobs, you know, just line up each morning and see if there's a job for the day. That helped get some money. She didn't like it much. Some people say that it is easier to be alone, but I'm glad I had her along. Then we had a baby, a boy, and that could have been bad, but the jobs began to get better. I heard of a better job from a friend and I changed. No, I didn't think about going back to the reservation. Jobs were even worse there. There are things in the city that I like — the museums, movies, things like that. There are things to do, and the jobs did get better. We have quite a family now. Three girls and two boys, and I can take care of them all. Some people say that it is easier if you are alone, but I am glad that I have my family. I take the children to the zoo, and things. My wife never has to work any more. I think I'd like some other cities too. I like Chicago, but I have visited some smaller cities like Green Bay, and I think I might like to live there. But I can say I like a city. — *Male, age 49.*

Well, I think an Indian ought to go back to his reservation and help the people there. It's not that I don't like Chicago, but I think if everyone young and educated leaves the reservation, who is going to run things? You know tribal politics can be damn dirty, and someone who knows something ought to go back and watch those guys. I am going back someday, but first I am going to finish my education and get some experience. — *Male, age 33.*

I came under the relocation program. I applied through the agency back on the reservation, and I came to Chicago to go to school. I went to a business school in a suburb, and I liked it out there. It was really beautiful, the trees and that. All the kids coming in for training lived at the Y. We don't any more.

I took secretarial training, and some of the teachers were good and some weren't. I used to think . . . I still think that sometimes they just passed us with good grades because they knew the BIA would go on paying. So maybe we really didn't get a very good education always. But I must have learned all right because I applied for a job as a secretary, and I got it OK, and I am still doing it. I think the relocation program is a good thing, but the BIA just never seems to do anything right. They really don't seem to take an interest in the students, and they ran us through like cattle, but the idea is still good. And some of the advisors are real nice and helpful. Well, anyhow, I have a job now that pays enough and I can save some money. It is my hope to go to college someday.

I think that people who really make it in the city and on relocation are people who are quite independent. If you are too dependent on the BIA or anyone else, you'll probably drop out and go back home. You have to have some idea or goal in mind. I want an education. I have traveled about a lot. I guess someone who had never been off a reservation might have a hard time, but I didn't. I don't know if I'll stay here, but I can't say that I don't like cities. There is so much going on, like if you want to go to these art places and if you want to go see one of the latest movies that's out and what not and things like the Buckingham Fountain, and things like that you never see anywhere. Also all the things you can learn from other people because they're all from different backgrounds, like on the job, you know, the boss finds out you're Indian, so he talks about his German history or something like this, and you kind of learn a lot from them too. That's what I like about the city. I don't like what is so dirty, and it's expensive. I think city people are sort of unfriendly. I mean you could fall over in front of somebody and I don't think they'd pick you up. — *Female, age 24.*

Unsuccessful Adjustment to the City

I wish we had never left home. This will never be a home to me. It's dirty and noisy, and people all around, crowded. The apartment is too small, and it seems like I never see the sky or trees. Seems like nothing goes right anymore. First my husband got sick and lost his job. He still isn't working. I have a job, but it never seems like we have enough money. Everything costs so much, shoes, clothes, books, and stuff like that the kids need for school. I have to get help from welfare and have to ask for things. But what can I do? I wish my husband would go back to work. Things would be different then. He says the doctors tell him he can't work yet. I guess they know, but he seems to be able to do the things he wants to do. I wish he'd take more interest in the children. They're always in trouble somehow. After I leave for work, I don't know what's going on. The girl has been picked up on truancy a couple of times, and the boys have gotten into trouble too. They've been up in juvenile court, but they got put on probation. The probation officer is a real nice man, and he tries to help me, but the boys don't listen to me. Next time they'll probably get sent to IYC [the Illinois Youth Commission], and that means reformatory, I guess. My husband ought to do something about them. He just doesn't know how to control them . . . he doesn't even try. I can't be there, and they don't listen to me anyhow. They did something bad. They stole because they wanted some money to spend. I can't give them any money. And once or twice, maybe more, they've gotten an older man to buy them beer and stuff because they're too young to buy it themselves. Well, back on the reservation maybe they'd get beer too, but then I don't think they'd get into so much trouble. They wouldn't get picked up by the police. Maybe the schools are better here, but half the time my kids just don't go to school. They start out, but they never get there — or else I guess they leave before school is out. I just don't know what to do with them. The counselor always wants

me to come and talk, but how can I when I have to go to work.
When the boys were in juvenile court, I had to take off from
work because the mother or father is supposed to go too. I just
don't know why my husband can't do more — just sits around
and drinks beer with friends. I don't like living here, but we
have no other choice. — *Female, age 48.*

I don't like living in Chicago. I'm here on the relocation training program, and I'm glad to learn a trade, but I sure don't like
the city. The BIA doesn't give us enough money to live in Chicago. It's awfully expensive here. But it's not just that. People
are different here — even the Indians. They don't talk to you.
Bus drivers are bastards, and I got lost on the "el" and no one
would help me. City people are in such a hurry. As soon as I
finish school, I'm going away — maybe back to the reservation,
but to a small town anyhow. I'd rather be in a small town and
not have such a good job as stay in the city. — *Male, age 25.*

Most of my life I've been coming back and forth to the city.
I'm thirty now. I used to stay with my mother's sister. When I
was a teenager, I thought the city was wonderful. My aunt was
married and had a family. Sometimes I had to babysit for her.
But I liked to come to visit. Then I got into trouble. That's how
I got these tattoos. In Bridewell [prison], for strong-arm robbery.
So, like I say, I'd stay here for a few years then go back for a
few years. I just couldn't get along either place really. I got
a lot of relatives both places, and pretty soon we'd start fighting
and I'd move on. Maybe I shouldn't feel that way, but I don't
belong any place. Do you ever get that feeling that you don't
belong? Well, I do, and then I start to drink. And I got married, but I didn't like her. I just don't fit in anywhere . . . relatives, marriage. And I'm always getting into fights, especially
with Puerto Ricans. The Indians here ain't like they used to be
when I was young. So I go back, but there's nothing to do
there. It's prettier than the city — but somehow even there the
people seem different and I come back to the city. Maybe I
ought to get my GED [General Education Diploma] — finish
my education, but I don't seem to be able to do anything. —
Male, age 30.

HOUSING PROBLEMS

Virtually no one claims he has been discriminated against because of his Indian ancestry. However, many Indians have large
families, and the larger the family the more difficult it is to find

suitable living accommodations. Some people claim that landlords will simply not rent to families with many children, a complaint also voiced by many people not of Indian extraction. Another housing problem appears to be the high rents which are common in the city. However, by far the most frequent complaint concerns the number of apartment houses infested with cockroaches. One father told me that the cockroach infestation was the only disagreeable thing about city life. Everything else, he said, he could cope with, but unless the entire building could be treated by an exterminator, cockroaches would move back into his apartment no matter how much insecticide he used. He believed that the landlord was unwilling to take the necessary measures to control the situation.

> I'll tell you one thing. People ought to start exterminating. Exterminating – you know – like whole buildings – cockroaches. The buildings here are really full of them. We never had cockroaches at home – bugs, yes, like flies and mosquitoes. But not cockroaches. No, I've never seen any rats here. I read in the papers that some people have rats, but we have cockroaches. We cleaned up the whole apartment, but still cockroaches.

Because of the large size of many families and sometimes because of actual size, the living quarters of many people must be considered small. The desirable ratio of living space, one room per family member, is sometimes achieved, but frequently it is not, especially in the case of large numbers of children and low family incomes. The number of people per dwelling unit tends to decrease as the socioeconomic level rises; it is the common pattern among the general population. In this, Indians are not unique. Crowded living quarters are the norm among all low-income groups in the city. Large numbers of people per dwelling unit, generally crowded conditions, and concomitant problems of order and tidiness are present among the Puerto Rican, Mexican, and Appalachian migrants in Chicago.

> You get an apartment. The landlord is good for a month or so, and then he just lets the building go. He don't try to fix up nothing. Now this is the second place we've moved, and the landlord wouldn't fix up nothing. I was asking for some screens to put on the windows, some putty I needed for that one win-

dow, and he wouldn't get it, he would just let it wait another
week. "Can't do it now," he says. "There's no money." And they
told me that he's got nine apartment buildings. I know it's really
because we got so many children, and he wants to get us out. —
Mother of ten children.

Conversely, comments like the following are typical of the
professional and semi-professional.

It took a little bit of looking, but we really didn't have any
troubles finding a nice apartment. I think the rents are high in
Chicago, but it is very nice where we live. There are quite a
few Indians in that neighborhood, and you can look out over
the lake. There are trees and grass, you know. I guess when
people have big families and not much money, housing is hard
for anyone, but we have only two children, and we didn't find
anyone objecting to our children. Our landlord is a real nice
guy, and he says he likes to have Indians in his apartment house
because we're the first Americans. — *Mother of two.*

CHILDREN IN THE CITY

Families of Indians are often large, and frequently the children
are raised in an atmosphere of permissiveness. Here, too, the
range of variation is great, and I have seen some parental attitudes as strict as any among any other ethnic group. Parents
often express concern over children growing up in the city,
although the adults usually believe that the city school system is
superior to rural, reservation, or boarding schools. Boarding
schools are used as a last resort for severe delinquency problems
or for those situations where domestic life is such that the children might suffer. In general, parents want to raise their children
at home, and most children accept schooling with about the
same enthusiasm as children elsewhere.

One thing about these schools I don't like. I don't know.
Seems like the kids don't get the right education. And when
they ask the teacher for help, you know, some problems they
can't figure out, the teachers get mad. One of my kids asked the
teacher for help and the teacher just bawled him out for not
paying attention and expelled him from school. He got sent
home, and they said he was expelled 'cause he didn't behave
in school. It's just the ideas of them not learning the problems,

and the teachers wouldn't help them out. But what I'd like to know is this: what good does it do to know how to work those problems? Every little thing the kids do they send them home or punish them. The teachers are no good and they keep asking for higher wages and raises. And my girl says the teachers cuss the kids. — *Mother of nine children.*

Oh, I think the schools here in the city are much better than the schools in the country. They're especially better than Indian schools. My children learn a lot more than I did when I was their age. Of course, it depends upon the school. Some of the schools in the ghetto may be pretty bad. I have read about that in the papers, but the schools my kids go to are real good, and the kids like school, and they get along well with the teachers and the other kids. — *Mother of four children.*

Numbers of families take trips on weekends to the large parks in the city, and to the zoos and museums, especially the Museum of Science and Industry and to the Field Museum where there is an outstanding collection of American Indian material. Concerned parents supervise their children's activities, and both mothers and fathers talk about traffic dangers and other city hazards for the little ones and express a desire for safe, supervised play areas for younger children.

Some adolescents have learned how to obtain alcoholic beverages, from beer to hard liquor, by promising some adult man a drink if that adult will make the purchase for the minors. Even if the underaged adolescents reveal to authorities the source of their supply, another wino, Indian or non-Indian, can usually be found to perform the same function another day. Thus, there is no difficulty in getting liquor and becoming drunk even if one is underage. It is usually in a drunken condition that the adolescent boys commit crimes ranging from petty misdemeanors to an occasional strong-arm robbery. Most juvenile delinquency, however, occurs in the form of truancy or running away from home. Dislike of school, boredom, and overcrowded conditions at home are the most frequent reasons the young give for this type of behavior. Working parents, and even some mothers who do not work, find it hard to keep tabs on the older children. There is no certainty that children will actually go to school when they set out in the morning, although, of course, most of them do. Never-

theless, truancy remains a problem in some families, especially
when there is no motivation toward getting an education or
when the expectations of accomplishment are low.

> Oh, I like school all right, but some of those classes, ugh.
> What good will they ever do me? My father has a good job at
> the factory, and he doesn't have a high school diploma. There
> are some teachers I really like, and I don't cut those classes,
> but let me tell you there are some where I just think I'll die
> before the bell rings. Yes, those are the ones I cut. My coun-
> selor gets mad, but seems like it is silly to take some of those
> subjects. My parents never say anything about my report card,
> but I guess my mother would like me to finish. — *Male, age 17.*

> I want to go to college when I finish high school. I would
> like to have a really good and interesting job. My parents en-
> courage me a lot, but it is really something I have thought
> about myself. I would like to be a teacher, and you have to go
> to college for that. I think I could do college work. My grades
> are pretty good, a little better than average, I think, and the
> counselor says I could get into college. I don't know about pay-
> ing for it except that I have heard there are some special schol-
> arships for Indians, and I have been hoping that I can get some
> help with money that way. — *Female, age 17.*

SOME ASPECTS OF
MARITAL RELATIONSHIPS

When the national economy is depressed, it is often easier for
women to obtain employment, especially among certain groups
where the men are only unskilled or semiskilled laborers. The
working women support the household, leaving the men to care
for the children and to do the household chores. In a society or
subculture where the men are supposed to be the breadwinners,
if not the "bosses" of the family, the result is a sort of emascula-
tion of the male. The strain and guilt feelings of failure to play
the role of head of the family may produce an increased tendency to turn to alcohol as escape. Frequently physical conflict
between the man and woman increases, that is, wife-beatings
increase. This strain is found not only among American Indians,
of course; it has been reported among Appalachian whites and
Puerto Ricans who live in the same areas containing the dens-
est Indian population and among other low-income groups

elsewhere. Marital strain from this economic cause has been recognized for some time. There is a high correlation between socioeconomic class, level of education, and certain strains in the
husband-wife relationship. Often the wife, having earned the
money, considers it hers to dispense. She may become quite
independent which adds to the husband's already exacerbated
male self-image. The additional insult of female independence
may be the cause of the increased wife beatings, the husband
using brute strength to demonstrate his masculinity.

Instead of belaboring this particular economic situation and
its impact on the husband-wife relationship, there is an alto-
gether different stress in the husband-wife relationship observed
in my counseling in domestic problems in Chicago which is of
interest. Marital problems which on the surface have a certain
similarity to those arising from the economic pressures just described have, upon deeper probing into the individual case,
appeared to result from differing relationship expectations of
males and females. This particular expectation differential represents only a small segment in the range of marital variation. Between certain married couples, however, the pattern has emerged
so frequently that it is worth examining.

As a preface, it is important first to describe the range of
expectations in the married life of Indians, one which does not
differ from the range found in the general population. There are
many marriages that are stable, in which the ties are firm and
fond. There are also unstable marriages resulting from unstable
personalities, unwise and hasty decisions, or economic pressures.
These unions are not unique. But there is one form of a marriage
conflict that is frequent enough among certain Indian men and
women to be worth some special notice. This is the conflict
which often seems to arise when reservation born and bred men
whose education is limited to high school or less marry women
who were raised in the city and went through the city school
systems and sometimes had advanced education.

Again, superficially, the relationship may seem very much like
that resulting from the economic stresses that select women over
men in the labor market. The manifestations may be a high level
of drinking by the man and occasional wife-beating. Also, there
is a noticeable absence of the male from the home during the

nonworking hours. The difference between these symptoms and
those formerly mentioned is that the man is employed, often at
well-paying and steady work. The defining condition that sets
this relationship apart is the man's usual absence from his
home. He holds a job, usually a very good job, is a steady
worker, and supports his wife and children, if any. If he drinks,
it is controlled social drinking that does not interfere with his
employment. After the daily job is over, however, he goes home
only long enough to eat, change his clothes, and then go out
again alone — that is, without his wife.

The situation almost inevitably results in great loneliness on
the part of the wife and a tremendous pent-up hostility toward
her husband. She may go out by herself or with some girl friends,
although the problem of baby-sitters may prevent this outlet, or
she may just stay home and watch television. These women
rarely go to bars by themselves; they have been taught that it is
not the nice thing to do. They are city-bred and grew up to
expect companionship in marriage and they would go to a bar
only with husbands and friends. But their reservation-raised
husbands have not grown up with the concept of companionship
in marriage. A wife means one of two things to them: a domestic
convenience to keep the house clean, cook, and care for the children; or a sexual partner (usually not their only sexual partner).

The following quotes are parts of two interviews with a couple.
The wife consulted me about her marriage, and what she had to
say is related first. I had some difficulty in getting her husband to
talk at all. He was not nearly so voluble, and to make his interview more meaningful, some of the questions asked him are included. His wife's interview, on the other hand, poured out
almost as though she could not stop. These two interviews demonstrate the polar expectations of marriage in a forceful way.
The mystery is, of course, why this couple and the others like
them do not discover their different expectations before getting
married.

The Wife's Story

My husband comes home after work. He has a good job,
$7.50 an hour. Most of the time he gives me enough money to
take care of the bills, and I can buy furniture and clothes too.

But this isn't what I thought of as marriage. Like I say, he comes home from work. He eats dinner, gets cleaned up and dressed up, and he goes out. He doesn't say, "Come with me." He doesn't even say where he is going. Some nights he doesn't come home all night. Sometimes he has even come home drunk and when I asked him where he'd been, he hit me.

I can't talk to him about it. My throat closes up. I think if I talk I'll cry or he'll say I'm nagging. I don't want to do either. But this is not marriage to me. A boy friend would pay me more attention than my husband does. We never do anything together. I don't think he can understand what loneliness is. Sometimes I think I'll go right out of my mind with loneliness. A boy friend would see more of me and be more considerate of me than my own husband.

We have been married four years, and most of the time it has been like this. I have heard other Indian women say this too, but I think it is different when they are more educated. I've had two years of college, but my husband has only a GED. When I was in college, I remember that couples did things together, they had parties together with other couples, and the husband seemed to care about what his wife thought. I don't think my husband even can understand what I think. I know that we are not always going to like the same things. I know that there are things I like to do that don't interest him, and the same goes for him. But there are things we could do together. Look . . . I think if it's a good marriage, we both give up something to gain something. All I feel any more is pain . . . and loneliness. It's an aching place in my stomach . . . a pit with no bottom. I'm even afraid now because he hit me.

He says very little to me. Days go by when he never says a word. I want to share with him. Share my life with him. Everyone gets moody sometimes — I know that. I can be sympathetic. He doesn't have to go and drink — or why can't two people go out together and try to be happy? I want him to be happy and I want to be happy. You see, I think like this: if other people are going to be so important that they are more important than your wife, then you should not be married. It is just day after day and week after week, and I'm left alone. I mean that — really alone — no one. He acts jealous if I have a girl friend, and if I ever went out with a fellow, he'd probably kill me.

What about a promise? Like when you get married, that's a kind of promise; it's a promise for the future. Marriage means future. It doesn't mean tonight or for a couple of weeks, not just today, but we will try through a lifetime. You don't get mad once and quit. He was the one who wanted to get married so much. I was not so sure. I knew there were quite a few Indian men who go off night after night and leave their wives. I have heard women talk. They are hurt too, but they never say anything. They are older women, but I wasn't raised to accept this. I wanted something real, worth trying for, to make permanent. "What do you want?" he says. "Everything has to change." But there's another way of looking at that too. Children grow up and change, but you can still love them and be with them. You have to learn how to take change. It doesn't mean that everything falls to pieces. Like I said, he'd probably kill me if I ever went out. I know that he goes to bars with women. I can just imagine how he would treat me if I went out with a man. But you see, I wouldn't do that because I don't think it is right. I mean, as long as I'm married, I've made a promise, and I won't break it. It's honor to me. They talk a lot about a woman being possessive. I don't want it to be like that. I want it to be shared. To plan together — to work toward something — that doesn't mean possession. I'm not possessing him any more than he'd be possessing me. I've told him this, and he says, "I don't know what you are talking about." So now I am going to get a divorce. I'd rather be lonely alone than lonely and scared with him.

The Husband's Response

If you listen to her, I'm a bastard. But men and women have different interests. What can we talk about? She wants to talk about the kid. So all right, I love my child, but I'm not supposed to raise her. That's a woman's business. I'm a man. A man goes out with other men. I don't want to say something that would shock you, but you've been around. You know what it's like. We go to a bar. Now, who wants a wife around telling him what to do. That's embarrassing when you gotta show everybody who's boss. I want to have some fun. I don't want her watching me.

Q. Suppose she paid no attention to you but instead danced and drank with some other man?

A. She'd have two black eyes. My wife belongs to me. She acts so people know I'm boss. Back home [on the reservation] a man goes with a woman, they settle down and raise a family.

She stays home and takes care of things. She doesn't go out and act like that.

Q. Suppose she thinks she has a right to make up her own mind?

A. She shouldn't have married me. My wife can take care of my home and kid. She better be there when I come home . . . no matter when I come home. I'm a man . . . these are the things men do. If I want a woman, what the hell, I don't have to marry her. But what would my friends think if I run home because my wife wants me there, because she worries. Like, what the hell makes her think that she's so important that I have to shape my life around her? She stays home and behaves herself or I teach her about a black eye or something.

Q. Suppose your wife loves you and wants to make a life with you and share and solve problems together? Does that mean she is trying to run your life? Should you have married her if you didn't want to share a life with her?

A. That's only what she thinks. Why don't women say this at first? What do you hear? "You're handsome . . . you're strong . . . I love you . . . and so on." So OK I've had lots of women. They all say the same things. They just want a husband.

Q. Suppose the woman was raised differently, educated, upper class. Wouldn't she expect something different? Suppose she believed in you, your life and potential, and wanted to see you make the most of yourself. Someone honorable, trusting, and faithful.

A. There are no women like that. They're after what they get just as men take what they can get.

Q. Does this mean that marriage cannot be successful in the sense that husband and wife can both be happy and share a life together?

A. Oh, maybe they can. You can get too old to go on running around. If your wife doesn't nag, if she keeps her mouth shut and does her job, that's good enough.

Q. But what about the woman? Did you ever think that she might want something more? Do you think she is less human than you? Do you think a woman could get lonely or scared, or insecure?

A. Look, in my life what counts is me. Why make me responsible for someone else's happiness. Come on . . . there's always another woman. I like to look around and say I could have any of those women, in bed, I mean. I wouldn't marry them. I might think that one looks like a real challenge, so that's the one I go after. Know what? I usually get her. What's my wife bitching about? After all, I married her. Anything permanent means that some woman is making demands on me. I'm free. No one is going to make demands on me.

Q. Does it occur to you that you are making demands on her too? She gives up something, you give up something, but there is a lot that you have together that you could not have any other way. Isn't there more to being a man than just taking a woman? Is that all that being a man means?

A. You are just trying to make me conform. No woman is worth making me change my life. I want to be free. Goals tie me down. I don't want to be dependent on another person, I don't want another person dependent on me, and I don't want any demands. I break no promises because I make no promises.

Q. Wasn't your marriage a kind of promise?

A. You're trying to trap me.

These interviews are typical in the outlooks expressed, but the respondents are more articulate than many with the same problem. There is very little mutual dependence or sharing in any of these cases. The male attitudes in cases of this sort may be the result of a breakdown of ego respect — others are held in little respect because one has little respect for oneself or for one's goals or abilities. It is a fear of failure, and a sort of self-fulfilling prophecy: "I can't live up to the expectations placed upon me, but rather than let other people say so, I will demonstrate it myself first." In this, it is quite different from the concept of the double standard. It is a face-saving device. It appears to be a display of public superiority to hide a private feeling of inferiority or inadequacy. The Latin American new to the city may experience a similar reaction when his cultural emphasis on *machismo* is met with a new response on the part of Latin American women who think in terms of sexual equality. There are doubtless many other similarities between this example and the marital behavior and expectations among other ethnic groups.

A reservation-raised man was asked what he thought about the different behavioral expectations discussed; then a much younger fellow, born and raised in the city, was asked to read the quotations and comment on them.

> This is an interesting thing you've asked about. Back on the reservation, any girl running around with lots of fellows was considered an easy mark. But when I moved to Chicago, I learned from the woman I married that in the city, the city high schools for instance, that a girl goes with lots of fellows. Not because of what I thought, but so she can choose the kind of guy she wants to marry some day — so she can have some idea of what the possibilities are. I would not have thought about this myself, but it is very sensible. To me, on the reservation there was really no question of a girl making a choice based on her own ideas of what she wanted. She was supposed to take what was available. A girl was supposed to marry and not run around. Meeting lots of guys to see what there was, was just running around. And a man really didn't seem to think about a woman as a friend when she married him. I mean there were other things, sex, raising the kids, keeping the house, but not really someone to have fun with like on Saturday night. That's when you went out with men. Well, I'm glad I have my wife. She is important to me. I have plans about what I want to do with my life, and she has a place in those plans. You might say we plan together. But there's lots of guys who can't see a wife as a friend. Like I say, on the reservation we were brought up to think different. — *Male, age 33.*

> It's hard for me to think of a man hitting a woman. I don't know what I'd ever do if my father ever did that to my mother. Oh, yes, I know it happens — but I hear about it among other groups than just Indians — and there are lots of Indian men who would be happy to stay in a nice clean home and spend the evenings with their families instead of tomcatting around. That's the way I want my life to be when I get married. I'm going to take my time, but when I decide, I hope it will be for the rest of my life. I mean, like, we'll like each other, really like each other. And I'd like to own a home — something real nice. Maybe even in the suburbs — someplace where you don't see cockroaches in the crapper. I will be happy to go home and work around the house. It will be a real home. — *Male, age 18.*

ALCOHOLISM

Unquestionably, drinking problems loom large among the Indians in Chicago. Habitual clients of the caseworkers at both St.

Augustine's Center and the American Indian Center come with drinking problems. A spot check by students on West Madison Avenue, which is considered the skid row of Chicago, revealed that about 5 percent to 8 percent of the habitués were Indian. This spot check should not be considered the last word, because it was done largely on the basis of visibility rather than acknowledged ethnicity. Nevertheless, that percentage represents a figure considerably in excess of the Indian to non-Indian ratio of Chicago inhabitants. Compared to the drinking at Indian bars in the Uptown area, the Madison Avenue crowd appears to be more consistently occupied with drinking, and less apt to have permanent or monthly residence. Most inhabitants of Madison Avenue take rooms by the night or week rather than by the month, and the missions familiar to the Madison Avenue scene are practically nonexistent Uptown.

Much has been said about Indian alcoholism, but not enough said about the many Indians whose drinking is controlled and therefore not a problem. Some bars in the city are known as "Indian" bars because the clientele is largely Indian. Indian drunkenness is focused in these and other bars, and consequently, Indian drinking is public drinking. Many non-Indian drinkers have a different drinking pattern that involves drunkenness under circumstances less apt to lead to public notice. Indians are only rarely solitary drinkers. Non-Indian drinking is most frequently done at home or at the homes of friends where they may sleep until sober enough to escape detection by the public. I can offer no statistical information on this subject, but only my own observations. The important point to be made here is that when drinking data about the two groups are gathered only from the police blotters, I do not think the situations are comparable. This source seems to be the only one for drinking statistics which are published comparing Indian inebriation to non-Indian.

Indians themselves have a lot to say on the subject of alcoholism. One of the most revealing statements was made by an alcoholic who is now an abstainer:

> It seems now almost as though I was taught to drink, like children are taught anything by the example of the grownups around them. I can remember sitting around the kitchen on weekends, and everyone would come in Friday after work, with

beer and sometimes liquor, and they'd start drinking. Me and my little brother, we'd just sit and watch them. I never thought about it, but I guess it always seemed to me the thing to do. Start drinking on weekends. And then, I guess I just drank other times, too, until it was just out of my control. So one day, I just said to myself, "You don't have to do this." And then I quit. Quit completely. But you know, I think lots of people start heavy drinking because they just grow up thinking that is the way to behave. They just don't know about anything else to do. — *Male, age 43.*

One immediately wonders whether drinking patterns or problems are changed when a person moves to the city. The consensus is that, if there is a difference, drinking is less of a problem in the city, although it is more apt to result in interference by authorities.

I think drinking is a social outlet for Indians; to meet another Indian, you go up to the bar and meet. I don't think there is more drinking in the city than there is in the country. In the city it's closer and there is more access to it. But I can't see that it is a racial problem. It's something that is learned; that's where there is the difference. I know this: in all your big cities, most of your Indians have relocated from reservations where they have already learned drinking ways. If Indians have an alcohol problem here, they had it back on the reservation too. The difference is that it is more obvious here because they get picked up more, whereas back on the reservation, they are in a place; they drink there, they stay there, and here they get out on the streets and get picked up by the cops. So people hear more about it. — *Male, age 33.*

I know I drink a lot. Sometimes I look awful. You don't know what it's like, drinking for a month straight like that, everyday. I've had DT's. Sometimes you see things that ain't there, stuff like that. You might think somebody is in a room with you and there ain't nobody there. That's why a lot of times when I was drinking for a long, long time, maybe I'd be sleeping, and I had to sleep with the light on, because if I didn't, if I'd turn the light off, I'd begin to see things. Even then I can't sleep. You come up from one of those drunks, seems like you're cold and hot at the same time. You're sweating, and it's such an awful feeling; it's sickening. I said to myself, time and time again, "I'm not going to do this no more. God, please help me, don't let me be this way no more." But I was doing this before I came to live in the city. See, if I'm here like this I go on the wagon, I quit drinking, because I find there is more to do, to keep your mind occupied and stuff like that. Rather if I was out in the country I'd just be laying around and stuff like that, nothing to do in the winter time, listen to the radio, and it's cold out, and so you drink. But here, at least you can go to a show or something like that. There's always something going on. I guess it's a problem of boredom. — *Male, age 31.*

Beer and whiskey are preferred drinks for those whose drinking is controlled social drinking, while the problem drinkers, those whose drinking may be said to interfere with their life functioning, tend to drink wine.

Do you know why an Indian drinks wine? Anybody who drinks wine in the city here drinks it because it is a cheap drink. You buy a pint, it costs you 55¢ and it's stronger than beer. Now beer costs you 40¢ a pint. If you buy a quart of beer it will cost you 65¢, but wine is 55¢ and that's why they drink it. We get it in a special place. If we buy it in some other place, might cost 70¢. Way up where I live, it's 70¢ up there, a pint of wine, but down here it only costs you 55¢. But I live in aristocratic country up there, you know. — *Male, age 49.*

INDIAN ORGANIZATIONS

There are two centers of organized Indian activity in Chicago: the American Indian Center and St. Augustine's Center for American Indians. The latter is operated under the auspices of the Episcopal church and is primarily a service organization dealing with welfare and psychological and religious problems. A priest appointed by the bishop of the diocese is the director of St. Augustine's, and he is supported by a paid staff.

The American Indian Center is a private organization, run by a board of directors elected by the Indian membership. Hired by the board of directors, a staff with an executive director actually operates the Center. The director is the only non-Indian staff member. The American Indian Center offers more diversified social, educational, and recreational facilities than does St. Augustine's and may be seen as a microcosm of associational networks for many Indians in Chicago. But if the Indian population is even close to the estimate of 12,000, there are many Indians who do not participate in programs offered by either the American Indian Center or St. Augustine's. Both organizations have a goal of expanding to reach more Indians in the city.

Welfare and counseling services of these organizations deal with financial and emotional problems which may arise from the move to city life, or which may represent long-term problems. The American Indian Center, housed in a large five-story building, provides a meeting place for a number of autonomous Indian organizations such as tribal clubs like the Winnebago Club and the Sioux Club. In addition, the Center sponsors a monthly powwow and frequently special powwows to celebrate specific events. Many Indians and non-Indians attend these gatherings regularly, even Indians who do not otherwise avail themselves of the Center's facilities. As one friend put it, "Powwows are important. Wherever you find Indians, you'll find powwows. We are fortunate to have a building with a room large enough to have a really good sized crowd." Other group activities carried on at the Center are Boy Scouts, Canoe Club, Alcoholics Anonymous, a summer day camp, a tutorial program for children after school, basketball, and other organized programs.

There does not appear to be any rivalry between the two centers serving the Indian population of Chicago. The organizations are complementary rather than competitive, and a number of people avail themselves of the services of both. Indian employees at St. Augustine's are usually members of the American Indian Center which is really, as the members like to point out, a center *of* Indians whereas St. Augustine's is a center *for* Indians. The American Indian Center would like to expand its coverage of the Indian population in Chicago, and it is not entirely for reasons of limited budget that expansion is slow. Although more and more Indians hear about the Center each year, there are still many who do not participate in any of its activities; it is not uncommon to meet Indians who have never heard of the Center.

> Lots of Indian people I know don't go to the Center. One reason I think is that they associate it with welfare, and people don't want other people to think they are on welfare. I know that there are lots of things going on at the Center besides welfare work, but I hear people with good jobs say that they wouldn't go to the Center because they don't need any services. I think there are other Indian people who have friends and they do everything with their friends and they don't think

about going to the Center. And there are lots of people who live too far away. It costs quite a bit to take public transportation, but even more, it takes lots of time to get to the Center from some parts of Chicago. — *Male, age 45.*

I don't think there's any 10,000 Indians in Chicago; I don't care what anybody says. But I do know that there's lots of Indians don't go to the Center. They don't need to get food and stuff. They've got jobs, and when they get home after work, they just want to stay home. Besides, you know what? Not all Indians go to powwows. I don't think they're so hot myself, and I certainly wouldn't dance. I've seen a few, but I'd rather do something else with my spare time. — *Female, age 28.*

PROTEST MOVEMENTS

Participation on an active level in any protest movement is almost entirely limited to teenagers and young adults, and not many of this age group can be considered active. One sometimes sees pins, printed or beaded, reading "Indian Power." Almost invariably these buttons are worn by younger people. Newspaper stories and some books have referred to "Red Power," but I have yet to see an Indian wear a button with that phrase on it or use the expression orally. Whenever there has been a discussion of protest and Indian power, two points are made: most Indians would not join a protest march (although a few have), and Indians in general do not like the term "Red Power" because they associate it (and think others associate it) with communism.

I've seen the kids wear buttons with "Indian Power" on them, but I don't know what they're doing; just some kids, you know. I think the younger people today are a lot smarter than we were when we were that young. But all it means to me is that there should be more Indian say. You know what I really think they mean? Just because they hear Black power, you know, and white power, well they want to come back and say Indian power. They just want to come back and say the same thing so that they got something to say too. Because they're a race too. If them guys is doing it, why can't the Indians say Indian power? But really in their minds and hearts, they don't know what they're talking about. — *Male, age 39.*

There are several ways of making your needs known. Marches are a way, I guess, but it would just embarrass me to march. If someone wants to do that sort of thing, it is up to him, but as for me, I would find some quieter way of getting my ideas across. — *Male, age 36.*

You couldn't get a handful of Indians to go marching around this town. I know it. There's enough Indians in this town that they can do anything that they want. You see the Indians when they travel; when they go down there to the park, they travel four or five in a pool. They have to. They're going into Puerto Rican territory. If you travel by yourself, you're the one that gets hurt. I don't know what you call Indian power. But that's power right there, when you got four or five men with you, when you're going down there. That's the only power I can see. And they don't bother you. It's just like I said that time. I walked down there by myself and I went down there and went to sleep. Five of those guys woke me up. I said, "What do you want?" "Get up." First thing I know, I got hit. I thought my eye was knocked out. The other guy was going to stab me with a knife, you know, because I was by myself. You can't go down there by yourself. So I guess that's what they call Indian power. — *Male, age 49.*

INDIAN IDENTITY

How do Indians explain what makes them "Indian" and keeps them "Indian" under circumstances that presumably result in a melting pot mixture rather than ethnic retention? The simple legal definitions of "Indian" as someone enrolled in a recognized tribal unit or someone of one-quarter Indian blood, i.e., one grandparent who was a full-blood, do not explain Indian identity. It is a difficult concept to verbalize. Even very vocal Indians have trouble stating what it means to them to be an Indian. "Gee, that's a hard thing to say. It's just different somehow," is a typical response. Two individuals, however, have been unusually forward in discussing their search for personal identity and meaning in life, both concepts being bound up in their minds with the concept of "Indianness." These two formulations are not presented as necessarily the result of urbanization, yet these people are city dwellers and have been for some time. Therefore, it is likely that the urban experience as well as their education has had some part in developing their philosophy.

There is something that I will tell you that is hard for me as an educated person, but with an Indian background. That is that I have a belief in signs. I can't get over this. Sometimes I can think that is good medicine, like maybe I heard about it in my childhood, and I only dimly remember, or maybe I thought it up myself because I needed some assurance. You see, I can think about this quite rationally, but by the old ways — I mean the things I heard long ago — it is important, how it is interpreted. But then education, I mean knowledge of cause and effect, interferes. What have these signs to do with human beings? Who makes the signs? I can say this and scoff, but then I remember that it is powerful medicine, and, you know, I'm not so sure. What do I really want to believe? Signs or causal relationships? Now here is a big point: I have met many people who are not Indians but who look for signs. I want something to give me comfort sometimes when I am scared or lonely. I am alone so much in the city, but I am not really sure that it is just the city. Maybe I would be alone or feel lonely anywhere. I would like to have someone important to me and know I am important too. I would like to know that we are a part of nature, of the natural order, that time may pass, but there is always us. And this is *the* thing, the one thing: we know this together. We're a part of nature, like trees have roots that have to grow from soil and be nourished. We have roots in each other and grow and are nourished. That is not a modern way of understanding, but it means a kind of security and trust that nothing else brings. When everything goes, we have each other — an understanding and physical contact that no one else in the world can give, not a parent, not a child. But we know and have our knowledge reinforced by signs in nature. Is this an Indian way of thinking? You have asked me what being an Indian in the city means to me. And my answer is what I have said. This is the loneliness that many Indians in the city face. But I have been reading about the loneliness of the individual in modern society, and I have to say that I am not sure that this is only Indian. It may be just that I tend to look for approval from the natural world. I never really talked about this with anyone else, so I don't know what other people think. But isn't it psychologically sound? If you believe that you will succeed, don't you have a better chance? Doesn't self-confidence help? I think maybe Indians can still seek this individual experience that validates life. How many others can do that? Sometimes people say that it seems as though an Indian can leave, quit, forget more easily than other people. I don't think this is so. It just seems that way because when you are little you learn to hide the scare and sorrow because we Indians do not have a tradition of easing pain by talking about it to everyone who comes along. The emotionally hurt Indian reveals his agony to only a very few. Maybe this helps explain the high rate of alcoholism among Indians. If you are drunk you can act out your emotions in a way that does not strip you naked. It is better to be drunk than sober if you are going to have an emotional explosion. — *Male, age 40.*

The following statement, really a monologue, was made by a woman who had wrestled with the identity problem. She had been drinking for several hours when she made these comments about her search for personal fulfillment.

How do you know what? Just keep moving — don't think too much. Action — moving — drinking — always something just so you get tired — don't ask questions — else maybe you cry and want to know why. You want something and don't know what and it hurts. And Jesus how it hurts. And why you're different because you can't want the things you're supposed to want. And if you could only understand it when it was all over, that would be something, but you never do. You just try not to let it hurt so much. Everybody tells you what you should do. No one asks what you want — how you feel.

Sometimes I think about my children. I do not think about them as often as I ought to, I guess, but it worries me. I ought to be able to say something that helps them . . . something that means something. But how can I? I don't know for myself. Things change so fast. Sometimes I think I know, and then it is all different. I could tell them, "These are the rules, the laws." But I know that things seem different to them. My life is run by what I learned twenty years ago. I know people who seem to have a little part of the world for their very own. I would like that for me. A safe place — quiet, good.

It is kind of like a play or a movie — standing off and seeing other people react and thinking that is just like me — but it is closer, and you have to decide. But no matter what you decide, you decide wrong because you can't be happy. You see too much. You are too many different people, and the world is not made to accept you as so many different people. You're supposed to decide and stick to it. What are you supposed to be as a person or as an Indian? I always wonder and sometimes I want to scream or cry or kick things or fight. Oh, I don't know who or what I am, and I really don't know how anyone knows these things. I was raised as an Indian, and I don't know what that means. I have to wonder what does it mean that I say I am an Indian. Maybe it is a way to escape what I really am. It's OK to say, "I am an Indian." Everyone likes that. It is a way of making an impression. People like to know Indians. But I am a human being too. It is a kind of fake — a way out — and I've never said this before — but it is a kind of fake — and a way of making an impression and being safe. But it is kind of corny, and I'd like to think it meant something . . . like this is a real live person who wants something.

I was raised to believe that I would do something to help humanity. I would never think of myself. That would be a good life. It isn't that way, no matter how you try. Something sneaks through. It matters. You want some things. I mean, what does a person mean to the rest of the world? And then I think, "Who really cares?" And this is something I just don't understand. It seems as though people should help each other and stop sadness, and say, "I'm here to help." I think that is the Indian way, maybe, but maybe not because there are lots of Indians who don't care either. Like all that matters is just one other person who believes in you. And then you look at the way it is, and wonder whether even one person cares. Oh, God.

SUMMARY

Indians come to Chicago from all over the United States and Canada. They come from vastly differing backgrounds, heterogeneous not only in tribal affiliation, but in socioeconomic and educational levels as well as in the degree of prior experience with urbanization. Accommodation to urban life does not appear to depend upon any of the above categories, but rather it seems to be highly individualistic and personalized. The accommodation factor is extremely difficult to measure, for two people of seemingly identical experience and background may react very differently to city environment.

If there is stability in the household, a strong family head, and regular income, adjustment problems are usually either minor or nonexistent. If, on the other hand, the family unit is broken by illness, divorce, unrestrained drinking, or any other major disorder, the whole family is usually affected, and the children especially will reflect the family instability with behavior characterized by truancy and delinquency. This behavior, unchecked, frequently leads to conflict with the law or the school system, and also to a general sensation of having no norms and not belonging. Early childhood experience in such an unstable family unit, whether this experience occurs before or after the move to the city, produces adults who do not know who they are or where they are going. By the time an individual with such a predisposition is an adolescent, he seems unable to control his life — indeed, he seems not even to comprehend that such control is possible. Adults coming to the city without a family, or at the most with a spouse, adjust best if the adjustment and problems are shared. Most people interviewed agreed that it was more comfortable and more secure to be able to discuss problems and goals with another person — the best person being a compatible and sympathetic spouse. The need for someone to share a life is apparent from a number of the foregoing quotations. Recognition and need of and by another person appears to solve, or at least alleviate, the identity problem.

Today more people of Indian extraction have goals and believe that they have some control over their destiny. They may rail at the BIA, the city government, or bureaucracy in general, for many reasons, but these Indians are no longer dependent upon them, at least not so dependent that they are afraid to manipulate these institutions. And that, perhaps, is the key to adjustment — increasing general independence on the part of Indians in the city. Whether independence is a characteristic of those who move to the city or whether it is a development after the move, the ability of the individual to remain flexible, to take misfortune in stride, to achieve a personal identity and meaning in life — this is the outstanding trait of successful urban accommodation. This independence allows the individual to manipulate his own cultural heritage as well as the cultures of the city to maximize his own options.

Within the matrix of city life there seems to be a detribalization resulting in a general identity as Indian, rather than tribal member, but this detribalization is also influenced by and reflects class structure. Some Indians are becoming members of general socioeconomic classes. This is shown in the group entering upper-class society as well as those who are swallowed up in the lower class as derelicts on skid row. Retention of a strong component of Indianness may be the result of a real pride in heritage, but it may also be a kind of defensive behavior or refuge. The range of variation is extensive.

The following statement embodies the thinking Indian's views:

> Being Indian to me is being myself. What person knows what has made him? I guess people of French or any other European ancestry feel the same way. Or Orientals. I don't think it is really different. It means that you belong to something, a group or some tradition. There are so many different kinds of traditions, and I don't know that one is better than another. Seems to me that the important thing is you know yourself. Not that it is an easy thing to do. But if you feel a part of something and secure in that belonging, then that's what it's all about. And I think this is a personal thing. I can't make it for anyone else — not even my own children, really. We all have to find it, and when we don't, then we're in trouble. Sure, I know sometimes people are impressed if I say I'm Indian and what my tribe is, but it's more than that. After it's all been said, it all goes back to your own image as a person. It's facing up to the basic things like responsibility, honor, and all that stuff. If you run away and call it the Indian way, who's going to get hurt? You are — that's who. I'm proud of my ancestors, but what I am depends on me.

BIBLIOGRAPHY

Ablon, Joan
    1964   "Relocated American Indians in the San Francisco Bay Area." *Human Organization* 23:296–304.
Garbarino, Merwyn S.
    1970   "Seminole Girl." *Transaction* 7:40–46.
Hurt, Wesley R.
    1961   "The Urbanization of the Yankton Indians." *Human Organization* 20:226–231.
Lovrich, Frank
    1951   "The Assimilation of the Indian in Rapid City." Unpublished M.A. thesis, State University of South Dakota.
Ritzenthaler, Robert, and Mary Sellers
    1955   "Indians in an Urban Situation." *The Wisconsin Archaeologist* 36:147–161.

Sasaki, Tom
    1960   *Fruitland, New Mexico: A Navaho Community in Transition.* Ithaca,
            N.Y.: Cornell University Press.
Verdet, Paula
    1959   "Summary of Research on Indians in St. Louis and Chicago."
            Mimeographed.
White, Robert
    1959   "The Urbanization of the Dakota Indian." Unpublished M.A.
            thesis, St. Louis University.

CHAPTER 5 the social environment
of the urban indian

PETER Z. SNYDER

INTRODUCTION

Although there has been some migration to cities by American Indians since the advent of urban centers, the major stimuli for such migration appear to be World War II and the Relocation Services Program of the BIA. The upheaval of World War II caused the exodus of many Indians from reservations into the armed forces and jobs in war-related industries. Through this exposure to and contact with the dominant society and its material goods, many Indians chose not to return to the reservations. Then in 1952 the BIA initiated the Relocation Services Program. Since that time some 100,000 American Indians have been relocated in one of thirteen (nine presently) urban centers in the United States.

The reasons for urban migration are multiple (Graves and Van Arsdale 1966), but all students of the phenomenon agree that economic necessity is *the* most influential reason in the decision to leave the reservation (Ablon 1964; Graves and Van Arsdale 1966; Hurt 1961; Martin 1964). The Navajo, who are the focus of this chapter, offer an excellent example of migration for economic considerations.

The Navajo reservation is economically inadequate to support the rapidly expanding population. The U.S. Public Health Service "uses a figure of approximately 2.30 percent for the annual net increases in Navajo population" (Kluckhohn and Leighton 1962:51). This is probably a fairly accurate estimate of population growth since at that time approximately 90,000 Navajos were on the reservation, and a recently completed Navajo tribal census reports some 120,000 as the total.

In addition to population expansion, the land itself is a limiting factor. Indeed, in the early 1940's nearly 12 percent of the reservation could be described as complete wasteland, 30 percent could support less than one sheep per 50 acres, 20 percent could support only one sheep per 17–25 acres, and only 20 percent could support a sheep on less than 16 acres. "Range figures for 1958 indicate a much smaller amount of good grazing lands: only approximately 5 percent will support one sheep on less than 16 acres. Nearly 50 percent will support one sheep per 30 to 65 acres" (Kluckhohn and Leighton 1962:49, 50). And so the depletion continues.

One solution to this economic pressure is migration. The Relocation Services Program was initiated to facilitate voluntary resettlement of Navajos and other Indians from economically depressed reservations to urban-industrial areas where wage-labor opportunities are more readily available. Three years of intermittent fieldwork among 135 Navajo relocatees at the Denver, Colorado relocation center is reported here, with emphasis upon urban social activities.

THE INITIAL URBAN
SOCIAL ENVIRONMENT

As stated above, like other American Indian groups the Navajo decide to migrate almost exclusively because of economic need

(Graves and Van Arsdale 1966). Once the decision is made, how do they select an urban center?

The literature on urbanizing nonliterate peoples throughout the world indicates the importance to the new migrant of having kin and/or friends in the chosen urban center. Kin and friends already living in the city provide an enclave into which the migrant can move upon arrival. This enclave aids him to adjust, socializing him to the new environment, teaching him the adaptive behavior necessary in order to meet this new milieu.

Secondly, the choice of urban center is believed to be related to the "closeness" of the chosen urban center to the home of the migrant. Replies of 134 male adult Navajo relocatees in Denver provide some interesting results, showing the choice of urban center is *not* predictable on the basis of closeness to home nor upon kin and friends in the city prior to migration. An examination of Table 5.1 makes this clear.

When answering the question "What were the reasons you finally came to Denver to live instead of some other city?" only 40 percent of the men said that it was close to the reservation (home). And only 17 percent responded that they had friends and/or relatives already there. Although the literature suggests a much stronger relationship between the choice of urban center and (1) proximity and (2) acquaintances residing in the city, the replies in Table 5.1 show only a little better than half — 57 percent or 77 — state these as reasons.

TABLE 5.1

Motives for Navajo Migration to Denver

What were the reasons you finally came to Denver to live instead of some other city?	*Number*	*Percentage*
Close to home	54	40
Friends, relatives there	23	17
Employment	24	18
BIA	6	5
Other	27	20

To gain further support to establish the validity of these findings, another set of data was compiled. Each respondent was asked if he had any friends or relatives in the city prior to his migration, if any friends or relatives had accompanied him, and if any had come after he had migrated. The results are presented in Table 5.2.

TABLE 5.2

Reference Group Type ᵃ *for Navajo Migrants*

	Number	Percentage
Previous reference group	69	52
Accompanying reference group	14	10
Following reference group	22	16
None	29	22

ᵃ "Reference group type" as used here means the close friends or relatives who have the most influence on day-to-day behavior and attitudes and who either precede, accompany, or follow the migrant to the city.

For theoretical reasons which follow below, the labels in Table 5.2 are given in terms of reference groups. The results are clear: 52 percent of the respondents reported a previous set of kin and/or friends residing in the city prior to their migration; 10 percent reported being accompanied by friends and/or relatives, and 16 percent reported that friends and/or kin followed them to the city. An *initial* reference group upon arrival is reported then by only 62 percent (83) of the respondents. This suggests that Navajo migrants in Denver do not fit the enclave pattern as reported in other areas of the world.

The total of 16 percent of the respondents reporting that their reference group followed them to the city supports the idea that *knowing* friends or relatives will be coming can provide enough emotional support to the migrant to keep him in the city whether he knows other Navajos or not. The literature is replete with observations about the emotional support afforded by previous or accompanying friends and relatives in the migration adjustment. Such support might, I hypothesize, also be generated by an anticipated reference group to follow, that is, the migrant knows others are on their way to join him and this is sufficient to sustain him until their arrival.

This still leaves 22 percent of the sample, or twenty-nine Navajos, without any reference group upon arrival in Denver and without the possibility of one arriving. The question is, how significant is this number? The cross-cultural urbanization literature leads one to believe that all migrants arrive either with, or into, an enclave of friends and/or relatives. But there is a lack of quantitative data in the literature to support such observations. We do not know to what extent kin in a city *are* prerequisites to subsequent migration. The literature presents no statistics on the number who do or do not have an enclave upon their arrival in the city.

Thus, the observation that 22 percent of the Navajo migrants in Denver did not have a reference group upon arrival may be "normative" cross-culturally, or it may not. Epstein's argument comes closest to this problem; he believes that *almost* every African arrives in a city having a known address, where he will live with a known relation who will meet him, take him in, feed him, show him the ropes, and help him to seek a job (1969:256). *Almost all* is not *all*. We then must suspect that a small minority of urban migrants do indeed arrive without a previous, accompanying, or following reference group.

A sample of 119 Spanish-American urban migrants to Denver provides some further comparative insight into the problem. Less than 10 percent migrated to Denver *without* a previous or accompanying reference group. Is the Navajo figure high? What is an accurate estimate of the number or percent of incoming migrants without friends and relatives? If we accept the Spanish-American data as a good estimate cross-culturally, why do so many more Navajos come alone to the city? We return to this question below in the discussion of the BIA role in urban migration and adjustment of not only Navajos, but all American Indian groups.

But first we shall briefly examine the twenty-nine Navajo "loners." Throughout the previous analysis, wives have not been considered as providing a reference group for their husbands. The critical role played by wives in the adjustment of the migrants has been amply demonstrated (McSwain 1965; Graves

Chapter 7 in this volume). Seven of the twenty-nine loners are married. Given that a wife is a reference group and provides emotional support, we can reduce the loner population from twenty-nine (22 percent) to twenty-two (16 percent), which approaches the Spanish-American data reported above.

The point here, however, is not just to reduce the loner population, but to demonstrate the significant role played by wives in the initial social adjustment — indeed, the total adjustment — of Navajo migrants in Denver. McSwain (1965) in several case studies examines in detail the wives' feelings and actions toward their husbands' social activities, particularly when they are related to drinking, as well as their economic role in managing the household budget. Graves (in this text) demonstrates statistical relationships between marriage and economic, social, and psychological adjustment. And, finally, in the diary of Andy Bodie, a Denver Navajo urban migrant, his wife's words emerge in his recollection: "I told her I met my brother on my way coming back. Told her I drunk beer at his apartment. Then she said the next time don't drink any beer or don't fool around with him because if he gets you drunk he might let you alone and you might get hurt. Don't bother to fool around with him she said. I said okay." But the subject was not dropped. Following a second drinking episode with his brother, Andy relates: "She said why do you like to drink with your brother? I said just to have a little fun. She said you shouldn't do that. Because he might get you in trouble. I said well, I won't do that anymore" (McCracken 1968:280–281, 315).

Finally, an overall view of the Denver sample shows some interesting data. If a migrant is married for all or part of the time in the city, his average stay is much longer than if he remains single throughout his stay (Table 5.3). Thus, marriage does indeed have a great effect on the length of urban residence. When these data are coupled with the work of McSwain (1965) and Graves (in this text), a rather complete picture emerges of the role wives can and do play in the adjustment of migrants. The importance of wives during the initial migration period means they should be considered as an accompanying reference group. Forty-four percent of the Denver sample are married.

Two factors, or variables, emerge: (1) kin and/or friends in the city, and (2) a wife. Through these factors we gain a great deal of insight concerning urban adjustment: married migrants stay longer; migrants who have a reference group (previous or accompanying) upon arrival also stay longer in the city than those designated as loners, an average of twenty-nine months versus twenty months, respectively. Viewed alone, these variables reveal little; it is the interaction, or interplay, of them that adds richness to the results.

TABLE 5.3

The Joint Effect of Marriage and Reference Group at Arrival on Length of Navajo Residence in Denver

	Number of Months (Mean) in Denver
Married and some kin/friends at arrival	61.5
Married and no kin/friends at arrival	46.5
Single and some kin/friends at arrival	21.6
Single and no kin/friends at arrival	27.1

Table 5.3 presents these findings. Besides supporting the earlier independent results that married migrants stay longer and people with a reference group at arrival stay longer, one significant relationship emerges. Those people who are married and have some kin or friends in the city upon their arrival stay in the city on the average of two and one-half to three years longer than the loners (unmarried and no friends or kin in the city at arrival). This finding alone is so significant that it should suggest future policy in the BIA Relocation Services Program.

These are not, however, the only social variables effecting success or failure in the city. Many other factors help us make finer distinctions and therefore more specific observations about behavioral science theory, or government policy. What are the other attributes of the initial social environment of the migrant? A few friends and kin in the city, though important, do not constitute an enclave and do not have the resources available in a large enclave to aid a new migrant's adjustment problems. In fact, the average size of a reference group at arrival for the Navajo is only one person. The enclave, then, is not just an associational network of a few kin and friends, but is a geographical area in the city inhabited by fellow ethnics or tribal affiliates. The best examples in American culture would be the Black ghettos, the Chicano *barrios,* or the Chinatowns found in larger cities. The enclave is relatively large in contrast to the initial reference group of kin and friends, who themselves may be recent migrants, and offers a core of established, long-term residents who can serve, and do in many cases, as experts or "gatekeepers" in locating housing and jobs, or can advise about problems that arise for the new arrivals.

THE URBAN ETHNIC ENCLAVE

The decision by a reservation Navajo to migrate to an urban area requires the abandonment of the traditional milieu in which he was reared. He must adjust to an entirely new *social* milieu, in which the closely knit, supportive structure of his reservation background may be attenuated or even absent. In reference group theory, urban migration can be conceptualized as a shift in membership group. Furthermore, this shift in membership involves a similar shift in reference group.

"Transitional reference group" is the term chosen to describe this phenomenon (Graves, Alfred, and Van Arsdale 1964:8). Formally, the transitional reference group can be defined as a sub-set of individuals with membership in two groups simultaneously — the group the individual is leaving (the reservation, or home) and the group into which he is moving. The members of this second group make up the urban ethnic enclave; during the transition period of a new migrant this group provides technical assistance, as well as support and identification.

The urban literature frequently contains ethnographic descriptions of such an enclave. But how does one make the concept operable in order to validate its reality? The procedure used for Denver Navajos follows.

Because the transitional reference group or enclave provides the migrant's first friends, helps him when he needs it, and introduces him to the demands of city life and the means learned for coping with these demands, the enclave is defined as *a group of people with a common ethnic background, who interact with each other at a high rate, and live within narrow geographical confines in the city.*

To explore further the existence of the enclave as defined, several variables were used to test the hypothesis that such an enclave exists in Denver among the Navajo.

Operational Definitions. The Urban Ethnic Enclave. The operational definition of the ethnic enclave is defined by several variables: (1) the number of the total population of Denver Navajos known by each subject, (2) the frequency of interaction with other Navajos, and (3) the geographic proximity measured in city blocks separating respondents.

Sociometric List. A list of all male adult Navajos known to be or believed to be in Denver on direct employment assistance at each data collection period was presented to the respondents. Each respondent was asked if he knew the person mentioned and if he had seen him in the last month. A score of 0 was given for not knowing the person mentioned, a 1 if he knew the person but had not seen him in the last month, and a 2 if he had seen him in the last month. A total of all scores gave the subject a sociometric score, a measure of his interaction-identification with the Denver Navajo enclave.

Interaction Frequency. Each subject was asked how often he "got together" with other Navajos, with other Indians, i.e., non-Navajos, and with non-Indians. From these data an interaction rate per month for each respondent with each of the three groups was computed.

Geographic Proximity. This is the number of blocks between each respondent's place of residence.

Time in Denver. Time in Denver from arrival to departure is expressed in months. BIA file information yielded the date of arrival in most cases and the date of departure in some. Where dates were not available from file information, self-report and key informant data were employed.

Several approaches, each employing a different set of relevant data, were utilized to establish the existence or nonexistence of the urban ethnic enclave. In the first method, eighty-three respondents (all adult Navajo male heads of households who were relocatees in Denver) were scored on the sociometric list employed to indicate the extent of interaction among Denver Navajos. None of the subjects knew everyone on the list; the mean ($\bar{X}$) number of acquaintances was seventeen; the highest number was forty-six, about half the Navajos then residing in Denver. The older, longer residents, it appears, may have begun to expand their reference groups and move out of the Denver Navajo transitional reference group. Therefore, we would expect this finding in interaction rates, high interaction with Denver Navajos being found among those just beginning the assimilation process.

The second approach, a sort of alternative measure of interaction, is afforded by a second set of data. If an enclave existed with high interaction rates, then we would expect that most Navajos interacted with other Navajos at a high rate, and there would be little other Indian and non-Indian interaction among this transitional reference group. But a muddling factor becomes evident for the first time — the length of *Time in Denver*. Indeed, the correlation between frequency of Navajo interaction and time in Denver is −.377, suggesting that the longer a respondent resides in Denver the *less* he interacts with other Navajos. This also supports the previous finding that Navajos in Denver do not know all other Navajos. The older residents have begun to assimilate, or at least expand, social interactions beyond Navajo tribal affiliates.

A median split on time in Denver provides us with some control over the data. Table 5.4 shows that those respondents with a low time in Denver (twenty-two months or less) have a significantly higher overall interaction rate than do those with high time in Denver (more than twenty-two). Two problems become evident, however. First, the "lows" do have a relatively high rate of interaction with other Indians and non-Indians, which is especially obvious in the corresponding mean figures among the "highs," who by our model would have been expected to interact more frequently with other Indians and non-Indians than the "lows." Furthermore, by recasting the "frequency of interaction" variables into proportions, a similar pattern is found, except that the "highs," when they do interact, interact more with non-Indians, although not significantly so.

TABLE 5.4

*Frequencies and Proportions of Interaction with Navajos,
Other Indians, and Non-Indians according to Length of Time
in Denver of Navajo Migrants*

Variables		Low Time in Denver (N = 65)	High Time in Denver (N = 70)	t and Significance of t Value
Total sociometric score	$\overline{X}$	27.4	27.9	0.13
	σ	18.6	20.1	N.S.
Frequency of inter- action with Navajos	$\overline{X}$	13.2	5.8	2.95
	σ	11.8	8.0	$p = < .01$
Proportion of Navajo interactions	$\overline{X}$	77.3	66.4	1.49
	σ	26.2	37.5	N.S.
Frequency of inter- action with other Indians	$\overline{X}$	2.6	1.4	0.98
	σ	5.9	3.7	N.S.
Proportion of other Indian interactions	$\overline{X}$	10.6	9.9	0.16
	σ	16.4	20.7	N.S.
Frequency of inter- action with non- Indians	$\overline{X}$	3.9	1.7	1.27
	σ	9.2	3.2	N.S.
Proportion of non- Indian interactions	$\overline{X}$	11.5	21.1	1.72
	σ	17.4	31.1	N.S.
Time in Denver	$\overline{X}$	5.3	54.3	12.75
	σ	6.5	31.5	$p = < .001$

N = no. of respondents
N.S. = not significant
σ = standard error of the mean

p = significant
$\overline{X}$ = mean

The tentative support for the hypothesis that an enclave existed among Denver Navajos can be explained in several ways.
First, those Navajos in Denver twenty-two months or less may
not have become acquainted with all the Denver Navajos they
would eventually know as time passed. A second possibility that
there is no social assimilation going on among Denver Navajos
and that they maintain a strong ethnic interaction-identity
throughout their Denver residence has been shown not to be
true. The "highs" do show a tendency to expand their interactions

to non-Indians even in the face of their overall drop in interaction rates. The third possibility that assimilation means cutting all association with tribal members, friends, and kin also does not seem true. In fact, in Table 5.4 interaction frequency with other Navajos is significantly lower for the "highs," but not absent.

Finally, the actual population sizes of the Navajo, other Indian and non-Indian subgroups tend to effect actual interactions. The larger size of the other Indian population and the extremely large size, in contrast, of the non-Indian population raises the probabilities significantly that a new migrant comes into interaction with both of these subgroups early in his urban experience. Furthermore, due to the small Navajo population in the city, the lack of a Navajo ghetto also places the migrant into more "contact" with non-Navajos. He cannot insulate himself from the total urban society; he has no ghetto in which he can hide, withdraw, or establish himself, isolated from the dominant urban society.

Turning to the third variable — geographic proximity — as an indicator of the existence of an urban enclave, a great spread in Navajo urban residences is observable. A subsample of fifty respondents examined as to their geographical proximity showed the average distance in blocks between them to be greater than nine blocks. But again, time in the city may lead to a dispersion of the ethnic enclave. Therefore it was necessary to use a control for time. Nevertheless, even among the "lows" in this sample (less than twenty-two months in the city), the average distance between them was found to be three and a half blocks, but with a range from zero (live in the same apartment) to eighteen blocks. These findings suggest a rejection of the hypothesis, but is a distance of three and a half blocks far in a large city? And with the small population of Navajos in Denver can they be expected to have "carved" out an area for a Navajo enclave?

In sum, three different approaches have been employed (one with an alternative) in an attempt to discover the existence of an ethnic urban enclave among Navajo migrants in Denver. We have been able to support its existence on a tentative basis. The need to rationalize certain findings, a shortcoming in the method, is not without foundation to the investigator, but we can see that other types of data, more in tune with the actual physical environment of the city might well have aided the tentativeness of the empirical data presented.

FUNCTIONS SERVED BY THE ENCLAVE

In the cross-cultural urbanization literature, observations about the functions served by the enclave for the new migrant are numerous. These functions ameliorate the problems of adjustment for the new migrant. Seen as a surrogate social structure transplanted from the rural situation, the enclave provides certain services: initial lodging, financial support, aid in finding employment, as well as moral support, protection from the insecurities of the urban environment, and in some cases enhancement of group distinctiveness and the maintenance in the city of traditional practices and beliefs.

The American Indian situation, however, is unique. Many functions attributable to the enclave are handled by the BIA. Not all American Indian urban migrants come to the city under BIA auspices, but in the Denver study only nineteen Navajos (14 percent) came on their own; the rest came under the Relocation Services Program.

How does the BIA become an "enclave"? Application for relocation services is voluntarily initiated on the reservation, or in many cases at one of the BIA Indian Schools, for example, Intermountain School at Brigham City, Utah. To each application is appended health, welfare, educational, and police records. Acceptance into the program lies in an evaluation of this application for various qualities, with most emphasis on an overall expectation made by the reservation office — Can the applicant be "expected to succeed"?

Once an applicant is accepted, a decision is made concerning his relocation site and his file is sent to the BIA office in that city. Upon a favorable review by the urban office, preparations are made on the reservation for the relocatee's departure and in the city for his arrival. Transportation, shipping of belongings, and subsistence costs are arranged and paid for by the BIA.

The relocatee is met on arrival, or in some cases, immediately goes alone to the Relocation Services Office. Several days of orientation and counseling ensue; these sessions range in subject from the use of buses, personal appearance, and medical insurance plans to the social climate of the city. Housing is located during this period, and a job is secured.

Services, both counseling and job placement, are extended for approximately one year, or until the migrant is significantly well adjusted to the urban scene to be expected to use community agencies. During this period, a social worker visits the residence of each migrant at the end of one month, then three months, and finally six months, to see how "things are going" and to offer help if problems have arisen.

The BIA is, then, an enclave because it provides many technical and economic functions usually ascribed in the literature to the urban ethnic enclave. But does it provide all? The previous discussion suggests that it does not. Of the migrants 62 percent have some reference group upon arrival (see Table 5.2) and in fact 17 percent stated that they chose Denver because they had friends or relatives already living there. These factors are certainly important to the migrant regardless of the BIA program and all its services.

Another factor associated with American Indian urbanization demonstrates the artificiality of the BIA relocation program. Cross-culturally, in unsponsored and unsupported urbanization movements, about 60 percent of all migrants are married, but among Navajo relocatees who have come to Denver since 1952 only 20 percent are married. Why?

The answer to this question is complex, although two factors probably provide a large part of the answer: (1) oversell and (2) quota. A large proportion of the Navajo relocatees — this would doubtless be true of other Indian groups as well — comes directly from BIA boarding schools. They have spent five years, if they were in the special Indian education program, or even twelve years (high school completed) in some cases, at a boarding school. The BIA makes every attempt to place graduates in the urban relocation program.

Several Denver Navajos stated that having completed school and the vocational training associated with it, they were asked in which city they wished to relocate; they were not offered the alternative of going home. Furthermore, in selling the idea of relocation to the new graduates, a much nicer picture of relocation, job placement, income, and benefits of urban living, is painted than most Navajos have experienced once they relocated in the city. A not uncommon example is found in relocatees who, armed with a welding "certificate" from Intermountain School, came to the city expecting to earn three to four dollars an hour. They found that either the job market was flooded with welders (most having experience which they lacked), or that the certificate meant nothing and first apprenticeship was necessary — if such an opening could be found.

This type of oversell was not, however, without reason. The natural environmental pressure of bureaucratic structures makes it imperative that the BIA justify its existence to Congress; therefore quotas must be filled. What better resource for filling of quotas than recently trained American Indian boarding school graduates who are still within the grasp of the agency?

The combination of these factors has led to the labeling of the Relocation Services Program as the "American Indian Fulbright Act," as well as an overrepresentation in the cities of young single American Indians whose commitment is in many cases open to question and, indeed, questioned by these relocatees themselves. "I came to have fun." "I am having a vacation before going home." "They told me at school I should relocate. Denver is the closest to my home."

From further examination, another effect of the BIA is found to be the patterning of initial social contacts among relocatees. In most urban centers, the BIA has a few contacts with industries and companies who will hire the inexperienced and poorly trained Indian relocatee. A new migrant is often placed with these companies and thereby meets others like himself. Furthermore, the BIA usually has developed contacts with a few boarding houses and apartment landlords who will rent to American Indians. Again through these previously structured channels, a new migrant gets to know others like himself.

This is not to say that these factors lead to negative aspects of migrant adjustment, but to point out that this unstated policy exists through the structure and resources that the BIA has in housing and job placement. If the policy of the BIA is to cluster or to put American Indian relocatees into contact with each other, that is acceptable; but if the policy aims toward dispersion of the relocatees into the general population, then the agency has failed. Neither alternative is better than the other; in fact, the best policy would be a combination of the two. New arrivals should be put in contact with older, established residents who can provide not only help in adjustment, but a positive role model of behavior and successful adaptation to urban-industrial living.

The fact that many migrants are young, single, and on their own for the first time off the reservation (except for boarding school) and that social sanctions are lacking against deviant behavior probably accounts for the overwhelming results presented by Graves (Chapter 7 in this text) concerning alcohol-related arrests. The lack of an enclave structure, of a surrogate social structure in the city, leaves the young, single, and non-committed migrant free to pursue his whims, to "sow his wild oats," all at the expense of the BIA and all without any form of social control or peer-sanctioning, except for local police and the drunk tank in the local jail. Thus, the young single migrant is overrepresented for various reasons. The reason for the extremely high return rate to the reservations of the Relocation Services Program relocatees is obvious.

SOCIAL INTERACTION PATTERNS

As a group, 66 percent of the Denver Navajo social interactions per month are taken up by other Navajos, 14 percent by other Indians, and 20 percent by non-Indians. Each respondent was also asked, "Where do you usually get together?" His responses for each group with which he reported some social interaction were scored as public, private, or both. The data, which appear in Table 5.5, show several interesting results.

First, Navajos tend to have just as high a percentage of private encounters with non-Indians as with other Navajos. Second, as was evident in percent of interactions per month, Denver Navajos interact more with non-Indians than other Indians and a greater percentage of these interactions is private. These findings lend some support to an earlier conclusion that non-Indians, being the majority in the city, are more available *to interact with* than other Indians who form a very small segment of the total urban population. In order to gain a more descriptive picture of what social activities were involved, these same data were

TABLE 5.5

Denver Navajos' Interaction Patterns

Denver Navajos' Interactions	Public	Private	Both
With other Navajos			
Percentage	34	48	18
Number	24	34	13
With other Indians			
Percentage	72	27	1
Number	21	8	1
With non-Indians			
Percentage	45	48	6
Number	15	16	2

subjected to a content analysis; the categories from this analysis appear in Table 5.6. The percentages in the table represent the proportions of responses made in each category; in most cases respondents made several responses about what activities were involved.

Among Navajos the greatest amount of social interaction takes place in each other's homes or downtown, with a minimum of drinking or meeting at bars reported. The picture is quite different when they are interacting with other Indians. There is an equal amount of home interaction and visiting the White Buffalo Council and the Denver Indian Center. The White Buffalo Council is a Pan-Indian organization in Denver which meets once a month; it is mainly fostered by Sioux, but members represent many Indian tribes. The Denver Indian Center also caters to all tribes and is run by a pastor and his wife. It is interesting to note that home interaction and White Buffalo Council or Indian Center interaction are second in intensity to downtown. Indeed, other Indian interaction does not seem as personal when contrasted to both other Navajos and non-Indians. The largest percentage of non-Indian interaction is in homes as it was with other Navajos; downtown is second in order, followed by meeting at church and in bars.

In order to gain even greater descriptive information about informal social activities each respondent was asked what he

TABLE 5.6

Location of Denver Navajo Informal Social Interaction Patterns

Denver Navajos' Interactions	In Own Home	At Homes of Friends or Relatives	At Church	At White Buffalo Council or Indian Center	At Parties, Houses, Dances, Wrestling Matches	In Bars	In the Mountains	At Bowling or Playing Pool	Downtown
With other Navajos									
Percentage	39	29	4	2	8	3	1	3	20
Number	46	22	5	3	9	4	1	4	24
With other Indians									
Percentage	19	11	2	19	9	7	0	2	30
Number	8	5	1	8	4	3	0	1	13
With non-Indians									
Percentage	24	22	10	2	7	10	0	5	20
Number	10	9	4	1	3	4	0	2	8

usually did when he got together with other Navajos, other Indians, and non-Indians. The categories were derived, as before, from the content of each respondent's answers. These data are presented in Table 5.7. Two categories account for over half the responses across all three groups: (1) talk, and (2) listen to the radio, watch television, or play cards. Playing pool and going to dances or movies, however, seem to be Indian activities that completely exclude non-Indians.

One interesting aspect of Tables 5.6 and 5.7 is the reporting of meeting at bars and of drinking as an activity. The smallest percentage of both activities is reported when interacting with other Navajos, and the highest with non-Indians. Furthermore, the overall incidence of drinking seems to be rather lower than one would expect. In fact, of the eighty-five respondents who reported that they drink, they drink rather heavily and, on the average, they report getting drunk about five times a year. Their arrest rates are quite high, the average being .72 times a year; 95 percent or more of these arrests are drinking-related.

Each respondent was also asked, "Do you belong to any clubs, athletic clubs, etc., here in Denver?" Only nine Navajos, or 8 percent, reported such an activity. Seven reported there were non-Indian members, and the other two said there were other Indians in the club. No exclusively Navajo organizations seem to exist among the Denver Navajos.

Twenty-four respondents reported attending meetings of the White Buffalo Council on an average of six times a year. These twenty-four Navajos account for 23 percent of respondents. This is not an insignificant figure, especially when coupled with a rather high rate of attendance.

Finally, of the total sample, only five respondents reported that they did *not* interact socially with other Navajos. The first, who had been in Denver for four years, made no statement about why he knew no other Navajos in Denver, but he was an alcoholic. The second, in Denver for nine years, said that he used to have Navajo friends at work, but now there were no Navajos. Another is a college graduate, the only one in the sample, who openly stated that he used the relocation program only to finance his family's move from the reservation because he already had a job. The fourth, in Denver for more than ten years, said he used to

TABLE 5.7

Activities and Denver Navajo Informal Social Interaction Patterns

Denver Navajos' Interactions	Talk	Listen to Radio; Watch TV; Play Cards	Drive Around	Go to Church	Play Pool; Go to Movies and Dances	Go to the Mountains	Drink	Go Downtown	Eat Out or at Home	Play Basketball, Baseball, Football	Go to White Buffalo Council
With other Navajos											
Percentage	35	13	6	2	17	3	3	10	8	2	0
Number	54	21	10	3	26	5	5	16	13	3	0
With other Indians											
Percentage	33	18	7	2	18	0	7	4	9	0	2
Number	18	10	4	1	10	0	4	2	5	0	1
With non-Indians											
Percentage	48	14	4	4	0	0	12	2	8	6	2
Number	24	7	2	2	0	0	6	1	4	3	1

have a lot of Navajo friends, but they drank too much; when he gave up drinking, he gave up his Navajo friends too. The last, in Denver nine years, also said he used to have Navajo friends, but he "got religion" and gave up drinking; he stated further that he prefers to stay away from other Navajos because they always borrow money.

THE URBAN SOCIAL MILIEU

Most of the urbanization studies in the literature treat the ethnic enclave as an undifferentiated group with essentially a uniform effect on all its members. It was felt, however, that greater analytic differentiation was possible. Indeed, when an enclave does not exist, as in this case study, it is important to know what the social organization of the migrant group is, for through this, the structural means by which to view adjustment is to be discovered.

Thus, through greater analytic differentiation we hoped to produce a model closer to reality, a model in which social adjustment would readily become observable. Most ethnic enclaves *are* broken down into small cliques on the basis of such criteria as age, marital status, interaction patterns, occupation, and urban residence. In fact when enclaves do not exist, I suspect cliques are the major social structure exhibited by migrant groups. The particular characteristics of the social clique with which a migrant becomes identified in the city is thereby likely to affect his assimilation, adjustment, and particularly many behavioral aspects.

In any review of membership-reference group theory the profound effects that primary groups have on the attitudes, values, and behavior of their members become obvious. Small social cliques are an excellent example of a primary group in which personal, face-to-face contacts are basic to the characteristics displayed by the group. These small social cliques then become of central importance in studying the values, attitudes, and behavior of the Denver Navajo.

Although primary groups may be quite fluid and therefore difficult to study in their natural setting, there may sometimes be more stability in the pattern of primary group interaction during periods of rapid change, where the traditional cultural context is deprived, removed, extinguished, or abandoned by individual choice, as in the case of urban migration. Under the stress of such self-imposed change, and the lack of an enclave structure, these groups provide the adaptive means to waylay stress and confront the subsequent problems. The primary group provides the context for induction of the new migrant into the urban milieu, and at the same time implants the attitudes, values, and behavior its members hold toward the city. Herein lies the power of the primary group.

In order to isolate these small groups or cliques a sociometric technique was employed. Each respondent was presented with a list of all Navajos known or believed to be in the city at the time of the interview. The respondent was asked if he knew each person, and if so, had he seen that person in the last month, and in the last week. These data were then subjected to a cluster analysis (BC TRY program), and clusters of people (or cliques) who knew each other and had seen each other recently emerged. Six cliques evolved from this analysis; supportive tests and outcomes validated the statistical reality of these cliques.

With the data about the six empirically derived cliques in hand, we examine it to see if social assimilation exists among Denver Navajos. To facilitate this investigation, t tests to determine statistically significant relationships in the data were run between all six cliques across a set of variables employed to measure social assimilation. The results appear in Table 5.8.

By ordering these cliques across the means of time spent in Denver from cliques 1 to 6, one might expect a linear increase or decrease in magnitude of each variable, such increase or decrease depends on the expected orderings resulting from a hypothesis that states that social assimilation will increase with time in the city. With this hypothesis, we would expect a decrease in total sociometric score, a decrease in Navajo interaction, and an increase in both other-Indian and non-Indian interactions. Table 5.8 shows the total sociometric score does decrease as expected, but significance is only found between clique 1 and cliques 3, 5, and 6; and between clique 2 and cliques 5 and 6. For frequency of Navajo interaction there is a slight decrease in the magnitude of the means, but clique 5 shows a sharp increase as does clique 3.

TABLE 5.8

Social Clique Membership and the Social Assimilation of Navajo Migrants to Denver

		Clique Numbers					
		1	*2*	*3*	*4*	*5*	*6*
Frequency of interaction with Navajos	$\bar{X}$	10.4	13.7	17.0	3.0	10.8	3.7
	σ	11.1	12.9	18.4	2.0	10.3	2.7
Frequency of interaction with other Indians	$\bar{X}$	0.5	3.8	0.0	0.0	1.6	2.4
	σ	1.3	7.8	0.0	0.0	3.1	4.8
Frequency of interaction with non-Indians	$\bar{X}$	0.2	3.4	0.0	1.2	4.0	1.9
	σ	0.6	7.5	0.0	1.9	5.0	2.9
Months in Denver	$\bar{X}$	18.3	23.3	25.7	43.0	58.9	60.2
	σ	12.8	18.6	3.1	16.2	37.5	42.5

Significance of Observed t Values

Frequency of interaction with Navajos	$2 > 6(p = < .01)$; $2 > 4(p = < .01)$
Frequency of interaction with other Indians	$6 > 3(p = < .05)$; $6 > 4(p = < .05)$
Frequency of interaction with non-Indians	$6 > 1(p = < .05)$; $6 > 3(p = < .01)$
Time in Denver	$1 > 5(p = < .05)$; $4 > 1(p = < .05)$; $4 > 2(p = < .05)$; $5 > 2(p = < .05)$; $5 > 3(p = < .05)$; $6 > 1(p = < .001)$; $6 > 2(p = < .001)$; $6 > 3(p = < .001)$

σ = standard error of the mean $\bar{X}$ = mean
p = significant

The only significant difference here is between cliques 2 and 5, and between cliques 2 and 4. Frequency of other Indian interaction shows no expected increase in means. Non-Indian interaction frequency, on the other hand, shows a slight increase from cliques 1 to 6; clique 2 exhibits the highest rate of all, and clique 3 reports no non-Indian interaction. We can only conclude that social assimilation is probably *not* simply a linear function of time in Denver.

SOCIAL CLIQUES AND ADJUSTMENT

This explication proposes that adjustment will be a function of the social clique to which a migrant belongs. Since these social cliques conform to the reality of the Denver-Navajo social structure and to a membership-reference group theory model, this process can be viewed more realistically, i.e., in closer conformity to the reality of urban adjustment among the Denver Navajo. Theoretically, we would expect that the clique, acting as a reference group, would instill upon its membership the adjustment pattern it poses as a reference group. Cliques should then differ from one another. However, it is possible that some of the cliques are enough alike to be but variants of one basic pattern. This is the case in one instance where two of the cliques are similar enough to be considered a *type*. All other cliques retain their distinct differences in one way or another.

In order to have some standard by which to judge the adjustment pattern exhibited by the six Navajo cliques, a hypothetical successful adjustment pattern should be presented. First, successful urban adjustment would be predicted by a firm background of preparation and experience. This would encompass not only schooling but the amount of vocational training and the particular skill learned. Furthermore, work experience would be important, as well as contact with whites and English language skills. Economically, the success pattern would be one of little unemployment, few job changes, and a long mean job length coupled with relatively high wages. Psychologically, the successful migrant would exhibit little stress and no alienation. He would be optimistic, see a future advantage to living in Denver, be economically oriented, and exhibit a high score on achievement motivation. He would also be internally controlled and nontraditional in viewing his own well-being and goals. The successful migrant would exhibit no drinking problems and thus would lack an arrest record.

Because of the large number of variables involved they will not be presented here, but each clique will be discussed in general, in its patterning across these variables, and the contrasts and differences between them pointed out, rather than their similarities. Furthermore, the discussion will center on the first three cliques and the differences among them. The other three cliques viewed briefly following discussion of the others, are small and therefore of minor importance. In fact, one clique no longer exists as the members have all returned to the reservation. Most Denver Navajos belong in the three major cliques and thereby these cliques exhibit the best picture of Navajo urban adjustment. By focusing on the three major cliques the tedious task of trying to view all six at once is reduced.

Major Cliques. Clique 1. In background variables, clique 1 exhibits average schooling, the lowest number of months of vocational training, and lowest premigration wage. In armed services experience and premigration contact with the dominant society, this clique has the second to lowest mean. This is also true of premigration work experience, highest premigration wage, age at relocation, and total contact with urban-industrial society when first interviewed. These Denver Navajos were the youngest when first contacted.

Once in Denver this group had the highest unemployment rate and the highest rate of job changes; this, of course, was coupled with a very low mean job length. Furthermore, they receive the lowest wages of any of the cliques and so borrow money at a high rate.

In terms of the psychological scales, they report the least stress. They are nontraditional and the most optimistic about their relative urban success. In behavior, this clique reports the second lowest number of times drunk in the last year, but they have the second highest arrest rate. Only about one-third of the sixteen members are married. They have been in Denver the shortest time and are thereby the least socially assimilated.

Clique 2. The second clique has thirty-three members and is quite similar in most variables to clique 1. In fact, a correlation between cliques 1 and 2 on these variables produces a correlation coefficient of .43 which is significant at the .05 level. However, there are some differences: clique 2 has significantly more months of vocational training, less unemployment once in Denver, and a much higher initial wage. Other differences are also apparent: clique 2 exhibits a lower frequency of job changes and little borrowing, but is more in debt than clique 1 or clique 3.

Clique 2 also reports a somewhat higher number of times drunk in the last year than clique 1, a few more drinking-related problems, but a much lower arrest rate. Again only about one-third of the members are married.

Clique 3. The last major clique has been in Denver as a group the longest. Seventy-five percent of the twenty-eight members are married. They have the highest type of vocational training and are a bit older, on the average, than some of the other cliques; otherwise, they exhibit average background preparation and experience.

In Denver this group has the highest mean for job length, and the highest present wage; they also report the greatest amount of debts. Psychologically, they exhibit a low fatalism score and relatively high achievement motivation. On the other hand, they see little future advantage to living in Denver.

In urban behavior this clique represents the highest number of times drunk per year and the highest yearly arrest rate. The interesting contrast here is the economic success and the extreme drinking and arrest problems exhibited by the members of this clique. Furthermore, this clique is the most socially assimilated of all.

To understand these three major cliques better, we will examine them ethnographically. The three minor cliques will be characterized only by the variables in the following section. The reader is asked to look at the major cliques more closely because of their size.

The first clique, in fact the first two cliques (correlation .43), are the young, unmarried Navajos. Much of their spare time including weekdays revolves around drinking. Because of this, they experience a great deal of absenteeism and lose their jobs frequently. These people generally have adopted the attitude that the city is a place to have fun and a job is necessary only for this end. They have little long-term investment in the city and leave at a frequent rate, only to be replaced by new arrivals with a similar attitude.

The third clique represents the married, economically well-adjusted older migrants. These people are well in tune with Anglo industrial society and are making a successful "go" of the city. Although they exhibit severe drinking problems and are arrested frequently, the drinking is weekend drinking characteristic of the blue-collar working class. Financially their situation allows them to pay bail and fines, so that arrests and drinking do not interfere with their jobs. Wives or girlfriends are often included in weekend activities.

Minor Cliques. Clique 4. This clique has only five members, four of whom are married. In background, this clique seems well prepared and experienced for urban adjustment; they have better than average schooling as a group, as well as more vocational training than any of the other six cliques. They have had relatively high armed services experience, contact with whites, and premigration work experience. They are a bit older in comparison with the other cliques at relocation and at first interview contact. Economically this clique has had the least job changes and the second highest present wage. Their background preparation probably accounts for these findings.

In psychological scales, this clique is found to be the least alienated; they report little psychological stress. Further, this clique exhibits the most internal, i.e., nonfatalistic, control of their own well-being, has the highest economic value orientation, and perceives the future advantage of Denver as a home. Rather surprisingly, they are not very optimistic and scored the lowest in achievement motivation.

Surprisingly, this clique reports the heaviest drinking — a quite high rate of drunkenness in the last year — and the most drinking-related problems. This is unexpected because of their seemingly well-adjusted economic and psychological patterns. In contrast to their obvious drinking pattern, they have the lowest arrest rate.

Clique 5. This group has nine members, only three of whom are not married. This clique offers a contrasting picture of background experience to that of clique 1. The members have the least amount of schooling experience and very little vocational training. But this group had much armed services' experience, the highest premigration contact, and the highest premigration work experience. The premigration wage is the lowest reported, but this clique also happens to be made up of the oldest migrants; age would place these migrants in an earlier period when wages were lower than they are now for the younger migrants.

In Denver this group has had a low unemployment problem, the least job changes, and the highest mean job length. This clique borrows at a high rate as a group and reported that debts are high; they have only average wages.

Psychologically, we find in this group a rather conflicting picture. They exhibit a high economic value orientation and relatively high achievement motivation. In contrast, but not surprisingly, they are the most alienated, report the most psychological stress, and are the least optimistic. Although they see little future advantage of Denver to meet their goals, they are the least traditional. This seems to point a clear picture of frustration of economic gain.

The group seems to have few behavioral problems since they report an average rate of alcoholic consumption and of times drunk, the least number of drinking-related problems, and a low arrest rate.

Clique 6. This clique is one of the most interesting. There are only three members and all of them have left the city. This clique has the most schooling of all the cliques, but on the other hand has the poorest vocational training and fewest months of vocational training. They also have very little pre-Denver work experience or contact with whites and yet have the highest pre-migration wage pattern and wages. Once in Denver, however, their wages are the lowest exhibited by any clique; subsequently they experience much unemployment, a high job turnover, and a low mean for job length. In contrast to this, they feel they should make a great deal more money per hour than most of the other cliques.

Surprisingly, this group reports the greatest number of psychological stress problems and yet are the least economically value-oriented. But again they are the most optimistic and see a fairly good future advantage of living in Denver, rather than on the reservation. In behavioral aspects this clique seems to have the fewest problems. They report the least drinking, say that they have not been drunk in the last year, and thus do not have any drinking-related problems. They do, indeed, have a fairly low arrest rate.

Coupled with good background experience and high premigration wages upon arriving in Denver this group received very low wages. It is not then surprising that they all left.

The six cliques, especially the first three, do indeed offer quite different patterns of adjustment after which a new migrant might pattern his own adjustment in the city. Since individual migrants are different, these cliques offer six reference group environments into which the new migrant might move, and with which he might affiliate depending on his predisposition toward his urban commitment. The three major cliques probably draw the most *new* members.

The cliques' patterns of drinking and arrests pose an interesting interpretive problem. Recalling the hypothetical successful adjustment pattern, we expected that adjustment and economic success would predict a low arrest record and little problem drinking. In characterizing clique 3, this was found not to be the case; this best adjusted, economically successful Navajo group had the highest drinking rate. In the absence of any obvious psychological problems, this outcome comes as a surprise. This assumes, however, the correctness of the premise that drinking is maladaptive for urban success. Without going into possible *causes* of this subcultural pattern, let us accept that it is a reality and poses no threat to the social or economic position of the lower-class workers involved and does not seem, as evidenced by clique 3, to greatly affect urban adjustment for Navajos.

VALIDITY THROUGH ETHNOGRAPHY

Having derived these social cliques empirically and characterized them in order to investigate the urban social assimilation and adjustment exhibited by the Denver Navajos, the question again arises: To what extent do these cliques correspond to the Denver Navajo social organization? That is, are these cliques *ethnographically* "real"? The statistical and ethnographic outcomes are harmonious as is shown below.

In order to accomplish this, a long-time Denver Navajo resident was enlisted as a field assistant to aid in the data collection. He was informed of the interest in *all* Denver Navajo informal social activities and not just those of the clique to which he belonged or of his own.

Because a list was available of the members of each social clique and their addresses, it was easy for the field assistant to make contact with any Navajos unknown to him. In this manner, all the cliques and most of their members were contacted. The inestimable value of the field assistant becomes apparent here. The field assistant, due to his ethnic identity, was able to gain immediate rapport with a previously unknown subject. With some individuals, more visits were necessary, but in most cases a single visit with a subject sufficed to gain an invitation to join him in an activity — almost always a group activity that included other members of a subject's clique. Through contact with almost all the Denver Navajos, we were able to isolate the interaction group of each individual, and these converged to a social and exclusive membership group of people. In engaging in multiple activities with each group, we were able to map ethnographically the interaction groups of an individual Navajo, and thereby the social cliques emerged. In all cases we were able to establish that the six empirical cliques were *real*, that the ethnographic membership groups did correspond to the empirical findings, and that activities were centered around such social groups.

A subsidiary dividend to this endeavor was the interesting picture of the Navajo urban life. In collecting the clique validation data, we were at the same time exposed to Navajo urban behavior; this revealed how the Navajo view the urban milieu and how they behave in and toward this environment.

An Urban Ethnography. Notes on Mobility. In general, Navajos change residence at a very high rate. Distances involved are small and indeed tend to be within a few blocks. The reasons for this are probably involved but we determined from various respondents that the object of moving was to be closer to their friends. In a very few cases the landlady explained that heavy drinking, noise, and nonpayment of rent had led to eviction. The high mobility rate of Denver Navajos is not unusual; it is also found among other minority and ethnic groups in the city and seems to be related to poverty and low socioeconomic status.

Notes on Informal Social Activities. Although the survey yielded many informal social activities reported by the respondents, it was found ethnographically that those data did not present a true picture. Almost all Navajo social activities involve drinking, and only in situations where drinking is illegal, such as movies, is it absent. Indeed, drinking often ensues following attendance at a movie. Parties, dances, and wrestling matches involve drinking, and there tended to be an overreporting of such activities. Most informal social activities center around drinking at bars or drinking at home while watching television or playing cards. Among the married respondents observed, drinking occurred more often at home.

Notes on Drinking. Navajo drinking in Denver tends to center around five bars. One of the bars is a "3.2" bar where the Navajos who are not yet twenty-one can drink. The other four are "neighborhood" bars frequented by blue-collar workers. Beer alone appears to provide the total alcoholic intake for the Denver Navajos. When asked why beer is consumed, two answers were the most frequent: beer is cheaper than wine or hard liquor; only alcoholics on the reservation drank wine or hard liquor. Though consumed in great quantities, beer was not seen as a sign of problem drinking or alcoholism. But drinking always led to being "high" and, in most cases, to drunkenness.

The bars tended to be meeting places, and a Navajo would move from one to another until he found some of his friends. Then as a group they would move from bar to bar; it was during this interim, when driving or in most cases walking from one bar to another, that arrests were made. The group was always loud and boisterous and called attention to itself; subsequently, the police would arrive and arrests for drunkenness and disturbing the peace would be made.

Married couples would occasionally be present, but in more cases, a married man would be alone. Much conversation and activity were centered around the many single Navajo girls in Denver. In fact, both the single and married men indulge in sexual affairs with single Navajo girls.

Notes on Social Integration. In general, little interaction was observed with people other than Navajos. In the bars there is very little non-Indian as well as other-Indian interaction. The longer time residents and married Navajos tended to exhibit the most social interaction with these groups.

Alienation or hostility toward the dominant white culture of the city was apparent once rapport had been established. A great deal of joking and kidding was directed toward me; when the Navajos became tired of my participation, they would speak in Navajo to exclude me. At the time I had enough knowledge of the language to understand much of the discussion; mostly it was directed toward activities and girls, but in not a few cases the discussion centered around me, the *billiigana* who asked so many questions.

The impressions received from the answers to such questions fell into two types. First, the city was fun — a place to drink, chase girls, and get money to do so from the BIA. The other type of answer dealt with getting money to buy things. Probably the most desired item was a pickup truck; the second, a television set. The money to attain these goals is not available on the reservation.

The overall picture from this ethnographic investigation is both happy and sad. Most informal social activities are fun; the Navajos drink a lot and get drunk, but this serves both a social as well as a "release" function. These activities cost money, however, and jobs are low paying, so by the end of a hard weekend of fun and drinking there is little money left to save toward buying a pickup or a television set.

The Denver Navajos harbor a great animosity toward the whites. The white man took his ancestors' land and by his prejudice blocks the Navajos' path to success. They are acutely aware of their inadequate training and experience, and are bitter toward the BIA school and white men in general because of this. Indeed, the American Indian is a unique cultural character. He is aware of the general public's romantic view of the Indian, and uses this to his advantage upon occasion. For example, in Denver prejudice runs high toward Spanish-Americans. Physically the Navajo Indian is not too easily distinguishable from the Spanish-American by most Denverites. If an uncomfortable situation arises in which the Navajo is identified as a "Spic," he is quick to point out that he is Indian and thereby obtains concern and apology from the whites. This was observed on several occasions, especially in bars when the drunk Navajo was being "escorted" out or was in a fighting mood.

Hostility within the Navajo group seems to be absent; this is

not true of all other minority ethnic groups against which prejudice runs high. Furthermore, the Navajos have learned the urban
milieu prejudices; they profess hatred of Blacks and dread identification as Spanish-Americans. These feelings probably serve in
lieu of the within-group hostility. Indeed, the Navajos maintain
firm barriers to outsiders, and their native language helps this
resolve.

SUMMARY AND CONCLUSIONS

The initial social environment of the Navajos in Denver has been
patterned by having kin or friends in the city at arrival as well as
by marriage. This discovery, however, does not provide a sufficient understanding of the social milieu of the migrant nor a
total picture of urban adjustment. Secondly, the BIA profoundly
affects both patterning and structuring of the Navajos' urban adjustment process.

An attempt to identify an urban ethnic enclave proved fruitless. The BIA role in the urban migration, initial adjustment, and
orientation process of new migrants emerged. It was not until
the true social organization of the Denver Navajo revealed itself
that an understanding of urban adjustment was achieved.

By isolating those groups in the city that act as the migrants'
reference group we have been able to capture the reality of the
urban adjustment and assimilation of the Denver Navajo. Behavior was patterned by the membership-reference group.

The application of the findings presented to other Indian
groups is limited, but not absent. The effect of the BIA is probably constant and equal across all tribes, but the particular social
organization varies. Navajos have been observed to be different
in urban behavior and adaptation from other groups, and this
clearly emerges in pan-Indian activities; the Navajos tend not to
participate in these organizations. Furthermore, they do not have
the tribal-based voluntary organizations such as those reported
among other Indian groups in United States urban centers.

Beyond this point, the comparative aspects must evolve from
observational data, since the research itself included only Navajos. Observations at pan-Indian gatherings revealed a great deal
of participation by Indians in general, but little by the Navajos.
The other-Indian segment of the American Indian population in

Denver was observed while collecting the ethnographic material previously presented. As with the Navajos, much informal social activity revolved around small group drinking in the various "Indian bars" in Denver. Discussions with this group revealed problems and attitudes similar to those expressed by the Navajo.

To depart from these statistical attempts to study, analyze, and categorize the adjustment of Navajo urban migrants in Denver, a personal view of such an experience by Andy Bodie portrays what it really means to be a Navajo in the city.

We left for Denver in October of 1966. When we were leaving, one of my brothers-in-law, he was going to Albuquerque, so he give us a ride to Albuquerque. When I first got to Denver I felt very strange. Marylin didn't because she had been up several times before, about two years ago. Things was simple in Phoenix. Up in Phoenix everything was very simple. When a person needs something, he gets something, but you have to work for it. Up in Phoenix when you work for about a day, you get paid on that day. You get paid right away. You don't have to wait two weeks for your pay.

Sometimes when I'm in Denver I wish inside that I could be back at home. I wish that it was over in Denver. At Phoenix they like Indians. They don't give troubles to Indians. Here is for the first time that I find people that don't like Indians. I suppose it's because the Indians were the first people that were here in the United States. The white people don't want for the Indians to have anything. Right now there's a lot of Navajos are richer than white people in the United States. They change their cars every year, and they got plenty of money, 'cause I see them when I go from place to place. They don't have to work. They get about $250 a week. Some white people don't like for Indians to work among them. All they want is to have white mans everyplace. Everyplace they want to see white man; they don't want to see no other people such as Indians. The white people don't want to share money with Indians.

Living in Denver isn't simple. I go to Christian church when I'm in Denver. I go to make people think that we're not superstitious about Navajo religion. I try to worship as a Christian. If we don't they'll probably think we're very superstitious in the Navajo way; so we have to try and do what we can so they won't think we're really superstitious about everything.

When I came to Denver I didn't think I'd have much trouble

after a while. I had a lot of money, but that was before I bought that car. It was a '59 Ford. After we bought that car it seems like the money just go by — just like losing a hour or something.

So I think that the most important thing that a man has is to have money. I have found in Denver that things are too high. Everything. Groceries, clothing, gas, and everything else is too high. Up in Phoenix they usually sell gas from $.18 to $.24 a gallon, and groceries usually are not high. Perhaps if you wanted to buy two pounds of pork chops it cost you $.89; up here it's, gee, a pound of pork chops it cost you $.79. We went up to the grocery store one morning up here in Denver. I asked that man how much it was. Heck, one-half pound, $.89; $.89 it was for pork chops. So I think groceries are too high up in Denver. Like clothing. Things are too high. I couldn't get myself a pair of jeans or a pair of Levi's. Heck, I got to work by myself. Gas, gotta buy gas every week; and I'm always short on money. Ever since we bought that car.

On the reservation we usually eat corn and tortillas; about twice a week we usually have mutton. We kill sheep and we butcher them. About twice a week we have mutton to eat with cornbread or either tortillas, and once in a while we have different kind of food to eat. Whites have different food every day. That's one thing I like about white people. We been eating white man's food up here in Denver. Another thing I like about Denver is the weather. It's warm. One thing I find about Denver and white people — on the reservation the Navajos, even those who make $250 every week, they wear the same clothes for about a week and then they change. They don't dare lose a quarter in drying their clothes or washing their clothes. But the white man don't do that. They change their clothes all the time.

One thing I've learned in Denver is driving the car. When you want to turn right, you have to wait for the light. In Arizona you don't have to wait for a green light. If you stop at an intersection with a red light, all you have to do is just look to your left; if there isn't a car coming, you just go ahead. The police don't bother you. Up in Denver you have to wait for a green light. They don't have any double turns either in Phoenix. If you want to turn you have to go clear to the right side or the left side to turn, and you can't turn in the middle of the inter-section.

In Denver a lot of different places I go white people usually look at me, stare at me. Some will come up to me and try to push me around. So what I think is people in Denver don't seem to like Navajos, especially when I wear my hat. They always come around and try to control me themselves and bump into me. I think they're trying to push all Indians around.

I don't like the way they live up here. Up here in Denver we have nothing to do but go to the movies and go to church and go to my work. When I'm working in Denver, I don't think about anything. Time just goes slow, that's why I don't think about anything.

After I left the reservation, I was thinking about how my parents were feeling back home. I was thinking about my grandmother because she was sick. I think I want to go back home and see my grandma and probably go back to Phoenix. I've got to get home right away or they'll think that I don't love them. If I get home right away, they'll think I love everybody.

When I go back to New Mexico I hope someday just to be living a good life – good homes, good transportation, and everything. And I hope I don't get living like those people in Gallup that laze around the corner and laze around in bars. I think it'll feel pretty good to get back on the reservation (McCracken 1968:115–118).[1]

BIBLIOGRAPHY

Ablon, Joan
    1964   "Relocated American Indians in the San Francisco Bay Area." *Human Organization* 24:296–304.
Graves, Theodore D.
    1966   "Alternative Models for the Study of Urban Migration." *Human Organization* 25:295–299.
Graves, Theodore D., Braxton M. Alfred, and Minor Van Arsdale
    1964   "A Study of Navajo Urban Relocation in Denver, Colorado." University of Colorado. Mimeographed.
Graves, Theodore D., and Minor Van Arsdale
    1965   "Values, Expectations and Relocation: The Navaho Migrant to Denver." *Human Organization* 25:300–307.
Hurt, Wesley R., Jr.
    1961   "The Urbanization of the Yankton Indian." *Human Organization* 20:226–231.

[1] Reprinted by permission of the author.

Kluckhohn, Clyde, and Dorothea Leighton
  1962   *The Navajo.* New York: Doubleday.
Martin, Harry W.
  1964   "Correlates of Adjustment Among American Indians in an Urban Environment." *Human Organization* 24:290–295.
McCracken, Robert D.
  1968   "Urban Migration and the Changing Structure of Navajo Social Relations." Unpublished Ph.D. dissertation, University of Colorado.
McSwain, Romala
  1965   "The Role of Wives in the Urban Adjustment of Navajo Migrant Families to Denver, Colorado." *Navajo Urban Relocation Research Report* no. 10, Institute of Behavioral Science, University of Colorado, Boulder. Mimeographed.
Snyder, Peter Z.
  1968   "Social Assimilation and Adjustment of Navajo Migrants to Denver, Colorado." *Navajo Urban Relocation Research Report* no. 13, Institute of Behavioral Sciences, University of Colorado, Boulder. Mimeographed.

CHAPTER 6   urban economic opportunities:
the example of denver

ROBERT S. WEPPNER

INTRODUCTION: THE URBAN EXPERIENCE

The migrant worker who leaves his rural home for the city can only be assimilated if his economic experiences there are not so disappointing that they extinguish his desire to adjust early in his attempt. Numerous studies have established this theory.[1] These economic experiences may include a multitude of occurrences during this crucial time in urban adjustment, and they may act separately or collectively to discourage the migrant. The impor-

[1] Two migration studies dealing with this subject are Beijer 1963 and Eisenstadt 1954.

tant factor these experiences share is that they operate early in the migrant's attempt to adapt to his new environment. His threshold of frustration is at its highest point then, but his expectations may be easily damaged when he meets unexpected obstacles. Such situations as trouble getting a job because of his unfamiliarity with the job market, wages lower than he expected when he gets a job, or his being "labelled" a non-Anglo by his employer or fellow employees may detrimentally affect his self-concept or restrict his choice of job roles. Any one of these may be the critical event that makes the individual fail to adjust and precipitates his withdrawal from the threatening new environment.

This "failure" to adjust to the urban economy precludes the migrant's assimilation into the city and its complex cultural system, and occurs when the migrant feels the economic system offers no satisfying job or no chance to become a permanent member of the labor force. Then he usually leaves the city, either to return to his home or to go somewhere else. On the other hand, if he gets a fairly high paying job that provides a reasonable standard of living, his chances for staying and for adopting the new culture and its values are greatly improved. This economic adjustment has been called a "way station to cultural integration" (Borrie 1959:101), which implies that it is one place on a continuum having cultural assimilation as its ultimate goal.

Economic adjustment also means the migrant must understand the job requirements. Coming to work regularly and at a specified time, maintaining a required level of production, and being somewhat depersonalized in the interests of the management's cost-profit standards are all part of adjusting. Job performance is a good indicator of how well the migrant has adapted. Once he is satisfied with his job and feels secure at work, he should be able to meet other aspects of the new environment and adjust to them. As one observer has noted, the economic aspects of a society go very far in determining the personality of its members. The process of "socialization" consists mainly of the internalization of value attitudes that make man "want to do what he is required to do by the social system under which he lives" (Weisskopf 1951).

FACTORS DISCOURAGING ECONOMIC
ADJUSTMENT AND CULTURAL INTEGRATION

Certain factors discourage the integration of migrants into new societies. The migrant who does not intend to settle permanently, for example, cannot be expected to integrate. The closer the migrant is to his home, the more frequently he can return; thus, whenever he encounters traumatic experiences in the city, he can return home for support (see Borrie 1959; UNESCO 1956; Jackson 1962). If his experiences are too overwhelming, he may decide to remain there and give up the attempt to settle in the city.

In addition to spatial factors, inadequate skills and incomplete knowledge of opportunities complicate the process of a migrant's adjustment. Some examples of this are found in Africa as well as in Latin America, where migrating workers tend to lack the skills necessary for industrial work. In the city, this lack forces them to work as unskilled laborers at low wages. The lack of incentives like good wages, job security, and prestigious positions results in low productivity in unskilled migrants. As a consequence, they are unstable in their job patterns and change jobs frequently, seeking only temporary expedients such as higher wages (UNESCO 1956). In such a shifting job market they are easily discouraged and can find no security upon which to build a new life. Their instability is further compounded because of their incomplete knowledge of actual employment opportunities in the city before they leave home. They are usually disappointed when faced with the reality of underemployment in the city, and this disappointment drastically affects their adjustment.

Much of migration literature gives the impression that migrants have a "short-run hedonistic" orientation to the future (Beshers and Nishiura 1961). This mode of orientation is determined by situational factors, such as day-to-day employment opportunities or dislike for one's boss or one's starting time. Since the individual has no long-range goals, any alternative job may be accepted to meet his immediate needs. Such an orientation does nothing to aid the migrant's economic adjustment.

Although these problems and others have been mentioned in

migration literature, there has been little systematic effort to make the concepts operable and the studies merely indicate what factors may have been operating to induce the migrant to escape his home environment and move to an urban one. Also in the studies, rather impressionistic statements are made about his life in the city. It seems to be agreed that young males have the greater tendency to migrate, but agreement is not universal as to the amount of education they have, i.e., whether the more educated or intelligent person is more aware of distant opportunities, and whether he is more capable of forming rational motives for migration. The fact remains, however, that the majority of migration studies have attempted to define what type of person will migrate, but few have discussed his chances for success after he gets to his destination. This chapter systematically explores the characteristics of Navajo migrants who are trying to adjust to working in Denver, and shows what a migrant worker encounters as the result of his efforts.

THE NAVAJO IN DENVER

The unrewarding reservation environment of the Navajos has induced many to abandon their traditional homes and migrate to more industrialized urban areas to work for wages. This migration has taken the form of either temporary off-reservation work or a seemingly more permanent type of urban migration. Until the late 1940's these migrations were the result of individual initiative; then in 1952, the BIA program of relocation assistance for Indian volunteers was initiated as an outgrowth of a successful job placement program begun in the late 1940's on the Navajo reservation. This Relocation Services Program provides individual Indians and their families transportation and moving expenses to industrial areas where year-round employment is available. In addition, living allowances are granted until the individual obtains employment, and other allowances are given for tools, equipment, household goods, and furniture.

In 1956, the program was augmented when the Eighty-fourth Congress enacted Public Law 959 authorizing the bureau to provide Indians with vocational and on-the-job training to meet the problem of unskilled migrants that had hampered earlier employment assistance activities. Under the auspices of this program, several hundred Navajo Indians have relocated in Denver from their reservations in Arizona, New Mexico, and Utah.

This group furnished an excellent opportunity for the study of migrating peoples' problems of urban economic adjustment, although the Navajos were somewhat better off than other migrant groups because they did have vocational training prior to their move and they had also learned the local language, English. But the overwhelming majority, if not all, were fluent in their native language and many were very traditionally oriented, that is, their families had traditional backgrounds of herding and farming and held traditional beliefs in the efficacy of native curing techniques.

The economic absorption of the Navajos into the Denver industrial community was complicated by more problems than just learning a trade or a different language. Their traditional values toward work and labor are believed by some to be incompatible with the Western work ethic because of their concept that labor is not a commodity, but should be given freely and also accepted in the same way (Ladd 1957). This attitude has changed somewhat as the younger Navajos have taken jobs on the reservation or in the cities and worked for wages. Even in this context, they are not completely integrated into the wage-labor system, for they may disappear from their jobs for days at a time to attend a ceremonial or help their families in a time of need, as several Denver employers reported.

The process of the Navajos' economic absorption is further confused and somewhat obstructed by the necessity for them to become more aggressive in their interpersonal relationships on the job. The Navajo tendency to avoid being aggressive conflicts with the demand of the Western European concept of competition. The traditional Navajo's economic theory assumes that there may be a potential abundance of goods if everyone works together to obtain this abundance. This belief rejects the Western idea of scarcity of goods; no Navajo cares to compete with his fellow man, for "it is assumed that a neighbor's success will contribute to one's own welfare" (Ladd 1957:253).

In considering the foregoing characteristics, it was felt that they would not distort the measures used in this study to predict the possibility of the migrant's success in the city. The Navajos are probably no more inflexible in adapting to the Western working ethic than any other migrant group, even though their traditional values are worth noting. Actually, their educational background and premigration wage-work experience revealed their potential for economic adjustment and eventual cultural assimilation. Other factors seemed, however, to operate against the Navajo's assimilation, subtle ones external to his premigration training or experience like the employers' perception of the Navajo.

RESEARCH SETTING

The data gathered for this study were collected both in Denver and on the Navajo reservation during a three-year period extending from the early part of 1964 to the end of the summer of 1966. Four distinct samples of respondents were involved: (1) Navajo migrants interviewed in Denver; (2) former Denver migrants interviewed on the Navajo reservation; (3) a matched comparison group of lower socioeconomic status white workers (Anglos), and (4) employers of Navajo and Anglo workers in Denver.

During the research period, 120 Navajo migrants who had been in Denver for varying periods, from a few days up to ten years, were interviewed. This group was believed to be representative of Navajo migrants to the city and included over 80 percent of all male Navajo migrants known to be living in Denver during this period. The summer fieldwork involved interviewing 124 former Denver migrants who had returned home after having spent some time in the city.

Finer discriminations were made in classifying the total of 244 migrants according to their levels of economic adjustment in an urban area; the migrants were divided into two groups, the economically adjusted and the economically unadjusted. The former category was made up of individuals who had been in Denver over eighteen months and were there when interviewed, and of returnees to the reservation who had been in Denver over eighteen months and were considered to have become economically adjusted in the city before they left for various reasons. These individuals (a total of 105) were lumped into a category designated "stayers." The other category was comprised of migrants who had come to Denver and then left before staying eighteen months; this group of 139 was called "leavers." Since the BIA will usually give a Navajo financial aid for one year after he migrates to the city, it was felt that if a migrant remained there six months after assistance ceased, he had, in fact, achieved economic adjustment.[2] Therefore, a period of eighteen months was selected as a criterion for economic adjustment.

The major sources of the data were the individual migrant's answers to a questionnaire constructed and administered by the staff of the Navajo Urban Relocation Research Project.[3] Each interview conducted elicited the Navajo's response to new job situations and his attitude toward the job. Present (or last) wage, absenteeism, and other indices of the migrant's economic adjustment were also collected, along with other psychological and social background data on each respondent.

In addition to these samples, a comparison group of Anglo workers was interviewed. The forty-one individuals in this group were matched to others in the Navajo group according to age, occupation, and wage level. Essentially the same survey questionnaire given to the Navajos was administered to the Anglo comparison group, with a few items deleted such as English language skills and expectations. It was felt that the addition of such a sample would give an excellent cross-cultural comparison between the groups and would point out similarities and contrasts in socioeconomic behavior.

Employer data were obtained from a short questionnaire constructed by me; employers were queried about eighty-two Navajo and forty-one Anglo subjects. The actual person interviewed was the one who knew the Navajo individual best — generally the group supervisor, although any supervisor who was too far removed from a subject was not questioned. For the purpose of this analysis, the supervisor will be referred to as the

[2] See Madigan 1956:7. Madigan discusses the one-year cut-off date of services. This definition of the "stayer" category seems to reflect best what the actual case in adjustment was, especially after the lengths of stay in Denver for the Navajo sample had been examined.

[3] The research reported in this paper was supported during its first year by the University of Colorado's Council on Research and Creative Work. Subsequent support has been received from the National Institute of Mental Health, 1-R11 MH01942–01, under the direction of Dr. Theodore D. Graves.

"employer," because in numerous instances, Navajos were employed in small shops where the owner was also the supervisor. The employer questionnarie contained open-ended questions that probed the supervisor's general opinions as to the competence, efficiency, and skill on the job of the Navajo and Anglo workers, and invited comments on their personal habits. The employers were asked about any particular problems with these workers and whether their disciplinary problems occurred more frequently than those of other workers.

The selection of the Anglo sample proceeded in this manner: the employers of Navajos were asked if they had Anglo workers who had certain attributes, such as being between the ages of eighteen and thirty, having roughly a certain wage level, and performing a certain type of job. This question varied with the products of the shop, but in each instance the attempt was made to equate these attributes to the Navajo sample. The job type corresponded to the Navajo sample in these areas: median values showed both engaged in semi-skilled occupations, and the median age of the Anglos was twenty-three compared to the Navajo age of twenty-four. The average Anglo wage was very close to that of the Navajos.

A COMPARISON OF THE NAVAJO WORKER WITH HIS ANGLO COUNTERPART

Initial Relocation Services Provided for Navajos. Navajo migrants do not have to rely on an informal "gatekeeper" who aids them in adjusting to urban conditions and in finding a job (as many Mexican-American migrants are forced to do) (Rendon 1968); they have, instead, the organized facilities of the BIA Relocation Center which acts as a clearing house to find them jobs and housing. The center provided them with a short orientation course that describes the Denver area and its environs, its recreational facilities, and social centers where Indians gather. If necessary, the office instructs them how to use public transportation, even to the point of how much the fare is and where to deposit it.

The BIA furnishes the newly arrived migrant with money to set up his household, to buy tools for the job, or to meet unexpected emergencies. Its counselors provide him with advice if problems of adjustment become unmanageable. Upon request, counselors also make periodic visits to the migrants' homes and help them with family problems.

Probably the most important function of the BIA office is performed by social workers familiar with the Denver labor market who know employers who can use the Navajo migrant's particular skills. These counselors try to find jobs in the areas in which the Navajo was trained, with as equitable a wage as possible. Often the applicant is taken to the place of employment and sometimes is guided through the intricacies of the job interview. At the very least, the staff calls a number of employers to obtain an interview for the applicant. This job-placement phase presented difficulties; the counselor was often hampered by having to offer to an employer a man possessing a poor grasp of English and no training, or a man with some training but not specialized enough to meet the potential employer's needs.

Indeed, more than one employer of Navajo workers reported to me that the Navajos were well-trained as far as their training program had gone, but it had not gone far enough. What should government training programs anticipate in trying to teach a Navajo to be a skilled arc-welder or an accomplished upholsterer? As an example, the largest number of Navajos with any kind of government vocational training were welders, but the welding of certain types of stainless steel and nonferrous piping required techniques that most of the Navajos had not learned.[4] Because of this lack, placement was not easy, but it was usually accomplished, even with certain incompatibilities that were particularly galling to the Navajo. Sometimes employers were reluctant to give the applicant a job in his field, and he was relegated to some other work. Several returnees on the reservation voiced the complaint that they had gone to Denver trained as apprentice welders, carpenters, or upholsterers and had been placed in jobs as parking lot attendants. One particularly vocal Indian returnee said he had trained for five years as a welder and had returned home when he was placed as a janitor; he felt this was beneath him.

Despite these criticisms, it must be recognized that the bureau

[4] From personal communication with supervisors at Thompson Pipe and Steel Company, and Colorado Builder's Supply Company, Denver, Colorado, 1965.

has Indians from other tribes to place; it has to contend with migrants who come completely untrained, inadequately trained, or dysfunctionally trained, that is, trained in an area such as agriculture, that is not in demand in the city. Within its capacity, the BIA provides many services to the Navajo migrant to ease transition into the Anglo working society. Yet Navajos fare rather poorly in the city; the data show that about half of the migrants in the samples returned home within their first three months in Denver.

Early Economic Experiences. This section describes the general traits of the Navajo migrant before he gets to the city and his early experiences in getting his first job there. When it is applicable, finer differences will be shown between the "stayer"-"leaver" categories described earlier; other greater differences between the Navajo and the Anglo groups will also be described.

The data from the study indicate over three years' difference in schooling between Navajos and Anglos (7.5 years versus 11.3 years). The government Indian training schools like the ones at Chemawa, Oregon, or Brigham City, Utah, attended by Navajos, emphasize a vocational training program along with other basic courses; an Indian completes his course after 1,080 hours of training over a two-year period. The Navajos' vocational training was similar to that of the Anglo sample in gross categories ranging from unskilled to skilled; however, the content of the training could not be determined except through interviews with employers, and they often reported that the Indians were not as thoroughly trained as Anglos.

As an additional point, thirty kinds of vocational training were listed by migrants and ran from welding to cabinetmaking, and from carpentry to silversmithing. Four independent judges content-coded these thirty from "unskilled" (an improbable, but logical possibility) to "skilled." They arrived at an 85 percent agreement, which was fairly high, and then the differences were resolved. In addition, the differences in vocational training type between Anglos and Indians were minimal, indicating that the comparison group of white workers had been carefully matched on the three criteria reported earlier.

The data show that when he finally got a job, the "leaver" had to wait almost three times as long as an Anglo to be placed in a position. To obtain this figure ("three times"), the amount of time the person spent unemployed was calculated and divided by the time he could have worked during the initial first half of his stay in Denver. The "free" time amounted to 37.3 percent of the average "leaver's" time after he arrived in Denver; a small part of this time was spent in the BIA's orientation program but most of this time was occupied in going from one potential employer to another or in seeking another job after having been laid off or fired. In comparison, the Anglo only had to spend 14.2 percent of his time in becoming fully employed; this figure closely matched the proportion of time "stayer" Navajos spent in obtaining work — 12.3 percent.

Although the Navajo "stayers" had more pre-Denver wage-work experience than the "leavers" (29.2 months versus 16.1 months), which might account for the latter's lesser ability to adjust economically, the low wages all the Navajos obtained when they worked certainly did not enhance their view of the Denver industrial community. The average starting wage for the Navajo sample in Denver in 1965 was a weekly rate of $59.20 for "stayers" and $52.00 for "leavers," compared to $65.50 for Anglos. Thus, Anglo sample members were hired at 10 percent higher wages than the "stayers" and 25 percent higher than "leavers." The low starting wage in Denver may have been doubly disappointing to the migrant Navajos who had work experience (both urban and rural), since the average highest pre-Denver wage they reported was $1.65 per hour, or $66.00 per week. Given the prospect of migrating to better one's position in life and then receiving a wage lower than one had received elsewhere does little to encourage the migrant to believe in the possibilities for economic advancement, nor encourage him to stay, hoping that in the long run he will improve his lot. On the average, Navajos received far below the general working wage for semi-skilled positions in Denver.

The frustration of the Navajos did not end in job-placement. As a measure of the Navajo migrant's tendency to remain in Denver, his first job there was matched to his vocational training to see if they coincided. This comparison was done by ranking the job and the training from unskilled to skilled for each migrant. Then this comparison was matched against his decision to stay in Denver or leave, using a Chi-square association test.[5] The calculation did not include those Indians with no vocational training, nor does it consider those with vocational agriculture training, which was felt to be nonadaptive to city working conditions. Only one-third of the migrants thus compared got a job that was similar to their vocational training. The disappointment to the majority of Navajos must have induced a large number to leave Denver. Table 6.1 shows there was a strong tendency for a migrant to remain if his first job was similar to his vocational training, and to leave if the two were dissimilar.

TABLE 6.1

The Tendency of Navajo Migrants to Remain in Denver and the Relationship between Vocational Training and Actual Jobs, 1965

Was vocational training the same as first job in Denver?	"Stayer"	"Leaver"
61 Yes	38	23
128 No	53	75
	$X^2 = 8.12 \ p < .01$	

X^2 = Chi-square
p = Significant

Thus it may be that the Navajo migrant's high expectations upon arrival in the city are quickly damaged when he is faced with such differences in wages and placement practices. Although the Anglo sample was also low in similarity of job to vocational training, its members had other support besides higher wages and less time needed to look for a job. They were in a familiar milieu and generally had some sort of kin or friendship network as a source of support and information about employment opportunities. The Navajo, on the other hand, found the Denver milieu very unfamiliar, had left many of their kinsmen behind

[5] A Chi-square association test seeks to test that the observed counts or frequencies do not differ from the frequencies expected in each category.

on the reservation, and had only the BIA as a source of information about jobs available.

Other Economic Experiences. Many Navajos had disappointing experiences early in their stay in the city and left rather quickly. The "leaver" had an average job length of only 2.7 months in Denver while that for the "stayer" was 21.3 months. The "stayers" reported an average of $80.80 per week before taxes for the highest wage received in Denver; the "leavers" had only earned $57.20 per week. In reference to the discrepancy in the average wage, many firms who employed Navajo workers hired more than one at a time; those who left Denver saw they were not earning as much as other workers, Navajo or Anglo, who had been working longer and thus making more money. This was reinforced for "leavers" when they saw that the Anglos were receiving even more than other Navajos who had been around longer. Anglos actually reported making $94.00 per week on the average.

Another interesting fact arose from the study of the BIA files.[6] Although it was not systematically recorded for every member of the Navajo sample, I found that even Navajos in skilled trades were not members of trade unions. When asked why he was not a union member, one Navajo welder replied that he had not "been asked to join." Since unions do not invite members to join their ranks, the employer of this Navajo was asked why he and some of his fellows were not union members; the only reply offered was that the Navajos were not considered skilled enough to join. Whether or not this was the actual reason, the fact remained that few or no Navajos enjoyed the benefits of union membership. This situation presents a disturbing parallel to other ethnic groups who are presently demanding union membership.

Multivariable Prediction of Economic Adjustment. Many of the economic measures, when taken one at a time, did differentiate migrants who made a successful adjustment from those who did

---

[6] Grateful acknowledgment is given to the former Commissioner of Indian Affairs, Dr. Philleo Nash, and to Dr. Solon G. Ayers and his staff in the Denver Office of Employment Assistance for their cooperation in making these data available.

not. The question remained whether the ability to predict which migrants would succeed could be improved by examining several measures simultaneously. A simple "pattern analysis" was found effective for this discussion.

Four economic measures were selected as being predictive of a Navajo's work adjustment in the city and also his overall success or failure — as evidenced by whether he stays in the city or leaves after a short period. These variables included two premigration attributes of the Navajo and two initial postmigration experiences of the migrant in seeking employment in Denver. These variables were selected because they had the greatest number of significant correlations with other economic measures considered, differentiated best between "stayers" and "leavers," and seemed representative of other various classes of variables measured.

The two most definitive measures of a Navajo's premigration conditioning for urban work were determined to be his amount of premigration wage-labor and the type of vocational training he had received, either under the auspices of BIA vocational training programs, through special armed services training, or other training programs. The two early experience variables in Denver were the percentage of time unemployed the first half of the migrant's stay and his starting or first wage.

The pattern analysis for the "stayer"-"leaver" differences is presented in Table 6.2. This table was constructed in the following manner: the two premigration and two initial postmigration variables were divided at the median and each subject was assigned a plus for each variable if his score was above the median. On the other hand, if his score fell in the range below the median for any of the predictor variables, he was assigned a minus. When all four variable values were taken together, there was a possibility of each subject falling into one of sixteen possible combinations. Thus, if an individual was above the median for the four predictor variables, he would have a pattern of four pluses and this pattern would be considered "optimal," or most favorable, for economic absorption. If the subject had a minus in any one of the four variables, he was classified as having one departure from the optimal pattern. A subject having two minuses would be placed in the two-departure category, and so on down the scale until those individuals below

TABLE 6.2

"Stayer"-"Leaver" Differences as Determined by
Premigration and Initial Postmigration Predictor Variables

	Migrant Category		
Departure Pattern	Number of Unadjusted "Leavers"	Number of Adjusted "Stayers"	Percentage of "Stayers"
Optimal	2	11	85
1 departure	16	28	64
2 departures	28	33	54
3 departures	47	19	29
4 departures	16	3	16
Overall X^2 (2 degrees of freedom)			26.94[a]
X^2 due to linear regression (1 degree of freedom)			26.12
X^2 due to departure from regression line (1 degree of freedom)			.82

[a] To test the significance of this association, an overall chi^2 test was calculated. This value was 26.94 with two degrees of freedom and is significant to the .01 level. Next, these particular data are treated as data in a bivariate frequency table and the regression coefficients are expressed in a form that involves the difference between the variates. This difference is the critical ratio for the linear regression of successive patterns of departures, as indicated by the percentages of "stayers" in each departure category. The value for the critical ratio is then squared and gives a value of 26.12, which is distributed as X^2 with one degree of freedom. This value accounts for that part of the overall X^2 due to linear regression. By subtracting the X^2 value due to a linear trend from the overall X^2, a value of .82 is obtained, indicating that only an insignificant portion of the overall X^2, is due to departure from the regression line (see Maxwell 1961).

the median in all the predictor variables were placed in the four-departure category.[7]

Then the percentage of "stayers" within each of these four categories was calculated. The hypothesis would lead one to expect that those individuals who have an optimal pattern will be most likely to make an economic adjustment to the city, and

[7] Median values used for pattern analysis:

Vocational Training Type		*Initial Unemployment*	
Skilled	+	9% or less	+
Semi-skilled or lower	−	10% or more	−
Amount of Premigration Work		*Starting Wage*	
More than one year	+	$1.35 or more	+
Less than one year	−	$1.30 or less	−

as Table 6.2 shows, 85 percent of them did. Of those individuals with four departures, only 16 percent of them remained in the city. The rest of the departure categories of "stayers" revealed no unexpected deviations in the trend toward a smaller percentage as the departures mount.

A further analysis, which is not given here, tested whether these two sets of variables were *both* contributing to the prediction of urban economic adjustment. It appeared that the subjects varied in their actual behavior (here the decision to stay in Denver or leave) as *both* premigration and postmigration factors operated for or against them, but postmigration experiences appeared to be the more critical determinants in the migrant's decision to stay than the premigration conditioning. The evidence seemed to be that when the premigration experiences were held constant, a change in the postmigration measures produced a much larger percentage of migrants who leave than when premigration measures are varied. In other words, whatever the Navajo's premigration conditioning may be, any unfortunate experience he has in the city in trying to find a job is likely to have a profound effect upon him in his first uncertain months there. Thus, the Navajo migrant who comes to the city with poor background and has had a bad experience in obtaining a job (long wait and low wages when he gets one) is not going to become economically absorbed or culturally integrated.

In every one of the economic measures made on the Navajos, such as wages, percentage of time employed, similarity of job to training, and others, there were differences between the "stayers" and "leavers" in the direction expected. That is, the "leavers" always had a poorer showing; they made less money, waited longer for a job, and were less highly regarded as employees than other Navajos who remained in Denver long enough to qualify as "stayers." Over half the measures displayed statistically significant differences that indicated the "leavers" were not as well prepared for the city, nor did they exhibit as good performance as the "stayers."

A close examination of these measures indicated the possibility of artifactual results, due to the adjusted "stayers" having been in the city longer and thus having had more time to improve their economic position. For example, the present job classification of the adjusted "stayers" may have been higher (more toward the skilled type) than that of the unadjusted "leavers," due to the fact that they had more time in the city to advance. In view of the slight upward mobility exhibited by all the Navajo migrants, however, this may not be such a problem, for an investigation of the type of job the migrant obtained when he first entered Denver and the type he held when interviewed showed that they do not greatly differ. Also, the mean job length of "stayers" may have been a much larger figure than that of the "leavers" because of their longer time in the city. It follows that present wage would be higher.

The important differences to consider are those between the Anglo and the Navajo groups. The breakdown of the Navajos into the two groups indicated that some Navajos can and do adjust economically. What Navajo-Anglo differences in things like wage levels and employer perceptions show is that there are many more difficulties for the migrant than might have been expected.

Evaluation by Employers. The perceptions of employers on how Navajos and Anglos performed their work were obtained through questions that probed for attitudes on how the subjects did their job and related to their fellow workers. The data were then classified by content-analysis; three independent judges examined their comments, and a series of categories emerged with almost 85 percent agreement between the judges.

The first question for employers was, "What kind of worker is (was) ———?" Answers ranged from "You can't find a better worker than the Navajo" to "You could only use them for the commonest type of labor." The easy facility with which white employers identified their Indian workers surprised the interviewers on more than one occasion, and it was difficult to control for subjective bias in the interview. The employers were extremely cooperative and many were willing to talk at length about their Navajo employees. A wide range of comments was obtained; these were divided into three categories: "favorable," "unfavorable," and "neutral." This neutral category represented comments which were either noncommittal or not related to the question.

The initial question and others were used to obtain more specific responses to other areas of the subject's work performance. Many responses to the initial question involved the Navajos' ability to take instructions; their general attitude was described as a desire to please and a willingness to learn new work processes. They were complimented on their lack of a tendency to "talk back," a characteristic that other workers exhibited, and the fact that they generally only needed to be shown how to do a job once. A reticence on the part of the Navajos to be vocal about their tasks was seen as an advantage in this context, but as a disadvantage in other job contexts.

The same data collected on the Anglos characterized them as being dependable and conscientious, often taking the initiative on the job — something employers said the Navajos would not generally do. Other categories concerning competence, efficiency, and skill on the job, although they may be hard to separate because of overlap, were probed. The employers' responses are summarized in Table 6.3 for comparison between Navajos and Anglos.

TABLE 6.3

Employer Perceptions of Navajos and Comparable Anglo Workers

	Navajos[a] (Percentage)	Anglos (Percentage)
Type of worker		
Favorable	62	88
Neutral	19	3
Unfavorable	19	9
Competence		
Favorable	78	66
Neutral	9	17
Unfavorable	13	17
Efficiency		
Favorable	60	62
Neutral	19	19
Unfavorable	21	19
Skill		
Favorable	63	79
Neutral	13	21
Unfavorable	24	0

[a] "Stayers" and "leavers" are combined.

What might be gleaned from this information is a feeling on the part of employers that Navajos possessed many favorable traits as workers, the primary one being an unquestioning attitude toward accepting instructions. Anglo workers were viewed as better and more skilled workers, even though their competence was less than the Navajos and their efficiency was about the same. The reasons for these perceptions on the part of employers cannot be analyzed from the present data, but these comments do show that these perceptions may condition the migrant's desire to remain in the city and probably are very influential in the decision he makes to stay or leave.

When the employer was asked what bad traits each Navajo subject had as a worker, 20 percent of the comments were that the individual had no bad traits and 6 percent of the responses were not pertinent. Employers reported that 14 percent of their Anglo workers did not have bad traits. The two groups are listed in Table 6.4 according to the bad traits mentioned by employers.

It appears that employers desire the trait of initiative among employees. In both the Navajo and Anglo samples, this characteristic received the most comments, and in fact a higher propor-

TABLE 6.4

Bad Traits of Navajo and Anglo Workers
according to Their Employers

	Navajos (Percentage)	Anglos (Percentage)
Lack of initiative	20	26
Inability to communicate (Doesn't understand. Speaks poor English.)	17	0
Carelessness (with equipment)	0	16
Drinking-related problems (Hangover prevents good work. The subject doesn't come to work because of drinking.)	13	0
Poor attendance or undependability	12	16
Lack of experience or poor production	11	9
Poor or antagonistic attitude	10	0
Talking or playing around	0	9
Other (not classifiable into any categories)	17	24

tion of the Anglos than the Navajos were rated down on this point. This suggests that "lack of initiative" on the job may not be a Navajo "cultural trait," as many Anglos near the reservation would argue, but a socioeconomic trait common to all persons, Indian or Anglo, in similar socioeconomic strata within American society.

The other categories are not directly relatable, but it appeared that the poor attendance complaint of the Anglo sample bore a resemblance to the Navajo characteristic of undependability, so the two were combined. In the Anglo sample, drinking was not mentioned once in response to this question. In the Navajo sample, however, it was the third most common source of complaint, commented on in 13 percent of the cases.

Another set of scales was given each employer to rate the individual Navajo or Anglo on his characteristics. The employer was asked to circle the number on a seven-point scale to indicate where he thought the man belonged according to measures of dependability, ambition, flexibility (ability to accept changes), consideration of others, and ability to plan ahead. These scales were devised by Alex Inkeles for use in cross-cultural evaluation of workers in Latin America and Europe (Inkeles 1964). Statistical tests run on the five measures indicated that Anglo employers rated Navajo workers significantly different from Anglos on four of the five scales.[8] Navajos were rated as less dependable, not as ambitious or desiring of getting ahead, unable to accept changes as easily, and more careless in not planning ahead. On

---

[8] The following t scores were run with the assumption $\sigma_1^2 \neq \sigma_2^2$:

	Anglo	Navajo		
Dependability	$\overline{X} = 5.51$ $\sigma^2 = 1.41$	$\overline{X} = 4.99$ $\sigma^2 = 2.87$	$t = 1.96$	$p < .05$
Ambition	$\overline{X} = 5.27$ $\sigma^2 = 1.85$	$\overline{X} = 4.29$ $\sigma^2 = 1.98$	$t = 3.69$	$p < .01$
Flexibility	$\overline{X} = 5.51$ $\sigma^2 = 1.21$	$\overline{X} = 4.64$ $\sigma^2 = 2.31$	$t = 3.59$	$p < .01$
Consideration	$\overline{X} = 5.80$ $\sigma^2 = .96$	$\overline{X} = 5.33$ $\sigma^2 = 2.79$	$t = 1.94$	N.S.
Plan ahead	$\overline{X} = 5.12$ $\sigma^2 = 1.71$	$\overline{X} = 4.01$ $\sigma^2 = 2.06$	$t = 4.26$	$p < .01$

the one rating of consideration toward the feelings of others, the Navajos were not significantly different from Anglos.

In general, the employers' comments indicated that the Navajo worker compared favorably with his fellow workers and was a competent, efficient, and skilled worker. On these specific questions, there do not seem to be major differences in the employers' responses to the Anglo and Navajo skills, efficiency, competence, and problems or bad traits as workers, even though there is a tendency for the Navajos to be rated a bit lower. Surprisingly, "lack of initiative" is no more a problem for the Navajo than for comparable whites, and communication problems, though more of a barrier for the Navajos, are also a problem for Anglos. The one problem mentioned that is much higher, is drinking among the Navajos.

After some long discussions with employers, it appeared that the Navajo, although exhibiting desirable characteristics, was seen as limited in his upward mobility by his unaggressive behavior. It might be maintained that this is a trait unique to the Navajo, or it might be argued that perhaps this perception is a stereotypic response to Navajos that employers use to rationalize their reasons for limiting his advancement. As was pointed out by O. Collins in his New England factory study, certain ethnic groups are relegated to definite positions which are difficult to transcend (Collins 1946).

If the Navajos suffer from the same discriminations directed against other minority groups, such discrimination may be more subtle and couched in terms like "lack of initiative." Then, too, if Navajos were seen as more undependable, unambitious, inflexible, and unable to plan ahead, such a perception on the part of the employer, if felt by the Navajo employee, could have deleterious effects on his desire to become a full-time worker in this Western economic milieu.

It is difficult to say whether the feelings of the employer were due to a definite discrimination against a minority group or were caused by the Navajo himself because of lack of recognition of his job responsibilities, or a meager repertoire for wage work due to cultural differences. Whatever the cause, there is a differentiation in the minds of the employers. Unfortunately none of the testing instruments used to gather data for this paper included questions that could probe such reasons since that type of testing was beyond the scope of this investigation.

To a large extent, stereotyped perceptions of Navajos by their employers may be true and valid observations of the Navajos' work behavior and, if so, may be inimical to additional good performance on the job if the Indian perceives the employers' estimate. It gives pause for reflection (but not proof, unfortunately) to see employers' reactions to two classes of workers, one red and one white, and to ponder what effect this force external to the Navajo has on him and if he is able to meet it adequately.

Since "leavers" did come to Denver with significantly less education and significantly less work experience, they were probably less prepared to succeed economically. This lack of preparation is reflected in their higher initial rate of unemployment, lower starting wage, and lower likelihood of getting a job of the same type as that for which they trained. It can be speculated as to what might have happened if they had not had these unfavorable initial experiences. On the other hand, they consistently received lower employer ratings on every index, which would likely result in lower wages, more unemployment, and shorter jobs later on, whatever their initial experience might have been.

Other Factors Conditioning Success for the Navajos. Success may be a nebulous thing for the Navajo migrant when it is defined by the sole criterion of whether the individual stays in the city or leaves. Because of the global nature of this measure and the fact that it is determined by outside observers, it may be too encompassing to indicate perfectly what is operating in the Navajo's world in the city, but it is an indicator of more important underlying factors. The migrant's failure to adjust may be because of a multitude of problems, ranging from inability to perform his work tasks to deviant behavior like drinking, which results in arrest. After either of these traumatic events, a Navajo may decide the city is no place for him.

Nevertheless, there are certain attitudes and behaviors that the Navajo exhibits that are quite closely related to economic adjustment in the city. Some are more behavioral in their nature and may be very influential on whether the Navajo can do his job well. The first of these attributes involved the linguistic ability of the Navajos, or how well they could speak English; this ability was determined from three measures. The first was a test in which every Navajo was given a set of pictures and asked to identify the correct picture when asked a question such as "Which is the triangle?" This was done for thirty different items and the correct number of responses was recorded for each subject's measure of English language skills (Lado 1957).

In another battery of modified Thematic Apperception tests (Michener 1965) given to the Navajo samples, a simple count of the number of words each subject uttered was taken from transcripts of the subject's tape recorded interview to determine his fluency relative to other members of the samples. Also, the number of grammatical errors he made was divided by the total number of words and he was assigned a score. By this procedure, the higher the score, the poorer the subject's use of English.

From all these measures of language ability, the "stayers" were tested against the "leavers," and in every case, the differences were significant. This means that one thing which was built into a "stayers" success was that he could speak and understand English better than other Navajos. This contributed greatly to his adjustment, although it cannot be said that it was causal in only one way. Success in the city most probably contributed to an improvement of the Navajo's English language skills, since, they worked together with Anglos. The fact that he was able to receive instructions better and communicate with his fellow workers and supervisors had to have a great impact on his job performance. Earlier, when employer perceptions were reported, they stated that communication problems occurred with Navajos about 17 percent of the time. It must be remembered that this statement applied to both "stayers" and "leavers" and the latter group probably accounted more for this figure.

One interesting attitude the Navajos exhibited as a group when compared to Anglos was the feeling that they, the Navajos, had very little control over external events (Jessor, *et al.* 1968). In other words, tests showed that the degree to which each Navajo felt he had personal control over the consequences of his behavior, or over the rewards and punishments which are the results of his behavior, was much lower than the Anglos. This may be roughly equated to the idea that the Navajo was more fatalistic about life and thus more prone to take failure without a personal struggle to ward it off. This belief system is quite common among many non-Western people. What is important to consider in the context of relocated Indian workers is that the Western economic system is postulated on the idea that every man is a master of his destiny, and Navajos did not fit the mold if the test was an adequate indicator. The employer ratings on the flexibility and the ability to plan ahead of their Navajo workers may have been conditioned by the Navajo's just being unable to handle changes or plan ahead, due to this fatalism.

Another characteristic related to the Navajos' feelings of external control and their inability to plan ahead was the fact that, compared to the Anglo workers, they had a very nebulous future-orientation. This measure was arrived at by asking, during an interview, subjects from both the Navajo and Anglo samples to look ahead for a minute and tell the interviewer five things they thought they would do or things they felt might happen to them in the future, and how long it would be before the event occurred. The results showed extreme differences between the Anglos and the Navajos. The Anglos were very future oriented and listed multiple events such as buying a car or a home and getting a raise. On the other hand, the Navajos in many cases could only list one event and they were very simple occurrences. Whatever the number of responses, generally they were economically conditioned.

The Navajos who went to Denver must have wanted to do well if their statements about the city and its advantages are considered. Both groups of Navajos felt Denver offered good economic opportunities and mentioned this fact more often than Anglos when they were asked what they liked and disliked most about the city. However, the Indians felt they were much lower on the scale compared to the average white man in Denver, a feeling that may have been conditioned by a number of factors but was not explored beyond asking them to rate themselves on a scale comparable to the average white man in Denver. On this scale the Anglo sample placed itself much higher than the Navajos did. From this statement and others on the part of the

Indians, the general impression was that although they felt Denver offered good economic opportunities and they probably would be better off there than on the reservation, they really did not see much hope of attaining a great deal in Denver. They came to the city and wanted to be successful, but they were not optimistic about obtaining their goals because they felt they were not equal to the white man and their chances for success were therefore effectively diminished.

SUMMARY AND CONCLUSIONS

The purpose of this study of the adjustment problems of Navajo Indian migrants is not to indicate that insurmountable obstacles are placed in their way. Irrational or unjust discrimination may operate against them because they are not Anglo-American, but such relative deprivations are not measured here. The Navajo came to Denver with a number of things against his interacting profitably with the Anglo culture. Although by his own statements, he wanted to get a good job and make a good living in Denver, he was not really sure he could accomplish this. Compared to the Anglo role model he wished to emulate, he felt he was very much below the average in Denver and he had much lower expectations of getting ahead economically than members of the Anglo sample.

Despite the fact that his cultural ethic valued hard work and thrift, the Navajo lacked an aggressive attitude, or as many employers stated, a lack of initiative. Perhaps the unaggressiveness was a result of social isolation; whatever the reason, it did not help to serve the Navajo's cause, even though the same complaint was made about Anglo workers. The employers may have categorized the Navajo as less ambitious because of his seemingly passive nature. He might be a very steady producer, but to many employers this was not enough.

Two other Navajo characteristics which may have worked against them were their short future time perspective and their belief that one has little personal control over external events. If they were not disposed to look to the future, they could not rate very highly with their employers on the ability to plan ahead on the job. In addition, if they would rather leave themselves to fate, it is not unreasonable that they might be viewed as somewhat less ambitious than Anglos. These characteristics must have been operating against all Navajos in the minds of employers; one manifestation of this was the lower wages Navajos received in the city.

The "stayer" Navajos did have fairly good training for various trades in Denver as well as a fairly good amount of pre-Denver wage-labor work. Along with these experiences, the BIA offered a job-placement service to all the Indians. Because of these factors, 43 percent of the sample could be classified as having become viable, contributing members of the work force. These were the "stayers" who exhibited an ability to use their experience and skills to support themselves after they were no longer eligible for government aid. Even though they may not be permanently situated in Denver, their presence there indicated that the Navajos' attempts to relocate were not met with total failure.

The largest percentage of the migrants did leave Denver because of many factors reported here. It must be remembered that many of the "leavers" who relocated to Denver were young unmarried individuals who came there directly after graduation from their training schools. Consequently, they were very mobile and could leave easily. Also, this group had fewer qualifications in things other than work experience; they could not speak English as well as the "stayers," which was proved by tests administered to them in interviews. It is obvious that this ability is critical to success in an English-speaking community. If Navajos have trouble in understanding instructions or communicating with others, they cannot perform adequately on the job or even enjoy their surroundings off the job. In addition, the Navajo faced social isolation because his conversational repertoire did not include sports, politics, or adequate fluency to understand jokes and puns. It is small wonder so many employers reported that Navajos kept to themselves at work and "always ate lunch over in the corner by themselves."

Some Suggestions for Easing the Indian's Burden. Any suggestions to help Indians would be likely to apply more toward those Navajos who fail in the city than those who are successful. They might, however, apply to all the Navajos, and are directed at avoiding the relocation of Navajos who are really not suitable or qualified to adapt to city living, i.e., those individuals who do not have the necessary characteristics and have the greatest potential for nonadjustment. If the poorer risk migrants are weeded out before being relocated, then their contaminating effect will not be felt by other, more qualified Indians, since the latter group may be misperceived as bad employment risks if the employers have had bad luck with other Indians in the past.

The government would not arbitrarily select those who should or should not come to Denver, but at the very least it should not encourage a Navajo who has an inadequate background by subsidizing his trip to Denver and having him fail. There are costs other than those monies expended in bringing the migrant to the city; social costs for the individual should also be evaluated. The severe disorientation the Navajo suffers in a new setting would be avoided, and any subsequent deviance such as excessive drinking would be lessened.

Some premigration characteristics should be evaluated before a Navajo is selected for relocation. The present investigation shows that the Navajo who failed to adjust in Denver might have succeeded if he had had adequate vocational training. Then, too, the research data indicated that "stayers," before coming to Denver, had worked a total of a year at jobs other than herding or farming, giving that group a broader work-experience base within which to operate and exposed him to working conditions similar to those in Denver. These two considerations, coupled with a requirement that the Navajo speak adequate English, would help him greatly and would also favorably condition his early experiences in Denver.

To educate out "passiveness" and to educate in "initiative" is difficult mainly because the two characteristics are so ill-defined and symptomatic of other factors. Therefore, a suggestion to reeducate the Navajo to behave more aggressively would be specious because of its impossibility. Even if it were not impossible, it may be inoperable because it might be incompatible with other cultural characteristics of the Navajo. Perhaps a reeducation of employers of Indians could be accomplished by some brief public relations literature on the good traits of Indian workers.

Economic adjustment or absorption may be seen as the initial phase of the process by which the migrant eventually becomes integrated into the culture he has chosen to adopt. Thus it may be generalized that economic adjustment also conditions other types of social behavior in the city. In order to test this hypothesis, data were employed for selected variables and a larger picture of the Navajo's potential for adjustment to city life and his cultural assimilation emerged. By the predictive potential of certain characteristics of migrants, potential workers can be trained adequately and reduce migration problems, both for the migrants, employers, and governmental administrators.

BIBLIOGRAPHY

Beijer, G.
     1963   *Rural Migrants in Urban Settings*. The Hague: Martinus Nijhoff.
Beshers, James M., and Eleanor N. Nishiura
     1961   "A Theory of Internal Migration Differentials." *Social Forces*
            39:214–218.
Borrie, W. D.
     1959   *The Cultural Integration of Immigrants*. Paris: UNESCO.
Collins, O.
     1946   "Ethnic Behavior in Industry: Sponsorship and Rejection in a New
            England Factory." *American Journal of Sociology* 51:293–298.
Eisenstadt, S. N.
     1954   *The Absorption of Migrants*. London: Routledge and Kegan Paul.
Inkeles, Alex
     1964   "Harvard Project on the Socio-Cultural Aspects of Development."
            Cambridge, Mass.: Center for International Affairs, Harvard University. Unpublished report.
Jackson, J. A.
     1962   "The Irish in Britain." *Social Review* 10:5–16.
Jessor, Richard, *et al.*
     1968   *Society, Personality, and Deviant Behavior: A Study of a Tri-Ethnic Community*. New York: Holt, Rinehart and Winston.
Ladd, John
     1957   *The Structure of a Moral Code*. Cambridge, Mass.: Harvard University Press.
Lado, Robert
     1957   *Linguistics across Cultures*. Ann Arbor: University of Michigan
            Press.
Madigan, LaVerne
     1956   *The American Indian Relocation Program*. New York: The Association on American Indian Affairs.

Maxwell, A. E.
   1961   *Analyzing Quantitative Data.* New York: John Wiley and Sons.
           (Chapter 4 has a discussion of trend analysis.)
Michener, Bryan P.
   1965   "The Development and Scoring of a Test of Need-Achievement of
           Navajo Indians." *Navajo Urban Relocation Research Report 6,*
           University of Colorado. Mimeographed.
Rendon, Gabino, Jr.
   1968   "Prediction of Adjustment Outcome of Rural Migrants to the City."
           Unpublished Ph.D. dissertation, University of Colorado.
UNESCO
   1956   *Social Implications of Industrialization and Urbanization, Africa
           South of the Sahara.* Paris.
Weisskopf, W. A.
   1951   "Industrial Institutions and Personality Structure." *Journal of Social Issues* 7:1–6.

CHAPTER 7   drinking and drunkenness
among urban indians

THEODORE D. GRAVES

INTRODUCTION

Finding an American Indian community anywhere in the United States today where a perceptive visitor will not be confronted by overwhelming evidence of excessive drunkenness and other forms of social pathology is almost impossible (Graves, in press). Nor can one talk with government officials, teachers, missionaries, or others in daily contact with Indians without this theme coming up. This is not just the biased judgment of non-Indian "outsiders"; most Indian leaders also recognize, and lament, the high rates of social problem behavior among their members, and many tribes spend considerable time and resources sponsoring alcoholism workshops, studies, committees, AA groups, and other

276   DRINKING AND DRUNKENNESS AMONG URBAN INDIANS

activities designed to deal with the more obvious manifestations of these problems.

Given this widespread recognition that drunkenness and associated social problems are endemic among Indians, surprisingly little empirical research has been devoted to the systematic investigation of this behavior, its causes, consequences, and possible cures. Indians are usually considered the province of anthropologists. But the typical anthropological study of American Indian drinking is likely to describe ethnographically the *form* it takes in various Indian communities, and the positive, integrative *functions* being served, rather than the social problems being created.[1] It is as if there were a deliberate conspiracy of silence among anthropologists to protect their Indian friends from embarrassment.

Such a strategy, however well-meaning, is of dubious scientific merit, and cannot benefit the Indian either. For the problem will not disappear by ignoring it. Only through recognition of the problem and study of its distribution and associations can we begin to understand where strategic intervention might be called for, and thereby initiate efforts for the alleviation of the problem.

This chapter presents a small portion of the findings from a thorough empirical study of drunkenness among Indian urban migrants, one of the few studies of drunkenness among American Indians.[2] The data herein form part of a larger investigation of the adjustment problems of Navajo migrants to Denver, Colorado, which my students and I conducted between 1963 and 1968.[3] This study examined a range of economic, social, and

[1] See, for example, Devereux 1948; DuToit 1964; Heath 1964; Honigmann and Honigmann 1945; and Lemert 1954.

[2] See, for example, Dozier 1966; Ferguson 1968; Graves 1967; Honigmann and Honigmann 1968; Jessor, Graves, Hanson, and Jessor 1968; Stewart 1964; Swett 1963 and in press; and Whittacker 1962 and 1963.

[3] The research reported in this chapter was undertaken within the Program of Research on Social Processes, Institute of Behavioral Science, University of Colorado. Initial support in 1963 was provided by the University's Council on Research and Creative Work, followed by a three-year grant from the National Institute of Mental Health (1-R 11 MH 1942).

Because this research was designed in part to serve as a training laboratory for social science graduate students at the University of Colorado, many people have participated in the data collection and analysis: Drs. Braxton

psychological factors involved in the adaptation of *any* urban newcomers, and also included investigation of nonmigrants living in the reservation setting from which the subjects came.

To report these data fully, or adequately to place Indian drinking problems within the broader social-psychological context is obviously impossible to do in one chapter, but at least the flavor of our findings follows. The data illustrate my thesis that the high rates of Indian drunkenness found both in the cities and on the reservations are not indications of an *Indian* problem, but a problem of the wider society within which Indians are trying to survive. That drinking problems are probably more acute among Indians than any other ethnic group in the United States is simply an index of the severity of the pressures to which Indians are exposed, and the paucity of their available resources. We must all bear responsibility for their situation.

THE CASE OF HARRISON JOE [4]

The case history of one Navajo Indian and his brief stay in Denver illustrates many problems that migrants face. Like most Navajo newcomers, Harrison Joe was in his early twenties and single when he arrived in the city. He had graduated two years before from the Special Navajo Program at Intermountain School in Brigham City, Utah. This program, now discontinued, was a five-year course for Navajos with little or no prior educational experience; it emphasized basic language skills and vocational training, and was all the education Harrison Joe had ever had. Nor had experience served as a substitute for formal education.

M. Alfred, Robert D. McCracken, Romola McSwain, Duane Quiatt, Peter Z. Snyder, O. Michael Watson, C. Roderick Wilson, and Robert S. Weppner; Avery G. Church, Mary Collins, William Hozie, Kenneth L. Kuykendall, Bryan P. Michener, George Oetinger, III, Carl Shames, Minor Van Arsdale, and Suzanne Ziegler. My debt to all these students is great.

A brief description of the strategy guiding the overall research is available in Graves (1966). Most of the material presented in this chapter appeared earlier in a different version, titled "The Personal Adjustment of Navajo Indian Migrants to Denver, Colorado," *American Anthropologist* 72 (February 1970):35–54. My manuscript for a book on the topic is in preparation.

[4] The case material presented in this section was collected in weekly interviews by Bryan P. Michener, supplemented by records from the Bureau of Indian Affairs and the Denver Police Department.

Harrison Joe, like the majority of Navajos who come to Denver, had never been in a city before. Other than boarding school, his only off-reservation experience comprised two months of picking potatoes in Idaho at one hundred twenty dollars per month.

At Intermountain School, Harrison Joe had received vocational training in upholstery, but this did not help him find a job near his reservation home. During the two years following graduation his only wage-labor was ten days' work for the tribe at ten dollars per day, so he decided to try relocation. Denver was his first choice because he had a relative there and it was close to home. The BIA agreed to pay his travel expenses and to help him find a job in the city, under the special government "relocation" program in operation since 1952.

On arrival in Denver on a Thursday morning, the first thing Harrison Joe did was to ask how to get to the BIA Office of Employment Assistance. There he was interviewed and given a haircut, and taken to a rooming house where several other Indian relocatees lived. His first weekly subsistence check was issued: thirty dollars; after he paid twenty-one dollars for room and board, this still left him with some pocket money. On Friday and Saturday the office staff also gave him job counselling and sent him on three job interviews which were nonproductive.

Although unsuccessful at finding a job those first few days, Harrison Joe had no difficulty finding friends. The first morning in town he met another Navajo at the bureau office, and his roommate at the boarding house was also Navajo. Thursday evening he went looking for his "uncle" (a young man about his age with two years of urban experience in both Chicago and Denver), but he had moved. On Friday Harrison Joe tried again, and this time found his "uncle" sitting in the park with some other migrants; the whole group spent the evening together. On Saturday afternoon another Navajo took Joe out to see the town, and later to watch television at his apartment. On Sunday Harrison Joe became acquainted with a Navajo who was a former roomer at his boarding house and who later became his closest friend; they went to the Pink Elephant, a popular Navajo bar, where they spent the evening with his "uncle" and other friends. On his way home, the evening was marred by a fight with another group of Navajos, who had taunted the shy stranger.

During his second week in Denver, Harrison Joe's only work was a five-hour job as a brickyard laborer and a day heaving cinder blocks. All his job interviews were unsuccessful, and he was beginning to feel discouraged. That Saturday, BIA subsistence funds again in his pocket, he set out to explore the town. Meeting no one he knew, he again dropped in at the Pink Elephant, where he spotted his "uncle" chatting with another clan brother from Gallup. This fellow was also a new migrant, had found no work, and had been beaten up; he, too, was getting discouraged and talked of returning home.

Harrison Joe's third week in the city was equally unsuccessful. By Tuesday the BIA had given up trying to get him work in upholstery, and instead got him hired as a cinch-maker in a saddle shop. The next day he was fired because he was too slow and came to work two hours late. On Thursday he tried to get a job on his own; because the lines were so long at the Colorado State Employment Office, however, he did not even get to fill out an application form. By this time he was so discouraged that after he picked up his BIA subsistence check, he decided to return home, and packed his bag. But instead he spent the evening talking with one of our researchers. On Friday morning when he stopped at the BIA office, he learned the staff had found him a job as a trainee leather-trimmer, to begin the following week, so he decided to give the city another try.

Saturday was an eventful day. He earned three dollars cutting lawns, so this money together with the nine dollar balance from his subsidy check made him feel expansive. He decided to wander down to Larimer Street, Denver's skid row, where other Navajos had pointed out a friendly bar. "Navajos, two of them, were around," he reported later, "and they bought some beers for me, and we started drinking." In typical fashion, each bought drinks for the others, and they moved from one bar to the next. Exactly what transpired during the evening is unclear; at some point Harrison Joe got into a fight and was badly bruised and cut on one arm; he may also have been slipped a Mickey Finn and rolled (his perception of the events), or perhaps he and his friends simply drank up his twelve dollars. "I don't know how much I drink," he admitted.

In any event, there were some "police standing there and me drunk. One Navajo took off. And I just sit there; don't know if I had been passed out. And I was in jail." Because it was his first offense, he was released Sunday morning, but was required to return to court Wednesday. Broke, tired, and hung over, he hiked to the house of a friend, who took him out for a couple of beers to sober him up; then he went home to bed.

Monday, Harrison Joe began work as a leather-cutter trainee. Tuesday he was fired. Wednesday he went to court and was given a ten dollar suspended sentence. Thursday he picked up his thirty dollar maintenance check from the BIA and, without a word to anyone, left town.

Harrison Joe is fairly typical of the majority of Navajos who come to Denver in search of better employment opportunities. Migration to the city places produces an emotional conflict in them. On the one hand, they want the material goods that their Western education has taught them to value, but limited job opportunities on the reservation prevent them from attaining these goods. On the other hand, they retain a deep emotional attachment to their kin and the reservation; the city offers few substitutes for these (Graves and Van Arsdale 1966).

The average migrant arrives in Denver with other handicaps. He has limitations of language, race, and culture; Indian education lags behind that of the American public at large. Therefore, not surprisingly, over half the migrants remain in the city less than six months. But often the migrant is equally ill-equipped to compete back home. The better educated Navajos who remain on the reservation command the best jobs. Thus the migrant is apt to slip into a cycle of urban migration and return, each phase of which ends in personal failure. Small wonder that large numbers of these "marginal men" seek release from frustration and failure in drunken stupor.

One index of the psychic difficulties that these migrants experience is the frequency with which they are arrested in Denver, almost always for a drinking-related offense. The high rate of Indian arrests in comparison with those of other American minority groups and the dominant white community is easy to

TABLE 7.1

Comparative Rates of Arrest of Various Ethnic Groups
in the United States — 1960

	Rate per 100,000 Population		
	Total Arrests	Alcohol-Related Arrests	Official Percentage Alcohol-Related
Total population (including all groups)	2,200	940	43
White	1,700	780	47
Negro	5,900	2,000	33
Indian	15,000	11,000	76
Chinese-Japanese	1,100	270	24

Source: Stewart 1964:61, Table 2.

document.[5] Tables 7.1 and 7.2 present figures based on official FBI statistics and census data for the nation at large and for Denver as summarized by Stewart (1964:61, 65); Indian arrests are ten or more times those for whites, and at least three or four times those for other minority groups.

Figures of the kind in these tables, however, are subject to the criticism that the population base on which these rates are calculated may be badly distorted. Particularly in an urban area like Denver, rapid Indian turnover makes accurate census-taking nearly impossible. Nonresident Indians temporarily in the city for recreational purposes may account for many arrests, and the urban Indian population is predominantly made up of young single males in the lowest economic strata of the population who are disproportionately liable to drunkenness and arrest. Their racial distinctiveness, furthermore, and their pattern of public drinking make their drunkenness particularly conspicuous.

To control for such factors in the study project, individual police records of 488 migrant Navajo males were collected, representing 94 percent of the known Navajo migrants in Denver

[5] See, for example, Ferguson 1968; Honigmann and Honigmann 1968; Jessor, Graves, Hanson, and Jessor 1968; Stewart 1964; Swett, in press; and Whittacker 1962.

TABLE 7.2

*Comparative Rates of Arrests of Various Ethnic Groups
in Denver — 1960*

| | Rate per 100,000 Population | | |
	Total Arrests	Alcohol- Related Arrests	Official Percentage Alcohol- Related
Total population (including all groups)	5,300	2,700	51
White (combining Anglo and Spanish)	4,800	2,500	53
Anglo	3,500	2,000	57
Spanish	15,000	7,000	46
Negro	12,000	3,600	30
Indian	60,000	51,000	86
Chinese-Japanese-Filipino	1,100	470	41

Source: Stewart 1964:65, Table 14, as corrected by Graves.

for the ten-year period 1953–63. In addition, similar records were collected on 139 Spanish-American male migrants (Rendón 1968) and on 41 lower-class Anglo males who occupied jobs in the city similar to the Navajos (Weppner 1968). Since Denver police consider Spanish-Americans their major problem-group, these subjects served to control for possible police bias in arrests, as well as for any problems of unfamiliarity with the city which a new migrant might suffer. The lower class Anglo group served to control for the possibility that Indian arrest rates were simply a product of a working class recreational drinking pattern typical of other groups in the same economic stratum.

Despite these controls against bias, the Indian group exhibited an arrest rate of 104,000 per 100,000 man years in the city, which is more than twenty times the Anglo rate (5,000) and over eight times the migrant Spanish rate (12,500). At least 93 percent of the Navajo arrests were for drinking-related offenses — far higher than the other two groups. Even this figure may be too low, however, if a careful follow-up were made of each arrest to check the possibility of alcohol involvement. In exactly such a study of 610 Indian arrests in San Francisco, for example, Swett found that "consumption of alcohol was a contributing factor, either to the offense or to the arrest, in every case" (1963:2). Furthermore, when the *types* of crimes for which Denver migrant subjects were being arrested were examined, arrest rate for serious crimes, whether against persons or against property, was clearly *lower* than for the population at large.[6] Obviously, Indians are not more "criminal" than other minority groups, as Stewart (1964:65) implies; they are simply more drunk.

THE STRATEGY OF EXPLANATION

An explanation of these gross group differences can be sought in two ways. The typical anthropological approach is to examine factors in Navajo history, or that of American Indians in general, to discover aspects of their cultural tradition, particularly with respect to alcohol use, that might explain their apparent low threshold for drunken excess (Heath 1964; Stewart 1964; Ferguson 1968). For example, such historical aspects would include: most North American Indian groups lacked aboriginal intoxicants; they acquired a taste for hard liquor within the context of a "frontier" society; and their long history of prohibition gave them little opportunity to learn and practice patterns of "moderate" social drinking (Dozier 1966).

The poverty of culture as an explanatory concept is apparent, however, on two counts. First, despite the depressing overall picture of migrant drinking, about half the Navajos who come to Denver never have a run-in with the police and appear to be keeping their drinking within tolerable limits. Yet all are products of this same cultural tradition. Recourse to specific features of a culture's development or to limitations in its adaptive behavioral repertoire simply fail to explain these significant intragroup differences.

Second, even if some satisfactory level of explanation of mi-

[6] Based on less adequate but tribally more diverse data on Indian arrests in the San Francisco Bay region, Swett (in press) came to essentially the same conclusion. These data agree with more casual observations dating back at least as far as the Meriam report (Institute for Government Research 1928:764).

grant Indian drinking were achieved through an appeal to unique features of Indian "culture," general understanding of drunkenness as a behavioral phenomenon would be advanced relatively little. Each "cultural" explanation of group differences is ideographic, an explanation that can apply only to that group (or very similar groups) in that place and time. But how then can drunken excess be explained among American Indian groups such as the Apache and those south of the border who *did* possess intoxicants aboriginally, or among half-breeds whose socialization to Indian tradition is often attenuated, or among the Eskimo whose cultural tradition and contact history are quite different? And cannot the American Indians' experience contribute to an understanding of the growing problem of drunkenness among their Spanish-American neighbors or, stepping farther afield, among educated South African Bantu?

The strategy of explanation adopted in the present study is quite different from the typical anthropological approach, and, I believe, far more fruitful in the long run. All analyses have been conducted within a single ethnic group, the Navajo, thus controlling for effects of cultural heritage. Drawing on more general social science theory about the social-psychological etiology of excessive alcohol use, analytic variables have been selected on which individual Navajo migrants may differ. Thus, whatever empirical relationships are found between indices of drunkenness and other structural or psychological variables among Navajo migrants have potential explanatory significance for other groups with drinking problems.

THEORY AND METHODOLOGY

The theoretical orientation adopted in this study is a synthesis of two major intellectual traditions. One embodies theories of psychopathology that treat drunkenness as one of many "neurotic" responses to conditions of psychic stress. Critical elements in these theories are such things as *conflicts* between competing but mutually incompatible goals, or the *disjunctions* that result from unfulfilled aspirations. The other tradition is made up of socialization theories that treat drunkenness as learned behavior. Critical elements are the social *models* provided and the pattern of social *reinforcements* and *punishments* by which behavior is socially modified and directed.

These two bodies of theory are complementary: each explains exactly what the other leaves out. Disjunction-conflict theories of psychopathology provide powerful psychological *motives* for drinking; social-learning theories account for the *channeling* of these motives into specific behavioral form. Their synthesis results in a true social-psychological theory, or "field theory," of urban Indian drunkenness (Yinger 1965).

The approach of this research has been to treat drinking as a rational and purposive act, an adaptive maneuver in a migrant's continuing efforts to achieve personal satisfaction. The determinants of this act are hypothesized to lie in the interaction between a particular set of objective conditions and a particular set of personal attributes for perceiving, evaluating, and coping with these conditions. Such a simplified "decision-theory" framework is straightforward enough when applied to such specific choices as whether or not to return home to the reservation (Graves and Van Arsdale 1966). But drunkenness is a *recurring* act; the interest lies not in whether a migrant drinks, but in how often he gets drunk. This requires a search for explanatory variables that can be related to group differences in *rates* of drunkenness, by increasing or decreasing the probability that certain categories of Indians will choose to engage in heavy drinking on many occasions and in a variety of situations.

Finally, a word must be said about the nature of alcohol itself. People drink for many reasons. An adequate theory of drinking behavior should therefore provide room for a diversity of individual motives, such as the many social-convivial ends consumption frequently serves. But drunkenness is a peculiarly attractive response to conditions of frustration and conflict; its narcotizing effects provide a simple, inexpensive, and readily available means for temporary escape from psychic misery. When trying to account for high rates of drunkenness within any group, these properties of alcohol must certainly be recognized.

Based on these theoretical considerations, four general hypotheses were formulated concerning sources of intragroup variation in Navajo migrant drinking behavior:

Hypothesis 1: Those Navajo migrants who are least successful in obtaining the economic rewards of urban life will display the highest rates of drunkenness.

The main thing the migrant to Denver is seeking is a better job than limited reservation resources can provide. Failure to obtain steady, well-paying work in Denver should therefore prove to be a major source of disappointment and frustration that alcohol could help him to forget.

Hypothesis 2: Those Navajo migrants with the greatest opportunity for acquiring skills for successfully holding down good jobs will display the lowest rates of drunkenness.

Failure on a job may occur either because it is too difficult (the migrant has been poorly trained), or because the migrant has limited personal resources (experience) for coping with job demands.

Hypothesis 3: Those Navajo migrants who experience the greatest disjunction between their personal goals and their expectations of achieving them, or the greatest conflict between competing, mutually incompatible goals, will display the highest rates of drunkenness.

Although a marginal economic position should be the major structural source of migrant motives to drink, migrants may differ in the way they perceive and evaluate their marginality. For a more complete understanding of the migrants' aspirations and of the reasons they may seek drunken escape, a direct assessment of these psychological variables is also required.

Hypothesis 4: Those Navajo migrants experiencing the weakest social pressures to drink and the strongest social controls against drinking will display the lowest rates of drunkenness.

In Denver the major social pressures and constraints relevant to a migrant's drinking stem from his wife and his Navajo peers. This fourth hypothesis directs an examination of the effect of these social relationships on migrant drinking behavior. In interaction with strong psychological motives to drink, these factors should provide substantial understanding of the high rates of Navajo drunkenness and arrest observed.

To bring empirical evidence to bear on these hypotheses, data were collected on 259 male Navajo migrants and former migrants, including essentially all who were living in Denver during 1963–66 (135), as well as a one-third random sample of all former Denver migrants who had returned to the Navajo reservation

(124).[7] The main instrument was a lengthy formal interview of about two hours' duration, which included background information, complete job histories, and a battery of psychometric and sociometric tests. In addition, interviews and ratings were collected from most employers of Navajo Indians in Denver (Weppner 1968), all migrant records from the BIA were abstracted, participant observation of Navajo recreational activities in Denver was conducted (Snyder 1968), and case studies in depth were made of representative migrant individuals and families (McCracken 1968; McSwain 1965; Ziegler 1967). From these data, findings of substantial internal consistency and reliability emerge.

In this presentation, arrest rates in the city will serve as the primary index of drunkenness (the "criterion measure"). Based on public records, these rates have the virtue of being "nonreactive" (Webb, et al. 1966) because they are not dependent on the subjects' memory or honesty; the records also extend over the entire period, whether short or long, that each migrant remained in the city. Thus arrest rates serve as a convenient and objective, if indirect, measure of drunkenness rates.

The possibility of using police records, however, was dependent on the particular circumstances of this research. For example, many middle-class white businessmen may get drunk as often as some of these Navajo migrants, but their drinking rarely comes to the attention of the police; arrest records would be useless as an index of drunkenness within this group. But ethnographic observations by both ourselves and others (Heath 1964; Ferguson 1968) have shown that the typical form Navajo drinking takes, its social and public nature, makes it particularly susceptible to notice by the police.

The use of arrest rates places some limitations upon the analy-

[7] Actually, only about half of these "returnees" were selected on a truly random fashion from a total list derived from BIA records. During the first summers of fieldwork, we had no idea how difficult it might be to locate specific returnees on the reservation. Consequently, the reservation was simply divided into areas and the attempt made to locate what returnees we could from each on a "quota sampling" basis, making an effort not to select only the most readily available. On dozens of economic, social, and psychological variables, these two returnee samples differed significantly no more often than would be expected by chance. They have therefore been combined, and all treated as a single random sample.

sis, however. In the case of the Navajo (and probably all urban Indians) the assumption that the greater the drunkenness the greater the arrest rate is not unreasonable, given the high percentage of arrests for drinking-related offenses and the predominantly public form of Indian drinking. But because the relationship between drunkenness and arrest is probabilistic rather than mechanical, *group* rates are more dependable than *individual* rates, making correlations between a migrant's personal attributes and his frequency of arrest unstable. This problem is exacerbated by the fact that many migrants, like Harrison Joe, remain in the city only a few weeks or months, so that the temporal base on which individual rates might be calculated is often very small.

To handle considerations like this, we have focused on and taken advantage of *differences* among the Navajo subjects in their background and behavior. (This is a departure from the normal anthropological procedure, which emphasizes *similarities* among subjects by characterizing the "typical" form of their beliefs or actions.) Migrants were given "scores" on each attribute which interested us, scores which varied according to how much of the characteristic they possessed. For example, subjects were scored for the number of years of schooling they had, and the amount of "achievement orientation" they displayed on a projective test.

To relate arrest rates to these scores, the following procedure was employed. First, the range of scores on some characteristic was split at some convenient point near the middle, and the migrants classified as high or low on that characteristic. The number of arrests were counted among those highs interviewed on the reservation, then multiplied by three (since this was a one-third sample), and added finally to the number of arrests acquired by highs interviewed in Denver (essentially a total sample). The same procedure was followed for estimating the number of man years the highs spent in the city; arrests were divided by man years, rounded to two significant decimal places, to yield an estimated arrest rate per man year for the highs. These steps were then repeated for migrants falling in the low category as well. In standard form these two figures were then converted to rates per 100,000 man years in the city (simply multiplying each by 100,000) to permit direct comparison with data such as those presented in Tables 7.1 and 7.2.

This procedure may sound complicated, but since it will be used throughout this chapter and is critical to the argument, it is essential that reader credibility is not lost at this point. The following demonstration may help to illustrate and clarify the procedure, and perhaps allay suspicions of mathematical legerdemain as well.

The arrest rate for the migrant population in Denver has already been presented above, and was based on actual records from almost the entire group. To estimate this same rate from the interviewed sample as an illustration, how would this estimate be calculated, based on the procedure outlined above, and how would it compare with the actual rate?

The 135 migrants interviewed in Denver had 245 arrests, while the 124 interviewed on the reservation had 137. Since this reservation group is a one-third sample of all returnees, their arrests are multiplied by three to get an estimate of the total returnee arrests: 411. When these are added to the Denver group, an estimate of 656 arrests for the total population is obtained. The actual number by count was 665, giving an error in estimate of about 1.5 percent. Similarly, for man years in the city: the group interviewed in Denver account for 352.5 man years, while the group interviewed on the reservation account for 86.33. Multiplying the latter figure by three and adding the two numbers gives an estimate of 611.5 man years in the city for the total migrant group. This compares with 639 man years by actual count, or an error in estimate of about 4 percent. Finally, to calculate the arrest rate, the estimated number of arrests, 656, is divided by the estimated number of man years in the city, 611.5, and multiplied by 100,000. This yields a figure of 107,000 arrests per 100,000 population, as compared with the actual rate of 104,000, for an error in estimate of less than 3 percent.

The question of the "statistical significance" of the data should be mentioned. Since arrests are not independent events, i.e., the same person may be arrested more than once, there is no statistical procedure by which the "significance" of a difference between the arrest rates of two groups can be tested. This problem is exacerbated by the unequal sampling ratios employed in the

Denver and returnee strata, since data from the latter subjects must be multiplied by three to provide population estimates, introducing further nonindependence. As a consequence, no tests of statistical significance will be presented in this chapter.

Instead, far more stringent criteria will be applied to an evaluation of the results: (1) is the magnitude of group differences in the arrest rate large enough to have *social* significance, and (2) is the *pattern* of associations consistent with a reasonable set of theoretical expectations? If these two criteria are met, then the issue of statistical significance would be irrelevant anyway. For those still concerned with the problem, however, some evaluation of the results can be based on the error in estimate of group rates just presented. If group differences in arrest rates are no larger than 3,000 to 5,000 per 100,000 man years in the city, for example, they are probably not large enough to be stable, and therefore not worth interpreting. But almost all the differences to be presented here are usually 20,000 or more. It is therefore unlikely that the interpretations are empirically unfounded, despite an inability to demonstrate the formal statistical significance of the results.

ECONOMIC FACTORS

As emphasized earlier, the major structural pressures to drink experienced by Indians in American society derive from their marginal economic position. The theoretical basis for this is found in the work of Merton (1957:131–194) and others. When goals are strongly held for which society provides inadequate means of attainment, in the view of these theorists, the resulting means-goals "disjunction" produces pressures for engaging in alternative, often nonapproved, adaptations, of which excessive drinking is one common form. In decision-theory terms, the anticipated rewards (goals) for engaging in socially approved behavior (means) are relatively low. The resulting disappointment and frustration leads to the selection of *other* courses of action that may not be so highly approved (such as drunkenness), but provide substitute rewards.

In another study employing a rural sample of both Indians and Spanish-Americans (Graves 1967a), it was found that among those strongly oriented toward the dominant society and its material values, those with poor and irregular jobs consistently had higher rates of drinking and associated problem behavior, as well as stronger psychological *feelings* of deprivation and alienation, than those with relatively steady jobs. By contrast, among those with relatively little commitment to the dominant group values, the kind of jobs held had practically no relationship to drinking rates or associated psychological feelings.[8]

Among migrant Indians, the situation is different than among these rural-reservation groups. Essentially all migrants are strongly attracted to economic goals, which is a major source of their dissatisfaction with reservation life and of their motivation to migrate. Furthermore, those who remain in the city longest display the strongest economic value orientation (Graves and Van Arsdale 1966). It was therefore hypothesized that any index of economic failure in the city would be associated with higher rates of drunkenness and arrest among all migrants.

This hypothesis was repeatedly supported, regardless of what measures of economic success were employed (see Tables 7.3 and 7.4). Wages have great psychological salience for these migrants, and the association between arrest rates and an indirect measure of feelings of *relative deprivation* which were derived from this fact should particularly be noted. When the migrant's starting wage was *lower* than the highest wage he had received before migrating, as was true for slightly over half of all migrants, it is probably fair to assume that he might begin to wonder if the many sacrifices associated with migration were worthwhile. This psychological situation, based on certain features of migrant social structure, is associated with a subsequent arrest rate of 116,000 per 100,000 man years in the city, more than double the rate of 54,000 among those migrants whose starting wages were at least as high as they had experienced before migration.

But absolute levels of economic achievement are also associated with arrest rates; jointly these form an even more powerful predictor. Those who experienced unemployment rates of 15 percent or more during their first few months in Denver and who

---

[8] See also Jessor, Graves, Hanson, and Jessor (1968) for the more general situation among nonacculturating groups as well.

TABLE 7.3

*Initial Economic Experiences in the City versus
Denver Arrest Rates*

	Proportion of All Migrants (Percentage)	Arrest Rate per 100,000 Population
Initial percentage employed		
More than 85%	50	73,000
85% or less	50	128,000
Starting wage		
More than $1.25 per hour	38	77,000
$1.25 or less per hour	62	93,000
Starting wage relative to highest premigration wage		
Same or higher than premigration	48	54,000
Lower than premigration	52	116,000
Combined pattern of variables		
Favorable on all three of the above	11	34,000
Favorable on two out of three	32	85,000
Favorable on only one indicator	41	88,000
Unfavorable on all three of the above	16	214,000

TABLE 7.4

*Subsequent Economic Experiences in the City versus
Denver Arrest Rates*

	Proportion of All Migrants (Percentage)	Arrest Rate per 100,000 Population
Subsequent percentage employed		
Full employment	66	66,000
Some unemployment	34	179,000
Present wage		
More than $1.35 per hour	45	57,000
$1.35 or less per hour	55	167,000
Present wage relative to highest premigration wage		
Higher than premigration	51	43,000
Same or lower than premigration	49	165,000
Combined pattern of variables		
Favorable on all three of the above	22	44,000
Favorable on two out of three	32	55,000
Favorable on only one indicator	33	157,000
Unfavorable on all three of the above	13	448,000

had a starting wage of no more than $1.25 per hour, which was the same as, or lower than, what they had experienced before migration (16 percent of all migrants), had an arrest rate of 214,000 per 100,000 man years in the city. By contrast, those with less unemployment and a higher starting wage (11 percent of all migrants) had an arrest rate of only 34,000 per 100,000, about one-sixth that of their less fortunate brethren.

Although these initial economic experiences in Denver are powerful predictors of a migrant's subsequent drinking problems, the association between economic position and arrest rate deepens with time in the city (Table 7.4). For example, those who continued to have periods of unemployment during their last few months in Denver and who were making less than $1.35 per hour (a wage no higher than 13 percent of all migrants had received before coming to Denver) had an appalling arrest rate of 448,000 per 100,000 man years in the city!

In part, this depressing relationship between economic position and arrest rate probably results from the fact that continuing deprivation is more psychologically disturbing than initial deprivation, a period when hopes may linger for better times to come. But it also derives from the effect of the migrant's drinking on his economic position. Complaints about their drunkenness is the major factor that differentiates employer ratings of Indian employees from those of whites in comparable jobs, and these complaints are clearly related to lower Indian wages or dismissal (Weppner 1968). As one employer put it, "He'd take off three or four days at a time because of drinking. We took him back three or four times, but hell, there's no use putting up with it." This feedback from the migrant's drinking behavior to the structural and psychological "determinants" that in turn give rise to it, is a theme pursued in this study, wherever time-linked data permit. Thus the development of a vicious cycle is traced from structural position, to personality, to behavior, a cycle that is difficult to break once set in motion.

BACKGROUND FACTORS

This developmental cycle does not begin in the city, however. Background preparation for urban life also contributes to economic success in Denver, and thereby to a better personal adjustment. The possible influence of a migrant's father (or father surrogate) in providing both direct and indirect training for successful wage labor, via processes of social learning and "modeling" (Bandura and Walters 1963) was particularly fascinating. The hypothesis was that successful parental wage-labor role models would be associated with better economic performance in the city by their sons, and therefore better personal adjustment. All the links in this chain of inference cannot be presented here, although this hypothesis received support at each point examined. Table 7.5 presents the end product, the association between parental models and subsequent urban arrest rates. Those migrants whose fathers provided economically successful wage-labor role models had arrest rates of 62,000 per 100,000 man years in Denver, less than half the rate for migrants whose fathers were engaged in more traditional reservation occupations and were economically unsuccessful as well (135,000 arrests per 100,000 man years).

Education and vocational training provide even more direct

TABLE 7.5

Economically Successful Parental Role Models versus Denver Arrest Rates

	Proportion of All Migrants (Percentage)	*Arrest Rate per 100,000 Population*
Father's occupation		
Father has nontraditional occupation (wage labor)	39	75,000
Father has traditional occupation (farming-herding)	61	97,000
Economic position of family of orientation		
Perceived as better off than neighbors	60	75,000
Perceived as worse off than neighbors	40	117,000
Combined pattern of variables		
Nontraditional occupation *and* family was better off	26	62,000
Mixed pattern	48	83,000
Traditional occupation *and* family was worse off	26	135,000

preparation for successful economic performance, and were therefore also expected to be associated with a better urban adjustment. The evidence in support of this hypothesis is presented in Table 7.6. Migrants with eight or more years of formal education which included skilled vocational training also had arrest rates of less than half those with less education and no skilled vocational training (51,000 versus 145,000 arrests per 100,000 man years in the city). It should be noted, however, that a small amount of education or training is associated with higher arrest rates than almost none at all! Perhaps this results from raising the migrant's aspirations higher than his level of preparation can help him achieve. Commonly these migrants, like Harrison Joe, who came to the city with semi-skilled training for which there is a limited market, expect to receive good jobs in their chosen field right away, and are disappointed when they do not.

Other forms of premigration experience were also implicated, but not always in the manner one might anticipate. For example, premigration wage-labor experience, though it usually re-

TABLE 7.6

Education and Vocational Training versus Denver Arrest Rate

	Proportion of All Migrants (Percentage)	Arrest Rate per 100,000 Population
Years of education		
11 years or more	14	33,000
8–10 years	31	75,000
5–7 years	45	128,000
4 years or less	10	87,000
Vocational training		
Skilled	41	66,000
Semi-skilled	45	117,000
None	14	83,000
Combined pattern of variables		
8 or more years of education *and* skilled vocational training	21	51,000
Mixed pattern	43	77,000
Less than 8 years of school *and* no skilled vocational training	36	145,000

sulted in better urban jobs, was also associated with higher arrest rates. From other data it appears likely that favorable premigration experience raises migrant aspirations higher than the reality of urban life can satisfy, thus producing a sense of "relative deprivation" among many otherwise "successful" migrants.

In summary, if we looked at no other variables than a migrant's economic position in the city and his preparation for urban life, we would still have achieved a major understanding of his drunkenness and arrest problems.

PSYCHOLOGICAL FACTORS

The previously reported finding that urban wages relative to premigration wages are a better predictor of arrest rates than absolute wage level indicates the importance of *psychological* processes in mediating this empirical relationship. Two types of psychological variables are of focal importance: personal *goals*, and future *expectations* concerning one's ability to achieve these goals.

The most successful technique for discovering the migrants' values involved a content analysis of four open-ended questions:

What are the things you like best about living in Denver?
What do you *not* like about living in Denver?
What do you like best about living on the reservation?
What do you *not* like about living on the reservation?

The answers to these questions did two things simultaneously for the investigation: (1) they helped define the *opportunity structure* of the city and of the reservation *as perceived by these migrants*, and (2) they provided a basis for distinguishing those migrants whose personal goals are most compatible with what the city can provide. The results of this content analysis have been reported elsewhere (Graves and Van Arsdale 1966), and demonstrate the overwhelming significance of *economic* opportunities in the city, whereas the reservation is characterized by the variety of social and traditional goals it can provide. From this sharp distinction in the perceived opportunity structure of the city and the reservation, the following hypothesis was derived: *those migrants who have a personal goal structure that is unrealistic in view of urban opportunities will experience the greatest psychological conflict about remaining in the city, and will therefore drink the heaviest.*

To test this hypothesis, migrant responses to these four questions were sorted into categories, and the proportion of economic-material goals mentioned was calculated for each subject. When divided at the median, those migrants with the weakest commitment to economic-material goals did indeed have higher arrest rates in Denver (Table 7.7).

To get at the other end of the value continuum and to provide a second, operationally distinct measure of migrant goals, a semi-projective measure of Navajo "traditionalism" was used, which Goldschmidt, Edgerton, and Nydegger originally developed. (See a related test by Goldschmidt and Edgerton 1961.) Subjects were shown pictures that contrasted traditional and modern scenes, and their responses to these scenes were again analyzed for content. Those subjects who displayed a strong orientation toward the goals of traditional reservation life also had higher

TABLE 7.7

Personal Values versus Denver Arrest Rates

	Percentage of All Migrants	*Arrest Rate per 100,000 Population*
Economic value orientation		
High economic values	50	84,000
Low economic values	50	96,000
Navajo traditionalism[a]		
Low traditional values	37	82,000
High traditional values	63	95,000
Combined pattern of personal values		
High economic values *plus* low		
traditional values	17	61,000
Mixed patterns	49	86,000
Low economic values *plus* high		
traditional values	34	117,000

[a] Based on a sample of approximately two-thirds of the protocols derived from projective instrument.

arrest rates in Denver (Table 7.7). Neither of these two value measures, moreover, bore any relationship to *actual* economic achievement in the city. Thus, a correlation between material values and good jobs could not account for the lower arrest rates, adding weight to the value-conflict interpretation. And when combined, these two value measures yield a substantial degree of association with arrests: those migrants whose goals are most compatible with urban opportunities have an arrest rate of 61,000 per 100,000 man years in Denver; those migrants whose goals are least appropriate have arrest rates that are almost double, 117,000 per 100,000 man years.

The source of this particular type of psychic distress and therefore of the migrants' drunken response lies in the fact that the pursuit of one set of goals (economic-material) through urban migration leads to inadequate satisfaction of another set of goals (social-traditional) that are often equally strong. Another way to measure this conflict and its consequences is through a self-anchoring scale of migrants' future expectations (Graves and Van Arsdale 1966). Those migrants who expect to do well in the city in the future but have no hope for success on the reservation have few doubts about migrating. They remain in the city longest and have the lowest arrest rates: 75,000 per 100,000 man years (Table 7.8). Those who expect to do well back home but not in Denver also have relatively low arrest rates: 81,000 per 100,000 man years. What conflict they feel is quickly resolved by a return to the reservation. Those who feel they could do well in either location are in a "double-approach" conflict reflected in an arrest rate of 93,000 per 100,000 man years. Those in the more devastating "double-avoidance" conflict who cannot anticipate personal success in either location have a far higher arrest rate: 179,000. This analysis provides strong empirical support for a "conflict theory" of drunkenness.

Also of interest were three personality traits at a fairly high level of abstraction that we believed would serve both to promote economic success and to control against selection of escapist behavior such as drunkenness (Graves 1966). These included feelings of personal control (versus fatalism), an extended future time perspective, and high achievement motivation. The first two were measured using modifications of

TABLE 7.8

Future Expectations versus Denver Arrest Rates

	Proportion of All Migrants (Percentage)	Arrest Rate per 100,000 Population
Future expectations if in Denver		
will improve in next five years.	65	82,000
will stay the same or get worse.	35	113,000
Future expectations if on reservation		
will improve in next five years.	48	90,000
will stay the same or get worse.	52	95,000
Interaction between future expectations for Denver and reservation		
will improve in Denver but not on reservation.	35	75,000
will improve on reservation but not in Denver.	18	81,000
will improve in either location.	30	93,000
will not improve in either location.	17	179,000

techniques developed for the Tri-Ethnic Research Project (Jessor, Graves, Hanson, and Jessor 1968; Graves 1967b). The third was measured by a TAT picture type projective test of our own construction, with the assistance of a Navajo artist (Michener 1965).

Contrary to expectations, these attributes of "industrial man" proved completely *unrelated* to economic success in the city, and for two traits the relationship with drunkenness and arrest was *opposite* the anticipated direction. Need-achievement will serve as an illustration. Those with high achievement motivation actually had *higher* arrest rates than those with low achievement motivation (Table 7.9). In interaction with the most potent measure of economic failure, the dynamics of this process are revealed more clearly. Among those migrants who probably perceived themselves as doing relatively well in the city (those making more money than they ever had before), high or low achievement motivation appears to be almost unrelated to arrest rates. But among those who probably felt economically deprived, such aspirations become critical: migrants with low need-achievement have arrest rates of 97,000 per 100,000. But those in

TABLE 7.9

Need-Achievement versus Denver Arrest Rates

	Proportion of All Migrants (Percentage)	Arrest Rate per 100,000 Population
Achievement motivation		
Low	49	64,000
High	51	86,000
Interaction between this need and		
economic pressures		
Present wage higher than highest		
premigration wage *and*		
a. low need-achievement	27	33,000
b. high need-achievement	23	39,000
Present wage same or lower than		
highest premigration wage *and*		
a. low need-achievement	21	97,000
b. high need-achievement	29	176,000

similar economic circumstances with high need-achievement have arrest rates of 176,000. Achievement striving is apparently not the adaptive trait teachers working with Indian students may believe; instead, for those with limited marketable skills this trait makes the inevitable frustrations of urban living that much harder to bear.

SOCIAL FACTORS

For a more complete understanding of migrant drinking, however, social pressures and constraints from peers and wives should also be taken into consideration. The social-recreational nature of Navajo drinking (Heath 1964; Ferguson 1968), common to most American Indian groups, was observed in Denver as well. In fact, recreational activities among migrants almost always involve some drinking — more often than not, heavy drinking and drunkenness (Snyder 1968). It is not surprising, therefore, that pressures from buddies to join them is the single most common explanation of their drinking problems given by Navajos themselves, both on and off the reservation. That this

is not the whole explanation is obvious from the associations between arrest rates and economic deprivation. But the Navajos'
excuse cannot be dismissed as pure rationalization, as was amply
illustrated by the case of Harrison Joe. To a young migrant
alone in the city, the social rewards for deciding to drop into a
bar with his friends may be very high indeed.

The empirical support for the influence of peer group members
on migrant drinking is strong (Table 7.10). Those with exclusively
Navajo friends in the city have arrest rates of 131,000 per 100,000
man years, substantially higher than those who spend at least

TABLE 7.10

*Informal Social Relationships in the City versus
Denver Arrest Rates*

	Proportion of All Migrants	Arrest Rate per 100,000 Population
Kin and friends at arrival		
None	47%	69,000
Some	53%	107,000
Friendship pattern in the city		
Some non-Navajo friends	51%	62,000
Exclusively Navajo friends	49%	131,000
Navajo sociometric score		
(those interviewed in Denver only)		
Relatively few Navajo friends	N = 56	38,000
Many Navajo friends	N = 56	66,000
Interaction between peer group		
pressures and economic pressures		
Present wage higher than highest premigration wage *and* some non-Navajo friends	28%	32,000
Present wage higher than highest premigration wage *and* exclusively Navajo friends	24%	77,000
Present wage same or lower than highest premigration wage *and* some non-Navajo friends	24%	113,000
Present wage same or lower than highest premigration wage *and* exclusively Navajo friends	24%	207,000

part of their spare time with non-Navajos (62,000 arrests).[9] Furthermore, this influence apparently begins as soon as the migrant arrives in Denver: those with any kin or friends in the city on arrival (other than wife) have a subsequent arrest rate of 107,000, as compared with a rate of only 69,000 arrests for those who arrive knowing no one. The case of Harrison Joe illustrates how this relationship comes about. Whatever positive function a Navajo reference group may serve in helping a new migrant adjust to a strange urban environment, it also serves to socialize him to a pattern of recreational drinking which is likely to get him into trouble and make his adjustment more difficult.

The establishment of Navajo drinking groups and the powerful influence they apparently have on members' drinking behavior can be understood in terms similar to the formation and maintenance of other types of "deviant subcultures" (Cohen 1955; Cloward and Ohlin 1960). Given the manifold pressures on many migrants to drink as an escape from the frustrations and problems generated by their marginal socioeconomic position, a pattern of drinking to oblivion is established, and continues to be strongly reinforced among core participants and others with similar psychological needs who may be drawn to the group. Such drinking groups are an attractive adaptation for migrants not only because of the escape that drunkenness may yield, but also because of the social solidarity created among participants. Furthermore, by flaunting the mores of the dominant community, group drunkenness provides an outlet for hostility toward white society which many Indians would like to join, but which has failed to accept them fully (Berreman 1964; Parker 1964). Once a pattern of group drunkenness becomes normative, however, it also serves as a standard of behavior for some participants who may not have the same psychological needs that generated the pattern in the first place. Thus the existence of the pattern itself, as mediated by the social pressures exerted by core participants, becomes a sufficient cause for the drinking behavior of others who come in contact with it.

[9] The use of sociometric data to define the strength of peer-group influences reveals similar results, but the measure is restricted to the subsample of migrants interviewed in Denver who remained in town long enough to develop stable friendships.

This interpretation gains support from the interaction between economic pressures and peer pressures. When migrants are doing relatively well in the city economically, even if their friendships are drawn exclusively from the ranks of other Navajos, their arrest rate is only 77,000 per 100,000 man years. The peer group pressures to get intoxicated are apparently *far greater,* however, when migrants are doing poorly in the city, and therefore they have a personal, psychological motive to get inebriated as well. Those with relatively poor wages evidently find the enticements of their Navajo drinking companions far more attractive, and have an arrest rate of 207,000, almost three times the rate of their economically more fortunate companions.

Counteracting these peer pressures are the constraints being applied by a migrant's wife. Keeping her husband's drinking within bounds is one of her major responsibilities (McSwain 1965). Some wives are obviously more successful at this task than others, but all with whom we spoke about this matter at least try. A measure of their success is seen in an arrest rate of only 56,000 among those married throughout their stay in the city (Table 7.11). This rate rises to 73,000 among those married during only part of their stay, and jumps to 124,000 among the three-quarters of all Navajo migrants who are single their entire time in Denver. The fact that only 20 percent of the Navajo migrants are married when they arrive is a major structural difference between them and other minority groups in Denver, which also helps to account for part of the radical difference in arrest rates between the Navajos and other groups. For example, 88 percent of the Spanish migrant comparison sample are married, though many first came to the city alone, and then called their family to join them after they found a job (Rendón 1968).

Since married migrants might be assumed to be older and more experienced, the alert reader may wonder if this relationship between marriage and low arrest rates is not simply a matter of better jobs. But somewhat surprisingly, marital status is *unrelated* to economic success in the city. As with many other variables investigated, however, the migrant's economic position is highly important for understanding the points at which wifely controls become most critical. When migrants receive relatively good wages, those who are married have arrest rates only about

TABLE 7.11

Marital Status in the City versus Denver Arrest Rates

	Proportion of All Migrants (Percentage)	Arrest Rate per 100,000 Population
Marital status at arrival		
Married	20	60,000
Single	80	106,000
Marital status during entire migration		
Married throughout stay	19	56,000
Married part of stay	6	73,000
Single throughout stay	75	124,000
Interaction between marital controls and economic pressures		
Present wage higher than highest premigration wage *and* married any time in city	14	39,000
Present wage higher than highest premigration wage *and* single throughout stay	37	55,000
Present wage same or lower than highest premigration wage *and* married any time in city	13	120,000
Present wage same or lower than highest premigration wage *and* single throughout stay	36	228,000

10,000 lower than those who are single. By contrast, when migrants are receiving relatively poor wages, those who are married have arrest rates 100,000 lower than those who are single (bottom of Table 7.11). The influence of a migrant's wife as an agent of social control appears to be far more important when he is badly off, and therefore highly motivated to get drunk, than when he is doing well.

Finally, the joint influence of social pressures and controls, in conjunction with a migrant's economic position in the city, reveals the value of approaching the explanation of urban Indian drunkenness from several directions simultaneously. For a migrant who is single throughout his stay in the city, associates exclusively with other Navajos, and earns no more than he had received previously, both the pressures and the temptations to drink heavily are great. Of all Navajo migrants to Denver,

18 percent fell into this pattern, and their arrest rate was 243,000 per 100,000 man years in the city. At the other end of the scale is a handful of stable migrants (8 percent) who were married throughout their stay in Denver, did not spend their spare time exclusively in the company of other Navajos, and were receiving the highest wages they had ever enjoyed. Their arrest rate was only 26,000, or approaching the range found among Spanish-Americans and Negroes. In the interaction between social variables and economic variables, therefore, it appears that most of the difference in arrest rates between Navajo migrants and other urban minority groups can be accounted for.

CONCLUSIONS

Unhappily, drunkenness has come to occupy a prominent place in the adaptive repertoire of both reservation and urban Indians: its narcotizing effects are leaned on heavily as a way of coping with feelings of personal inadequacy and failure by temporarily escaping from them. This is, of course, only one of many functions of alcohol use, and one which most drinkers, Indians and non-Indians alike, are aware of and depend on from time to time (Jessor, Graves, Hanson, and Jessor 1968; Jessor, Carmen, and Grossman 1968). Indians, like other people, also drink for social reasons, but for them recreational drinking groups have become a prominent feature of the urban Indian scene. This feature has resulted in rates of drunkenness and associated problems far higher than those of other American groups, even those also occupying marginal positions within society. The question raised by many observers is: Are not these high rates the result of a cultural predisposition among Indians to hide from their problems in drunken oblivion rather than to seek "more constructive" alternatives?

This is not my reading of the facts. Generally speaking, recourse to a group's "culture" to explain their behavior simply serves to conceal ignorance of the underlying processes in operation. Alternatively, the typical structural conditions within which a group's problems of adaptation arise can be examined, along with the personal resources generally available for coping with them. When viewed in this way, I find no convincing empirical evidence that there is something unique about the way Indians use alcoholic beverages, or that other people in similar circumstances would not behave in a similar fashion.

This chapter has served to document the basis for such a conclusion. In the research project on which it is based, a deliberate attempt was made to seek an explanation of excessive Indian drunkenness in terms of structural and psychological variables that are also relevant to non-Indian drinkers, such as the type of parental role models, premigration training for successful urban employment, and marital status. After it was shown that better prepared Indians have far fewer drinking problems than those who are less prepared, the Navajos' high drinking rates in comparison to other urban groups can be understood in light of the fact that their preparation for successful, unstressful urban living is far poorer. Almost a third of the comparison group of Spanish-American migrants studied in Denver, for example, had fathers who were employed as semi-skilled wage laborers or better (Rendon 1968); most Navajo wage labor of the last generation was purely unskilled manual work. A third of the Spanish-American migrants also had essentially completed high school (eleven years or more), whereas only 14 percent of the Navajo migrants got this far in school. Eighty-eight percent of the Spanish-American migrants were married; only 20 percent of the Navajo were. The first job in Denver for 15 percent of the Spanish-American migrants was skilled, whereas only 6 percent of the Navajo were able to do this well. If these substantial differences between the Indian urban migrants and the other working-class groups with which they are in competition were controlled, little difference in their drinking behavior would remain.

The analysis of Navajo drinking groups reveals they have much in common with other ethnic groups, though in some respects these groups appear to display unique cultural features as well. The typical Navajo social drinking group is seen as an adaptive response to certain structural conditions that also give rise to similar groups within other tribes, and among many non-Indian peoples as well. In addition, the drinking group's departure from conventional middle-class norms reveals dynamics that provide theoretical linkages with such well-studied phenomena as delinquent gangs and drug-use circles. Furthermore, when groups of Indian migrants who are peculiarly susceptible to the social pressures exerted by members of these drinking cliques are defined — single Navajos whose marginal economic position in the midst of affluence generates strong feelings of relative deprivation, and whose friendships are drawn exclusively from the ranks of their fellow Navajos — arrest rates are more than twice as high as those for Navajo migrants in general. By contrast, married migrants with a stable urban adaptation who are not socially mapped into these groups have arrest rates close to those of other minority groups in the city and only a fraction as high as the overall Navajo rate.

Thus it would appear that the vast majority of Navajo drunkenness, at least in Denver, can be accounted for *without recourse to the fact that the subjects are Indians.* These findings have greater theoretical and applied implications as a result. Particularly significant is the fact that many of the critical determinants examined in this chapter are structural variables over which society can exercise some measure of control.

Even though this is a statistical analysis, it has potential policy implications for persons working with individual migrants, as long as the *probabilistic* relationship between variables is kept in mind. This may be illustrated by returning to the case of Harrison Joe, the migrant whose history is presented in this essay. A summary of his background attributes and urban experience is presented in Table 7.12. On five of the six "predictors" discussed in this paper, Harrison Joe appears poorly equipped for success in the city. Only the fact that his father was a silversmith, a marginal case of "wage labor" at best, might possibly suggest success.

If funds for the relocation program were limited, discouraging such "poor risks" from coming to the city might be advocated purely on the basis of a cost-benefit analysis. One might also argue that encouraging people to migrate despite a poor prognosis may be doing them a disservice. Resulting failure may have serious long-range psychological and social consequences, setting these "poor risks" on an endless spiral of migration and return, marked by frustration, failure, and drunkenness at every turn.

As in all statistical decision-making, one must consider the cost

TABLE 7.12

Harrison Joe's Profile on Key Variables

	Prognosis
Predictors	
Father was a silversmith (considered wage labor)	+
But family perceived as worse off than neighbors	−
Five years of education (special Navajo program)	−
Semi-skilled vocational training (upholstery)	−
Unmarried	−
Had a friend in Denver on arrival	−
Initial urban experience	
62% initial unemployment	−
Starting wage was only $1.25 per hour	−
But this was higher than he had earned before migration	+
Subsequent urban experience	
Continued high unemployment rate throughout stay	−
Wages never rose above $1.25 per hour	−
Though this was higher than premigration wages	+
Maintained an exclusive Navajo friendship circle	−
Was arrested for drunkenness within three weeks of arrival	−
Returned home almost immediately thereafter	−

of letting a migrant come to the city and being wrong versus keeping him away and being wrong. Some applicants with poor qualifications *do* succeed in the city, and the bureau quite properly is reluctant to cut them off from their chance. It would be far better to encourage such applicants first to take advantage of BIA-sponsored basic educational and vocational training before embarking on direct employment assistance. At the very least, special counselling and follow-up should be provided for high-risk applicants after their arrival.

This survey's results have many other obvious applied implications. The role of economic marginality in the migrant's adjustment problems is fundamental. Repeatedly, factors such as marriage, peer pressures, and a variety of personality variables contribute to the migrant's drinking problems when the migrant has a poor and unstable income, whether this contribution be positive or negative. If these economic hardships could be solved, other factors would assume minor importance. What the migrant needs is not more psychological counselling (Ferguson 1968) or more wholesome recreational outlets (Dozier 1966), but better jobs. Any limitation in his personality or cultural repertoire for coping with his adjustment difficulties becomes irrelevant if the economic basis for these difficulties can be dealt with.

But the research also makes clear that urban migration is not the best way to solve the economic limitations of reservation life. Experience with migrants indicates that most would prefer to live and work near their reservation homes. Forcing them to seek employment in large urban centers only adds to their adjustment problems in many ways. Indian critics of BIA policy have often suggested that federal funds now invested in relocation might be better spent in improving reservation opportunities and promoting Indian jobs in surrounding communities. With this judgment I am forced to agree.

BIBLIOGRAPHY

Bandura, Albert, and Richard H. Walters
    1963   Social Learning and Personality Development. New York: Holt, Rinehart and Winston.
Berreman, Gerald D.
    1964   "Aleut Reference Group Alienation, Mobility, and Acculturation." American Anthropologist 66:231–250.
Cloward, Richard A., and Lloyd E. Ohlin
    1960   Delinquency and Opportunity: A Theory of Delinquent Gangs. New York: Free Press.
Cohen, Albert K.
    1955   Delinquent Boys: The Culture of the Gang. New York: Free Press.
Devereux, George
    1948   "The Function of Alcohol in Mohave Society." Quarterly Journal of Studies on Alcohol 9:207–251.
Dozier, Edward P.
    1966   "Problem Drinking among American Indians: The Role of Socio-cultural Deprivation." Quarterly Journal of Studies on Alcohol 27:72–87.
DuToit, Bryan M.
    1964   "Substitution: A Process in Culture Change." Human Organization 23:16–23.
Ferguson, Frances N.
    1968   "Navajo Drinking: Some Tentative Hypotheses." Human Organization 27:159–167.
Goldschmidt, Walter R., and Robert B. Edgerton
    1961   "A Picture Technique for the Study of Values." American Anthropologist 63:26–47.

Graves, Theodore D.
  1966   "Alternative Models for the Study of Urban Migration." *Human Organization* 25:295–299.
  1967a   "Acculturation, Access and Alcohol in a Tri-Ethnic Community." *American Anthropologist* 69:306–321.
  1967b   "Psychological Acculturation in a Tri-Ethnic Community." *Southwestern Journal of Anthropology* 23:337–350.
  1970   "The Personal Adjustment of Navajo Indian Migrants to Denver, Colorado." *American Anthropologist* 72:35–54.
  1971   "Culture Change and Psychological Adjustment: The Case of the American Indian and Eskimo." In *Adaptation, Adjustment, and Culture Change,* George DeVos (Ed.). (In press.)
  1971   "There But For Grace: A Social-Psychological Study of Urban Indian Drunkenness." (In preparation.)
  ———, and Minor Van Arsdale
  1966   "Values, Expectations and Relocation: The Navajo Indian Migrant to Denver." *Human Organization* 25:300–307.
Heath, Dwight B.
  1964   "Prohibition and Post-Repeal Drinking Patterns among the Navajo." *Quarterly Journal of Studies on Alcohol* 25:119–135.
Honigmann, John J., and Irma Honigmann
  1945   "Drinking in an Indian-White Community." *Quarterly Journal of Studies on Alcohol* 5:575–619.
  1968   "Alcohol in a Canadian Northern Town." Paper presented at the Annual Meeting of the Canadian Sociology and Anthropology Association.
Institute for Government Research
  1928   *The Problem of Indian Administration.* Baltimore: The Johns Hopkins Press.
Jessor, Richard, Roderick S. Carmen, and Peter H. Grossman
  1968   "Expectations of Need Satisfaction and Drinking Patterns of College Students." *Quarterly Journal of Studies on Alcohol* 29:101–116.
Jessor, Richard, Theodore D. Graves, Robert C. Hanson, and Shirley Jessor
  1968   *Society, Personality, and Deviant Behavior. A Study of a Tri-Ethnic Community.* New York: Holt, Rinehart and Winston.
Lemert, Edward M.
  1954   "Alcohol and the Northwest Coast Indians." *University of California Publications in Culture and Society,* vol. 2, no. 2.
McCracken, Robert D.
  1968   "Urban Migration and the Changing Structure of Navajo Social Relations." Unpublished Ph.D. dissertation, University of Colorado.
McSwain, Romola
  1965   "The Role of Wives in the Urban Adjustment of Navajo Migrant Families to Denver, Colorado." Unpublished M.A. thesis, University of Hawaii.
Merton, Robert K.
  1957   *Social Theory and Social Structure.* Glencoe, Ill.: The Free Press.
Michener, Bryan P.
  1965   "The Development and Scoring of a Test of Need Achievement

for Navajo Indians." *Navajo Urban Relocation Research Report* no. 6. Mimeographed.
Parker, Seymour
    1964   "Ethnic Identity and Acculturation in Two Eskimo Villages." *American Anthropologist* 66:325–340.
Rendón, Gabino, Jr.
    1968   "Prediction of Adjustment Outcomes of Rural Migrants to the City." Unpublished Ph.D. dissertation, University of Colorado.
Snyder, Peter Z.
    1968   "Social Assimilation and Adjustment of Navajo Migrants to Denver." Unpublished Ph.D. dissertation, University of Colorado.
Stewart, Omer C.
    1964   "Questions Regarding American Indian Criminality." *Human Organization* 23:61–66.
Swett, Daniel H.
    1963   "Characteristics of the Male Indian Arrest Population in San Francisco." Paper presented at the Annual Meeting of the Southwestern Anthropological Association.
    1971   "Indian Deviance in the Urban Area." Section II of James Hirabayashi (ed.). (In preparation.)
Webb, Eugene J., Donald T. Campbell, Richard D. Schwartz, and Lee Sechrest
    1966   *Unobtrusive Measures: Nonreactive Research in the Social Sciences.* Chicago: Rand McNally.
Weppner, Robert S.
    1968   "The Economic Absorption of Navajo Indian Migrants to Denver, Colorado." Unpublished Ph.D. dissertation, University of Colorado.
Whittacker, James O.
    1962   "Alcohol and the Standing Rock Sioux Tribe. I. The Pattern of Drinking." *Quarterly Journal of Studies on Alcohol* 23:468–479.
    1963   "Alcohol and the Standing Rock Sioux Tribe. II. Psychodynamic and Cultural Factors in Drinking." *Quarterly Journal of Studies on Alcohol* 24:80–90.
Yinger, J. Milton
    1965   *Toward a Field Theory of Behavior: Personality and Social Structure.* New York: McGraw-Hill.
Ziegler, Suzanne
    1967   "An Urban Dilemma: The Case of Tyler Begay." Unpublished manuscript.

CHAPTER 8

involvement in an
urban university

FRANK C. MILLER

INTRODUCTION

Indian education was a rather esoteric subject a few years ago, of interest to the Indian people, to at least some of the educators involved in it, and to a few scholars, but it was not a public concern. Today there is a growing awareness that the state of education for American Indians is, in the words of a subcommittee of the United States Senate, "a national tragedy — a national challenge." The reports of this subcommittee (Senate Subcommittee on Indian Education 1967–68, 1969a, 1969b) are the latest volumes in an unbroken tradition of analyses of the problems in Indian education. In spite of excellent reports, penetrating diagnoses of causes, and constructive recommendations, the problems remain unsolved.

This chapter examines one effort toward a solution of some aspects of the problem. The Department of American Indian Studies at the University of Minnesota was created in 1969 as a response to an explicit definition of need, a definition shared in large part by concerned Indians and non-Indians alike. The development of the department will be analyzed in the light of important cultural, social, and educational trends in the region and in the nation. This account will be a case study of rapid innovation that will have, it is hoped, implications for other realms of educational change.

A *METHODOLOGICAL NOTE*

The materials in this chapter are not the result of "research" in the usual sense, and the account is existential as well as anthropological. What is said here comes out of an experience of active involvement; it is not an outsider's detached study of a series of events. I was chairman of the ad hoc committee that proposed the establishment of the Department of American Indian Studies, and also chairman of the advisory committee that planned its program while a staff was being recruited. This chapter is a personal view of events in which I was an "observant participator," not a "participant observer." It is not, of course, a complete account; my selection of what to describe has been guided by my conception of what is important and relevant. It also contains some analysis of the dynamics of change, although this has deliberately been kept to a minimum. This account is offered as grist for other people's theoretical mills, but it is also hoped that it may contain some practical guidance for those who are concerned about the problems of Indian education.

At the outset, I want to state my views about the value of data reported by "observant participators." There is no doubt that the potential for selectivity and subjectivity in observations is greater than in the usual sort of anthropological research. Yet I would argue that there is possibly a difference in degree, but certainly not in kind. All anthropological observation is selective in that it is guided, however implicitly, by theoretical assumptions. An anthropologist's data are always limited to some extent by his particular role as a fieldworker in a particular cultural setting, and by the contacts he is able to establish in that setting.

In any case, since I was far too busy as a participant to "do research" on the events reported here, no attempt has been made to broaden the base of my data. This limitation should be weighed against the fact that I occupied a certain vantage point in observing the events, a vantage point that would not have been available to a detached observer.

THE NATURE OF THE PROBLEM

The Department of American Indian Studies was created in response to a set of social conditions and educational problems that spanned the university, the community, the region, and the nation. Broadly conceived, the essence of the problem is the difficult situation of American Indians in American society. Whether that situation is viewed as the product of exploitation by a capitalist political economy (see Chapter 2 by Jorgensen in this volume), as the result of incomplete acculturation, or as the product of other factors, most observers agree that the Indian people are the most deprived minority group in the United States. Indian communities have the highest rates of virtually all the indicators of poverty — dilapidated housing, a high number of persons per room, use of contaminated water, incidence of disease, unemployment, and school dropouts.

During the past three years, the problems of Indian education have come to national attention through the work of the Senate Subcommittee on Indian Education. The hearings and the report of the subcommittee document the conclusion that the state of education for the first Americans is a national tragedy. On behalf of the subcommittee, Brewton Berry (1969) surveyed the voluminous literature in the field. After discussing the nature of the problem, his conclusion is "that formal education is failing to meet the Indian's needs, that there is widespread dissatisfaction with its results, and that the schools are falling short of their goal of preparing the Indian to participate effectively in American society" (Berry 1969:30).

Most of Berry's report consists of an extensive discussion of the causes of the failure. He does not attempt to isolate the most important causes; rather, he considers the ways in which the background of the students and the patterns of their schooling contribute to the problem. Teachers tend to be inexperienced, if not

ill-prepared, lacking formal certification, parochial, insensitive
to cultural differences, and sometimes burdened with stereotypes
about Indians. The little research that has been conducted on
the attitude of Indian parents toward education frequently refers
to apathy and suspicion. Wax and Thomas (1961) argue that
what is interpreted as apathy is actually an ethic of noninter-
ference. Regardless of how such orientations are interpreted,
there is a growing acceptance among Indian parents of the need
for education. The research surveyed by Berry does not raise the
issue of how much Indian parents actively encourage and support their children in school.

Berry considers the view that Indians fare poorly in education
because they are "culturally deprived," and concludes that

> . . . if "cultural deprivation" is equated with "cultural vacuum,"
> the concept would seem to be not only erroneous but even
> harmful and regrettable. But if it is interpreted as implying an
> impoverished home environment, poor health, undernourish-
> ment, and unfamiliarity with those experiences which contrib-
> ute to academic achievement and successful adjustment to
> American society, it would seem to have considerable validity
> (Berry 1969:49).

Clearly, the second interpretation would be more appropriately
described as "economic deprivation."

There is a diversity of opinion among both Indians and scholars — categories that are, fortunately, not entirely mutually exclusive — about the degree of persistence of traditional Indian
culture. But many agree that the schools' emphasis on punctuality, competition, and individual achievement places Indian
children at a disadvantage, especially children from traditional
families.

A large minority of Indian students do not use English as a
native language, and most scholars agree that the language barrier is a major handicap for such students. The problem of the
language barrier is greatly compounded by the inability — perhaps it would be more appropriate to say unwillingness — of the
schools to deal with the issue. In the recent past, pupils in federal boarding schools were whipped for using an Indian language,
even among themselves. The response to linguistic differences

has become less brutal, but hardly more sophisticated, in most schools attended by Indians. At least today recognition of the problem is growing and scattered efforts are being made to cope with it.

Related to cultural and linguistic differences is the matter of self-image. Three hundred years of disastrous culture contact have left a legacy of low self-esteem and alienation among many Indian groups. Berry quotes several researchers, including James S. Coleman (1966), who believe that these are two of the major factors in academic failure.

Finally, there is the question of the nature of the schools themselves. One of the most striking impressions gained from reading the literature is that numerous and repeated efforts have been made to explain academic failure by variables internal to the Indian or inherent in the Indian's situation, but that few scholars have considered the orientation, the programs, and the quality of the Indian schools. A notable exception is a monograph by Wax, *et al.* (1964), which includes some searching criticisms of the schools on the Pine Ridge reservation in South Dakota. The Senate subcommittee has corrected the omission; its report deals intensively with the failure of both state and federal schools, to deal effectively with the special challenges of Indian education.

Current knowledge does not permit the identification of any factor or set of factors as the most important cause of the problems in Indian education. The weight of the evidence seems clearly to suggest that Indian students suffer from the handicaps of poverty and linguistic differences, that some traditional Indian values are inconsistent with the motivation and behavior demanded by American schools, and that the schools themselves and their teachers are poorly equipped to deal with the special problems of Indian education.

To view the situation in a somewhat different way, formal education has not been integrated into Indian culture with the exception of the eighteenth century Cherokee, the Rough Rock Demonstration School, and the Navajo Community College. Frequently students must leave home in order to be educated; wherever there are schools in Indian communities, they are intrusions of the wider society. They will remain intrusions until they are modified in structure, orientation, and curricular content, or until Indian communities lose their distinctive character.

THE LOCAL AND REGIONAL CONTEXT

The University of Minnesota serves a state and a region in which American Indians are the largest racial minority group, even though they are only about 1 percent of the total population. The five states in what the local media call the "Upper Midwest" (Wisconsin, Minnesota, Iowa, and the Dakotas), along with the two adjacent provinces of Canada, contain one of North America's major concentrations of Indian people. The Chippewa (also called Ojibwa) predominate in Minnesota and Wisconsin; in the latter state there are also Oneida and Winnebago, and in the former several small communities of Sioux. A small group of Fox reside in Iowa; large numbers of Sioux and others live in the Dakotas.

In this region, as in the nation as a whole, perhaps the most important recent development in Indian affairs has been the rapid increase in the rate of migration to cities. The growth of urban Indian populations has occurred within the context of increasing movement off the reservations. This movement has been going on to some extent ever since reservations were created, but it was only a trickle until World War II. Then many men entered the armed forces and others found work in defense industries. After the war, most service men and defense workers returned to their home reservations. Some of them had come to see the world in a different perspective, became dissatisfied with reservation life, and consequently left again, some only temporarily, but some permanently. During the Korean War, the same process took place, and it is being repeated again with the United States' involvement in Southeast Asia.

The BIA relocation program has contributed somewhat to migration away from reservations. Although it has never involved large numbers of people, it has served as a channel for the relocation of Indians in large cities. The program has not contributed directly to the increase of the urban Indian population in the Upper Midwest because the BIA, as a matter of policy, has not placed people in this region's cities. The policy is sometimes justified on the grounds that the relative proximity of cities to reservations would make it too easy for people to return home without making a realistic attempt to adjust to city life.

During the past ten years, the Indian population in the cities of the Upper Midwest has increased greatly, although the absolute numbers are still small. Meriam (1928) estimated that six hundred Indians lived in Minneapolis and St. Paul in the mid–1920's; the number had increased some, but not greatly, by 1950. Then the rate of expansion began to accelerate, and present estimates of Indians in the Twin Cities range between 8,000 and 10,000.

The accelerating movement off the reservations may be attributed to several factors. Indian populations are growing rapidly because birth rates remain high and death rates, while still high, have been lowered by the increased availability of modern medicine. Reservation resources have never been adequate to support their residents, and there is less and less economic incentive to remain. Finally, education and the mass media have had a growing impact on many in the younger generation. For good or ill, the enticements of urban life are increasingly visible.

At the primary and secondary levels, education for American Indians in the Upper Midwest presents a varied picture. Federal boarding schools are found only in the Dakotas. In the remainder of the region, Indian children attend public or parochial schools, sometimes located on the reservation, sometimes off. In Minnesota, Red Lake is the only reservation with a population large enough and concentrated enough to have its own high school. Elsewhere in the state, several Indian communities have grade schools that forward their graduates to high schools off the reservation, schools in which the Indian students usually form a small minority. A study of such a system has been made by Harkins (1968).

The interests and priorities of the University of Minnesota were another dimension of the context in which the Department of American Indian Studies was created. The president of the university, O. Meredith Wilson, had a deep interest in, and concern about, the situation of the Indians. He was chairman of the Commission on the Rights, Liberties, and Responsibilities of the American Indian, which had been established and supported by

the Fund for the Republic in the wake of the application of the
so-called "termination policy" being applied by the United
States government in the 1950's. The commission consisted of
some noted administrators and scholars in Indian affairs who
conducted an extensive survey of Indian problems and a general
reappraisal of the status of the Indian people and of government
policies toward them. The final report (Brophy and Aberle 1966)
is the most comprehensive treatment of the subject by a study
commission since the Meriam report in 1928.

President Wilson's concerns were shared by few of the other
members of the university; the only staff showing any significant interest was that of the Department of Anthropology. It had
a long and distinguished tradition of teaching and research on
Indian cultures, both historic and prehistoric, but relatively
little attention was paid to the contemporary situation. At that
time, there was not one full-time faculty member outside of
anthropology whose primary scholarly interest involved some
aspect of American Indian affairs.

The academic neglect of the contemporary Indian situation
contrasted sharply with the rapidly growing awareness within
the region during the 1960's of the special problems of the area's
largest minority. But awareness did not necessarily mean understanding. There was growing public interest in, but little knowledge about, the nature of Indian culture, the impact of
government policy, and the sources of the problems faced by the
native Americans, who increasingly were saying that the essence
of the "Indian problem" was white people's ignorance about
Indians.

THE FIRST EFFORTS FOR CHANGE
IN THE UNIVERSITY, 1964–66

Toward the end of 1964, President Wilson appointed a committee on American Indian affairs, under the chairmanship of Mat-
thew Stark, Coordinator of Human Relations Programs in the
Student Activities Bureau. Stark was also adviser to Project
Awareness, a program to promote educational enrichment and
vocational motivation in an Indian community in the northern
part of the state, conducted in the summer by university volunteers as a social-service project.

The composition of the committee reflected the state of affairs at the time. In the first place, as a university-wide committee, it was extremely small. I was the only one of the few faculty members with a primary interest in any aspect of American Indian life who served on the committee; the other members were professors with general interests in minority groups or in problems of social change, and middle-level university officials with both professional and personal concerns about the situation of American Indians in American society. Secondly, during the two years of its active existence, there were no members of Indian descent. So far as I know, no one of Indian descent was on the university staff at that time, and it was highly unusual for nonmembers of the university to serve on university committees in those days. During various periods from one to three students, all non-Indians, served on the committee. The absence of Indians on the committee seems almost incredible from today's perspective, but it must be said that the temper of the times was such that it did not seem curious to members of the committee.

The committee set for itself the following tasks:

1. To prepare a summary of present university activities in Indian affairs.

2. To review requests for university assistance in helping to meet various problems facing American Indians.

3. To establish communication with tribal councils and with educational and governmental agencies concerned with Indian affairs.

4. To conduct research and action programs.

5. To assist American Indian students in making satisfactory educational progress at the university.

6. To gather information about university courses relevant to Indian affairs.

7. To recommend new courses and programs.

As the committee met and continued its discussions, a serious lack of basic information about local Indian affairs became apparent. The committee prepared and distributed a brief questionnaire to Indian organizations and Indian-serving agencies, asking them about their membership, goals, programs, and suggestions for the role of the university. Although the committee did not contain any representatives from the Indian community, or any nonuniversity members of any sort, it was seriously interested in basing its recommendations, at least in part, on a broad definition of needs and problems not limited to the perceptions of a few university staff members.

The questionnaire yielded some useful general information, but it was not an adequate instrument for communicating recommendations about possible roles for the university. Therefore the committee decided to hold a statewide meeting of representatives of Indian organizations and Indian-serving agencies. The meeting, held in October, 1965, was extremely well-attended, with representation from virtually all relevant groups and by a significant number of interested individuals without any particular group affiliation. The meeting yielded about fifty suggestions, general and specific, about what the university might do in the domain of Indian affairs. The major tasks for the committee during the 1965–66 academic year were to work through the suggestions, to organize them into a coherent framework, and to discuss them with representatives of appropriate units of the university.

The final report, completed in June, 1966, included a number of basic themes. There was general agreement about the need for better education in American Indian affairs in order to increase the average educated man's awareness of contemporary issues including their background and proposals for their resolution. The special educational needs of professionals such as teachers, social workers, and public health personnel, who work with Indians were also considered. The report recommended improved preparation in basic professional training and more opportunities for in-service training for people in mid-career.

The report dealt more extensively with the need for improved educational opportunities for the Indian people themselves. The committee saw the necessity for programs to reduce the dropout rate in elementary and secondary schools, and to prepare Indian students better for post-graduate training and college. At the former educational level, there were recommendations for increased scholarship aid, expanded counseling, and tutorial and other supportive services. Specific recommendations were made for more adult education and the content of such educational programs.

The committee considered the service role of the university, one that is traditional in land-grant universities and has been increasingly appreciated in recent years by other kinds of institutions as well. In this realm, the report recommended that the university might assist Indian tribal councils in various ways — by making technical personnel available and by holding workshops and training institutes. It also suggested that the university furnish the same sorts of services for Indian community-action programs, which were rapidly growing at that time under the auspices of the Office of Economic Opportunity. The special needs of the growing numbers of urban Indians were discussed briefly in the report, as was the need for improved legal aid for both urban and reservation people.

Finally, the report considered information-processing and research. The committee keenly appreciated the lack of any centralized source of information about Indian affairs in the region, ranging from the culture and history of the tribal groups to salient contemporary issues of governmental policies. The report recommended that an Indian center be established at the university as a facility for the preparation and distribution of pertinent information. It advised that the three high priority research topics were Indian languages, urban migration, and the impact of education on Indian populations, in both reservation and urban contexts.

The report was submitted to President Wilson, who circulated it to deans and department heads of units to which recommendations in the report had been directed. His covering letter urged them to find ways of implementing the recommendations, but it contained no assurances that university funds might be specifically allocated to such purposes.

The chairman of the committee and a few members followed up the report's distribution by individual conferences with those deans who had responded favorably to the president's letter. The reports conveyed back to the committee indicated varying degrees of interest, but no strong commitment to a vigorous course of action. The group met a few times during the 1966–67 aca-

demic year, but it was apparent that its report had generated
little interest.

CHANGES IN THE CONTEXT, 1966–68

Although the 1966 report did not seem to have much impact,
other events and developments within and without the university
were setting the stage for a revival of the entire issue of Indian
education. With the continuing growth of the civil rights movement came increased national concern about the status of minority groups. The difficult situation of the Indian people within
American society was becoming increasingly difficult for the nation to ignore, particularly in Minnesota, whose citizens considered the state to be politically enlightened. Some prominent
politicians had a special interest in Indian affairs. Hubert Humphrey, then Vice-President of the United States, had been made
an honorary member of the Red Lake Band of Chippewa Indians when he was United States Senator from Minnesota; his
role as one of the leading spokesmen for the needs of Minnesota
Indians had been assumed by his successor in the Senate, Walter
Mondale. The concerns of politicians were reinforced by the
mass media in the Twin Cities, which devoted increasing attention to the reporting of Indian affairs. That segment of the public
that was politically aware heard more about Indian problems
than ever before.

The Indians themselves were becoming more involved in the
political and social life of the state; individuals were emerging
in key roles, in both public agencies and community organizations. In the Twin Cities the number of Indian organizations
proliferated as migration accelerated, and the Urban Indian Fed-
eration was formed to facilitate communication among them. One
of the most visible groups was the American Indian Movement
(AIM), the first militant Indian organization in the region and
one of the first in the nation.

In 1968 the Minnesota State Department of Education appointed Will Antell as Director of Indian Education, whereby he
became the first person of Indian descent to hold the position.
The state department also formed an Indian Education Committee, composed entirely of Indian people, to advise on policy issues and program development. The Minneapolis school system

created its own Indian Advisory Committee, and in 1969 appointed Ted Mahto, also of Indian descent, as the system's first consultant on Indian education. The schools in Minneapolis and many other communities showed growing interest in incorporating more adequate information on Indian history and culture in the curriculum.

Indian people as a group also became more involved in education. Although the dropout rate in secondary schools remained high, every year more Indians graduated from Minnesota high schools. The number doubled in six years, from 111 in 1962 to 233 in 1968 (State Department of Education 1968:43). Increased urban migration is also reflected in the figures; seven Indian students graduated from Minneapolis high schools in 1962, twenty-three in 1968. According to the same report, there was a steady growth in native Americans attending college with the assistance of federal, state, tribal, and private scholarships; in 1967–68 the figure was 172, while the year before it had been 147. These figures do not include students without scholarship aid, but they no doubt represent the majority of Indians in college.

During the first part of the 1960's, the main campus of the University of Minnesota in Minneapolis–St. Paul experienced the same increase in Indian students. They probably could have been counted on the fingers of one hand in 1960, but by the academic year 1967–68, their number had increased to twenty-five. Then, in the spring of 1968, Martin Luther King was killed, and a scholarship fund was created in his honor to be used for the support of disadvantaged students of all races. Partly as a result of recruiting efforts associated with the Martin Luther King Fund, there were forty-five Indian students at the university in 1968–69.

As the numbers grew, the activities of the American Indian Students Association expanded. Its focus was the educational situation of native Americans, rather than off-campus political and social issues; it became concerned about university curriculum and its neglect of contemporary Indian affairs.

The university itself underwent internal changes that helped to lay the groundwork for later developments in Indian affairs; the most important was the selection of a new president. Malcolm Moos was appointed to that post in 1967 when O. Meredith Wilson resigned to become director of the Center for Advanced Study in the Behavioral Sciences. With a background as a professor of political science, a speech writer and advisor to President Eisenhower, and director of the Ford Foundation's Program in Law and Government, President Moos was committed to a greater involvement of the university in community life and to a larger role for the university in teaching, research, and service directed toward the major social issues of the day.

The Center for Urban and Regional Affairs (CURA) was established as one of the principal means for promoting greater attention to problem-solving and community involvement. Fred E. Lukermann, Assistant Vice-President for Academic Affairs and a man who was to play a central role in future developments in Indian affairs, became acting director and served until John R. Borchert, Professor of Geography, assumed the directorship.

The unit of the university that assumed the largest initial role in Indian affairs was the Training Center for Community Programs. Early in 1967, it established a small Indian Affairs Center federally funded by the Department of Health, Education, and Welfare. When Arthur M. Harkins became director of the training center later in the year, he initiated a long-range program of research on the current status of the Indian populations of the region, with a primary focus on urban Indians.

The training center also gave technical assistance for the planning of Indian Upward Bound, which became the only Upward Bound program in the nation operated by an all-Indian board of directors. The University of Minnesota has served as fiscal agent, but the board of directors has complete responsibility for setting policy and conducting the program. As the brochure for the program states,

> Indian Upward Bound is leading an Indian Uprising. We're urban Indian students, parents, foster parents, grandparents and friends leading an uprising against prejudice, ignorance and poverty.
>
> Through Indian Upward Bound, we're getting special help with school and with the problems of living in the city. We're fighting for independence, finding out who we are, learning to be proud of our own culture and our long history. And dis-

covering that we have a lot to give to our people and our country . . . if we'll work at getting a good education (Indian Upward Bound, n.d.).

The Training Center for Community Programs and such projects as Indian Upward Bound established important precedents for Indian participation in university-based programs. These activities were subsumed under the Center for Urban and Regional Affairs as it developed.

THE ESTABLISHMENT OF THE DEPARTMENT

The establishment of the Department of American Indian Studies was not an isolated phenomenon. It should be viewed within the context of the growing nationwide movement for ethnic studies programs, of which the most numerous and the most visible have been concerned with Afro-American studies. The movement first made itself felt at Minnesota in the spring of 1968, when the Afro-American Action Committee requested the establishment of a Black studies' program and a number of other changes at the university, including more scholarship funds for Black students; the proposals were referred to the existing University Task Force on Human Relations.

The following fall, the American Indian Students Association, under the leadership of G. William Craig, began preliminary discussions with university administrators about the need for a more adequate curriculum in American Indian studies and more involvement in Indian affairs. In succeeding months, various individuals and groups informally discussed the need, but no formal proposals were presented to the university.

Then on January 14, 1969, a group of Black students occupied the central administrative building; speedier progress in the development of Afro-American studies topped their list of demands. During intensive negotiations that spanned forty-eight hours, the administration of the university agreed to progress faster toward the goals urged by Black students, and the students agreed to end the occupation.

The negotiated settlement of the Morrill Hall occupation perhaps represented something of a breakthrough; at least it indicated that the university was prepared to implement programs to which it had previously given a verbal commitment. In any case, there seemed to be a favorable atmosphere for rapid progress. About two weeks after the occupation, a meeting was held, attended by Donald K. Smith, Vice-President for Administration, Assistant Vice-President Fred Lukermann, other university officials, a number of Indian students and representatives from the Indian community, and interested faculty. The agenda consisted of a general discussion of needs and possibilities in the realm of Indian affairs and Indian studies; some of the basic themes, which gained importance later, emerged during this meeting. First, a number of Indian participants emphasized their conviction that the principal beneficiaries of further development of American Indian studies would not be Indian students themselves, although Indian students would have an important stake in such a development. Rather, the beneficiaries would be the thousands of non-Indians who comprised the overwhelming majority of the university and of the state, and whose knowledge of the complexities of Indian affairs was generally extremely limited. From the beginning, the proponents of Indian studies differed somewhat from the proponents of Black studies, since the latter placed a stronger emphasis on the special academic needs of Black students.

A second theme was the symbolic and practical importance of Indian languages. In the context of the general discussion of gaps in the university's curriculum, I casually suggested that there was no reason why the university should not teach the Chippewa language as a regular language class; some of the Indians present responded enthusiastically, and after pointing out that they had never thought such a thing possible, they said there would be great interest within the Indian community for such a course. The outcome of this first meeting was a consensus that the university should proceed further to consider the need for the development of American Indian studies and other aspects of the university's role in Indian affairs.

In March, President Moos and E. W. Ziebarth, Dean of the College of Liberal Arts, appointed the Ad Hoc Committee on American Indian Studies. It was designed to include faculty members, Indian students, and Indian people outside the university. The broad base of the committee is indicated by the following list of members, which includes titles and positions as of the date on which the committee was appointed:

Faculty: Hyman Berman, Director of the Social Science Program and Associate Professor of History; Dean A. Crawford, Professor of Secondary Education, Duluth; Edward C. Defoe, Associate Professor of Pediatrics; David L. Graven, Professor of Law; Arthur M. Harkins, Director, Training Center for Community Programs and Assistant Professor of Education; E. Adamson Hoebel, Regents' Professor of Anthropology; Jerome Liebling, Professor of Studio Arts; Norman W. Moen, Assistant Dean and Professor of General College; Thomas M. Scott, Associate Professor of Political Science; and Frank C. Miller, Chairman, Assistant Dean of International Programs, and Professor of Anthropology.

Indian students: Gregory W. Craig, President of the American Indian Students Association, Beverly Rogers, Delores Snook, Richard Tanner, and Vince Tookenay.

Indian community representatives: Will Antell, Director of Indian Education, State Department of Education; Chris Cavender, Director, Indian Upward Bound; and Rosemary Christiansen, Upper Midwest Regional Educational Laboratory.

Gerhard Weiss, Associate Dean for Humanities in the College of Liberal Arts, was asked to meet with the committee to serve as a consultant on procedures for implementing any report that might be forthcoming.

The Ad Hoc Committee first met on March 28, 1969. After extensive discussion of various aspects of the need for Indian studies and of procedures for adopting new courses and programs, some Indian members reaffirmed points they had made in the general meeting. They emphasized a great interest in the possibility of establishing Indian language courses, which they saw as one means for helping to promote better communication between Indians and whites. They remarked that one of the main problems Indians meet is white people's ignorance of Indian history, culture, and affairs in general; they mentioned that teachers, social workers, and other professional people who work with Indians often have limited understanding of Indian patterns of behavior or of the special status that Indians occupy within American society. The committee discussed but did not take any action on a number of general issues, including the desirability of a bachelor's degree in American Indian studies, the location within the university structure of such a program, and the relationship between general education for undergraduates and specific training for professional people who intend to work in Indian communities in one capacity or another. The meeting closed with the creation of a subcommittee to work on a specific proposal for curriculum development.

The subcommittee met weekly during the month preceding the next meeting of the full committee. The complexities of developing a new Bachelor of Arts degree were discussed from many points of view, and some of the details of the proposed Chippewa language course were worked out. As chairman of the committee, I contacted Professor Howard Law of the Department of Linguistics, who had offered his help earlier, to discuss the possibilities of offering a Chippewa course. He agreed to guide the development of teaching materials; this was a major task since Chippewa is not one of the well-studied Indian languages. There is no adequate dictionary nor grammar of the language, and many dialectical differences complicate any attempt to teach it. In consultation with Professor Law, the subcommittee decided to suggest that the course be taught jointly by a graduate student in linguistics, who would handle the technical linguistic details, and one or more native speakers of Chippewa, who would serve as expert informants and handle many of the class drills in pronunciation and like matters.

The full committee, at its next meeting, approved the subcommittee's recommendation that a Chippewa language course be established and that a sequence of five quarters be offered eventually, enough to satisfy the language requirement of the College of Liberal Arts. The proposal for a Bachelor's degree in American Indian Studies within the College of Liberal Arts was adopted in principle. After discussion of the dimensions of such a degree, the subcommittee on curriculum was asked to work out the details; there was a strong feeling that the curriculum in Indian studies should not be limited to the College of Liberal Arts. For example, new courses were being developed by Professor Moen and Mr. Craig in General College, essentially a junior college within the university and the academic unit in which a significant proportion of Indian students begin their higher education. The committee voted that courses in General College would be considered part of the total program in American Indian studies, regardless of the particular organizational form that the degree in the College of Liberal Arts would take.

During the next two meetings of the full committee on May 14 and May 21, the subcommittee proposal for the specific content and structure of a degree was approved for submission to the normal channels for curricular change. The final draft of the proposal recommended that a new department be created to offer the degree in American Indian studies. The need for the new department was placed within the context of the history of Indian-white relations within the region and the nation:

> When the University was chartered in 1851, the Chippewa and the Dakota owned half of the Territory of Minnesota. In that year, seven years before the Territory became a State, the first Indian reservation in the area was established. Since that time the American Indians in Minnesota and throughout the western part of the United States have suffered from the loss of most of their lands, the destruction of their traditional economic base, inconsistent and discriminatory government policies, and inferior opportunities for education. In spite of these adversities, Indian communities and Indian culture have persisted in Minnesota and in other parts of the United States. Today Indians are the largest minority in the state.
>
> Educational institutions in general and the University of Minnesota in particular have a special responsibility to offer to the people of the state, both Indian and non-Indian, an education that is adequate to deal with the complexities of contemporary Indian affairs. Initially the proposed curriculum in American Indian Studies will place an emphasis on, but will certainly not be limited to, the kinds of issues that have special relevance in the State of Minnesota and in the Upper Midwest. These issues will be treated in a broad cultural and historical perspective that will include consideration of Indian groups in other parts of the United States (Ad Hoc Committee on American Indian Studies 1969:1).

The proposal emphasized that American Indian studies should not be limited to Indian groups in the United States, but should also encompass the rich cultural heritage of native Americans in

Latin America. The proposal suggested five specific goals for the department:

> 1. To offer undergraduate education, including a B.A. degree in American Indian Studies, that is based on sound scholarship and that contributes to an understanding of contemporary problems and issues.
> 2. To offer upper division courses that will contribute to the training of students in education, law, medicine, public health, social work, and other professional fields. Such courses would be part of the general education of such students, and would be especially useful for those whose careers will involve work with Indian people.
> 3. To offer upper division courses that will contribute to the preparation of graduate students planning research on topics related to Indian Studies.
> 4. To serve as a resource base for programs conducted in cooperation with Indian communities and organizations.
> 5. To make the University more open and inviting to Indian students (Ad Hoc Committee on American Indian Studies 1969: 2–3).

The curriculum proposed consisted of three categories of courses. The first category would be courses in General College, which would be open to students from other colleges; as lower division courses, they would not count toward a major. The second category would be core courses, listed as American Indian Studies in the College of Liberal Arts' catalog, which would include new introductory courses of an interdisciplinary nature, advanced courses that would not fit neatly into one of the established departments, various kinds of experimental courses, undergraduate seminars, and independent study. The third category of courses would be new and existing courses in other departments of liberal arts and in other colleges, courses concerned primarily with American Indian populations. The specific role of these courses in the new undergraduate major was left open to determination by the new department.

The Ad Hoc Committee intentionally left the question of the structural base of the new curriculum until the last possible moment. When the committees on Afro-American studies and

American Indian studies were initially formed, the general assumption seems to have been that they would propose new B.A.
degrees, but that the structure proposed would be interdisciplinary programs rather on the model of foreign area studies or
American studies. The latter, in particular, has a long and
rather distinguished history at the University of Minnesota. Some
of the members of the Indian studies committee, including myself, had serious reservations about the virtues of the interdisciplinary program as a mode of academic organization; there
appears to be ample evidence that such programs frequently lack
both a firm financial base and a faculty with a full-time commitment to the program, so they tend to lack vitality and continuity. Consideration of the question of structure was postponed
for two reasons: first, to reach a consensus about the content of
the curriculum seemed to be of primary importance; second, the
committee on Afro-American studies, having been appointed
earlier, was further along in its deliberations and the Indian
studies committee wanted to see what the initial reactions to its
proposals would be. The Committee on Afro-American Studies
proposed a departmental mode of organization; when this proposal was accepted by the Social Science Divisional Council, the
first step in the review process, the committee on Indian studies
rather quickly came to a consensus that a new Department of
American Indian studies should be proposed.

Two arguments favored a department over a program. The
Afro-American Studies Committee had emphasized that interdisciplinary programs seemed to have a kind of "second-class
citizenship" in the university. As a matter of empirical fact, some
interdisciplinary programs had experienced a rather troublesome
history within the College of Liberal Arts. To the Black students
in particular, departmental status as a symbol of full acceptance within the university structure seemed to be an important
consideration. On the Indian studies committee, the students
were most concerned about this same point, although their concern was shared by the rest of the committee.

The committee was equally anxious to establish an academic
organization that would be an effective means for accomplishing
the goals set forth. The arguments in favor of departmental rather

than program status were succinctly listed in the committee report:

> First, the Committee believes that an integrated curriculum can be offered successfully only if there is a core faculty with a primary commitment to that curriculum. A departmental struc-ture would be the best way of ensuring the maintenance of that commitment.
>
> Second, if the department is to serve as a resource base for community programs, staff with the necessary talents, training and experience will be required. Again, a department seems to be the best mechanism for acquiring and maintaining such a staff.
>
> Third, a commitment to community involvement will make demands on staff time that could not be met by faculty with basic appointments in other departments.
>
> Fourth, at the University of Minnesota departments seem to have more continuity of financing than the programs.
>
> Finally, departmental status symbolizes "first-class citizen-ship" in the University. Rightly or wrongly, any other status is taken to signify something less (Ad Hoc Committee on American Indian Studies 1969:3–4).

After the final proposal was adopted by the full committee on May 21, the pace of events moved rather quickly. The academic year was nearing its close, and the various councils and com-mittees in the College of Liberal Arts concerned with the cur-riculum had been exceptionally busy. Nevertheless, under the leadership of G. William Craig, the Indian students on the com-mittee urged it to move vigorously and to attempt to obtain final approval of the proposal before the year ended. Dean Ziebarth and the associate deans cooperated fully and agreed to call the necessary meetings. On May 27, the proposal was approved unanimously by the Social Science Divisional Council; the next day it was accepted by the Humanities Divisional Council with one dissenting vote; a few days later, the All-College Council, the final step in the collegiate review process, approved the pro-posal with one dissenting vote. Finally, on June 7, the Board of Regents accepted the proposal with enthusiasm and officially established a Department of American Indian Studies.

THE DEVELOPMENT OF THE DEPARTMENT

The development of the department is another story, one that has just begun. All that I shall attempt to do here is to describe briefly some of the initial steps.

Dean Ziebarth appointed a search committee to locate a chairman for the department, and an advisory committee to guide its development until a full-time staff could be appointed. In order to continue the precedent established in the formation of the Ad Hoc Committee, both committees included faculty, Indian students, and Indian community representatives.

Since the department was established too late in the year to obtain a full-time staff for 1969–70, the advisory committee arranged for a number of new courses to be taught by existing staff in various fields. The committee continued to place a high priority on Chippewa language courses. Gilles Delisle, a graduate student in linguistics working under the direction of Professor Howard Law, began to extend the existing but inadequate grammatical analyses of Chippewa and to create teaching materials, both major enterprises, but the course was ready to begin in January 1970. Gilles Delisle was assisted in the teaching of the course by Delores Snook, who was the new president of the American Indian Students Association, a member of the advisory committee, and a native of the Red Lake reservation in northern Minnesota, and by Mrs. Rose Foss and Mrs. Winifred Jourdain, also natives of reservations in the northern part of the state. Student and staff feedback indicates that the course has gone extremely well, and that the combination of linguists and native-speakers makes an effective teaching team. The course was being extended in 1970–71 to satisfy the language requirement in the College of Liberal Arts; as far as I know, it is the only instance where an Indian language can be used to satisfy a formal language requirement.

In General College, G. William Craig was appointed as a lecturer to assist Professors Norman W. Moen and Dorothy L. Sheldon in developing three new courses concerned with Indian arts, Minnesota Indian history, and contemporary Indian affairs.

In the College of Liberal Arts, there were four new Indian

studies courses for 1969–70, in addition to the Chippewa courses. I introduced a course entitled "The American Indian in the Modern World," with several sessions conducted by visiting speakers of Indian descent. A course on urban Indians that had been introduced by Arthur M. Harkins the preceding spring in the social science program was subsumed under the offerings of the new department and taught by Harkins, Craig, and Richard G. Woods of the Center for Urban and Regional Affairs. Woods also taught a course on industrialization and unemployment. An undergraduate seminar on "Contemporary Issues in Indian Affairs" was offered by Professor Roger Buffalohead, the first full-time staff member in the Department of American Indian Studies.

Most of the 1969–70 academic year was devoted to the search for staff, with a strong effort to locate scholars of Indian descent. In the appointments made for 1970–71, a pattern of cooperation with other departments emerged. Professor Roger Buffalohead, the Acting Chairman of the Department of American Indian Studies, is a member of the Ponca tribe and formerly director of the American Indian Culture Program at the University of California at Los Angeles. He is a historian, and the Department of History was consulted about his appointment in history as well as in Indian studies. George Morrison, a native of the Grand Portage reservation in Minnesota, is an artist; he teaches courses on American Indian arts in Indian studies, and classes in painting in the Department of Studio Arts. Timothy Dunnigan, anthropologist and linguist, has general responsibility for the development of Indian language courses; he works closely with the linguists and the native speakers who have contributed greatly to the development of these courses.

CONCLUSIONS

This chapter has described in some detail a university's response, over a number of years, to changing perceptions of the situation of American Indians in American society. Now I should like to consider what of general significance is revealed by the events at the university. The contrast between the rather fruitless efforts of 1964–66 and the apparent success of more recent proposals is striking and likely to be instructive. The principal limitation is that this is only one case study, and there is no way to control variables in order to demonstrate a determinate relationship among them. Still, if institutions and men had to wait for conclusions based on controlled comparisons in order to act, institutions might wither and men might starve. The analysis of experience may be useful, even if it does not satisfy the canons of the strict methodologists.

A comparison of the two efforts toward greater university involvement in Indian affairs immediately reveals variation in a number of dimensions. The general social and intellectual context of the university, both regionally and nationally, underwent major changes even in the short space of time between 1966 and 1969. What has come to be called "the crisis of the cities" began with many eruptions of violence in urban ghettos during the summer of 1966. The civil rights movement led to the "Black revolution," with its emphasis on Black pride, Black power, and local community control. The status and role of ethnic and racial minorities were reexamined as the nation began to abandon the myth of the "melting pot." Although Black people were the focus of these developments nationally, Indians became increasingly "visible," especially in areas such as the Upper Midwest. There was a new level of concern about social issues abroad in the land.

The most striking difference between the 1964–66 and the 1969 committees was the total absence of Indian members in the former, and their major involvement in the latter. The 1969 committee was established partly as a result of the efforts of G. William Craig, then president of the American Indian Students Association, who pointed out to university officials the need for more attention to contemporary Indian affairs. The Indian members of the Ad Hoc Committee and its curriculum subcommittee contributed to the formulation of the proposal for a department in at least three ways. As the participants who were most closely in touch with the Indian community, they were able to communicate the range of opinions in that community about the nature of the "Indian problem," and they brought a sense of urgency that came to be shared by most committee members. The Indian members contributed to the emerging consensus about the goals of the proposed program and the role of the

university in Indian affairs in general. They also made useful suggestions about the content of the program and courses that
should be offered.

The sense of urgency communicated by the Indian participants
was an essential ingredient in the rapid formulation of a proposal. G. William Craig has described accurately the role that the
Indian students played:

> We never resorted to threats of violence or intimidation. We
> pushed hard, we demanded to be heard, and we were careful to
> act in a gentlemanly manner so as not to alienate anyone who
> could help us.
>
> As the program was developing we became nags. We
> bothered a lot of people. We knew what we wanted in an
> academic sense — a solid department with highly qualified aca-
> demics on the staff (Pentelovitch 1970:6).

Faculty involvement varied in the two periods. The efforts for
change during 1964–66 were carried out primarily by university
staff who were not full-time members of the teaching faculty,
yet many of their suggestions for change were directed toward
the teaching units of the university. By way of contrast, of the
ten staff members on the Ad Hoc Committee in 1969, nine were
tenured members of the faculty, and five of these were in the
College of Liberal Arts, to which the proposals were directed. As
chairman of the committee, I was chairman-designate of the
Anthropology Department, the one department in the university
which might have a vested interest in the field of Indian studies.

Generalizing about the general stance of the Minnesota faculty
vis-à-vis new educational programs is difficult. Although neither
the space nor the evidence is available to document the assertion, I have a strong impression that the faculty is receptive to
innovation and responsive to certain kinds of demands for change
from outside the university.

The final comparative dimension is the orientation of the university administration. In 1966, President Wilson had a deep personal concern about the status of the Indian people, but the
administration did not seem to have any particular interest in

further involvement in Indian affairs, and there were no indications that funds would be available for new programs. In 1969, the commitment of the university was clear. President Moos, in both public speeches and administrative decisions, was attempting to move the institution toward greater responsiveness to social needs. The central administration advised appropriate committee chairmen that funds would be available for new programs in areas such as Indian studies. Assistant Vice-President Fred Lukermann had the responsibility within central administration for helping to develop these new programs.

The experience at Minnesota demonstrates that, at least in certain circumstances, a university can move quickly to create new educational programs. The Department of American Indian Studies was established ten weeks after the first meeting of the committee. The key to rapid innovation was an effective combination of Indian involvement, faculty concern, and administrative commitment. The ultimate orientation of the new department will be set by its staff. My view of the relationship of the academic world and the American Indian is that the Indian people throughout the United States are becoming increasingly resistant to scholarly work that only serves the interests of the academic world. The claim that much research has been exploitative, that it has used the Indian people as subjects but has contributed little to their communities, cannot be dismissed as militant rhetoric. The wisest academic response to the growing criticism of anthropology and other disciplines would be not a self-righteous defense of the virtues of pure knowledge, but a new willingness to cooperate with the Indian people in a common effort to develop their communities and to improve education at all levels, for Indians and non-Indians alike.

As we contemplate a greater involvement of the university with the community, it would be well to remember human, and particularly academic, frailties. Professors are primarily scholars, not stalwart makers of a new world. Their primary product is knowledge, occasionally tempered by wisdom. Their contribution to the improvement of Indian conditions, and of the human condition, will depend upon the quality of that knowledge, and how well it is tempered by wisdom.

BIBLIOGRAPHY

Ad Hoc Committee on American Indian Studies
1969   "A Proposal for a Department of American Indian Studies."
        Minneapolis: University of Minnesota. Mimeographed.
Berry, Brewton
1969   *The Education of American Indians: A Survey of the Litera-
        ture.* Washington, D.C.: U.S. Government Printing Office, pre-
        pared for the Senate Subcommittee on Indian Education.
Brophy, William A., and Sophie D. Aberle
1966   *The Indian, America's Unfinished Business: Report of the Com-
        mission on the Rights, Liberties, and Responsibilities of the
        American Indian.* Norman: University of Oklahoma Press.
Coleman, James S., *et al.*
1966   *Equality of Educational Opportunity.* Washington, D.C.: U.S.
        Government Printing Office.
Harkins, Arthur M.
1968   *Public Education on a Minnesota Chippewa Reservation.* Wash-
        ington, D.C.: United States Office of Education.
Indian Upward Bound
n.d.   *Indian Uprising.* Minneapolis. Mimeographed.
Meriam, Lewis, *et al.*
1928   *The Problem of Indian Administration.* Baltimore: The Johns
        Hopkins Press, for the Institute for Government Research.
Pentelovitch, Bill
1970   "American Indian Studies." *Minnesota Daily,* February 23,
        1970.
Senate Subcommittee on Indian Education
1967–68 *Hearings.* Washington, D.C.: U.S. Government Printing Office.
        5 vols.
1969a   *Field Investigation and Research Reports.* Washington, D.C:
        U.S. Government Printing Office.
1969b   *Indian Education: A National Tragedy — A National Challenge.*
        Washington, D.C.: U.S. Government Printing Office.
State Department of Education
1968   *Annual Report 1967–1968: Indian Scholarship Program.* St.
        Paul: State Department of Education.
Wax, Murray, *et al.*
1964   "Formal Education in an American Indian Community." *So-
        ciety for the Study of Social Problems.*
Wax, Rosalie H., and Robert K. Thomas
1961   "American Indians and White People." *Phylon* 22:305–317.

PART 3

to stay or not to stay
in the city

INTRODUCTION

The major thrust of Part 1 was to present important historical precedents and developing urban-industrial ideologies that have played instrumental roles in the urbanization of native American peoples, whether on reservations, in small rural colonies, or in city enclaves. In Part 2, a number of case studies portrayed the manner in which Indians become a part of the urban milieu of the city and how they develop strategies for coping with the occupational, legal, educational, and other urban social institutions.

This final section looks at the many complex factors that enter into an Indian's decision either to stay in the city or to return to a rural reservation community. As Jorgensen and Nagata pointed

343

out in Part 1, the influences of the urban metropolis have also been important in creating new problems in the rural reservation communities, rural colonies, or agency towns.

The perspective of a single family is used to dramatize the factors involved in an Indian's choice of residence — urban vs. reservation. As William H. Hodge points out in Chapter 9, there are many disadvantages in taking such a particularistic view. But the family case study shows how complex such decision-making can be, and has the advantage of demonstrating the operation of many personal and cultural forces in the life-styles of individuals.

There are obvious problems in making generalizations based on one study, but our focus is on understanding how human beings — in this case a family of Navajos — resolve the problem of determining their location in space. Hodge shows clearly that the actual resolutions to remain in an urban setting or to return to a reservation setting may vary considerably within a single Indian family. Thus, the factors Hodge describes in this case can be seen as an embodiment of the complex forces involved — forces that other students of American Indian life would recognize and acknowledge to be present in particular cases known to them. Hodge does not intend to persuade the reader to accept his case study as a type from which to derive generalizations about decision-making relating to American Indian residence. But there is no reason not to accept this case as a valid portrayal of the forces many Indian families face as they weigh the merits of remaining as city dwellers against those of returning to their rural reservation communities.

CHAPTER 9   navajo urban migration:
an analysis from the
perspective of the family

WILLIAM H. HODGE

INTRODUCTION
This chapter presents an Indian rural-urban migration model
that may be used for analyzing Indian migration data, a model
first developed from a study of Navajos who were residents of
Albuquerque, New Mexico, during 1959–61. The general features
of this model are briefly described. Then a case history of an
urban Navajo migrant is presented to give primary descriptive
emphasis to a single individual, Walter Higgans; some attention
is also given to members of his family, particularly his siblings
and parents. The family is used as a framework within which
effective comparisons may be made of the factors that promote
or retard migration. Since individuals in a given family are

compared, such variables as heredity and the sociocultural environment are controlled so that differences in decisions about
migration that exist between individuals assume a much greater
significance than those among a number of isolated individuals
selected on some other basis.

Such a comparison should not be considered to be definitive
for a number of reasons; the most obvious is that an examination
and comparison of selected aspects of the lives of a family's members can do no more than suggest the operation of a variety of
factors whose interrelationships are of a highly sophisticated and
subtle nature. Such a comparison, however, is worth making for
at least two reasons: first, detailed and organized descriptive
data concerning urban American Indian migrants have not yet
been readily available to students of the modern urban experience; second, a heuristic evaluation of the rural-urban migration
scheme developed in an earlier study (Hodge 1969) can be made.

The chapter also attempts to portray the lives of a number of
contemporary Navajo Indians, viewed as human beings who
share some characteristics with all other men. At the same time
they are distinct in their own right, since they are people who
are valiantly attempting to preserve a particular ethnic identity
as a part of a discrete lifeway in the face of formidable odds.
They have met with varying degrees of success in their efforts,
and face a challenging and perhaps threatening future. Their
odysseys have not yet ended.

THE RURAL-URBAN MIGRATION SCHEME

Before a discussion of the frame of reference for analyzing the
Navajo migration data, it should be emphasized that the model
to be examined is an adaptation of a very general one that has
been used by many social scientists in a wide variety of contexts.
Germani states:

> It is usual to analyse rural-urban migration in terms of push-pull
> factors. Migration is then considered to be the outcome of
> interplay and balance of expulsive forces existing in the country-
> side and of attractive forces operating in the city. Different
> combinations of such forces may result sometimes in population
> movements having the same direction. Thus, it has been fre-
> quently observed that, while rural-urban migration in developed
> countries is related mainly to increases in the labour demand

created by urban industrial growth, in many developing nations
mass movements towards the cities take place even when such
new and better employment opportunities are extremely low
or even completely lacking. In this case we have a different
combination of forces in which the weight of the push factors
in the countryside is much stronger than the pull factors in the
urban areas. In other instances we may even find situations in
which rural conditions, although actually improving, are still
insufficient to countervail overwhelming incentives irradiating
from the cities. Analogous mechanisms may be used of course
to describe not only the existence and degree of rural-urban
migration, but also the lack of it (Germani 1965:159–160).

Germani then goes on to say that such a perspective is naive,
especially if migration differentials are to be the central focus
of study. In this situation not only must push and pull factors be
examined, but the social, cultural, and subjective conditions
under which such factors operate should be considered. Such
variables should be given equal scrutiny both at the place of
residence and at the destination of the migrant.

With Germani (1965:160–163), I view migration as a process
having a three-layered structure: an objective level, a normative
level, and a psychosocial level. The objective level consists of
push and pull factors, the nature and conditions of communications, plus accessibility and contact between rural and urban
areas. The normative level of the migration process amounts to
an assessment of the ideal norms and values associated with
migration, in particular the desirability or undesirability of available residential niches and their associated behavior patterns in
a rural and urban setting. The psychosocial level is an extension
of the normative level in that the attitudes and expectations of
concrete individuals are taken into account. In this particular
exercise, all three levels function as a general frame of reference
to the extent to which available data will permit.

My particular use of this approach differs from Germani's because I do not view Indian migration as essentially a one-way
trek from countryside to city, the place where Indians, either as
individuals or members of families, lose their distinctive ethnic
identity and join an anonymous urban mass via processes con-
veniently and vaguely referred to as "acculturation" and "assimilation." Other students of the contemporary urban Indian also

take a position similar to mine (Uchendu 1966 and Ablon 1963). The work of Brian du Toit (1968) and the authors of papers in an anthology edited by Hilda Kuper (1965), which is devoted to an examination of urbanization and migration in West Africa, differ from Germani in the same manner, despite the different ethnic settings involved. My particular formulation of migration from the reservation to Albuquerque also has additional refinements which are discussed below.

MIGRATION PATTERNS — NAVAJO RESERVATION TO ALBUQUERQUE

Most students of modern Navajo life are convinced that, for a given Navajo, the reservation and the city form parts of the same system, in which he occupies a sometimes stable, sometimes shifting place. This urban and reservation Navajo system can be said to consist of two interrelated orbits, a reservation orbit and an urban orbit. With the exceptions cited below, a Navajo simultaneously experiences push and pull forces toward and away from the urban orbit and toward and away from the reservation orbit.

TABLE 9.1

Push and Pull Forces in the Albuquerque-Reservation System That Determine Residence and Migration Patterns

Forces That Pull Individuals	*Forces That Push Individuals*
Away from Urban Orbit toward Reservation Orbit	*Toward Urban Orbit from Reservation Orbit*
Congenial family ties	Poverty
More relaxed atmosphere	Friction with relatives
Chance to use urban-acquired skills to best advantage	BIA schooling influences
Appearance of traditional niche unavailable before	Non-Navajo spouse
Appearance of nontraditional niche unavailable before	Extreme physical handicap
Inability to make a living regarded as satisfactory in the city	Military service
Language barriers	
Unfulfilled obligations to reservation kinsmen	

TABLE 9.1 (continued)

Forces That Pull Individuals	Forces That Push Individuals
Away from Reservation Orbit toward Urban Orbit	*Toward Reservation Orbit from Urban Orbit*
Opportunity for job	Unsatisfied job aspirations
Escape from unsatisfactory reservation life	Lack of satisfying interpersonal urban relations
Higher standard of material living	General dissatisfaction with urban way of life
Medical care	Navajo spouse
Urban preference of, or for, children	
Language barriers	
Inability to make a living self-defined as satisfactory on the reservation	

Where a Navajo happens to be at a given time is viewed as the net result of the various forces involved. A number of points should be stressed. (1) Push and pull forces account for movement or its absence within the system, working either singly or in combination. (2) This formulation is oversimplified, since other orbits do exist, e.g., pueblo, rural "Spanish," planned seasonal movement between the reservation and specific nonurban employment like railroad work and harvesting seasonal crops. (3) The urban Navajos termed "permanent-resident" (cf. Hodge 1969:2–3) by definition constitute a stable part of the urban orbit; they are not subject to the various forces, while those termed "nonpermanent resident" — the traditionals and Anglo-modified types — most certainly are.[1] (4) The reservation orbit

[1] It is appropriate to repeat here my definitions of traditional and Anglo-modified types of Navajos. For a more extensive discussion, see Hodge (1969:2–6).

　　. . . A Navajo is traditional because he was reared in a traditional Navajo milieu and had a closed reservation background. A closed reservation background is one which includes few or no Anglo contacts during an individual's formative years. Such a backround implies a total absorption in and a total commitment to the traditional way of life. . . .
　　. . . Such a Navajo marries a Navajo woman who was also reared in a traditional Navajo milieu and had a closed reservation background. His reservation contacts reinforce and maintain his traditional status. If a traditional Navajo works off the reservation at seasonal labor, the majority of his contacts, with the possible exception of his employer, are with other traditional Navajos. If he lives in a city on

consists of two types of reservation communities: the traditional where a traditional pattern of life is followed, and the transitional where a combination of traditional Navajo and some white patterns of behavior more or less cohere. (5) The specific examples of the push and pull forces have been taken from the life histories, supplementary field notes, and other materials gathered during my two-year fieldwork in New Mexico. (6) The explanatory power of this scheme is tentative or heuristic. The intent was not to derive postulates to account for the residence patterns of all Albuquerque Navajos. The specific examples of pushes and pulls do not necessarily operate to determine the residence choice of a given Navajo. Some factors may be more important than others in determining type of residence, and therefore should be weighted. Such a task, however, was beyond the scope of that study and is left to future, more quantitative modes of analysis; the attempt here was made merely to indicate the kinds of forces at work, their operation, and their possible effects.

In the case history of Walter Higgans,[2] some factors obviously had a more immediate influence than others in determining where he has lived and will live. Why these variables assumed such importance are discussed. Underlying the discussion is the assumption that much of an individual's behavior is due to the fact that he occupies a particular place in time. With residential changes come behavioral changes, but change and permanence in residence with attendant behavior patterns can be best evaluated if viewed from the perspective of the life cycle. In effect,

---

a temporary basis (and urban residence can only be regarded as temporary for Navajos in this category), his interpersonal relations are also, for the most part, with other traditional Navajos. . . .

. . . Most Anglo-modified Navajos have had a closed reservation background for the first few years of their lives and have then undergone nontraditional experiences such as boarding school both off and on the reservation. . . .

Many of the Navajos in this category remember their early years on the reservation as unpleasant, because they feel that they were taken advantage of by older siblings or parents. They were often forced to remain at home to care for livestock while others in their family went off the reservation for schooling or relatively lucrative seasonal labor. They were given tedious jobs with little or no material reward. Navajos with this sort of background state that they want nothing to do with their kinsmen when they return to the reservation. . . . (Hodge 1969:3–4).

[2] All personal names and most place names are fictitious.

place and time cannot be disassociated if a valid understanding is to be gained of the relationship between migration, residence, and behavior.

With the factors of residence and migration given prime importance, the relationships between the variables of the individual and his milieu are critical. Urban and reservation and/or rural life for an Indian is not a random experience but is ordered by temporal, cultural, social, and other dimensions. It is a difficult matter to determine how much descriptive material should be presented to provide an adequate setting for a given individual. In addition, the most significant ties between an Indian and his spatial surroundings are frequently not obvious. At what point does a detailed life history become only a sequence of vaguely related facts and not a body of organized data suitable for useful and specific analysis? A generic answer to this question probably does not exist, and each situation must be decided on an empirical basis.

WALTER HIGGANS: THE NAVAJO RESERVATION AND ALBUQUERQUE

The Navajo reservation is located in the northeastern portion of Arizona and extends into southeastern Utah and a limited area of western New Mexico. Navajos also live in the smaller, isolated communities of Ramah, Alamo, and Canyoncito, all in New Mexico. The Navajo reservation comprises a total land area of 24,000 square miles, about the size of West Virginia. The reservation consists of mountain ranges, mesas, and large expanses of eroded desert land. At least 100,000 Navajos spend most of their lives eking out a marginal existence based on limited horticulture, stock-raising, wage labor, and some form of government relief. Despite the fact that Navajo country has a number of natural and mineral resources that are being commercially exploited to a degree, the reservation has been overcrowded and underdeveloped for at least the past fifty years. Hence, large numbers of Navajos must find temporary and/or permanent residence away from the reservation. Frequently such residence is located in a city.

In examining the life of Walter Higgans, an initial look at what Clyde Kluckhohn (1951:223–238) refers to as "some premises of Navajo life and thought" provides a useful framework for an understanding of much of the Navajo's behavior. The traditional Navajo view of life can be described in terms of premises, the first of which is subdivided into a number of formulas:

Premise 1. Life is very, very dangerous.
    Formula 1. Maintain orderliness in those sectors of life which are little subject to human control.
    Formula 2. Be wary of nonrelatives.
    Formula 3. Avoid excesses.
    Formula 4. When in a new and dangerous situation, do nothing, or
    Formula 5. Escape.
Premise 2. Nature is more powerful than man.
Premise 3. The personality is a whole.
Premise 4. Respect the integrity of the individual.
Premise 5. Everything exists in two parts, the male and the female, which belong together and complete each other.
Premise 6. Human nature is neither good nor evil — both qualities are blended in all persons from birth on.
Premise 7. Like produces like and the part stands for the whole.
Premise 8. What is said is to be taken literally.
Premise 9. This life is what counts.

These premises and their implications structure, in a meaningful and satisfying way, the world of the traditional Navajo for which Higgans was raised. During his intermittent forays into the nontraditional world these premises have proved less useful. A major theme tying together his total experience to date has been that of an individual who has acted and reacted to life around him in a consistent fashion, but the rewards of such behavior have varied radically according to the time and place in which he found himself. Out of necessity, his choice of path from a number of feasible alternatives has been that one which was the least painful, and not that which seemed to him to be the most desirable and rewarding. He has shifted from one undesirable situation to another, realizing that while it may be no better than the last, it will at least be different and therefore more attractive for a time. It would, however, be a serious mistake to view Higgans as a helpless victim of circumstances who has been tossed from one dilemma or catastrophe to another by a mindless fate. Paradoxically enough, his behavior has mirrored a close adherence to the traditional realm referred to above precisely because he has been so vigorously challenged by events of non-Navajo derivation. He has been forced to rely upon traditional reactions to nontraditional situations simply because they were the only responses known.

Walter Higgans is a lightly built, short-statured individual with a relatively dark complexion. His ears were pierced for earrings. When I first knew him, he "was either forty-two or forty-six — I really don't know which and I don't worry about it." His hair, like most Navajos of that age, was jet black. He had the habit of looking over and past one's right shoulder when engaged in conversation; if asked a question requiring an extended, involved answer, he often stared at the floor or off into space when answering. He was a heavy cigarette smoker. He usually dressed in sports clothes that were either new or in good repair. He moved with an easy relaxed grace, and his usual expression was one of wary inscrutability. Both other Indians and whites who were casual acquaintances regarded him as quiet, pleasant, and unknowable.

At the onset of my fieldwork in Albuquerque in August, 1959, Higgans was teaching at the Albuquerque Indian School. He owned a modest but comfortable home, was married, and had three adolescent daughters. In order to understand the significance of his position in a modern non-Navajo world, it is necessary to retrace his life to this point, and then consider briefly what has transpired in the ensuing eleven years. Much of his life history was tape-recorded, and while his command of spoken English was adequate, much of the meaning of his discourse was conveyed by hand gestures, facial expressions, and periods of silence. Accordingly, what follows is an integrated blend of his transcribed statements and my interpretative comments. Stressed are the events and the supporting details that he emphasized. While there are obviously omissions and gaps in his account, there is good reason to believe that his story is reasonably accurate.

Higgans' immediate family has a highly varied composition (see Figure 9.1). This variation is, at least in part, due to the different responses each member has made to a wide variety of stimuli stemming from life off the reservation. Such responses,

352

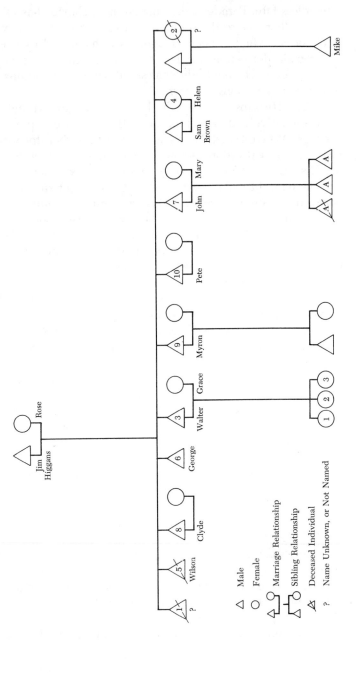

Figure 9.1 The Family of Walter Higgans

△ Male
○ Female
△—○ Marriage Relationship
└┬┘ Sibling Relationship
⧄ Deceased Individual
? Name Unknown, or Not Named

in turn, have been conditioned by the factors of age, sex, and personality structure.

Walter is the oldest surviving son in a family of ten children. His older brother died soon after birth; an older sister was killed in a car accident shortly after she had given birth to a son, Mike. A younger brother was killed when an intoxicated Navajo bus driver lost control of his vehicle which then rolled down a mountainside.

His surviving sister Helen, like most of the other members of the family, has a strong traditional orientation. She is also a hand-trembler and those who know her well are convinced that she has additional supernatural powers, e.g., the ability to predict the future and to detect witches. As a hand-trembler, they believe she is able to diagnose diseases and to determine which singer or ceremonial practitioner can cure a given illness. This kind of diagnostician is referred to as a hand-trembler because during the diagnostic procedure her hand — and sometimes entire arm — trembles and points in the direction where the appropriate practitioner can be found. Helen is disturbed by the fact that she has this particular talent; the physical aftereffects of the "trembling" are frequently painful, and being this close to the realm of the supernatural is potentially very dangerous for her. She and her Navajo husband Sam speak little or no English, seldom go off the reservation, and gain a precarious living via limited horticulture and livestock-raising.

Another brother George is also a hand-trembler, but the reaction of his peers to this characteristic, especially his brothers, has had unfortunate results because he has been "embarrassed and made to feel real bad." George is also the only son who showed little or no interest in going to school. At the age of eighteen (in 1946) his discontent reached a point where he began to disappear for long periods of time. He would be seen briefly by a family member or a close friend in one of the small towns bordering the reservation; he then disappeared from these places, and the family heard nothing of his whereabouts for several years. His sister Helen, because of her special powers, often stated that she had "seen" George in the San Francisco area; he appeared to be in good physical health but she felt that he would not be coming home for some time. He did unexpectedly return during the blizzard of December, 1967. He offered no explanation for his leaving the reservation twenty-one years before, and merely said that he had been living in San Francisco during this period but now had decided to come home.

Walter's brother John, by attending a number of BIA and church-sponsored schools, earned a high school diploma and then served in the marine corps during World War II in the Pacific. Following this, he enrolled in Haskell Institute at Lawrence, Kansas, and went on to the University of Missouri for a degree in journalism. His undergraduate training was followed by a period of graduate school at an Oklahoma university. In 1951, John married a girl from that state who was one-quarter Cherokee and who had a generalized pan-Indian background. During the next three years he worked as a reporter for a number of leading newspapers throughout the country and subsequently moved to Albuquerque to work for a newspaper there. After a period of five years he took a job with the Navajo tribe at Window Rock and has since alternated between federal and tribal jobs on and off the reservation. His work has always had an immediate connection with Navajo interests, and he has often expressed his preference for residence in the Southwest, on or near the Navajo reservation. He once attempted to explain his frequent changes in residence to me:

> Well, it's like this. I've also wanted to help out the tribe, I guess, because the Navajo way is best, provided you can work some of the things from the white way into it, like good sanitation, modern housing, cars and pickup trucks. So I decided that I needed some of these things and to get them you have to get a good education off the reservation. I wanted to be in newspaper work because if I was, that's how I could tell a lot of whites about what was good about Navajos and what we needed help with . . . like so much sickness all the time, and not enough water most places, and some whites comin' around like a few of the contractors and not doing their jobs like they should. I wanted the public to know all about this, so I went to college and got a degree in journalism. But if you work in town, your boss expects you to work night and day, especially if you are a reporter. When five o'clock in the afternoon comes, I don't want to work some more; I want to play. I don't want a lot of money — I just want a lot of friends. Lots of money just makes life too complicated, especially when you don't have it and lots of people around you do.

I remember when I first came to town to live, I saw everybody drivin' new shiny cars around and that made me want to get one, so I did. Then if you have a good car, you got to have a nice house to go along with it and lots of nice clothes and furniture and all the rest of it. And of course you can't afford to pay for this stuff all at once, so you have to make time payments. You just get everything paid for and then it wears out, and you got to go through the whole business all over again. You do this three or four times, and then you wake up one day and you are old, about sixty maybe. You realize that you have been workin' for a lot of other people that you bought things from and not yourself. You really haven't lived.

But when you are workin' for the tribe or the government on the reservation, there is always all this politics. Somebody gets mad at somebody else. No sooner does a person get a job or get elected to an office than somebody else is tryin' to get his job. And things happen sometimes that you know are wrong, but you can't do anything about changin' them. Maybe nobody can do anything. No matter how hard you work it can be this way. After a while, you get so tired of it, that you leave and work in town. Then after some months or years go by something happens on the reservation. Maybe a new tribal administration gets elected, and things look good because you grew up with some of these people and you know that they really want to help like you do. So you get a job back there, and then find out again that it isn't so much the people but it's the whole system. No matter how good the Navajos might be, the BIA has to OK everything that happens, and most of them don't really try to find out what the tribe wants. But then lots of Navajos outside of the tribal council think they shouldn't have to do anything. Somebody else should just give them everything. It's a mess. It probably will be for quite a while until the situation improves.* [3]

John and his wife have adopted three Navajo orphans.

Another brother Clyde is junior in age to both Walter and John. He acquired a high school education essentially the same way as John. After army service in World War II, he enrolled at the University of Denver and was awarded a degree in civil engineering about 1952. He then joined a large steel fabrication company in Dallas, and is currently the head of its drafting de-

---

[3] An asterisk at the end of an extract indicates a transcribed, tape-recorded conversation.

partment. Soon after going to Dallas he married a white girl and seems to lead a very comfortable and satisfying life.

Clyde is the most engaging extrovert that I have ever met. While he is able to find the ridiculous side to almost any situation, he has a great deal of self-discipline and is regarded by all who know him as highly intelligent. He seems to have been born with a great disdain for esoteric areas of Navajo ceremonial life.

> When I was ten or eleven years old I used to have a lot of fun every time that they had a *yeibeichei* [night chant] dance. It lasted eight days and nine nights, and especially on that last night I used to sneak on to the end of the line of the masked dancers, and here all the other Navajos would be just holdin' their breath and I'm out there makin' faces at everybody. After a couple of times of that, some of the older people came to my old man and said, "Look, we know that your boy is good at heart but he has been doin' some bad things. So the next time we have a big ceremony around here, we want you to send him out to that sheep camp way on the other side of the mountain and make him stay there until everything is all over with." And that's just what the old man did.
>
> I remember another time back home and it was in the winter, and we heard this weird noise outside the hogan. Somebody said, "Is that a ghost?" I said, "Naw, it's just a stray pussy cat," and, boy, did they all get mad at me. Those people [his family and friends] get riled up at the craziest things.
>
> One time I really shook up everybody around where we lived. There was this old man who lived all by himself and he didn't come around very often and everybody except me thought that he was a witch. One day I walked right up to his place and we sat out in front and at first he was pretty quiet and didn't say much, but then I got him to talkin' about the number one subject — women. And pretty soon he was laughin' and jokin' all over. There wasn't anything wrong with him. He just wasn't treated right by other people.*

He also appeared to have little respect for, or interest in, the more mundane aspects of reservation living.

> The old man, now, maybe he's never been to school, can't speak English, and almost never goes off the reservation, but he's pretty smart. He told John and me that we should try to get in a position so that we could decide whether we wanted

to live on or off the reservation, and then go do it. That's why he was after us so much to get a lot of school and get to know a lot about white ways of livin'. Me, I don't like the reservation except to come back to visit the folks and see my brothers once in a while. There is nothin' goin' on around here that really interests me, and most of these people are a big pain in the neck. They don't want to work. They don't want to take care of themselves. They're always lookin' for a handout from the government or somebody else. And when they do work, it takes them forever to do anything.

When I first got out of the service, I went to work for the tribe for a while because I wanted to help out, but I soon got sick of that. I'd get up early in the morning, work hard all day long on some project that the tribe wanted done and try to get the people around here to join in. They'd almost never do it unless they could see that there was something in it for them right away. After a while I got disgusted and decided that I was stupid to work myself half to death for somebody who didn't care about it. So then I went to college and got a job off the reservation. Livin' in Dallas is just about right for me because if I was any closer, there would be too many kin folks around my neck, but it is close enough for me to get back in a hurry if I have to. I've lived in Dallas about ten years now, and in that time I've seen only two Navajos once in a park. I walked by and didn't say anything to them.*

The fact that Clyde has frequently worked as an informant and interpreter for anthropologists may partially account for his irreverence for traditional Navajo life, but his brothers stated that this had been his general attitude before he had contact with anthropologists. Further, there is no evidence to suggest that his service experience influenced his general orientation.

Myron and Pete are the youngest brothers, Pete being the youngest sibling; they are in their early thirties. Both have the equivalent of a high school education and have agreed, perhaps with the urging of the other members of the family, to remain on the reservation and be immediately responsible for their aging parents who are in their mid-seventies. In return for assuming this obligation Myron and Pete will equally inherit their parents' possessions, which will include certain water rights, land suitable for grazing and/or horticulture, and a large number of sheep and cattle. John and Clyde each contribute forty dollars a month toward their parents' living expenses. Because they have been given a free choice of residence by their family, they have agreed not to share in their parents' estate. While this arrangement seems to be generally satisfactory to the Navajos involved, the wives of John and Clyde often question its fairness. Walter did not contribute cash to support his parents because he was then a self-supporting university student.

Myron and Pete are married to Navajo women with backgrounds similar to their own. Myron takes care of some of the farm work that his father can no longer do, and he is occasionally employed by the tribe and the federal government on a part-time basis. Pete does most of the agricultural work, but non-relatives are usually hired by the family to take care of the sheep. Both brothers appear to be ambivalent about their more or less permanent reservation residence. One example vividly illustrates Pete's discontent with his lot. Early on a Sunday morning in November he was watching a "combined night chant and fire dance."

> This was just to the east of Yellow Sand itself. I remember lookin' at my watch and seeing that it was 2:00 A.M. This was the last thing that I remember. I blanked out completely. The old man told me a lot of times not to jam up in a large crowd like that because that is when there is the best chance of being witched. I didn't believe him before now, but I guess that this has convinced me. During the rest of that day and on Monday I blanked out some more. All at once I would wake up and be some place doing something and not know how I got there. I talked to the old man and he decided that I might have some white sickness as well as this witch trouble. So he decided that I should go to this white hospital in Albuquerque first and see if they could find out if anything was wrong with me. But he said that I should say nothin' about this witch business because if I did, some doctor might put me in a nut ward for a long time.*

He was sent to the Bernalillo County Indian Hospital for an examination but no physical or organic abnormalities were found after four days of extensive testing. He then returned home and with his father's guidance began the long and involved process of traditional therapy as a victim of witchcraft. When I asked why he thought that a witch would attack him, he replied:

> Well, I guess that I knew it was coming because I haven't felt right in my mind [mentally comfortable] for a long time. About two months ago my wife heard a loud knock at the front door and when she opened it, no one was there. Then my job as a dormitory attendant at the BIA school isn't very good because I have to keep yelling at everybody all the time and that disturbs things. There are some other boys who live not too far away, and they are very jealous because I won so many prizes at the rodeos last summer. I never bragged about this or anything, but they are still jealous of me. Maybe if I can get the job of postman which will be open pretty soon, I will like that better maybe.*

Some time later John mentioned that most of the neighbors at home were jealous of his younger brothers because of their future inheritance and that Pete had always seemed to be afraid of witches to the point that he never went outside his house after dark unless it was an absolute necessity. He added:

> I remember one night this cow of ours got stuck in a fence and broke its neck. My Dad wanted Pete to go outside and shoot it right then but he wouldn't do it. He went out the next morning and shot it, but we all had to listen to it yell all night. That was a real pain.*

Several months later while they were driving back from the reservation to Albuquerque, John mentioned that Pete's witch trouble had the net effect of making many aspects of traditional belief and life much more attractive to him than they had previously been. For example, when hunting deer, he now follows most of the traditional rituals as described in W. W. Hill (1938), and his luck has supposedly improved to an impressive degree. He also thought that since his interests had shifted in certain areas, reservation life itself would eventually become more palatable to him.

Neither Myron nor Pete has lived off the reservation since he has become an adult.

The father, the genealogical senior male of this family, is indeed an impressive person. He is over six feet in height, with a lean but well-muscled figure. Despite his age, about 76, he has an erect, energetic, and alert bearing that has apparently made him irresistible as an "extra" to a number of Hollywood movie

directors who have made films in this area. One of his sons
gleefully recounted to me:

> All the old man had to do was kinda walk around in the back-
> ground where the camera was pointing and scowl a lot. And
> just for that they paid him money. He thinks that all those
> Hollywood guys are real crazy.*

His sons knew few of their father's relatives with the exception
of their paternal grandfather.

> That old man was really somethin'. He was one of the real
> old timers who never forgot about Fort Sumner [where about
> 50 percent of the Navajos were forcibly relocated by the gov-
> ernment during 1864–68]. He said that he had to go there when
> he was a boy. Then when this stock reduction program came
> along about 1932 or so, he really was tough. He wouldn't cut
> down on his sheep, horses, and cattle no matter what the whites
> said to him. He kept his stock hidden mostly, but once they
> caught him. They put him in this wagon with a lot of chicken-
> wire over the top and hauled him off to jail. He never forgot
> that. Other times he would be on one side of the arroyo and
> these damn government inspectors on the other, and he would
> just laugh at them. For a while he had this mule named "John
> Collier" [the then Commissioner of Indian Affairs who had
> initiated the program]. And just about every day he'd beat the
> hell out of that damn mule. He liked that.*

The father, Jim Higgans, was elected to the tribal council as a
delegate from Yellow Sand for several years. Even when he is not
in office he is regarded as a strong authority figure for the community which has long been noted as one of the more politically
sophisticated areas of the reservation. Whites as well as Navajos
respect him as a man who is patient, wise, and always willing
to consider the feelings and rights of others. He seems to be
unusually perceptive about his own position in a changing, uncertain, and often threatening reservation situation. When a BIA
official once asked him, with a son interpreting the conversation,
why he had not taken advantage of some sort of educational
program, he replied:

> By the time that schooling was really available here, I was
> too old, maybe in my late fifties, and I had too many respon-
> sibilities toward my relatives. But suppose that this hadn't been

so? But suppose that there had been enough school around and say that I would have gotten an education, maybe eighth grade or better? What would I have done? The only place open for me off the reservation would have been doing some kind of job like washing dishes in a restaurant or working in a filling station. I wouldn't want that. Life here hasn't been really good since the twenties and I suppose that it will get worse, but being here is really the only way I know about, or want to know about. So I stayed here and I always will.*

Jim Higgans and his wife have, of course, made brief shopping visits to the nearby reservation border towns and occasionally to Albuquerque to visit John and Walter. At such times his son Myron drove his father's pickup since he could not drive, and his wife rode in the open back of the truck. She was forced to do this since her husband and not she owned the truck; she usually objected to this mode of travel and her husband did not like to take long trips without her, so the parents seldom traveled off the reservation. Their inability to speak or understand English may have further contributed to their sedentary life. John did take his parents along on an extended tour of the northwestern United States during summer vacation in 1952. The only appealing aspect of off-reservation life then was the slot machines in Reno, Nevada, largely because both parents were exceptionally lucky when they played them.

This, then, was the family situation when I first came to know Walter and some of his brothers: two brothers and one sister had died; one brother lived in Dallas; two were in Albuquerque; one was in San Francisco; and two were on the reservation, along with a married sister and her children. The reservation brothers maintained separate modern residences in the Yellow Sand area. The sister lived in a hogan with her husband which was located not too far from her parents' hogan. The urban-dwelling brothers maintained contact with the others in their immediate family as their salaried jobs permitted.

John and Clyde called their father at least once a month. Since their father's hogan had no telephone, this necessitated calling Myron's or Pete's home on the chance that he was visiting there, or calling one home and asking the brother to have their father there the next day. The father called John and Clyde collect about twice a month, usually to discuss some aspect of federal politics or other developments of national importance. Because he could neither read, write, nor understand English and depended upon verbal communications from his Navajo associates, these developments often were relayed to him in a highly confused form. For example, he failed to understand why the federal government often gave so much money to foreign countries, but never seemed to get anything back. He argued that Washington should buy these countries outright, "and then they could do anything they wanted to with them." One of the recent topics for telephone discussion was "this new politician LSD. I have heard a lot about JFK and LBJ, but they just mention LSD and never say what he does." The brothers talked to Myron and/or Pete at the same time they called their father. Walter and his father exchanged calls with about the same frequency. The brothers never sent letters to relatives on the reservation, and John and Clyde almost always communicated with each other by telephone.

Clyde visited the reservation about once a year, but usually without his wife. John and Walter (during the periods when they lived in Albuquerque) went to Yellow Sand about once a month, as weather and the condition of reservation roads permitted; this amounted to eight or nine visits a year. Myron or Pete, either with or without their wives, usually came to Albuquerque once a year for a twenty-four-hour visit. To my knowledge the father and mother have never gone to Dallas.

When Walter, John, and Clyde did visit the reservation, they made little or no effort to contact relatives besides their parents and siblings. All three stated that they had to spend more time doing farm work than visiting with their kinsmen; apparently, Mike, Helen, and Sam Brown are an undependable source of help for Jim Higgans.

Walter and his brothers said very little about their mother's relatives beyond the fact that she was the second daughter born into a family of six sisters and one brother. One daughter and two sons of her oldest sister briefly attended the BIA school in Albuquerque, but apparently none of them have profited from this experience. They remained at the school a very short time and then returned home to resume the traditional reservation style of life. The remaining members of the family have a similar kind of orientation.

The data suggest that these individuals were not important to Walter's family since they seldom, if ever, saw them and they were not regarded as a potential source of aid. Most of them lived in a community about thirty miles west of Yellow Sand.

Jim Higgans and his wife, sometimes in company with Helen and her dead sister's son Mike, followed as closely as possible a traditional round of life. Winters were spent in their hogans with outdoor activity regulated by the weather and the needs of their livestock. Shearing sheep and selling their wool marked the beginning of summer; then followed a period of slowly moving up the sides of Rabbit Ears Mountain to their warm-weather sheep camp. Here the group lived in a "shade" or modified lean-to. This mountain area has always provided sufficient water and forage for the sheep and their owners. With the coming of fall in late September, surplus lambs born that spring were sold along with some cattle, and the return trip was made back to the hogan at the foot of the mountain. This routine was broken by attendance at a number of sings, or curing ceremonials, and an occasional rodeo, or by brief trips to visit relatives living in similar sheep camps. Additional aspects of their lives resemble closely descriptions by W. Y. Adams (1963), Dyk (1938, 1947), and Sasaki (1960).

WALTER HIGGANS TELLS HIS STORY

Walter Higgans' life story is presented below chronologically, through his taped, transcribed account, interspersed with editorial comments which amplify and focus his commentary.

> Well, I was born on the reservation somewhere in between Yellow Sand and Blue Notch around a place called Green Lake. I've asked about where I was born but I never did get a correct answer. I picked my birthdate as October 12, 1917, because it was very easy to remember since it is Columbus Day. When I was young I saw mostly Navajos, not many whites at all. There were a few missionaries, some trading-post operators, and once in a while a white truck driver would come through, but that's about it. John, Clyde, and I would sometimes go to this white Presbyterian Sunday school class. I guess the old man [his father] thought that you couldn't know too much about religion, any kind of religion.

Then when I was five years old I was sent to the BIA boarding school at Yellow Sand. I remember that on the first day they asked us what our names were so that they could write it down someplace, and of course you don't tell your Navajo name, especially to a white. So I just told them that I didn't know. Then this schoolteacher said that they would call me Walter Higgans, and she wrote that down on a big tag, tied it with a string, and put it around my neck. That's how I learned about the name that I use most of the time now. I was there about two or three weeks, and then the boys' advisor told me that since I was too small to even climb into a chair or get into bed by myself at night that I should stay back at home for another year.

Then I went back home and herded sheep and helped out other ways for another year. The next year they thought that I was big enough so I went back to the Yellow Sand school and stayed there until I had completed about the sixth grade.*

Higgans said nothing about this period of his life other than that he was in school most of the time. His brothers stated that he always seemed to be very shy, especially toward those outside his immediate family. He was also interested in traditional ceremonial practice and learned as much as was possible for a boy his age. But he seldom if ever discussed his feelings about ceremonialism with anyone and often became angry if he was directly asked about them. He was only moderately successful in his school work and had much difficulty learning English. When I knew him in Albuquerque he mentioned that he still was not comfortable with the language and preferred to think in Navajo; he seemed to be able to express himself adequately both in writing and in speech however. Since his father was relatively wealthy, having livestock, farm land, and close kin connections with other equally wealthy families, Walter must have had sufficient food, clothing, and shelter. Because of his father's active and prominent political participation, it is also reasonably certain that he had an early, constant, and extensive exposure to tribal and federal political activities during the late 1920's and early 1930's.

Most people in Yellow Sand community experienced a similar childhood, without privation, due to the following development. Commercially exploitable amounts of oil, coal, and natural gas were discovered in the area about 1922, and since these resources were located on federally controlled land, private enterprise had to work through Washington to gain access to them. In turn, the government felt itself bound, legally and morally, to make certain that the tribe received reasonable social and financial benefits from such exploitation. This obligation meant that some sort of effective representative tribal government must be created so that the Navajo tribe as a whole would profit, rather than a few fortunately placed individuals who could conceivably be "bought off" by various corporations. Just how to create a responsible and representative tribal government from the remnants of traditional political structure surviving after the effects of forty years of federal paternalism is a problem yet to be solved. But in striving for such a goal the Navajos of Yellow Sand have acquired a keen interest in tribal and federal activities, especially the manipulation of wealth and influence and the possible rewards that both can bring. Much of Walter's behavior during his early and middle adult years reflects his early political conditioning.

In 1931, when he was about thirteen years old, he was sent to the Albuquerque Indian School as a student and enrolled in the seventh grade. Again, he did not mention his school activities or his reaction to the city. Since students were legally permitted off campus only a few days out of the calendar year, it is possible that he had little interest in, or awareness of, what occurred outside the school environment. In September, 1933, his school record file notes: "Interested in things agricultural." In 1935 he had completed the tenth grade; he had also developed the habit of excessive drinking, and did not appear to be enjoying his life at school. Again, his file states: "Somewhat shifty — doesn't apply himself as well as he might." In May, 1935, it was recorded: "Walter Higgans returned to the school on Monday morning from the reservation at 3:15 A.M. in a state of intoxication — suspended from school two weeks more." The explicit reasons for his behavior are not known to me, but they may well be correlated with the unsettled conditions on the reservation growing out of the depression and the stock-reduction program. Inter-sibling rivalry and conflict may have also contributed to his dissatisfaction, as well as the harsh, arbitrary discipline prevalent at Albuquerque Indian School during this period. At any rate, he dropped out of school for about two years.

Sometime during 1935–40 he was exposed to the ceremonial use of peyote:

> I happened to be up in southwestern Colorado around Ignacio where the Utes are and I just accidentally ran across this meeting where they were eating this stuff and praying a lot. I decided that I didn't want anything to do with it because it really wasn't Navajo. We believe that you don't have to be doped up or anything like that to pray. Besides, there was enough trouble around as it was, and most Navajos where I lived didn't like peyote either.*

Some of the "trouble" may have been associated with his fear of witches. He would not admit to ever having been attacked by witches, but his brothers mentioned that he had always been afraid of them. With the previously mentioned exception of Clyde, all of Jim Higgans's family regard witches as a potential or actual threat.

Walter tells of further experiences after leaving Albuquerque:

> I went back home and didn't come back to Albuquerque. I stayed on the reservation and got into this Civilian Conservation Corps. I did all kinds of work on the roads, and then sometimes would get assigned to emergency conservation work, like trying to stop erosion and things like that. Then in 1938 when I was somewhere in my twenties, I started the eleventh grade at the Yellow Sand BIA school and finally graduated in 1940. I had hoped to go to a radio communications school in Washington state. This was for something with the government connected with forestry. About five or six of us were selected to go, but then I didn't have any choice of what to do. I was called up by the draft, the Selective Service, on January 22, 1941. Between the time I graduated from high school and went into the army I worked back with the CCC.*

His service experience of four years' duration was, indeed, a mixed blessing for him. He acquired a wife, a number of physical and emotional injuries, and the ultimate conviction that off-reservation life held far more dangers than rewards for him.

> I got inducted at Santa Fe, New Mexico. From there we were sent on to Fort Sill, Oklahoma, and I was there for about two or three months. That's where I first met this girl that I later married. Then I got transferred to Abilene, Texas. It was Camp Barkley. Then I was put into the 45th Division, 180th Infantry,

Company F. So we had three divisions there. The 179th and 180th were from Oklahoma, and the 157th were from Colorado, and 158th were from Arizona. These were all National Guard units, and they were filling up to capacity with Selective Service people like me. We were in Texas until 1942.

I kept writing this girl. She was at a small Indian school and we kept writing. I met her again when I was stationed in Abilene, but then in April 1942, I got transferred to Fort Devens, Massachusetts, for almost a year. From there we got sent to Pine Camp, New York, which is near Niagara Falls. They give me about ten days' leave including travel time and I took it. I knew that it was impossible to get out to the reservation and back in that time, but I went any way. My Dad had been tryin' to get me out of the service, but he wasn't able to and I wanted to see him and this girl.

At that time there were buses and trains packed with people all the time. It was hard even to get standing room in some places. So, I took the train from Pine Camp and came back out here to the reservation and that alone took me four days. At that time this girl was goin' to the University of New Mexico here in Albuquerque, so I stopped here on the way to Yellow Sand and stayed over night and then went on out there the next day. I visited my parents for three days and then I had only three days to report back to camp, so I started back. I knew that I was going to be AWOL because I couldn't make it in three days, so I went AWOL for a month and stayed in Albuquerque and got married to this girl. My parents didn't know a thing about it until the FBI or somebody came out to Yellow Sand looking for me. I spent about two weeks in Hobbs, New Mexico, and then I decided to go back.*

Here his account differs from that of one of his brother's who stated that their father, after much persuasion, convinced Walter that it would be better for everyone if he went back to the army voluntarily rather than be caught by federal authorities and returned as a prisoner.

I used my old furlough paper and my old round-trip ticket that I bought which was still good and I went all the way back to Pine Camp on that. I was checked several times by the military police on the train, and why they didn't realize that I was AWOL I'll never know. They just told me to go ahead. So I went all the way back into camp. The guards at the gate looked at the papers and sent me in. I reported to the company captain, and he thought that I had been brought back under guard.

I was sentenced to six months in the guard house and loss of two-thirds of my pay it was. That all shows on my discharge paper. We were all sent down to Camp Pickett, Virginia, and I was in the jug there. They left me alone in there for twenty-two days, and on the twenty-third day the captain asked me if I wanted to get out now rather than serving the full six months' time. The catch was that the division was moving to Camp Patrick Henry, and that's the debarkation for all overseas duty. So the company commander was really interested in me to go along. So I told them that I didn't want to get out. I would be glad to stay right where I was. But they talked me out of it. I still can't figure out why they wanted me to go along. So we all got on this ship finally, and about half way out in the middle of the Atlantic Ocean I got this official notice that I was released from all confinement. I wasn't in the brig or anything. So they really did me a big favor I guess.

So we went to North Africa, and it took us about a month to get across. When we landed we didn't do very much fighting. It was just cleaning up like. And then we did some more training and did a landing in Sicily. This was in June 1943. I wasn't actually wounded, but I got hurt there. At one place in this battle I was carrying the barrel of a 60 mm. mortar. We were crossing this bridge over a dry riverbed, and then right in front of us this machine gun opened up on us and everybody headed for the railing or over it. At first I hit one side of the bridge wall and I looked across and saw that the boys on the other side were really getting it, so I ran across to the other railing and jumped over into the riverbed. I don't know what happened. I guess that the barrel hit me in the groin and along my right side. When I came to I was in the middle of the battle. When the firin' stopped, I got up and went with the ones who were left and I didn't feel a thing until that night when it started hurtin' and I couldn't walk.

I ended up in the hospital for a little while, but before it was even healed up, I was thrown back into the company again. It was just in time for this place called Salerno which is up in Italy in September, 1943. By about January, 1944, we had fought up to Cassino and that was about as far as we went because of the stiff opposition. Then they pulled us out of the line and we went back to Salerno for further training, as if we hadn't had enough of that already.

Later that same month we made a landing at Anzio, which is just a little closer to Rome. There wasn't too much opposition there from the Germans, and we pushed them maybe twenty to thirty miles back almost to Rome, but they counterattacked with panzer tanks and pushed us back to within four or five miles of the beachhead again. Luckily I wasn't captured, because a lot of the boys there were. My bunch that was left stayed there all the rest of the winter, and then in June we jumped off and got to Rome and went past. A little past Rome, I got wounded and ended up in this hospital near Naples. I am leaving out a lot of stuff here because — you know [gestures and facial expression indicated that he didn't want to supply additional details].

I got back to the company just in time for some more practice landings at Salerno. My wound, which was in the left leg, was not healed up much, but that didn't make much difference. I am a little hazy about details because then I was just interested in thinking about coming out alive and not where I was or where somebody else was. Then we landed in southern France, around Nice I guess it was. Up pretty close to Switzerland we hit the Alps Mountains. Then eventually we wandered around the Black Forest area [?]. That was close to San Die, near a place called Epinal [?] or something like that.

Around there I got captured. I didn't have to be captured, but I did because I followed orders. Well, through all this time I was squad leader once in a while and acting platoon leader sometimes, but then I would always get busted [demoted in rank for insubordination]. I was busted about four or five times. Sometimes I didn't carry out orders because the orders were stupid. I wanted to do things the way I wanted, not the way that they wanted me to. Like they would tell you to move when it was a mistake to move, and sometimes I refused to go, so they busted me. So up around Epinal I decided that I would follow their stupid orders and get captured just to show them [his superiors] that their orders were wrong. We were up in the line and it was the night of October 5th/6th, just before my birthday. We were supposed to have a week's rest, but we didn't have no rest all through France.

The Germans were tryin' to come down this mountain road and we were supposed to try to stop them. We went into this heavy thick forest area where everything was so thick that you couldn't see far at all. But the Germans kept sending out patrols, and there was firing back and forth, in patches like. Then everything cut loose. While those patrols were keeping us busy, their tanks had moved up practically right on top of us and they were so close you could hear the recoil from their guns when they fired. So we started to fall back slowly and we had been doin' this for about three hours, and all of a sudden the platoon on our left ran through us and they were yellin' that the tanks had moved in and were coming this way fast. They had only .30 caliber machine guns, and you can't fight tanks with that. They left all their stuff behind. We went down into this big arroyo where they had been.

About that time, I was a squad leader, a buck sergeant. I talked to the platoon leader and he talked to a lieutenant and the captain of the company, and they said to go get all the equipment that was left back up there, but nobody would go because the tanks were too close. So the captain talked to the battalion commander, and he said to go back up and hold the line. By that time three of us, and one of these was a cousin of mine from Blue Notch, we had already gone up there and brought back most of the rifles and grenades that they had left there. Then the telephone line got knocked out with all the firing. So two of us were sent up in the direction of the tanks to fix the telephone wire. There was lots of cover — something like ferns growin' about shoulder high — and this other guy got separated from me. All at once there were two Germans standin' right behind me and I was captured.*

Along with about sixty other prisoners, he was transported in a freightcar to a prison camp to the east of Berlin. The trip took several days and all occupants of the car had to stand up during this time. After a number of brutal interrogation sessions at the prison camp and a period of thirty days' solitary confinement, he was placed with the rest of the prison population. Walter was vague about why he was given such brutal treatment and mentioned only that he had refused to tell his captors anything but his name, rank, and serial number. The remainder of his stay was uneventful, but the camp food grew steadily worse in quality and quantity, and in January, 1945, Higgans along with twelve others from his barracks escaped while they were being moved on foot from one camp to another.

We escaped because they were going to move us into Berlin, and we didn't want to be caught in the middle of the fighting. We got through the Russian lines and into Poland to Danzig, because we had heard that that was an open city. But that place was torn to pieces, so then we headed down to Warsaw and then from there to Lodz. And from Lodz we went across to Kiev. All this time we were walking, and while this was going on I got arrested about twelve times, because I was walking with these white boys and the Russians wanted to know who I was. They didn't even know that I was an American and that I was born over here. They'd throw me in jail and put me through interrogation by somebody who could speak English. I kept tellin' them that I was an Indian, but they would just laugh and say that there were no Indians over here and I had to convince them. They finally turned me loose one place and then I'd get arrested at the next town. After the twelfth time, I asked them to give me a pass. The Germans had taken all our identification from us. When I was in jail, the others were good enough to wait for me. There was twelve of them, and I was the odd one, the thirteenth.

We finally walked down to Odessa and, boy, I never seen such an awful lookin' bunch of people in my life. We had been tradin' our clothes for food, but we were still half starved and almost naked on top of that. This was toward the end of March 1945, when we got down there.*

Higgans and his companions, after considerable effort, found an American ship and managed to convince its officers that they had escaped from the Germans. They were then put on a British ship bound for an Italian port and eventually returned to the United States. He and a large number of other soldiers who had escaped through the Russian lines were sent to Santa Barbara, California, for three weeks of an "intelligence debriefing." They were told to say nothing about their contacts with the Russians for at least a year because there were hundreds of other escapees still wandering around the Russian countryside who might be made to suffer if the Soviets heard any comments critical of their behavior toward Americans.

Walter was discharged from the service in July, 1945, but was told to return to the nearest Veterans Administration hospital for periodic treatment of a severe stomach disorder developed as a result of his treatment while in Germany and Russia. His weight had dropped to ninety-five pounds.

His emotional condition was even worse. He returned to his parents' home on the reservation and was the principal patient for an Enemy Way sing (this ceremony is believed by tradition-

ally oriented Navajos to be effective in the treatment of illness
brought about by contact with dead people and/or events closely
associated with death and violence). Its beneficial effects for
Walter were slight. He manifested considerable resentment
toward anyone in authority and stated repeatedly that at this
point in his life he wanted to be left alone to do only what he
felt like doing.

> I didn't want to be pinned down to a particular place for
> any time at all. I didn't even want to listen to anybody talk
> most of the time. Right about then I got to thinkin' that I had
> spent just about all my life tryin' to do what somebody else said
> I should do. The biggest jump that I ever had to make was
> from reservation life into school here in Albuquerque. Then
> goin' into the army was just about as bad. Then tryin' to decide
> what I wanted to do when I got out that was bad too. I had to
> have some way to earn my livin', but I just didn't want to have
> to decide anything right at that point.*

Possibly in response to his wife's urging, he enrolled in a business school in Albuquerque in August, 1945, with the G.I. Bill
paying his tuition and part of his living expenses. Because of his
disturbed emotional and physical state he found it impossible to
concentrate on his studies, despite the fact that the school made
many allowances for his behavior. He could not keep awake in
class, and he found it impossible to sleep well at night.

> The minute I'd fall asleep, I'd be goin' through it all over
> again. Be back there in Germany and Russia or walkin' through
> Poland. Those damn Ruskys were terrible. I'd never be their
> prisoner. You would just look at them sometimes and they
> would knock you down and kick you and beat on you until
> they got tired of it. Those Germans were a lot better. At least
> they would have to have a good reason for beatin' you. They
> were right when they kept tellin' us that sooner or later we
> would have to fight the Russians, and I'd dream about that too.*

After a few months of this, he decided that he was wasting his
time and returned to the reservation to take a job with the
tribal government. He was given a low-paying position near his
parents' home at Yellow Sand; because of the salary, he was
forced to leave his wife and daughters in Albuquerque. After a
few months he felt he was being overworked, so he resigned.

He then returned to Albuquerque and took a job at the Indian school working as a "teacher-interpreter." His wife continued to work at various jobs, but the birth of their daughters had curtailed her earning capacity. Higgans took some courses in education at a small unaccredited Roman Catholic college during the summers and at its night school. After he had earned approximately seventy hours of credit, he was offered a teaching job at a BIA school on the reservation at Toadlena. His family accompanied him to the reservation; his wife soon found that reservation life for her had its shortcomings. The isolation from larger cities and the physical inconveniences were difficult for her to adjust to or accept. Walter was also notified by the Veterans Administration along with thousands of others that unless he soon enrolled in college again, he would lose his remaining educational benefits.

The family returned to Albuquerque and he secured a job as a dormitory attendant at the Indian school; his working hours were arranged so that he could enroll as a part-time student in education at the University of New Mexico. He used up the remaining two years of schooling that he had left under the G.I. Bill, but found himself with a considerable number of courses left to complete. One might conclude from this fact that he had failed courses or possibly dropped several before completing their requirements. He was awarded a Navajo tribal scholarship which paid his tuition and a small portion of his living expenses; the family, however, was forced to rely on his wife's earnings to survive. In all, he took a little longer than six years to earn his bachelor's degree in education.

When he agreed to act as my informant, Walter was employed as a full-time instructor in the Navajo Special Education Program at the Indian school. This program is designed to fit the equivalent of eight or nine years of education into five years; it was developed when the government discovered that a large number of young married adults on the reservation had spent little or no time in school, and therefore their earning capacities were virtually nil. Most of these persons had failed to attend school because of inadequate facilities during 1935–50. This special program aimed at preparing Navajos to fill a limited variety of unskilled and semi-skilled jobs. The students are taught to read, write, and speak English on an elementary level, and are exposed to such subjects as world geography and history, arithmetic, and other areas commonly associated with an elementary school curriculum. Some time is devoted to preparing students for such jobs as service-station attendants, waitresses, and kitchen helpers. In practice, a great deal of class time is spent discussing, in Navajo, the bewildering complexities of off-reservation life.

While he taught there, Higgans took an active part in leading such discussions. These deliberations led him to develop additional insight into his own sense of ethnic identity, his life goals, and the personal consequences of having moved abruptly from the Navajo reservation to the white urban world when he was neither emotionally nor intellectually prepared for such a change.

> I sit in front of these people in class and most of them are about like I was back in the 1930's. They don't have any idea at all about what it takes to make it off the reservation. These people can't see any reason for having their work graded A, B, C, or whatever it happens to be. They don't understand that this white world is all competition. If you are going to get what you want off the reservation, you have to be a little smarter than somebody else and work a lot harder than they do. Nobody can be equal and just live like Navajos want to. If you don't get part of somebody else's share of the good things, like money, clothes and all that, somebody's going to get a good part of your share of these things. You just can't stand still and relax.

> And these students, they kept asking me all the time, "Why does it have to be this way? Why can't everybody just go along relaxed and help each other out if you are a relative and enjoy life?" I don't think that I've been able to convince very many, if any of them, that it's a good thing to compete, and if I have, I've made trouble for them in a way back on the reservation when they go home. People will tell them that they have forgotten how to be Navajos and that they are actin' like the whites do. I don't think that I've convinced myself that it's good to compete. I guess that if I hadn't gotten this education, I would have been in more trouble than I have had off the reservation in the past. But I really had to go through a lot to get this degree.

> To know English well enough, to make the right kind of connections with all these facts so that you can pass exams and then remember what relates to what in the white way, and all the time you gotta keep thinkin' this different way. It's like every

place you go off the reservation is one big classroom where things keep happenin' that seem stupid. Like hurryin' all the time every place, and if you get behind you got to make up time. You never stop this rush. You got to have money for just about everything and to have money you got to work at a job whether you want to or not.

Most of the time you feel all alone here in town because everybody else is all alone and on their own. That's because of this competition all the time. You know that there are a few other Navajos in town, but we don't stick together at all. I'm not sure why this is. We don't trust each other much, I guess. Maybe that's because we all came from different places on the reservation and aren't related and didn't know each other until we met here in some way. Just seein' somebody in town and you know he's a Navajo, too, that isn't enough.

I think tryin' to learn the Navajo ways [traditional beliefs and practices] and at the same time bein' made to learn about the white way is what got me messed up right from the beginnin' almost. I've just about decided that now that I know somethin' about white ways I'll use them just when I have to and be Navajo.

This education business for Navajos is necessary, but it has got to be improved. The way it is now, it doesn't help a student live better often enough. The whole thing is, you just can't look at the student alone. You got to talk to the family where he comes from, and then that gets you into a whole lot of questions and problems. Sometimes it comes down to this. If he is goin' to do really well in school, he has practically got to stop being a Navajo, and that's all wrong. I wouldn't know what to do, but somethin' else has got to be tried soon.*

This conversation occurred in the spring of 1960 and may have marked one of the first times that Higgans had consciously articulated to a comparative stranger his desire to return to find a permanently satisfactory niche on the reservation. Further indications of this trend of thought had occurred about a year earlier when he again began to take an active and intelligent interest in tribal affairs. This interest was marked by his efforts to register off-reservation Navajos for the coming tribal council election and by his contribution to the formation of the Albuquerque Navajo Club.

The Navajo tribe permits Navajos who live off the reservation to vote by absentee ballot in the election, held every four years, of the tribal council chairman, vice-chairman, and a particular representative from their home district. The election of 1960 aroused considerable interest among Navajos everywhere because of the growing realization that the development of reservation resources could directly benefit Navajos, and that the council would take an active role in such a process.

Higgans, early in January, 1959, began to compile a list of resident Albuquerque Navajos who wanted to vote in the coming election. This effort involved locating individuals and families and recording their names, city and reservation addresses, plus their tribal census numbers. He also informed them that a voting place was to be selected and its location announced shortly before the election. He had some help from a few local Navajos in this endeavor, but the central impetus was his.

About this time, the office of the public health service withdrew free hospitalization privileges at the local Indian hospital from the city's Navajos; strangely enough, free care continued to be given to resident Pueblos, Apaches, and other Indians, and those Navajos living on the reservation were still treated in Albuquerque without charge. The Albuquerque Navajos were incensed at this development, and the public health officials were besieged with protests. The only response the Navajos received was the statement that the kind and extent of services offered depend upon the decision of a local office, which, in turn, is based upon "budget limits and other matters." Once more, the Indians faced a familiar and common enemy, the federal government. From this resentment and the interest created by the coming election, an Albuquerque Navajo Club was formed. Walter Higgans was elected its president because he was already known to many who attended the first organizing meetings, since he had helped register them for the tribal election. He was also one of the few Navajos in town willing to assume the responsibility for running such a club. The nature of this group is characterized briefly below. (See Hodge 1969 for more details.)

> . . . *The Navajo Times* (February 1960:6) states that the purpose of the club is "to provide general information concerning current and proposed tribal regulations, the various projects being considered by the Tribe and provide a means whereby those Navajos living off the reservation may get together and get acquainted with one another."

. . . During the period of my study (1959–61) the first two goals were stressed rather than the last. The meetings of the club did bring some of the local Navajo residents together, but very few got acquainted by this means. Those who did were of comparable socio-economic status. There were never more than twenty-five to thirty members who paid the dues of $1.00 per year. Of this number, not more than six or seven people were willing to do any work. . . .

. . . Meetings were rambling and aimless. Traditional Navajos did not feel comfortable there because Navajo was seldom spoken. The [other members] resented translating the proceedings into Navajo "because it makes the damn meeting last too long." Without translation, the meetings lasted between three and four hours. Those attending were highly aloof toward each other. Families arrived separately, sat together, and then left immediately after light refreshments were served. As one informant put it, "They just sit there like stumps. You'd think that they were mad at or scared of each other." The only charitable project that the club undertook was to collect small amounts of food and clothing to give to the "poorer Navajos" in town during the Christmas season. During the two holiday periods that I lived in Albuquerque, the club asked me to select the families to receive these gifts and then to distribute them. I was also asked to make a brief report regarding this distribution early the following month. No other interest was shown in the recipients (Hodge 1969:43–44).

Walter worked hard to be an effective president, and while there was a certain degree of self-interest behind his efforts, he did have a genuine desire to try to help other Navajos in town. For example, he was very influential in getting the tribe to provide two free issues of clothing per year for Navajo school children whose parents lived in Albuquerque; prior to this, clothing was given only to reservation students. His efforts to have the tribal council provide a chapter or clubhouse for the Albuquerque Navajos were unsuccessful. The council also refused to extend other benefits to those in town, but all Albuquerque Navajos were aware of the fact that if they returned to live on the reservation, they would be eligible for all tribal welfare services.

Higgans became quite disgruntled about the tribe's lack of interest in off-reservation Navajos and the failure of town residents to become involved in club activities. "Maybe Window

Rock [the council headquarters] wants to forget about us and maybe most people here in town don't want to be Navajos anymore," he once lamented. When he had completed his work for his B.S. degree, his dissatisfaction with town life seemed to increase, and his daily routine and spare-time interests reflected a kind of closeted existence. During 1953–57 while he attended the university on a part-time basis and worked at a full-time job, this narrow range of activities is understandable; however, once he had graduated, this withdrawal becomes more difficult to account for. He described his daily routine as follows:

> Well, first in the mornings we get up around about six o'clock, sometimes about a quarter of. My wife and I get up at the same time. We let the kids sleep until a little later on. We make them get up about seven. I have my breakfast early before the kids do, and then I leave the house to catch a bus here to work at the Indian school and get here shortly after seven. Then I come to my classroom here [where this interview was being taped], and I review my lesson plans. I generally have them made out a week or two in advance. I review what I am going to do for the day. Many times I have a conference with the vocational instructor or with some other teacher about some of my students. We try to keep our activities correlated. All this happens before nine.
>
> Then at nine they start school. Well, I usually turn in my absentee report a little after nine to the office, and we start off with the regular schedule. Some boys work in the filling station in the morning and some come to class here. Then in the afternoon they switch around. The girls who are waitresses in the cafeteria leave a little after eleven to go to work, and then some of the boys leave to go to work in the dish room or in the kitchen. About twelve the rest of us go to lunch. I'm off until about ten minutes of one and I come back here and go through about the same thing in the afternoon until about three or so. We usually have our movies or education films on Fridays.
>
> I leave the school grounds about 4:30, or wait until 5:00 when the wife comes to pick me up if I ask her to. Then, as soon as it's ready, we have our supper and after that I watch the six o'clock news on television. We go to bed around 10:00. That's about it.

Some of his spare time was occupied with his responsibilities as president of the Navajo Club. It is significant that he had few casual social contacts with Navajos outside the club and virtually none with whites living in his neighborhood. His colleagues at the Indian school sometimes held quasi-formal parties on or before holidays or on special occasions. Although he attended most of these events, he seemed to form few close relationships with other teachers. He often remarked on the many abrasive conflicts between Navajo and pueblo staff members but failed to offer reasons for such hostility. Presumably, there were other kinds of factions within the school that also played some role in his alienation.

He and his wife attended a Presbyterian Church near their home once or twice a month, and on rare occasions, Walter ushered during a church service. When he did visit a bar or tavern, he usually drank alone; such visits were infrequent but seldom produced salutary results. At home, he spent two to three hours a week watching various sports events on television. The remainder of his spare time was devoted to reading such magazines as *Life, Look,* the *Reader's Digest,* and novels having a Western setting. It seems reasonable to assume that the shallowness of Walter's city life was due to the fact that he really wanted to live on the reservation in what I call a "transitional community," which is a place where some aspects of traditional Navajo life can be combined with wage labor and many off-reservation conveniences like modern housing and sanitation.

His house was a six-room, frame stucco building in good repair; it contained the same kind of furniture found in other middle-class homes in Albuquerque. His wife enjoyed their well furnished modern kitchen equipped with most of the usual cooking appliances. They owned their home, and Higgans also drove a late-model station wagon which was in good condition.

Early in 1961 his chronic dissatisfaction with an urban existence resulted in a quarrel with his superiors over the nature of the training program, his future as a staff member in Albuquerque, and a number of other things. He left the Indian school and was given a teaching job on the reservation. In 1961 then, Higgans returned to the reservation for what he hoped would be a permanent relocation and has remained there doing good work in one BIA school or another. He has been promoted to a supervisory level and appears to be satisfied, in all respects, with his situation. His wife seems to have accepted reservation living gracefully. His daughters are now attending universities; whether they will want to live on the reservation or not is an open question. Since their only intimate contact with traditional Navajo life has been through their father and his kinsmen, it would be surprising if they do make a permanent home there. Perhaps if they married Navajo husbands who worked for wages and enjoyed off-reservation living conditions, they might spend their lives in Navajo country, but this is only speculation.

Walter recently said:

> I'm gettin' along in years. I'm 52 now. If I had the chance to go to someplace like Phoenix or Albuquerque and work in education in some way at much more pay than I'm getting now, I wouldn't do it. I can teach the way I want to out here and live the way I want to. You really can't live like a Navajo in town and you can't teach other Navajos who feel the same way you do.

From the perspective of his own life history, his conclusions would seem to be irrefutable.

SUMMARY AND CONCLUSIONS

The stated purpose of this chapter has been to assess the utility of a particular model used to analyze Navajo reservation–urban migration in order to gain a better understanding of Navajo migration patterns. This model had previously been used to explore the migration of an aggregate of Navajo men from various places on the reservation to Albuquerque.

Migration as used in this chapter can be defined rather simply. Migration is the movement of people, either as individuals or groups, from one spatial location to another; such movement occurs in time as well as space. The significance of migration can be understood only when viewed from the perspective of the life cycle; for many, it begins with birth and ends with death. Certainly for most Navajos, the human experience is structured by movement or motion (see Astrov 1950).

Admittedly, the analytic approach used here is arbitrary and artificial since the Navajo "extended" family exists within the context of certain residential and kin groups. The residential groups are the household, camp, and outfit, while kin groups consist of named, dispersed, matrilineal clans, which for certain purposes are formed into various clan groups. Since the cardinal purpose of this exercise is to explore reservation–urban migration patterns of some members of one family, the nature and functioning of these other units have no immediate relevance. Those who are interested in the total matrix of Navajo social structure are encouraged to read Aberle (1961, Adams (1958), Downs (1965), and Lamphere (1970).

Migration patterns are discussed below, using the individuals emphasized in the earlier part of this chapter.

The first-born son died as an infant and was scarcely regarded as a member of the family; he obviously cannot be considered as a part of the migration situation.

The second-born daughter in the family died in childbirth; she and her husband regarded life on the reservation as the only suitable residence, and had she lived longer, she probably would have remained there. The fact that her husband and son have not moved away supports this contention.

The fifth-born child, Wilson, was killed in a bus accident. At the time, he had completed about eight years of schooling, and was in his late teens. His preference with regard to residence was not mentioned to me by any of his brothers.

George, the sixth-born child, has manifested a perplexing kind of residence, leaving the reservation abruptly at the age of eighteen and returning under equally dramatic circumstances when he was thirty-nine. Unsatisfactory relations with his siblings may partially account for his reservation exodus. None of the other family members were willing even to speculate about why he returned. Apparently, no one was sorry to have him come back, but the Higgans family would not be particularly disturbed if he left again.

John left the reservation for the first time at the age of eighteen for three years' service in the Marine Corps. After his discharge, his education at Haskell Institute and the University of Missouri kept him away for several more years. His work as a reporter for newspapers in Kansas City, Albuquerque, and the San Francisco area following his marriage further oriented his residence off-reservation. After sixteen years living off the reservation, John took a job with the Navajo tribe at Window Rock, Arizona, for a period of four years. Four years later he then moved to the Phoenix area and became a consultant for the

Community Action Program of the Office of Economic Opportunity where he worked for three years until he was transferred to the reservation. If his current employment continues to be stimulating but not burdensome, he may well remain on the reservation for the remainder of his working life. It would be surprising if he did not retire there since his interest in traditional ceremonial practice and Navajo traditions in general has increased considerably during the ten years that I have known him. Correspondingly, his distaste for selected aspects of white off-reservation living has become more pronounced, e.g., hard work and punctuality as virtues in themselves, the competitive lust for material possessions and particularly their use and display, and the superficial and impersonal nature of social relations. There is no reason to believe that both trends will not become more evident with the passing of time. His wife also seems to have acquired a taste for the kind of reservation life that combines satisfactory living conditions with various modes of traditional Navajo action and thought.

Clyde Higgans, like his brother John, left his reservation community at the age of eighteen to join the army in 1945. After serving two years, he returned to the reservation to take a job with the tribe. A few months as a staff member of the tribal government convinced him that some of his colleagues and most of his constituents were really not interested in putting forth enough cooperative effort to make possible, by his definition, a satisfactory reservation life. He enrolled at the University of Denver in 1948 and received a degree in civil engineering four years later. He then moved to Dallas where he has worked as an engineer to the present time. His distaste for those features of reservation life that irritated him in 1947, seem, if anything, to have increased markedly. His white wife appears to have little interest and less understanding of Navajo culture. Both will probably be permanent off-reservation residents.

Helen and her husband Sam Brown cannot conceive of life off the reservation. With their parents, they view the off-reservation world as a place where other Navajos may go to travel and sometimes live, but never as a place where they might reside. Those aspects of living that they desire are of and in the fabric of traditional Navajo existence. They view as having a limited but appropriate utility those things that come from the white world such as medical practice and transportation, which can be used with the help of the other members of their immediate family.

The younger brothers, Myron and Pete, have never lived off the reservation or been in the military service. Both speak good English and seem to have a reasonably sophisticated understanding of the reservation and the non-Navajo world. But because of the obligations toward their parents which apparently they have willingly assumed, they will probably spend the rest of their lives on the reservation in the Yellow Sand community. It is conceivable that they might leave the reservation after the deaths of their parents, but this would appear unlikely since they are already in their thirties and will be even older by that time. A careful study of the available published and unpublished materials concerning off-reservation Indians and Eskimos (Hodge 1968) suggests that most Indians who spend a significant portion of their lives away from their home communities as adults, began such residence at an earlier age. Not enough is known about Myron's and Pete's current and future aspirations to speculate about their future residence.

Walter Higgans is undoubtedly now a permanent reservation resident. The fifty-two years of his life can be viewed as an extensive preparation for a highly specialized reservation niche, that of a coordinator of Navajo-modified white formal education, dispensed largely within the residential context of Navajo country.

The grandchildren of Jim Higgans may or may not follow the examples set by their parents with regard to residence. Mike seems to be the most likely candidate for full-time reservation living since he has had little formal education and has shown little or no interest in what occurs beyond the horizons of the Yellow Sand community. The children of John and Walter are more difficult to consider in this respect. My guess is that Walter's daughters would be less likely to spend much of their adult lives on the reservation since they have grown up in Albuquerque and have a mother who can accept, but not readily enjoy, Navajo life in a traditional or modified form. John's adopted children are now not more than seven years of age. If their father spends most of the remainder of his life on the reservation, they might well follow his example; if he continues to maintain his pattern of two to four years of reservation residence followed by periods of equal length in a city, it would be extremely difficult to predict the adult residence patterns of his children, given the data available now. The children of Myron Higgans are approximately the same age as those of John; they may or may not follow their father's example with regard to residence and migration.

The affinal relatives of Jim Higgans are not considered here because little is known by me about them, and they do not appear to maintain close ties with his extended family.

In sum, the situation with regard to migration and residence for the living members of Higgans' family is as follows: he will remain on the reservation as a permanent resident as will his parents, his sister, brother-in-law and their son, plus his two younger brothers, Myron and Pete, and their families. John and his family will probably stay on the reservation, but he is able and willing to return to the white world should his reservation niche become unsatisfactory. Clyde and his wife will not live on the reservation. Little can be said with certainty regarding the residence and general behavior of George. Finally, nothing need be added to the previous remarks concerning Jim Higgans' grandchildren.

The individuals who have been considered here fall into two general categories: those who have moved off the reservation and those who have not. An adequate migration model must be able to account for both situations. The model in its present form does this only in an indirect fashion. If the various pushes and pulls are equal in strength, no movement at all may occur. If this were the case, however, the individual might be placed under such an emotional strain that he could not function adequately and/or in a socially acceptable manner. The migration behavior of those manifesting deviant or abnormal behavior is well beyond the limits of the model.

From an examination of the data presented in this chapter, it is obvious that off-reservation migration is not a unitary or monolithic process. There are different kinds of migration, probably because different factors or pushes and pulls vary in importance from person to person. The model, in its present form cannot account for this variety of types, largely because the nature of the data have made it impossible to effectively weight the various factors regarded as pushes and pulls.

Further, the model is synchronic in a de facto sense in that the various pushes and pulls were taken from different life histories and then meshed together much in the same fashion that a biologist would illustrate cell division by showing a number of fixed slides, each being a particular phase of an on-going process. A time perspective is vital if a more realistic notion is to be gained of the nature of Navajo reservation–urban migration. As mentioned, the life cycle is crucial for such an understanding. Certain pushes and pulls may be important in one stage or phase of a Navajo's life, but of little or no significance for migration or nonmigration at another time.

Jim Higgans, as the head of Walter Higgans' extended family, seems to have kept around him enough children who as adults have been able to maintain and extend his personal interests with regard to property, community prominence, and emotional support. In turn, he has helped them in their varied activities and concerns and has promised additional, future rewards. Correspondingly, certain sons had to be encouraged to leave home because of the limited nature of Jim's resources. Those who were regarded in this fashion, Walter Higgans, plus John and Clyde, have spent at least a significant portion of their lives away from the reservation. Although Higgans has returned on a permanent basis, he can exist independently of his father's material support. The same may be said of John if he continues to live indefinitely on the reservation. Clyde's permanent off-reservation residence may occasionally be a source of regret for his father, but it is not a serious threat to the existence of the family per se. The fact that he regularly sends his father small amounts of cash undoubtedly makes his absence more acceptable.

At this point, what can be said as to the relationship between the variables of migration, residence, and behavior, at least with regard to the data presented in this chapter? These three variables seem to vary independently. There seems to be only an incidental kind of interdependence between the time and place where an individual finds himself and how he behaves, at least as far as many of the basic aspects of his life style are concerned, i.e., attitudes, values, or sentiments with regard to relations with the supernatural; a preference for various kinds of consumer goods and services such as cars, clothing, and entertainment; and the kind of vocation followed.

Even a casual reflection upon the triumphs and failures, the rewards and penalties woven through the texture of these Navajos' lives shows the emphasis placed by them on motion, travel, and migration as being intrinsically good.

They are one with Kipling who said:

> For to admire an' for to see,
> For to be'old this world so wide —
> It never done no good to me,
> But I can't drop it if I tried! [4]

BIBLIOGRAPHY

Aberle, David F.
  1961   "The Navajo." In *Matrilineal Kinship,* David Schneider and Kathleen Gough (eds.). Berkeley: University of California Press.
Ablon, Joan
  1963   "Relocated Indians in the San Francisco Bay Area. Concepts of Acculturation, Success and Identity in the City." Unpublished Ph.D. dissertation, University of Chicago.
Adams, William Y.
  1963   *Shonto: A Study of the Role of the Trader in a Modern Navaho Community.* Bureau of American Ethnology, Smithsonian Institution. Washington, D.C.: U.S. Government Printing Office.
Astrov, Margot
  1950   "The Concept of Motion as the Psychological Leitmotif of Navaho Life and Literature." *Journal of American Folklore* 63:45–56.
Downs, James F.
  1965   "Social Consequences of a Dry Well." *American Anthropologist* 67:1387–1416.
Dyk, Walter
  1938   *Son of Old Man Hat.* New York: Harcourt, Brace.
  1947   "A Navaho Autobiography." *Viking Fund Publications in Anthropology,* no. 8. New York.
Germani, Gino
  1964   "Migration and Acculturation." In *Handbook for Social Research in Urban Areas,* Philip M. Hauser (ed.), Paris: UNESCO, pp. 159–178.
Hill, W. W.
  1938   "The Agricultural and Hunting Methods of the Navaho Indians." *Yale University Publications in Anthropology,* no. 18. New Haven: Yale University Press.

---

[4] From "For to Admire" from *Rudyard Kipling's Verse: Definitive Edition* by Rudyard Kipling. Reprinted by permission of Mrs. George Bambridge, Doubleday & Company, Inc., Methuen & Co. (London), and Macmillan Co. of Canada.

Hodge, William H.
  1968   "Urban Indian Bibliography — Canada and the United States." Un-
         published in personal files. Mimeographed.
  1969   "The Albuquerque Navajos." *Anthropological Papers*, no. 11. Tuc-
         son: University of Arizona Press.
Kipling, Rudyard
  1940   "For to Admire." *Rudyard Kipling's Verse, Definitive Edition*.
         Garden City, N.Y.: Doubleday, p. 455.
Kluckhohn, Clyde, and Dorothea Leighton
  1951   *The Navaho*. Cambridge, Mass.: Harvard University Press.
Kuper, Hilda (ed.)
  1965   *Urbanization and Migration in West Africa*. Berkeley: University of
         California Press.
Lamphere, Louise
  1970   "Ceremonial Co-operation and Networks: A Reanalysis of the
         Navajo Outfit." *Man* 5:39–59.
Sasaki, Tom T.
  1960   *Fruitland, New Mexico: A Navaho Community in Transition*.
         Ithaca, N.Y.: Cornell University Press.
du Toit, Brian M.
  1968   "Cultural Continuity and African Urbanization." In *Urban An-
         thropology: Research Perspectives and Strategies*, E. M. Eddy
         (ed.). Proceedings, *Southern Anthropology Society*, no. 2. Athens:
         University of Georgia Press.
Uchendu, Victor C.
  1966   "Navaho Harvest Hands: An Ethnographic Report." Food Re-
         search Institute. Stanford, Calif.: Stanford University. Ditto.

PART 4   conclusions

INTRODUCTION

Many issues become apparent from this selection of essays. We can touch upon only a few of them, hoping that the reader will become involved in resolving some of them. A few questions are raised to point out some of these issues and to show how the authors address themselves to these concerns. The possibilities for their expansion are many.

The first question is: Are Indian problems in the urban environments related to cultural incompatibilities between Indian segments and the dominant urban ideologies, or are the problems presented here "third world" problems that encompass all the socially and economically deprived irrespective of cultural factors?

None of the authors would deny the significance of cultural

differences; it would not only be anthropological sacrilege, but it would be gross misuse of available ethnographic facts. Yet it is interesting to see the kind of arguments being put forth. Officer, because of the nature of the task requested of him, focuses directly on federal government–Indian relations over the years and could readily point to such cultural incompatibilities as attitudes about land occupancy and ownership, procedures for arriving at binding decisions, and means for instructing young. He shows how these cultural differences both impeded healthy social relations and provoked attempts to formulate policy to govern relations. Yet most of his discussion focuses on the structure of federal policy rather than on the nature of native cultures.

Jorgensen, while giving a useful historical description of Indian-white incompatibilities, prefers to relate Indian impoverishment to the structural and ideological stranglehold of the metropolis rather than to failures of Indians to "acculturate." In this sense, impoverishment or, as he refers to it, underdevelopment has tended to be most seriously felt in rural satellite communities, whether by Indians or others. It is an Indian problem largely because many Indians were coerced to live in rural isolation and were subject to the debilitating effects of the metropolitan economic-political structure.

Nagata recognizes the metropolitan areas' debilitating effects on agency towns and reservation communities — much as other small rural towns in America "suffer" from being only partly urbanized. Yet he does point to examples of cultural incompatibility, such as Hopi city dwellers who return with their children for Kachina rituals because life in the city is *kahopi* without this form of ritual identity resolution. The cultural life of the city does not provide this for *some* Hopi. Culture, then, is still an important factor in considering the adjustments of persons, but it does not explain or account for the persistence of impoverished conditions.

Garbarino maintains that Indians are pretty much like any other minority group, regardless of cultural background, in meeting (or failing to meet) the demands placed on them by urban life.

Snyder points out that the adjustments that Navajo migrants

make to Denver are better understood not in terms of Navajo cultural tradition, but rather in their relationship to the BIA.

Although Weppner notes how Navajo culture lacks the notion of a scarcity of goods or does not stress competitiveness or aggressiveness, he emphasizes that Navajos prove to be as flexible as other migrants in changing these orientations. Thus, lack of economic success is not so much due to incompatibilities in cultural orientations as to the attitudes of employers toward Navajos.

Graves, in accounting for Navajo drunkenness, seeks his explanations not in unique features of Navajo culture or its incompatibility with white culture but in structural and/or psychological variables that are common to other groups where drinking is a problem.

Miller has little to say about cultural incompatibilities but demonstrates how social conditions among Minnesota Indians prompted Indians and their white sympathizers to innovate educational change.

Hodge, who in his family case study emphasizes the role that cultural traditions play in decisions about where to locate one's residence, offers evidence to lend support to the idea that other factors apart from Navajo cultural incompatibilities with white culture can be used to account for variation in migratory patterns within a family.

The next question poses this: Is the acculturation model adequate to explain the state of impoverishment, deprivation, and personal alienation that *seems* to characterize so large a number of native Americans, or must we seek our explanations by investing more time and energy to a critical study of American institutions?

All the essays tend to look at structural factors, that is, features of the American system of institutions, to account for the difficulties Indian migrants experience in urban America rather than to appeal to some form of acculturation continuum — although the reader will detect differences in the thrusts of the authors' arguments. It seems that the authors have suggested that we employ strategies other than acculturation theory to study Indians in contemporary urban America most fruitfully.

The next question is: Shall we attribute the frustration, futility, and apathy so frequently thought to be characteristic of dislocated urban migrants to failings in social structure and social organization, or do we assess these symptoms to result from failings in the cultural mechanisms available for personality integration?

Once again, the emphasis has been on discrepancies in the American social structure. Officer's chapter obviously stresses the history of structural relations between federal government and native populations, and in retrospect, we can all detect some of the structural discrepancies that have seriously affected Indian populations. Jorgensen is quick to argue that it is not a failure of natives nor their cultures to achieve a final stage of the acculturation that is the source of their personal and social dilemmas; rather, it is due to the character of American social structure. Nagata, likewise, argues that Hopi frustration is not because of inflexibilities of Hopi character structure but because it is the nature of urbanization in America to incompletely and inefficiently urbanize the rural areas; it is a problem of social structure and organization.

Garbarino feels that Indians suffer the same structural inadequacies as other minority groups in the relationship between them and the larger society surrounding them.

Snyder and Weppner both suggest that a much more successful adjustment to urban life could be made by Indians if the relocation program of the BIA were to be overhauled. They cite "oversell" of relocation by the BIA as a factor in bringing poorly equipped migrants to the city, but the BIA *must* send migrants to cities in order to justify the existence of the relocation program within the bureaucratic structure.

Graves argues that personal goals and future expectations are important in predicting successful adaptation to the city, but because there are many Navajos who do adapt, there seems no good reason for suggesting that Navajo culture fails to provide mechanisms to integrate a reasonably successful and adaptable personality. He prefers to see the problem in the opportunity structure which suggests, once again, structural discrepancies in the metropolitan system.

There are other questions to be raised which would allow the reader to identify other important facts about Indians in cities. Is it entirely a matter of who has or does not have social, economic, and political power, or are there other cultural-ideological factors not related to power structures that explain the present dilemma of contemporary urban-oriented Indians? Does the lack of understanding of urban Indians suggest that we need more sophisticated sociological techniques including such things as better sampling, better demography, better surveys, and greater use of quantification, or do we still need more traditional ethnographic approaches and particularistic case studies? Do we achieve greater understanding by restricting our time horizon to the current scene, or are time depths essential to that understanding? Finally, are we more correct in emphasizing the maladaptive aspects of urbanization process, or are there more cases of successful adaptation than allowed by our emphasis on social problems?

These selections have sought to generate a number of basic questions, to provide descriptive data, and to present some analytic interpretations. We hope that they have succeeded in arousing an interest in a vital contemporary concern.

The final word in this text comes appropriately enough from an Indian. John W. Olson offers his view of the urban Indian's problems, based on his experience as a social casework director at the Chicago American Indian Center.

CHAPTER 10   epilogue: the urban indian
as viewed by an
indian caseworker

JOHN W. OLSON

Family and individual counseling services are provided at the
Chicago American Indian Center under the programs of the
Family Services Department. Through these programs, guidance,
counseling, supportive activities, direct assistance, and referrals
to appropriate city and private agency resources are available for
people facing personal and family crises with which they are
unable to cope. It has been the longstanding policy of the Indian
Center in these situations to attend to the immediate needs as
effectively as possible and to help those who seek assistance to
gain greater insight and motivation so that such problem situations are less likely to recur.

Because the Indian Center serves all ages and both sexes, it is not strange that almost any human problem may be brought to the Center by someone who is in need of assistance, and the range of specific services is extremely wide and varied. However, in casework we see only a segment of Indians who come to Chicago. Others — the vast majority — do not seek aid from our Welfare and Family Services Department; these can be considered the "invisible majority" — the people who do not appear in journalistic accounts about Indians in the city. They are people who are prepared educationally, emotionally, and socially for the experience of urban life. Casework deals with the population that is largely unprepared. It is this population that is the concern of this final chapter.

Also coming to the Center for emergency aid are people who live within such a narrow margin of savings that any fluctuation in the national economy has severe repercussions for them. During periods of full employment, they make a living, but with any recession, they need supplementary income or food which we try to supply. With this kind of crisis assistance, people in this category will usually be able to manage until there is an economic rebound.

The three major factors determining the reaction to city life of the people who receive most of the Center's attention in Welfare and Family Services, are educational background, employment opportunities, and psychological stability. These factors are, of course, complexly interrelated. For instance, employment possibilities depend upon the level of prior education and experience, and psychological factors impinge upon the motivation to get an education and stay on a job. However, the three factors can be separated analytically. I will treat them as independent variables first, then try to tie them together in a summary.

EDUCATIONAL BACKGROUND

For some time educators have been aware of the poor quality of the Indian schools and the meaningless curricula perpetuated by all too many school systems, on both federal and local levels. Unfortunately, the fact of awareness has not been sufficient to produce any large-scale change. The geographic isolation of the reservations, the low pay scales in small towns near the reservations, and the lack of intellectual stimulation and companionship have all tended to select for the less motivated, less well trained teachers. In addition, even dedicated educators who have been willing to give up social and financial advantages available elsewhere have all too frequently been ignorant of the cultural heritage and life-styles of their Indian students. This ignorance often results in the higher attainment of non-Indian students in mixed schools because the teachers are ill-equipped to handle the real academic problems of the Indian children, and it has tended to produce the stereotype of the stupid or unambitious Indian and the attitude that the Indian child was just not capable of attaining the same level of scholarship as the non-Indian child. Often very little of the curriculum is even remotely pertinent to the living conditions of Indians; such a curriculum generates no interest in learning and no motivation for achievement in the academic situation.

To a significant degree, educational goals have been fashioned to conform to the competitive achievement orientation of the American middle class and to the attainment of material wealth. Although Indian students often desire the material things of life, the means to this end remain vague in their minds, and the delayed and obscure rewards of education are not associated with a high level of academic achievement. Scholastic competition is an alien concept in the old life-style of Indians and has never been instilled as a value in most Indian households. Consequently, pressures in school to compete for grades or rank merely result in stress, tensions, or passivity. The lack of achievement orientation is, of course, not an inborn trait, but it is instilled in children early enough and firmly enough to make it difficult to eradicate or to modify. Ignorance of valid means to future goals may appear to non-Indians as aimlessness, and too frequently Indian children internalize that erroneous view of themselves, eventually concluding that they are less worthy and less capable than non-Indians. This tacit acceptance of themselves as inferior has been referred to as psychological castration of Indian youth.

There is, furthermore, reason to believe that the most competent Indian students are precisely those who drop out of the school system. They leave school because of boredom, because of irrelevance of the educational situation to their own needs, and because of their perception of the futility of their efforts — they can foresee no better life with an education than without one. Their talents are never challenged, their creativity never stimulated. They tend to think of school as confinement and punishment, not as opportunity.

Anyone with an inferior education is at a disadvantage in most labor markets. Employment potential in the city depends upon the prior training and experience of the individual; it is also affected by the individual's willingness to conform to the wage-labor standards of the employment market. For the inexperienced and uneducated there are only unskilled or semi-skilled positions. Jobs in these categories are low-paying and tend to be more directly affected by the national economy than employment in the skilled trades and the professions. In welfare work our clients are almost entirely from the unskilled and semi-skilled classes. During recessions we have many people out of work and looking for work. Joblessness in the city seems to aggravate the difficulties of city living. Rent, services, and goods are all usually more expensive than in the country, and the custom of moving into a household of relatives in time of need is often out of the question in the city where living space tends to be restricted and not expandable. Therefore urban life· is apt to be considered more difficult and less desirable at those times when the job market is depressed.

EMPLOYMENT OPPORTUNITIES

Most Indians originally come to the city because of greater employment opportunities, and it is true that even during recessions there are more and more varied sources of employment in the city. However, the cushioning effect of a kin group in which one may find temporary sanctuary is frequently absent in the city. This lack may not be grasped for what it is by the individual, but rather he may see the city situation as unfriendly and even personally threatening.

People coming to the city are often entering into an employment situation unlike any they have experienced on the reservation where available work is seasonal. With seasonal periods of free time, Indians have been accustomed to a pattern of travel-at-will to visit friends and relatives, to attend powwows and other ceremonials, or simply to see new places. Indians accustomed to such a degree of travel autonomy come into the city without the motivation to work at a job eight hours a day, five days a week. A compromise which is often struck is the daily pay job at which one works by the day and where there are no expectations of continuation by the employer. Jobs by the day allow persons to maintain freedom of movement, and they pay enough for immediate individual needs. Day laborers tend to be more transient both within the city and between the city and other areas. However, these jobs are low-paying and uncertain to the degree that they will not support a family, and they are the positions first to feel fluctuations in the national economy. Although they have appeal in some sense, they do not offer job security or any of the fringe benefits such as pensions, sick-time, paid-vacations, etc. In times of full employment, on the other hand, the ready availability of day labor may keep a person from looking for steady work — he can always get a day's pay through one of the day-labor employment offices.

Daily pay work is often sought by women to supplement other sources of income. For people with very little education and little or no training, day labor is often the only work available. If a worker is fortunate enough to gain steady employment, he still may face the disruption of strikes. There have been several strikes of long duration in Chicago within the last two years. Even with the help of union funds and occasional day labor, the strike may destroy the domestic economy because few families among the laboring class have savings to see them through periods without regular pay. Nevertheless, there is employment when the strike is over. Day labor jobs on the other hand are not as certain.

PSYCHOLOGICAL STABILITY

The psychological factors are too many and too complex for anyone but the professional psychologist to comment upon with authority. However, there are some aspects encountered often enough to suggest that they are important factors in the urbanization of American Indians.

When Indians are together on a reservation or in a small town close to many friends and kinfolk, they may have a number of conflicts, but they rarely have problems of personal identity; their images of self are usually accurate in the sense that they have only to look at the friends and kinfolk and see models for behavior. On this basis, one person can predict the behavior of others and can predict his own probable future with some degree of accuracy. With the move to cities, many Indians have lost the traditional image and with it their psychological stability. The surrounding people now act differently. No longer do the traditional models exist to point the way. Of course, there are many Indians who have realistic expectations of city life, either through prior experience with urban living or through the news media or education. However, for those people who come to the city with unrealistic expectations, the urban experience can be psychologically shattering.

Thus, the question of "Who am I?" becomes all important to those people because their expectations no longer coincide with reality. Even some highly educated people have found it difficult to achieve an accurate self-image. People with the problem of identity-quest may learn to answer "I am an Indian," and find in that answer a psychological security which they could not achieve in facing the anonymity of the city by being merely another body in the general population. They may find a new awareness of "Indianness" — may begin to seek out other Indians and become more conscious of "Indian" identity than they had been back on the reservation. "Indian" identity may become more important than tribal affiliation. On the other hand, tribal connections may tend to become intensified. Either way, individuals attempt to combat the loss of self-esteem by becoming "somebody." Whereas other people may define themselves in terms of profession, socioeconomic class, or school or club affiliation, the newly urbanized Indian develops a concept of self around the idea of cultural heritage, and that cultural heritage gives him roots and a sense of belonging. The Indians who have come to think of themselves in terms of occupation, or any of the categories of identity other than ethnic, have become invisible as far as *Indian* identity is concerned. They probably have Indian artifacts as decorative objects in their homes, and they recall their backgrounds in the way European immigrants do. They are, however, no longer really members of the Indian community. It seems to me that for many people, identity as an Indian is important in developing personal security when other sources of security are absent.

Where there is conflict, for whatever reason, and an individual cannot make one primary identification for himself, clinging instead to shifting identities, then he has real problems. He becomes the chronic drinker, the anti-social escapist. The confusion between traditional life-style and contemporary urban life is not satisfactorily resolved, but rather the individual tries to escape from life and refuses (or is emotionally unable) to achieve a modification in his behavior that would allow accommodation to the new social and economic conditions. I do not think this response is limited to Indians; it appears among many ethnic groups trying to adjust to and find meaning in contemporary urban society.

TWO CASE STUDIES

Two examples from my own professional experience illustrate the interaction of educational, occupational, and psychological factors, and show the range of the Indian urban experience.

The first case is that of a man whose lack of education and training was the major handicap in his adjustment to living in Chicago. Although there were certain psychological aspects to his reaction to urban life, in general he was positively motivated to settle down in the city and spend the rest of his life there. In his early sixties, this man came from a southeastern reservation with the last of his children. The others had grown up, married, and left home some time before. He had had only a grade-school education and could barely read and write. He had learned no trade and had no skills; his experience had been confined to agricultural labor, largely in cotton fields.

During his first weeks in Chicago, he lived with his daughter and son-in-law, but before long, other relatives joined them. Strains on available space and money caused the old man to search for employment. He was not quite old enough to qualify for social security help, and at the time he came to the city, there was a year's residence requirement before eligibility for general welfare assistance. The old man had heard of the American Indian Center and came hoping that Indians could help him find work. He felt backward about his poor command of English and feared that his language handicap would make it difficult for him to find work. In reality, his spoken English was adequate, and it was unlikely that any job for which he would be suited would depend upon written work. Nevertheless, he felt unsure of himself.

We gave him job referrals, directions on how to get to interviews, and enough money to pay for fares to and from three prospective jobs. He was turned down by all three places, because of his age in two cases, and because of his inability to read and write English in the third. The referrals continued for almost one year, and the man learned to get around the Uptown area of Chicago during the daytime; he still dislikes going out after dark. At the end of his first year in the city he became sick, but by that time he had fulfilled the residence requirements and was able to get general assistance from Cook County Welfare. He and his wife are still in the city, usually caring for a grandchild or two, and they frequently have their own son and his spouse staying with them. In spite of what might seem to many to be very trying experiences, the man and his wife both prefer the city to the reservation.

At the other end of the spectrum, there is the case of a man who had, on the surface, much in his favor. His level of education was distinctly above average, and one would have expected relatively little trauma in his urban accommodation. However, psychological factors, difficult for me to assess, intruded and rendered his education and native abilities useless.

In his mid-thirties, the man was the son of divorced parents who were from two different reservations. He had been raised by his maternal grandmother who provided spiritual and social guidance; she had died when he was in his early twenties. He served in the armed forces after completing his public school education; his young brother who was very close to him died in the service due to illness. This man's childhood and adolescence with his grandmother were pleasant, and he remembered that time of his life as one when he was taught responsibility. His grandmother's training counteracted the neglect and permissive attitudes of his real and stepparents. As a small boy he had seen his parents abuse each other physically and verbally, but he felt secure under his grandmother's care and her teachings of right and wrong.

His school grades had been very good, and he entered one of the larger universities in the state. In college he began to display psychological problems, overindulging in alcohol and neglecting his studies. After one year at the university, he dropped out and began a nomadic life, never staying more than a few months in any one location. By the time he arrived in Chicago he had begun to supplement his drinking habits with prescription medicines, amphetamines, and barbituates, a practice known as "popping pills." He has been arrested several times for drug use and alcoholism and has been referred to different agencies for treatment. He has even committed himself to hospitals for therapy, but has never stayed for the full course. He fears his dependence on drugs and alcohol, but he also fears what he has seen of treatment centers. He has in-depth knowledge of life in a derelict environment because he rarely has enough money to live elsewhere. In spite of his educational qualifications, he cannot keep a job. He comes to Chicago, leaves, and returns again, a true wanderer with no real home.

SUMMARY

The three primary conditions affecting urbanization of the Indian have been explicated above. Not all Indians encounter severe problems in moving from country to city; probably the majority do not. It is not Indians alone who encounter problems — they merely represent a segment of the multitude of individuals who are more or less forced into urbanization without proper preparation.

A minimum level of educational preparedness seems to be essential for a successful move to the city. A person must be able to speak and write an acceptable form of noncolloquial English grammar. The problem no longer is that the Indians speak their own language instead of English, but rather that they lack adequate training in acceptable English. In addition, there are certain skills that constitute minimal conditions for steady employment. It is impossible to separate the problems of education and employment; they are intertwined.

Added to the educational and occupational problems are the numerous psychological components of the human personality. Problems of identity and awareness of self, of purpose, of realistic means to desirable ends, of flexible attitudes — all enter into the total configuration. So complex are the interrelations that predictions of success or failure when based on superficial knowledge are futile. The causes of problems brought to us are so complex that we must work on a crisis orientation — trying to solve the problems as they occur rather than trying to predict and prevent them. We have good intentions, but the truth is that we still do not know enough. However, we believe that the decisions should be made by Indians, not by others. Other people have attempted to make our lives for us; now it is time for us to take an active rather than passive role in Indian directions.

index

Humphrey, Hubert H., 324

Indian communities: Alamo, 353; Canyoncito, 353; Chinle, 152; Farmington, 123n, 151; Fort Defiance, 123n, 148, 154; Fruitland, 123n; Hotevilla, 146; Keams Canyon, 118, 121, 128, 146n; Moenkopi, 115–157; Old Oraibi, 118; Ramah, 353; San Juan, 124; Shiprock, 136n, 148; Shongopavy, 137, 148; Shonto, 150–151; Toadlena, 377; Tuba City, 61, 115–157; Window Rock, 136n, 148, 151–152, 154, 156n, 358, 381–382, 385
Indian Court of Claims, 108
Indian identity, 58, 131, 147, 148, 199–202, 217–218, 348, 349, 378, 394, 404, 405
Indian lands: acquisitions of, 10, 13–17, 19, 20, 26, 38, 70, 103; allotment of, 23, 25, 27, 32–35, 43, 55, 69, 96, 99, 101, 122; economic development of, 51; exploitation of, 71, 80, 82, 83, 85, 86, 87, 90, 93, 95, 103, 108, 109, 153, 315, 353; fee patents, 23, 37, 38, 39, 40, 55; heirship, 38, 99; leasing of, 31, 38, 42, 55, 79, 82, 83, 97, 129, 153; management of, 5, 128; policy patents, 39; sale of, 40, 97, 99, 144; in severalty, 24, 30; titles to, 40; trust patents, 37, 38, 40
Indian policy, British, 9, 10, 12
Indian policy, federal, 4, 6, 9, 11, 18, 20, 22, 26–29, 32, 33, 37, 39, 42, 43, 44, 47, 49, 57, 69, 72, 83, 394
Indian power, 170
Indian Upward Bound Program, 326–327
Indian wars, 32, 92, 93
industries and industrialization, 3, 70, 80, 83, 108, 116, 121, 128, 147, 149, 151, 152, 153
intoxication, 12, 108, 126, 131, 132,

intoxication (*Cont.*)
151, 170, 193–196, 237, 275–311, 383, 395, 405

Jackson, Andrew, 14, 16, 19
Jefferson, Thomas, 13, 14
Jourdain, Winifred, 335
juvenile delinquency, 185

King, Martin Luther, 325
kinship and associational networks, 137–143, 144, 145, 146, 150, 222–227, 256, 384, 385, 387, 388, 389
kiva, 146, 147
Knox, Henry, 20

Law, Howard, 330, 335
legislation: Act of 1802, 21; Act of 1871, 30; Area Redevelopment Act, 51; Burke Act, 34, 37; Bursum Lands Bill, 40, 41; Coke Bill, 33; Curtis Act, 36; Dawes Severalty Act (General Allotment Act), 33–37, 69, 70, 95; Homestead Act, 32; House Concurrent Resolution 108 (Public Law 280), 47, 48; Indian Claims Commission Act, 44, 45, 71, 72, 79, 101; Indian Removal Act of 1830, 5, 11, 17; Indian Reorganization Act (Wheeler-Howard Act), 43, 44, 71, 72, 97, 99, 118; Johnson-O'Malley Act, 43, 108; Navajo-Hopi Rehabilitation Act, 121; Omnibus Act of 1910, 37, 38; Ordinance of 1786, 11; Public Law 959 (Indian Vocational Training), 248; Trade and Intercourse Acts, 12, 19
Leupp, Francis, 37, 38
liquor (*see* intoxication)
Lukermann, Fred, 328, 339

McIntosh, William, 15
McKenney, Thomas L., 16
Madison, James, 14, 25
Mahto, Ted, 325